Other books by John Nichol

THE UNKNOWN WARRIOR

A Personal Journey of
Discovery and Remembrance

JOHN NICHOL

**SIMON &
SCHUSTER**

London · New York · Sydney · Toronto · New Delhi

First published in Great Britain by Simon & Schuster UK Ltd, 2024

Copyright © John Nichol, 2024

The right of John Nichol to be identified as the author
of this work has been asserted in accordance with
the Copyright, Designs and Patents Act, 1988.

3 5 7 9 10 8 6 4

Simon & Schuster UK Ltd
1st Floor
222 Gray's Inn Road
London WC1X 8HB

Simon & Schuster: Celebrating 100 Years of Publishing in 2024

www.simonandschuster.co.uk
www.simonandschuster.com.au
www.simonandschuster.co.in

Simon & Schuster Australia, Sydney
Simon & Schuster India, New Delhi

The author and publishers have made all reasonable efforts
to contact copyright-holders for permission, and apologise
for any omissions or errors in the form of credits given.
Corrections may be made to future printings.

A CIP catalogue record for this book
is available from the British Library

Hardback ISBN: 978-1-3985-0944-3
Trade Paperback ISBN: 978-1-3985-0945-0
eBook ISBN: 978-1-3985-0946-7

Typeset in Sabon by M Rules

Printed and Bound in the UK using 100% Renewable
Electricity at CPI Group (UK) Ltd

MIX
Paper | Supporting
responsible forestry
FSC
www.fsc.org
FSC® C171272

for Sophie

CONTENTS

*This book is dedicated to all those warriors,
known and unknown, who made the ultimate
sacrifice during the First World War*

ACKNOWLEDGEMENTS

Many people offered their valuable time and considerable expertise while I researched and wrote this book. As ever, it is impossible to thank everyone individually, but I am eternally grateful to you all.

My sincere thanks also go to:

Fellow authors: Andrew Richards, Mark Scott, Richard van Emden, Tim Kendall, Justin Saddington, Jarra Brown and Professor Lucy Easthope. And David Railton KC, for his time and access to the family archive.

The Very Reverend Dr David Hoyle, Dean of Westminster Abbey; Canon The Reverend Dr James Hawkey, Theologian and Almoner; Ruth Cohen; and Dr Tony Trowles, Head of the Abbey Collection and Librarian.

Garrison Sergeant Major Andrew 'Vern' Stokes, Professor Dame Sue Black, Canon Alf Hayes, Andy Smith, Nikki Scott, Mary Fowler and Jenny Green, for helping me better understand some of the stories, experiences and emotions surrounding the First World War accounts I read.

The Western Front Association works tirelessly to ensure the First World War is kept in the public eye. From the organisation, Richard Hughes, David Tattersfield, Dr Matt Leonard, Jonathan Vernon, Jill Stewart, Rocky Salmon and Ralph Lomas all gave advice and guidance. And special thanks to Richard, Jill and David, alongside historian Professor Peter Doyle, who read an early draft of the book and offered their gratefully received expertise, corrections and comment. Any errors which remain are mine alone.

A number of eminent historians offered thoughts on the book and I am grateful to Katja Hoyer, Dr Robert Lyman, Andy Saunders, Dan Snow and Terry Whenham for their time and expertise.

The wonderful team at my fantastic publisher Simon & Schuster, for their encouragement, advice and expertise, and to Michael Wright for his time and assistance.

I am always grateful to my friend and agent of over thirty years, Mark Lucas, for his sharp eye for detail, writing expertise and wisdom.

My wonderful wife Suzannah and daughter Sophie, who are always there with much-needed love and support.

* * *

I was assisted, or read accounts, by many other researchers, authors and historians who offered invaluable information and contacts. It is impossible to name them all, but the following provided important leads, insights, pictures or advice:

Becky Clark, Dan Cope, Colin Dean, Dan Ellin, Michael Gavaghan, Dave Gilbert, Neil Hanson, Peter Hodgkinson, Christina Holstein, Chris Howe, Dr Rod Mackenzie, Juliet Nicolson, Terry Norman, Reverend Ray Pentland, Mike Peters, Craig Phillips, Dr Iason Tzouriadis, Julia Weymouth.

PROLOGUE

I am standing outside Westminster Abbey with a group of my fellow ex-prisoners of war from the 1991 Gulf War. We are suited and booted, medals glinting in the July sunshine. The flags flutter in the breeze behind us, across Parliament Square. I trace the stiff outline of the invitation in my jacket pocket with my fingertips as we wait to be ushered inside. It feels like something of a miracle to be here. Everyone who has fought in a foreign war has one dream above all others: coming home. And now here we all are – senior officers, junior airmen and airwomen, test pilots, chaplains, princes, dukes, Second World War veterans in wheelchairs, widows with determined smiles, and humdrum ex-Tornado navigators like me. All lining up in pressed shirts and polished shoes for a service to commemorate 100 years of the Royal Air Force.

It's also supposed to be a celebration. But everyone attending will have had comrades who lost their lives in war or in training, including some whose bodies have never been found. There is something about these great ceremonial occasions, with their silences, their symbolism and their ancient language as familiar as a pre-flight checklist, that can make the grandest public event feel deeply personal, too. Sometimes uncomfortably so, if you are catapulted into the past.

Edward I climbed these three low steps to the Great West Door for his coronation in 1274. So has almost every monarch since. Many were later carried up feet-first for their funerals.

Time after time, century after century, sombre crowds have gathered here, each man and woman connecting privately with a public sense of loss. In 1603, six knights carried the body of Queen Elizabeth I past this very spot, straining beneath the weight of a lead casket topped with her robed effigy. 'Westminster was surcharged with multitudes of all sorts of people in their streets, houses, windows, leads and gutters, that came out to see the obsequy,' wrote the chronicler John Stow, 'and when they beheld her statue lying upon the coffin, there was such a general sighing, groaning and weeping as the like hath not been seen or known in the memory of man.'[1] There is nothing starker than a coffin – a body in a box – carried with great solemnity, to take the doubt out of death. And nothing more evocative than the field of tiny wooden crosses, each one bearing a poppy, that blooms here every Remembrance Day.

We shuffle out of the sunlight and into the pale stone magnificence within. Somewhere in the distance is the tomb where they laid Elizabeth I to rest. Elsewhere lie Edward the Confessor, Sir Isaac Newton, Chaucer, Dickens and Stephen Hawking. Since 1066, it has been the location of the coronations of forty English and British monarchs, a burial site for many of them, and the venue of at least sixteen royal weddings since 1100.

Sir Winston Churchill is memorialised by an etched grey slab at our feet. My eye is drawn to the shiny rectangle of black marble beyond, guarded by a neat rampart of poppies, which marks the grave of the 'Unknown Warrior'. As we hover in the area chatting, a more knowledgeable friend tells me that it is the only memorial stone in the abbey which no one ever walks on. And that when the Duke of York (later King George VI) married Elizabeth Bowes-Lyon there in 1923, she placed her bouquet on it in memory of her brother Fergus, killed eight years earlier during the Battle of Loos, who at that time had no known grave.[2] The Queen Mother's spontaneous act of remembrance was echoed by her daughter after her wedding to the Duke of Edinburgh in 1947. Princess Anne followed suit in 1973, as did Sophie, Countess of Wessex, in 1999. Kate, Duchess of Cambridge, continued the tradition in 2011, as have many royals since.

I am embarrassed to admit that, despite attending countless services in Westminster Abbey, I have never properly examined the grave before. So today, surrounded by so many Known Warriors, I feel the need to stop and read the inscription. But it's too late; the ushers are tapping their watches. *Please move inside, ladies and gentlemen; the royal family will be here soon.*

Taking my seat, I glance across the aisle at the uniformed figures lined up opposite us; celebrated military figures, the weight of their service measured out in medals and gold braid. So many medals. So much service. I wonder if I deserve to be here, a fossil dug up from the sands of a foreign conflict fought and forgotten long ago. Some of the attendees are too young to remember that first Gulf War in 1991 when I was shot down and captured, let alone the Falklands in 1982.

In the distance to our left, the minor royals are already beginning to file into the abbey, sidestepping the Unknown Warrior almost without a second glance, before turning to make dutiful small talk with the beaming clerics and officers lined up to greet them. Across the aisle, I wave at a familiar Bomber Command veteran in a wheelchair. With his hair as white as parachute silk and long row of medals on his chest, he is an old friend with whom I have shared many cups of tea – and glasses of red wine – over the years as we discussed the Allied bombing campaign in the Second World War. Today, he has asked me to help him leave the abbey at the end of the service when we make our way to Horse Guards for the more convivial rituals of the day. No doubt more tea and red wine will be involved.

Westminster Abbey must have known many sombre silences in its thousand-year history. But today, thankfully, the Great West Door has been flung open, allowing the dazzling sunlight and the excited chatter of the crowds to venture in on the breeze.

The BBC is broadcasting live coverage of the whole day, featuring archive footage of past conflicts, as well as interviews with veterans old and young, widows and serving warriors too. As more members of the royal family arrive, ladies in pastel colours bob and curtsey. Princes hand their peaked caps to equerries. Politicians attempt to look as if they do this every day, though the darting eyes of some give them away. Prince William and the Duchess of Cambridge arrive. More smiles; more small talk. The Prince of Wales walks in and steps smartly around the grave of the Unknown Warrior, while Camilla clasps her hands, looking fiercely cheerful beside him.

Now a fanfare of burnished trumpets cuts through the thick air. We all rise and turn our heads, staring – while pretending not to stare – towards the Great West Door. Led by the Dean of Westminster Abbey, the Queen – looking neat and spry in her suit of blue-and-turquoise silk – walks in without the aid of a stick. Out of the corner of my eye, I watch her careful footwork on the abbey's polished stones as she steers a path around the poppies surrounding the black slab which blocks her processional route.

Once again I find myself strangely drawn by this mysterious grave, somewhat ashamed to realise how little I know of its origins.

* * *

Later, when the sounds of the organ voluntary are tumbling out from the decorated pipes above our heads, I collect my wheelchair-bound veteran and push him slowly down the aisle, chatting about the service, the royals, and the next part of the day. We are both keen to move on to the red wine aspect of the celebrations.

As we reach the grave of the Unknown Warrior he raises his hand. 'Let me just take a moment, John,' he says, quietly.

Many of his Second World War comrades are still missing, decades after the end of the war. Of the 125,000 Bomber Command aircrew who took to the skies, 55,573 were killed. Around a meagre 50:50 chance of survival. Countless numbers were never seen or heard of again. 'As long as you need,' I reply. I have lost quite a few friends myself, but for me, it is the haunting notes of the Last Post that normally bring sad memories to the fore.

While the rest of the congregation sallies out into the sunlight, and my white-haired companion bows his head in silence, I'm now able to closely examine the gilded inscription carved into the jet-black slab of Belgian marble:

BENEATH THIS STONE RESTS THE BODY

OF A BRITISH WARRIOR

UNKNOWN BY NAME OR RANK

BROUGHT FROM FRANCE TO LIE AMONG

THE MOST ILLUSTRIOUS OF THE LAND

AND BURIED HERE ON ARMISTICE DAY

11 NOV: 1920, IN THE PRESENCE OF

HIS MAJESTY KING GEORGE V

HIS MINISTERS OF STATE

THE CHIEFS OF HIS FORCES

AND A VAST CONCOURSE OF THE NATION[3]

I have *read* it before, but today is the first time that the words truly resonate. I suppose I'd always just thought it was symbolic, like the Cenotaph. Embarrassingly, the penny only now drops. There really is the *body* of an unknown soldier under there. I feel I should have known this. How did this man get from the killing fields of the Western Front to central London? Did they bring him straight from a First World War battlefield? Which one? Or did they dig up a body after the Armistice? And what makes him a warrior, rather than a soldier?

'He could have been an airman or a sailor,' murmurs the mind reader in the wheelchair. 'Nobody knows who he was.'

As I think about this, he points out a ship's bell, embossed with 'HMS VERDUN', hanging silently on the pillar beside us. '*Verdun* was the destroyer that brought back his body in a special coffin from France,' he says, 'with an escort of six other ships, as if he were royalty.' I stare at the grave while my 94-year-old friend begins to tell me about the large crowds that filled London that day in 1920; about the special places reserved for the widows whose husbands and *all* of their sons had been killed in the war. About the honour guard of servicemen wearing the Victoria Cross, our country's highest award for courage in the face of the enemy, who lined the aisle. Again, why don't *I* know any of this story?

He gestures towards the translucent Union Jack which hangs high and limp and almost unnoticed above the throne of Edward the Confessor, in the alcove to the left of the Great West Door. 'The Padre's Flag,' he says, reverently. 'Still stained with the blood of the fallen, it was draped across the coffin ...' His voice falters and stops. Is he thinking about *this* Unknown Warrior, or the hundreds he must have known personally during his own war years?

As I grapple with the enormity of what it represents, an idea is forming in my mind.

Sometimes the past can seem so remote; sometimes it seems like yesterday. Here, today, this humble Unknown Warrior is challenging me to connect the two; to join the dots between our lives today and all those innocent young men blown into fragments no more substantial than the poppies we pin to our coats each year.

So many names without bodies. So many bodies without names.

How did an anonymous corpse from the First World War come to be carried up the steps just in front of us, to be buried among the kings? Why did such vast crowds turn out to witness the passing of an unknown body in a box? And how does the Unknown Warrior still exert such a powerful hold upon us today?

The idea of placing myself in his boots is not a comfortable one. But as we walk slowly away from Westminster Abbey, amid the churning traffic and the tourists wandering through Parliament Square, I am determined to find out more and, if possible, retrace the life and journey of the Unknown Warrior.

THE ROYAL ALBERT HALL, LONDON
NOVEMBER 2022

The worldwide Covid pandemic halted my search for answers. As did writing a book about a more modern conflict involving my colleagues on the Tornado force during the 1991 Gulf War, and another about those whose lives have been saved by ejection seats. But I have had some time to research a little more about the First World War. I was staggered to discover the stark reality of the casualty figures: around 10 million military deaths, nearly 7 million civilian; 21 million military personnel wounded.[4] One of the heaviest losses of life on a *single* day, 1 July 1916, occurred during the Battle of the Somme, when (although figures vary) the British Army alone suffered around 57,000 casualties – dead, wounded and missing.[5]

These losses are on a scale almost too terrible to comprehend. But it was another fact which rocked me.

Commonwealth War Graves Commission files show that 526,816 British and Commonwealth soldiers of that 'Great' War have no known resting place. Of those, 338,955 have never been buried at all, while 187,861 do have graves but have not been identified.[6] What scale of devastation, what level of brutality, could result in more than *half a million* men having no known resting place? All those families unable to mourn properly, with no tangible location to focus their grief.

* * *

Following the death of the Queen in September 2022, I was honoured to be invited to pay a short tribute during the Royal British Legion's November Festival of Remembrance. In front of the new King, and a TV audience of millions, I had the privilege of talking about his late mother's dedication to a life of service for our nation.

Then, on the fortieth anniversary of the conflict, we went on to remember the sacrifice of those who lost their lives during the 1982 Falklands War. I watched as Mary Fowler, dressed in black and standing alongside an image of her father projected onto the floor, explained how, when she was only fourteen, he was killed aboard HMS *Coventry* during an Argentinian air attack. With thousands in the hall, and countless more watching around the world, she read aloud from the final letter she ever received from him, her voice cracking as she struggled to contain her emotions:

Dear Mary,
  By the time you get this letter, your birthday will have come and gone. I'm sorry I can't be with you, but I shall be thinking of you.
  I suppose your mum is a little upset so I would like you to look after her.
  I'm afraid I do not know when I shall be home again. But let's hope it's not too far away.
  Well love, that is about all for now, so till next time, God bless and take care of yourself.
  Love, Dad xxx[7]

They were his last words home. I didn't bother trying to contain my own emotions; tears were streaming down my face.

Mary told me afterwards that her pain was made infinitely worse by the fact that when he and many of his friends went down with the ship, their bodies were never recovered. She had no grave to visit, no place to contemplate a life without him, nowhere to grieve. As a young serviceman, I had watched that war unfold on TV, seen ships sinking into the freezing waters. I had even been deployed on a Task Force vessel later that year. I now realised that though I knew about the death toll, I hadn't really thought about its wider resonances.

The similarities between Mary's experience of loss in 1982 and that of the relatives of the Great War's Unknown Warriors in 1918 thrust my earlier promise to investigate the story more sharply into focus.

Sometimes the past can seem so remote; sometimes it seems like yesterday ...

CHAPTER ONE

DEATH AT HIGH WOOD

HIGH WOOD, THE SOMME
SPRING 2023

I don't really believe in ghosts.

Even so, as I trudge across the former First World War battlefields of the Somme in northern France, north-east of Amiens – across these grim, cheerless acres whose vague hills barely even seem worth heading for, let alone dying for – I spot something that stops me in my tracks. It is just a tuft of sheep's wool, snagged on a barbed-wire fence. Nothing more. But I suddenly feel the kind of prickling uneasiness that makes me want to turn around.

Nothing. No one here. Not alive anyway.

I step into the serene beauty of the 'London Cemetery and Extension' across the road from a thick wood. This burial ground was first established in September 1916 when a military padre and his men buried forty-seven bodies in a shell hole in the days after the 'battle of High Wood'. The fighting here that month was a mere glimpse into the Battle of the Somme that year, and just a minuscule representation of the battles of the four-and-a-quarter-year war. After the autumn fighting, it grew to become the third largest cemetery on the Somme, with 3,873 First World War burials, of which 3,114 are the remains of unidentified soldiers. Its soil is rich with the blood of the missing. And it is only one of thousands peppering the landscape of France and Belgium. These lines of perfect white headstones, with their gracefully cambered tops, and their neatly pruned flowers and shrubs adorning each grave, evoke a quiet sense of order and symmetry which must be the exact, diametric opposite of the deafening chaos in which the deaths of those that they memorialise took place.

Exactly where I stand.

As I walk along the rows of graves marking those who died on just one day – 15 September 1916 – I can feel the sun beating down on the back of my neck. My shirt is sticking to me with sweat. But all around me, there is a surprising coolness about this scene. The dazzling white stones gently shade the graves at their feet, and the greenness of the leafy plantings confirms how well cared for they are.

Listening to the slight breeze flattening the grass, I struggle to imagine what it was like to stand on this spot in 1916. I realise that I need to know exactly what those men saw and heard, and tasted and felt when the earth and sky were erupting in a maelstrom of shot and shell. If I'm honest, part of me would rather not think about it at all.

It all happened so long ago, but I am determined to make this journey into the past.

High Wood, The Somme
15 September 1916

Breathing hard, Anthony French pressed his face into the soft, damp soil as fragments of earth and metal spattered his back and helmet. His ears were drumming so violently that he could not tell if the barrage was lifting. Thunder rolled in his brain.

'UP!' the Corporal roared again.

Clenching his teeth, French managed to stumble another few yards into the flashing haze. 'Dark fountains of earth reared and fell before us. Smoke wreathed among us. Fumes of phosphorus and cordite fouled the violent air. Unsummoned tears distorted my vision and would not be brushed away.'[1] And all the time the body of his best friend was lying there, abandoned, somewhere in the mud behind him. Who would bring Bert back now?

As he staggered over the cratered earth, French stole a glance left and right. Where were the tanks? The dense line of khaki was now reduced to a few blurry dots. And still, from the rising ground on their half-left, in the direction of High Wood, came the staccato chatter of the machine guns. *Where are the bloody tanks?* 'Desolation of spirit gave way to a rising, fuming, blazing anger fed by primitive, overwhelming emotions, an unspeakable hatred of all mankind.' Time after time, the men flung themselves down at their Corporal's command, dragged themselves up to advance a few more strides and then dropped again in the tangle of blasted wire.

And then, just like that, they were clambering into the ruin of what – only minutes before – had been the enemy's frontline trench. Amid the adrenaline-fuelled blur of red and grey, French was dimly aware of flayed and mutilated bodies, twisted into impossible positions like rag dolls. Some had their guts and brains hanging out. He saw amputated limbs and a severed head still encased in its grey steel helmet.

Doing their best to avoid the gore, the men took sanctuary amid the warm, wet horror. Eventually, a signal sounded, ordering them to drop back. Someone joked that perhaps it was the cookhouse call. And now French and his comrades were floundering across the torn landscape once more. Turning, firing, swearing, falling. Turning, reloading, firing, scrambling. Turning, panting, swearing, dying. In the distance, French could see the blasted hulk of a tank, 'incongruous and forlorn', poking out from a shell hole like a fag-butt from an ashtray. Blue sky and gaping earth. That was when the German artillery shell exploded. 'I ran right into it. My world was steeped in a brilliant blood-red monochrome, and in that all-enveloping flash I hung, body and soul, my mind still free and functioning and most urgently desiring to receive an order, a signal.'

It felt as if the earth had risen up and struck him square between the shoulders, knocking him unconscious.

THE SOMME
JULY 1916

If you wanted to choose a single moment in the First World War when the killing was at its cruellest, you would be hard-pressed to beat 7:30AM on 1 July 1916, the start of the Battle of the Somme, when thousands of young men leapt gamely from their trenches, only to discover that woolen uniforms offer precious little protection against machine-gun bullets. Although numbers vary for obvious reasons, it is said that by the end of that first day, 21,392 British soldiers had been killed or were missing; 35,493 were wounded and 585 had been taken prisoner.[2] One man was killed every 4.4 seconds.[3]

But if that was the worst *time*, what about the worst *place*?

One hotly contested vantage point at which, month after month, the carnage had unfolded is the leafy wood I visit on a hot spring day over 100 years later. The most violent things happening today are the wind whipping round my ankles and a distant passenger jet slashing a white contrail across the sky. It was very different back then. 'We never saw anything quite like High Wood,' wrote one soldier. 'It was a wood only in name – ragged stumps sticking out of churned-up earth, poisoned with fumes of high explosives, the whole a mass of corruption.'[4]

Standing on a ridge only 100 feet above the surrounding plains, halfway between Calais and Paris, this unremarkable clump of trees is not exactly high. But it was high enough to give the Germans a commanding view and a murderous arc of fire. The Allies had tried pretty much everything to capture High Wood. On 14 July 1916, a cavalry charge sent a combined British–Indian force, armed with lances, into the jaws of a fortified German position heavily armed with machine guns. As one officer described the scene: 'It was an absolute rout. A magnificent sight. Tragic.'[5]

The staff at headquarters then tried other ways of blasting the enemy out of High Wood. They dug tunnels and planted explosives beneath them. They set up the 'Livens Large Gallery Flame Projector'. Weighing 2.4 tonnes, with a crew of seven, it could incinerate the enemy from 90 metres. On one occasion, they ordered ten machine-gun teams to direct continuous rapid fire into the wood for twelve hours solid. They managed to trigger a million rounds between them, although it took frequent barrel changes and four 2-gallon cans of water, many of the soldiers' water bottles and every urine tin in the vicinity being emptied into the gun-jackets to keep them cool enough not to jam.[6]

Despite all these efforts, High Wood remained in German hands. Now, for the next big assault, on the entire line between the villages of Flers and Courcelette, just to the north of High Wood, General Haig resolved to play what he hoped would be the Allies' trump card. Haig was the commander of the British Army in France, and for the first time in history, on 15 September 1916, he was going to send the 'Landship' or, as it would soon become known, the 'tank', into battle. This brand-new (and hitherto untested) weapon was, Haig felt sure, just the thing to break the stalemate on the Somme. The idea was that instead of employing an artillery barrage to creep slowly over the terrain in front of the advancing infantry, four tanks would be sent straight through the wood, mashing and blasting everything in their path, with the infantry following in their wake. The man responsible for the tank's development, Ernest Swinton, was adamant that the primitive British machines were not yet ready to be tested in battle. One senior officer on the spot had risked his life to crawl as close as possible to the territory over which the tanks would have to advance. He had seen the shattered tree stumps, poking up like pillar boxes. He had seen the cavernous shell craters, each deep enough to swallow a grocery van. Success was far from certain.

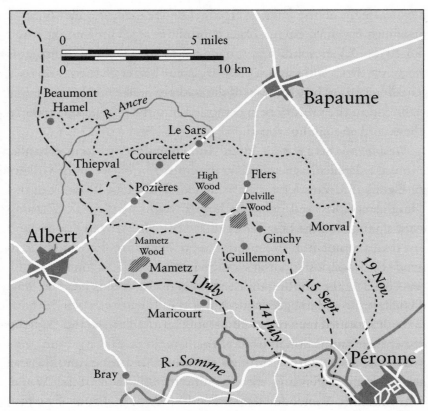

BATTLE OF THE SOMME FRONT LINES, JULY–NOVEMBER 1916

ALBERT, THE SOMME
2023

My journey in the footsteps of the First World War warriors takes me to Albert – 80 miles north of Paris – a landmark for all the young soldiers who came through here en route to the front lines at High Wood and elsewhere. I stop for a bite to eat at a restaurant opposite the great church where many might have prayed before moving up to the trenches.

Despite being a modern town, with pedestrians bustling about their busy lives and parking spaces devilishly hard to find, the memory of the conflict is still very much alive. Largely brick-built, like so many of the villages in northern France, its shell-blasted buildings may have been replaced and the basilica immaculately repaired, but Albert's street pattern and road layout will have changed very little from the town visited by all the soldiers whose stories I have been following. Many of them may have sat and swigged from their canteens in this very spot, gazing up at the gilded Madonna glinting in the sunlight at the top of the church's spire. I eat my *ficelle picarde* (as far as I can tell, a ham and mushroom pancake cunningly labelled as a *spécialité régionale*), while a pair of ancient field guns threatens a ghostly bombardment from just beneath the church steps. Stylised images of poppies are everywhere. There is even a bar called the Lest We Forget.

I take a moment to step inside the cool shade of the church. Just inside the door, a sign announces that the beautiful stone statue of the Virgin Mary cradling the dead body of Christ, his head leaning on her arm, was damaged by the fighting in June 1915. I wonder how many uniformed men must have stood here back then and thought about their mums, longing to see them again.

On one street corner stands the shiny statue of a Tommy, rifle at the ready, defending the entrance to the town's First World War museum. Someone has painted him dark green, as if he just fell out of a box of toy soldiers. One of his Australian comrades, immortalised in bronze, clutches an entrenching tool in front of the restored church. And a cheery-looking *poilu* (literally 'hairy', the nickname given to the unshaven French soldiers) stands guard over the rebuilt railway station. But these are nameless individuals, extracted from the hordes who passed through this place in 1916. Their frozen outlines give no sense of the flesh-and-blood characters, laughing and joking, who arrived here a century or more ago, and who must have gawped in awe at the buzzing hive of activity that the town had become, a month after the start of the battle raging on its doorstep.

ALBERT
SEPTEMBER 1916

Even by mid-September 1916, the quaint market town – a centre for pilgrims since the Middle Ages – had been shattered and was now a jumble of cratered streets and ruined houses. Beyond the rubble lay a vast British supply depot, transport hub and base camp. As far as the eye could see there were miles of tents, bivouacs, limbers and horse lines. Huge dumps of supplies and ammunition covered the ground, and between them, wherever there was space, stood the ferocious, roaring hulks of the big guns, devouring the great piles of shells stacked around them. It is incredible to think that this vast armed camp could exist just a mile or two behind the trenches, well within the range of the German heavy artillery. Only a few patrolling aircraft and the observation balloons tugging at their windlasses offered any protection from enemy spotters.

Here were canteens, bath-houses, water points and pontoons. Over there was the grim dysentery compound with men bent and straining over biscuit tins. Close to the road stood the casualty clearing station, where long lines of scarecrows wrapped in scarlet bandages were queuing to discover if they were fit to return to battle and be blasted some more. And that was the trouble with Albert. The war was laid bare. The soldiers amassing here, waiting to head for the trenches of the Somme, could not help but notice the faces of the ones staggering back from them. Dirty, unshaven, their tattered uniforms white with chalk and grey with mud, their faces grey with exhaustion.[7] The men watching them out of the corner of their eyes knew that Albert was their last stop before being sent to some of the deadliest hotspots 'up the line' – that jagged snake of trenches, bodies, barbed wire and shell holes that marked the raw, chafed border, every yard of it disputed, between Tommy and Fritz; King and Kaiser; us and them.

One man staring deep into the heart of the killing and chaos of September 1916 was the Reverend David Railton, an Oxford-educated army chaplain or 'padre', whose job was to carry a Bible rather than a rifle and to offer spiritual support to the men as best he could. Like many of the men in Albert, Railton had already spent months in the trenches. Like them, he had witnessed death and destruction on a scale which no man – including the twinklingly erudite vicar of Folkestone, whose parents had both been leading lights in the Salvation Army – should ever have to see.

Albert's great basilica, though blasted by shellfire, dominated the town, with its statue of the Virgin Mary still clinging precariously to the top of its tower. Hit by a shell, the Madonna had toppled forwards until she was horizontal, so that she now jutted out like an eerie gargoyle. Everyone and everything had to march past this disturbing landmark on their way to face the hell of the trenches.

Everyone meant cheery Londoners like Bert Bradley, a young soldier in the Civil Service Rifles – a volunteer battalion of Whitehall clerks and men from City offices – whose tenor voice was the pride of the platoon and made all those who heard it want to join him in song. Bert's girlfriend had recently sent him half a pound of milk chocolate and a tin of preserved cherries. He was now making himself popular by sharing the chocolate with some of the other chaps. One square may have gone to young Alec Reader from Wandsworth, a promising cross-country runner who had lied about his age and given up his job in the post office to enlist at the age of seventeen. Soldiers had to be eighteen, and although many under that age continued to serve at the front, Alec's secret was now out and the army had agreed to release him from active service. The release papers were due any day. In the meantime, he tried to ignore the crashing of the guns as he wrote another letter to his mum with a stub of pencil, balancing on the copy of *Treasure Island* he'd borrowed from his school library. He had already written to her more than seventy times during his service in France.[8]

Everyone also meant men like Harry Farlam, a grocer's assistant from Derbyshire, writing a letter to his wife, Annie.[9] And it meant Sidney Wheater from Scarborough, who was known for his speed and played hockey for Yorkshire.[10] Though Wheater was the youngest of five brothers, he was the only son of his father's second wife. His birth must have seemed a kind of miracle to her, as she was already forty – somewhat elderly to give birth in those days – when he arrived. At the opposite end of the social scale stood – a little apart from the other men, in every sense – the dashing Raymond Asquith, the eldest son of the Prime Minister. Unfeasibly handsome, brilliant and well connected, Asquith was an immaculate symbol of Britain's gilded youth. He had it all, give or take a little bit of friendliness, humility and human warmth, which even his best friends acknowledged.[11]

Day after day, in their various battalions, the men began to move out. The grocer's assistant and the Prime Minister's son were heading for the villages Guillemont and Ginchy, on the far side of High Wood. The padre, Bert the tenor and young Alec Reader, still clutching his copy of *Treasure Island,* together with Sidney Wheater, would be marching in the direction of High Wood itself.

It was not an enticing prospect.

High Wood
September 1916

Some of the men heading into battle were ordered to bivouac near Mametz Wood a few miles east of Albert. Bert chose this moment to share his tin of preserved cherries with his close friend Anthony French; French was not impressed by their surroundings. 'The place stank of death and residue of poison gas. The trenches had been cut, blasted and cut again by British and German troops in turn. To reach our concave wire-netting bunks in the lice-infested dugouts we had to pass through trenches reported as cut through corpses. As if to confirm this horrifying tidbit, from the side of one there hung a hand and forearm.' From this high point, surrounded by abandoned positions and tangled heaps of barbed wire, the men had a good view of the surrounding country. Behind them, at regular intervals, came the flash and bellow of a mighty gun. French decided that the rushing sound of its shells was 'like a ghost-train cleaving the sky'. Alongside them, the wood's limited surviving greenery seemed reassuringly familiar. Where they would shortly be going, however, was another world.

High Wood was a scene of apocalyptic desolation. Nearly every feature of the landscape had been wiped away by the bombardments of the previous days, weeks and months. North-east across the plain and away on both flanks as far as the eye could see, the horizon was fringed with the flashing of the guns. This, as they tried not to remind themselves, was where they were heading. Most of these men were already shattered. Either physically, like Sidney Wheater, the Scarborough hockey player, who had been wounded in the arm at the Battle of Loos a year earlier, or mentally, by the incessant shelling, like Irishman Tom Kettle, barely healthy enough to be in the army, let alone an officer in the front line.

Kettle was a brilliant academic, orator, barrister, poet and Member of Parliament, known as one of the finest minds of his generation. A reformed alcoholic, he had signed up to fight despite his chronic ill health. Kettle's charm made him immensely popular with the men. A tall, slim fellow, with a wide humorous mouth, sparkling dark eyes, and a brogue that would charm a bird off a tree, he was one of those people who just seemed to be able to get on with everybody. And now, fighting with the Royal Dublin Fusiliers, he still smarted from his early experiences of life in the trenches where – as he put it in a letter to a friend – 'the bombardment, the destruction and bloodshed are beyond all imagination'.[12] He had made a monumental effort to cure his alcohol addiction in order to be able to join up, but the pressure was beginning to tell. 'My ears are becoming a little more accustomed to the diabolism of sound, but it remains terrible beyond belief,' he wrote to his wife, Mary. 'The strain is terrible. It continues from hour to hour and minute to minute. It is indeed an ordeal to which human nature itself is hardly equal.' He also had a 3-year-old daughter and was desperate to see them both again. 'The heat is bad and the insects and the rats, but the moral strain is positively terrible. It is not that I am not happy in a way – a poor way – but my heart does long for a chance to come home.'

People dealt with the strain of trench life in different ways. Friendships such as the intimate bond between Bert Bradley and Anthony French helped, as did the joking and joshing – the gallows humour – that became a part of daily life. There were letters from home, too, sometimes with small luxuries tucked inside. Bert Bradley had also received a pipe from his girlfriend, complete with some dark shag tobacco, to go with the cherries and chocolate.

Charles Royston Jones, who had worked in the shipping department of the Board of Trade, wrote to his parents on Sunday, 10 September, assuring them that he was 'quite in the pink' and that he had received their parcel. He ended: 'PS. I want some safety razor blades as soon as poss, as I have run out of them also.'[13]

Excited to have been promoted to the rank of Lance Corporal, Harry Farlam, the grocer's assistant, wrote to his 'dear wife', Annie, in Derbyshire on YMCA writing paper emblazoned with red triangles and the words 'ON ACTIVE SERVICE' at the top. 'I must say that we are having a pretty rough time at present,' he admitted, 'but I keep coming through all right. I will now conclude with fondest love and kisses, from your affectionate husband Harry.' After his name, Farlam proudly wrote and underlined the word 'Corporal', before adding: 'PS. Don't forget to send me the notebook, as it is a *necessity*.'

The battlefield padres helped with morale, too. Railton had brought a gramophone out to the trenches with him and would play records to ease the tension. 'All goes well,' he wrote to his wife. 'I have had the gramophone rushed up at every halt today.'[14]

Another padre, Rupert Edward Inglis, who had played rugby for England, distributed large quantities of cigarettes and chocolate. Both chaplains spent as much time as they could chatting to the men.[15] 'Railton would natter to us on all subjects, take a hand at cards and finally prayers,' commented one soldier. 'His easy manner made him immensely popular with us all.'[16] Sometimes even just talking could have a positively medicinal effect, as Rupert Inglis found in his work assisting the surgeon carrying out rushed operations at the field hospital near Ginchy. The padre wrote to his daughter:

*The men have generally had morphia given to them. But
they do not often give an anaesthetic in a Field Ambulance,
so it is very often very painful for the poor chaps having
their wounds dressed and attended to. A man often suffers
a lot anticipating he is going to be hurt, and by talking to
him and interesting him – about all sorts of things, cricket,
football, boxing – you can often take his mind off it. The
other day we had a Welshman who had some very painful
wounds. As a rule Welshmen do not stand pain very well,
but this man was very keen on football, so he and I carried
on a violent discussion about football and the man got
through it splendidly. Then the surgeon found he had
something more to do to the Welshman, so he came over
and said, 'Come along – my local anaesthetic – I want you
to talk some more football.'*

Even the men who were not wounded were very often foot-sore from
the endless miles of marching which had brought them, via various
circuitous routes, to Albert – a strategy intended to confuse any
German spies who might be sending secret messages about where
the British were heading. But mostly it just confused the soldiers.
Worse, it had a sapping effect on morale. Young Alec Reader had
already spent time in a military hospital with septic feet. And Tom
Kettle's batman (the young soldier assigned to look after an officer)
Robert Bingham – at eighteen, just a few months older than Alec
Reader – was suffering, too.

For David Railton, the worn-out soldiers in his battalion reminded him of horses who would rather be thrashed than go one
step further. The padre had to watch aghast as some of them, reaching a bend in the road, simply marched straight on and tumbled, fast
asleep, into a ditch. Orders were that no one was to fall out unless
unconscious, or else he would be treated as a deserter. In spite of
this, fifteen men stopped marching out of Railton's battalion alone.
Ten were unconscious, and the rest had feet so broken and bleeding
that no more movement was possible. For Railton, marching beside

them, it must have been tough to watch. 'One brave laddie actually held out until the end,' he told his wife in a letter, 'and then collapsed and was found to have no skin on his feet at all. They were just raw.'[17]

In Anthony French and Bert Bradley's company, it was a point of honour never to stop marching and break ranks, except to drop, incapacitated, in one's tracks. 'In sweltering heat, some died where they fell,' declared French, bluntly. On the other hand, the rhythmic intensity of the long marches was the one thing that could help soldiers to sleep. The men would still be moving mechanically when they entered their billet. And if the way had been hard and long, French and Bert would drop, fully equipped, onto the floor of the empty room, and instantly fall asleep.

Sleep was certainly a challenge in the trenches. Nights might be quiet at times, but the peace could still be shattered by the roar of various shells. Wondering if they might still be alive in five minutes' time, let alone by the morning, the men, when not on duty, would either sleep standing up, or lie on sandbags and ammunition boxes – anything that would help them to remain a few inches above the ankle-deep mud that turned many trenches into sewers. Lice were an itchy, scratchy fact of life. Rats freaked the men out, too. 'You lie in your dug-out,' wrote Tom Kettle, 'famished, not for food (that goes without saying), but for sleep, and hear them scurrying up and down their shafts, nibbling at what they find, dragging scraps of old newspapers along, with intolerable cracklings, to bed themselves. They scurry across your blankets and your very face.'[18] 'Had rat hunt all night,' one officer recorded in his diary. 'Couldn't sleep for the damned things.'[19] Another was just dozing off in his hammock when he felt a sharp pain in the knuckle of his middle finger, right hand. The rat, he grimly deduced, had mistaken him for a dead man.[20] More than anything, however, it was the constant shelling that kept men awake. Even if you weren't being woken for sentry duty every four hours, or being volunteered for one of the dreaded night raids on the enemy, the sporadic yet continual gunfire meant that there was always the chance – at any time of day or night – that the next projectile to arrive overhead could have your name on it.

* * *

In the fortnight before the great assault on the heavily defended enemy lines around High Wood, several smaller attacks were planned. The Germans were holding other woods and neighbouring villages which had been earmarked for capture before the main attack could take place on 15 September. In particular, the two villages of Guillemont and Ginchy, a couple of miles south-east of High Wood, were perched on a hilltop overlooking the extreme right of the British lines. Like High Wood, this wasn't much of a hill. But it was still high enough to command panoramas of the eastern end of the British section of the battlefield, from where the enemy machine guns and artillery could use the heights to block any further British advance.

On 3 September 1916, Tom Kettle and his Royal Dublin Fusiliers dug in as best they could in a network of abandoned trenches near Guillemont, awaiting their orders. The men from Ireland could have had no idea that so many of them were about to die in the forthcoming engagement that a national committee would, years later, erect a granite cross weighing 4 tons to their memory at Guillemont.

The same for the Londoners at High Wood.

The South Africans at Delville Wood.

The Australians at Pozières.

The Newfoundlanders at Beaumont-Hamel.

Every village and copse around High Wood would one day have a future as a regimental mortuary for one nation or another as they strove to lend a sense of permanence to the memory of brief lives so quickly snuffed out. So many unknown soldiers, forgotten as they fell. Known unto God, yes. But known, too, to all those mothers and fathers and children and schoolfriends and lovers and wives who were sitting at home, waiting for news.

In the descriptions of how this regiment did this, and that

division did that, it is easy to forget who these people were. Few of
them were battle-hardened professional soldiers, welded to their
rifles from birth. The so-called New Army of 1916 was made up of
cheerful, hard-working citizens from all walks of life, who had been
quietly sorting letters in the post office or representing their school
at cross-country when General Kitchener pointed his finger from
the poster on the wall and the call to arms came through. These
were the men who were doing their best to be brave as they waited
outside Guillemont, Ginchy or High Wood with shells exploding all
around them. Minutes became hours. Hours became days. Days felt
like weeks. The men were asked to do nothing except patrol, dig
and endure the constant shelling which caused most of the deaths
during the war.[21]

Knowing that something big was close at hand, Tom Kettle threw
himself into that special fervour of activity which comes upon the
man who knows that he is running out of time. On the morning
of Sunday, 3 September, he wrote a 'last letter' to his wife, Mary,
together with a heap of instructions about how his works were best
to be published and appointing her as his literary executor:

My Dearest Wife
The long expected is now close at hand. I was at Mass &
Communion this morning at 6.00, the camp is broken up,
and the column is about to move. It is no longer indiscreet
to say we are to take part in one of the biggest attacks of the
war. Many will not come back.

Should that be God's design for me you will not receive
this letter until afterwards. I want to thank you for the love
and kindness you spent and all but wasted on me. There
was never in all the world a dearer woman, or a more
perfect wife and adorable mother. My heart cries for you
and Betty who I may never see again. I think even that it is
perhaps better that I should not see you again.

God bless and help you! If the last sacrifice is ordained
think that in the end I wiped out all the old stains. Tell Betty

*her daddy was a soldier and died as one. My love, now at
last clean, will find a way to you.*
  Ever your husband Tom

Tom checked the letter he hoped would never be delivered, put down
his pen and steeled himself for the attack to come. Later that day,
the assault on Guillemont, 3 miles to the south-east of High Wood,
began with a massive artillery bombardment.

The Irish pipers were busy from early morning. They
played 'Brian Boru's March', 'The White Cockade', 'The Wearin' o'
the Green' and 'A Nation Once Again', not that it was easy to hear
them above the thunder of the guns. For the soldiers peeking up out
of their trenches to watch the shells explode, it was an extraordinary
sight. The only way you could tell where Guillemont once stood was
from watching the colour of the earth thrown up by the fearsome
bombardment. A fountain of dark earth meant open countryside.
A spume of red brick dust showed where the pretty Picardy village
used to be. How, some of the Irishmen wondered, were they supposed to capture a village that had ceased to exist?

The main infantry attack began and, by the following morning,
the wasteland-formerly-known-as-Guillemont had been secured.
Casualties were severe. The brigade lost 1,147 officers and men out
of a total of 2,400. Yet Lieutenant Tom Kettle had lived to fight
another day and, on Monday, 4 September, was still desperately
trying to tie up loose ends. Frontline action tends to have this effect
on people. Somehow Kettle found the strength and peace of mind
to write and rewrite a poem for his daughter, Betty, in case the
three-year-old never saw her father again. It wasn't much, but it
was from the heart. Another letter he hoped would never be read,
but at least something for the little girl to know that her daddy had
been thinking of her if he didn't make it through the day. '*In wiser
days, my darling rosebud ... You'll ask why I abandoned you ...
To dice with death,*' he wrote, before urging his beloved daughter
to understand that if he had indeed joined '*the foolish dead*', he had
died not for King or country. But for her.

Unfortunately, every Allied success on the Somme tended to be followed by a vicious German counter-attack. On the morning of Thursday, 7 September 1916, Kettle's battalion, without leaving their trenches, lost another 200 men and seven officers to shellfire just outside Guillemont. Kettle was swiftly promoted to be commander of B Company. A few hours later, he led them in yet another attack. The stench of the bodies that covered the road was so awful that one of his friends described brushing foot powder on their faces in an attempt to mask it.[22]

Once again, Kettle managed to survive the fighting. Perhaps the tide was turning?

* * *

Ghastly by day, ghostly by night, High Wood had become known as 'the rottenest place on the Somme'.[23] A pestilential killing field, littered with the unburied bodies of so many men and horses that the place had its own noxious smell, High Wood's very name could strike fear into the heart of the toughest soldier. Too many of them had lost comrades there. All of them knew the wood's fearsome reputation as they approached it via Albert on 13 and 14 September. And here, before they reached High Wood itself, 'on the threshold of stark tragedy', as Anthony French put it, 'all light-heartedness fled'.

Even for men who had by now spent several months in various trenches and who had even begun to get used to the din of bombardments, the thirst, the rats, the lice, the mud and the lack of sleep, their first experience of the landscape between Pozières and Ginchy, on either side of High Wood, was unforgettable. For French and his friend Bert, the smell was as bad as the sights. 'The stench of dead mule almost overwhelmed us. The bloated bodies of these wretched beasts sprawled in grotesque postures and hampered our progress through the cutting. One animal still showed movement and was shot by its driver.' Grim work went on all around them. 'Pairs of stretcher bearers with expressionless faces picked their way through the rubble, their burdens hidden under greatcoat or blanket. A shell screamed above us and burst dully over the hill. Still in step we plodded on.'

Two months previously, when High Wood had been the scene of a cavalry charge, 130 horses and their riders had been cut to pieces by German machine guns. The carcasses of these horses were still lying where they had fallen, along with at least 100 of the men who had ridden them, quietly rotting in the shade of what was left of the trees. 'Yea, though I walk through the valley of the Shadow of Death,' muttered Bert, 'I will fear no evil.' Yet more unburied bodies lay further down the hill in various stages of putrefaction. One young driver, leading a horse team, did what he could to miss them. 'Strewn up the hill, in rows like corn that had been mown, lay hundreds of our chaps that looked as though they had run into a machine-gun nest. It was a warm muggy day and the poor chaps' faces and exposed flesh were smothered in flies. The smell was awful. They lay so thick we simply could not avoid running over some of them. The horses stepped over them, of course. But we could not help the wheels going over a few.'[24]

And the buzzing of the flies was only the half of it. Worse was when the eggs that had been laid inside the corpses hatched out into armies of maggots, crawling from ears and eye sockets and open wounds. Even the living were not immune. The Medical Office at a local Field Ambulance unit tasked with patching up the wounded was appalled to see one unconscious soldier arriving with part of his brain protruding from a hole in his skull, seething with maggots. Another was lying with a loop of gut sticking out from his uniform, the result of a bayonet wound, which had been lightly dressed with gauze, beneath which there was another wriggling mass.[25]

* * *

Today, as I gaze out over the smooth expanse of grass that carpets the slope leading to High Wood, I cannot help but imagine the bloody rubbish heap that it must have been 100 years ago, after two months of fighting. The discarded rifles with bayonets rusted to the muzzle; the shovels, water bottles and steel helmets; the maps trodden into the mud; the bones and limbs sticking out of the earth; the cotton bandoliers of small-arms ammunition; boxes of bombs, of Very lights, odd rounds of Stokes shells, flares, entrenching-tool handles, stretchers, petrol tins for water, odd pieces of clothing, empty tins of bully beef, groundsheets. 'It was one vast dump of discarded war material,' a disgusted soldier observed, surveying a similar scene near Ypres, adding his commanding officer's rule of thumb: 'You can tell a shell hole by its contents; two Mills bombs and a lump of faeces.'[26]

On the evening of 14 September 1916, as dusk descended, Padre David Railton wrapped up the treasured Union Jack he used in his services, his wooden cross, and his two squat candlesticks, then tramped his way up the crowded communication trench to the front line. There, wherever he could find space and men eager to receive him, he spread his flag over a stack of ammunition boxes, ready to minister to his military flock. Smiling at the dirty, weary faces gathered around him, he lit the candles and, in their dim, flickering glow, did his best to bring the spirit of the Last Supper into the stinking trench.[27]

Other padres, including the ex-England rugby player Rupert Edward Inglis, were doing much the same thing, using the same familiar words in trenches and dugouts all along the front. 'The blood of our Lord Jesus Christ, which was shed for you,' Railton intoned loudly enough to be heard over the drumming of the guns, 'preserve your body and soul unto everlasting life.' As he did so, each man answered 'Amen', some of them surprised to hear in their own voices that special firmness and fervour that come to the man who knows he may be about to die. Between communion services, feeling something similar, Railton found a moment to scribble a note to his beloved wife. 'We have got *there*,' he told her. 'Our men are waiting their turn. A good few are inwardly anxious but they put a cheery face on it all. Many guns are just behind me. The vibration is so great that spoons jump in the sugar case or teacups. God help us all.'[28]

Just a few days earlier, Irishman Tom Kettle had been scribbling another letter in his dugout south-east of High Wood, when he received the orders he had been dreading. Once again, he was to be in full readiness at midnight. The Dublin Fusiliers were to attack Ginchy, another pile of brick dust similar to their previous battleground at Guillemont, except perhaps a few yards closer to Germany. Kettle's 18-year-old batman, Private Robert Bingham, was with him at the time. While the great orator and academic wrote one last letter to his brother Larry, young Bingham sat on an ammunition box, adjusting his boots and puttees. His feet were still sore from the endless marching of the preceding weeks.

Ironically, it was Larry who had written to the authorities in April 1916, begging them to allow his brother to go to war, despite the poor health that was the legacy of his alcoholism. 'Tom's one chance of putting himself right and starting a new page is to remain in the army and go out to the front with his men,' he concluded.[29] Five months later, Kettle's letter to his brother was a full-hearted valediction. He must have known that these might well be the last words he would ever write:

> *If I live, I mean to spend the rest of my life working for*
> *perpetual peace. I have seen war and faced modern artillery,*
> *and know what an outrage it is against simple men. We*
> *are moving up tonight into the battle of the Somme. The*
> *bombardment, destruction and bloodshed are beyond all*
> *imagination, nor did I ever think the valour of simple men*
> *could be quite as beautiful as that of my Dublin Fusiliers. I*
> *have had two chances of leaving them – one on sick leave,*
> *and one to take a staff job. I have chosen to stay with my*
> *comrades.*

Looking up, Kettle watched Bingham closely. The boy had now removed his boots.

'Let me see those feet again, Bingham.'

'They's all right, sir. Just a bit red, really.'

Kettle looked into the boy's eyes.

'We need to get you to a doctor, Bingham.'

'I can go in the morning, sir. I'll be going on leave soon.'

'No, Bingham.' Kettle scribbled a chit and handed it to the young man. Then he gave him his watch for safekeeping. 'I want you to go now. Right now. You understand? Go to the hospital at Battalion HQ, and tell them I sent you.'

They stared at each other for a moment.

'Yes, sir. I think I do. Thank you, sir.'[30]

Alone now, in the closest thing to silence that an artillery bombardment will allow, Tom Kettle gazed down at the page he had written. Then he picked up his pencil and added a few more words. 'I am calm and happy but desperately anxious to live. Somewhere the Choosers of the Slain are touching with invisible wands those who are to die.'[31]

* * *

The artillery bombardment that preceded High Wood, along a line stretching between the villages of Courcelette and Flers on either side, was the most concentrated yet attempted on the Somme. Launching the offensive two months previously, the guns had fired around 200,000 shells a day. Now, in the days leading up to the 15 September attack, they blasted out almost 300,000 shells per day, and at a considerably narrower target.[32] With such a bombardment underway, there was no need to whisper. Waiting in the deep blue-grey light which heralded the dawn that Friday, some men were laughing and joking in strangely high-pitched voices; others were white and tight-lipped, with flashing eyes and jerky movements. All were keyed up for this great moment of their short, young lives.

Alec Reader, Bert Bradley, Anthony French and the other soldiers of the Civil Service Rifles were glad, for the first time ever, that their trenches were so crowded. It had been a windy night and, shivering in their damp uniforms, it was a comfort to be able to huddle close together and try to warm up. They hopped from foot to foot in an attempt to get the feeling back into their toes.

Their packs had already been named, numbered and stored in a shell hole. Some doubted that they would ever see them again, but Alec Reader had stuffed his library copy of *Treasure Island* into his, all the same. The men had each been issued with 120 rounds of ammunition, two grenades, an extra ration and either a pick or a shovel. As a 'bomber', entrusted with flinging grenades, Alec Reader was also weighed down with a large bag, a bit like a horse's nosebag, containing several Mills bombs. One or two men had changed into their clean spare shirts. Canteens were filled with foul-smelling water swilled out from petrol cans. Rifles were cleaned for the third time.

Anthony French wasn't cold, but he was still shivering as a water bottle of rum was passed hand to hand, the sky ahead turning grey. 'I woke Bert but he shook his head. When I took a swig and passed it on, he smiled. He knew I couldn't stand even the smell of it. We laughed quietly, I stopped shivering and didn't care about anything or anybody.' The officer looked carefully at his watch. French felt for his emergency rations. Bert checked his chinstrap for the third time. In another sector, Alec Reader shut his eyes and stopped hoping for a miracle. Too late for those release papers to save him now. Then, in a low voice, an officer said: 'Keep your eyes on me; and remember, over the top together. Keep in line with even spaces. Leave no gaps. Keep walking and listen for orders. Remember, over together. And good luck.'

'And to you, sir,' Bert said.

No movement.

No sound.

Only a deathly stillness.[33]

* * *

Early in the Battle of the Somme, the Allies had developed a strategy known as a 'creeping barrage': firing a wall of exploding shells which moved forward slowly over enemy positions while the infantry followed close behind. The idea being that any Germans not wiped out by the preceding three-day bombardment would now be forced to stay under cover during this latest onslaught, as the British soldiers advanced upon them.

At 6:20AM precisely, the creeping barrage was launched along almost the entire battle front, with just one significant gap in it. Anthony French was awed by 'a whining and a whistling and a vast tearing of the air and a tremendous roar as, from hundreds of thousands of hidden barrels, the first shells crashed and burst'. To their left and right, the air was full of the express-train whoosh of the shells' approach, the long, shattering thunder of their detonations and the whine or whistle of their metal shards while the fumes of high explosive were carried on the morning breeze. None of these shells, however, was being aimed straight ahead of them into High Wood itself which was deemed to be simply too close to the British forward trenches to risk a heavy bombardment. Not only this, but a creeping barrage might endanger the slow-moving tanks, which were supposedly going to perform the same task as the artillery.

Where were the blasted tanks?

Too late to worry about that. Not now, when the whistles were blowing – they couldn't actually hear the whistle, but they could see their officer blowing it – and they were all scrambling up over the parapets of their trenches, buzzing with panic and adrenaline, over and out into the blurred horror that lay between them and High Wood. 'In a moment every man was up and over and firmly on his feet,' recalled French, 'gauging equal distance with his neighbours, yet looking straight ahead. With pounding heart I stole a glance at Bert, ever a model of courage and tranquillity.' His friend looked as calm and unruffled as ever. He even had his pipe sticking out of his breast pocket. That glance would become a snapshot image engraved in French's consciousness for the rest of his life.

Stretching away to the left behind his best friend, he could see the line of helmeted men striding across the churned and devastated earth. Behind them, he was dimly aware of ravaged tree stumps and exhumed roots, just discernible in the misty light of morning. But here, still in sharp focus, strode the comforting figure of his friend, Bert Bradley, 'sure-footed; rifle and bayonet at the trail; head pressed forward; eyes peeled for the first sight of his old adversary, profile delicately outlined against the sky'. Reassured, French was about to look ahead once more when, suddenly, cutting through the earth-shaking roar of the artillery, he heard the vicious twang of a rifle bullet.

Another snapshot: his friend frozen to the spot. 'I saw Bert pause queerly in his stride and fall stiffly on his side and slither helplessly into a hole with blood streaking his face.' There was no cry or shriek of pain. One moment Bert was there. The next moment, he was not. 'I must have gone toward him as he fell,' recorded French, 'for I was on my knees beside him with his head in the crook of my arm when a sharp voice ordered me to keep going and not break the line.' Somehow French stumbled back to his feet and hurried to fill the Bert-shaped gap in the line. But he knew that Bert was dead, and that he would never see him again.

Approaching High Wood, the truth was dawning. The tanks had tanked. One had got lost en route. Two had got stuck in the wood itself. Another had swerved off course and opened fire on a trench full of Allied soldiers, killing and wounding several of them.[34] As a result, a desperate situation was getting out of hand. The soldiers who had managed to reach the German lines were now exposed to withering fire from their flanks, with the added danger of potentially being cut off and surrounded. Someone had to do something, and fast. Lieutenant Colonel Hamilton, the commanding officer of David Railton's battalion, at once leapt into action. Cometh the hour. Hamilton was deeply admired, even loved, by those who served under him. Railton himself referred to him as 'our dear Colonel' while describing an occasion when Hamilton gave up his tent for his men during a storm. He knew his men were dying in their droves. He could not stand by and watch. Swiftly organising a party of men, they made a courageous attempt to rush the enemy front line. In a few seconds Hamilton too had been killed, and alongside him, shot to pieces, lay every single man who had dashed forward with him.[35]

'Man after man went down to that awful machine-gun fire of the enemy,' recalled one soldier involved in the action that morning. 'Within 50 yards of the trench we left, there was but a bare handful left of half a company. I looked behind to see the second half of the company come on, led by the company officer, who as he neared us shouted, "Get on, damn you!" Just then he fell dead. Our platoon officer led us on. He had a walking stick in his hand, a revolver in the other and a smile set on his face. A big fine-looking man he was. Men were falling on all sides, some in their death agonies. The officer's runner stopped with a terrible scream, crumpled and fell behind a tree stump. The platoon sergeant next collapsed and began crawling back to our lines. In between the groans and cries of the men and the eternal awful fumes of cordite, that 100 yards to Fritz's line is the most fearful memory I have.'[36]

The screams of the men would haunt many of the troops fighting there for the rest of their lives. As one soldier recorded: 'That day I saw sights which were passing strange to a man of peace. I saw men in their madness bayonet each other without mercy, without thought. I saw the hot life's blood of German and Englishmen flow out together, and drench the fair soil of France. I saw men torn to fragments by the near explosion of bombs, and – worse than any sight – I heard the agonised cries and shrieks of men in mortal pain who were giving up their souls to their Maker. The mental picture painted through the medium of the eye may fade, but the cries of those poor, tortured and torn men I can never forget. They are with me always. I would I had been deaf at the time.'[37]

At around 11AM, in a final throw of the dice, a mass mortar barrage was directed at the eastern part of High Wood, where the German defences were at their thickest and most intractable. The eight teams inflicted a continuous barrage on the Germans which saw each mortar launch almost half-a-ton of shells over the course of the quarter-hour. The battle was turned on its head and the German machine guns were silent at last. Amid the smoke and noise and brutal chaos unleashed from the mortar emplacements, two companies of riflemen attacked High Wood once more. A few minutes later, German soldiers started stumbling into the open with their hands above their heads.[38]

* * *

Four days after the main attack on High Wood, Mary Kettle received a telegram from the War Office:

DEEPLY REGRET TO INFORM YOU LIEUT T M KETTLE WAS KILLED IN ACTION SEPT 9, THE ARMY COUNCIL EXPRESS THEIR SYMPATHY.

And that was it. One of the most brilliant minds in Ireland, a husband and father, snuffed out, just like that. Tom Kettle was one of over 4,350 casualties recorded by his division at Ginchy between 7 and 12 September 1916. We do not know exactly when Mary received the last letter her husband had written her. But it must have been around the same time. She now began writing to Tom's friends and colleagues in the army; to anyone who might be able to give her some information about how and where her husband had died, and, more importantly, where his body was buried. For a while, she heard nothing at all. And then at last one of his colleagues wrote to her from a field hospital on 14 October, apologising for not having done so sooner:

I was just behind Tom when we went over the top. He was in a bent position and a bullet got over a steel waistcoat and entered his heart. He lasted about one minute and he had my crucifix in his hands. He also said: 'This is the seventh anniversary of my wedding.' Boyd then took all Tom's papers and things out of his pockets, in order to keep them for you. But poor Boyd was blown to atoms in a few minutes, and the papers and all went. The Welsh guards buried Mr Kettle's remains. Tom's death has been a big blow to the Regiment, and I am afraid I could not put into words my feelings on the subject.[39]

At least now Mary had some information about *how* he had died, but in the chaos of the ongoing fighting, Tom Kettle's temporary grave and his remains would be lost. He was already one of the 'unknowns' and his daughter Betty, who was just three years old when he died, would have nowhere to mourn and commemorate her talented father.

* * *

Long after the tiny scrap of French land which was High Wood had been taken on Friday, 15 September, the fighting in the area continued. Bert Bradley, Anthony French and Alec Reader's 47th (London) Division alone lost more than 4,500 men and officers in casualties during the four days of the heaviest combat, out of a fighting strength of perhaps 8,500.[40] And at Ginchy, the razed village where Tom Kettle had met his end, the 'Choosers of the Slain' would touch with their invisible wands another of the most gifted and dazzling characters of the age. Late in the afternoon, Raymond Asquith, son of the Prime Minister, was shot in the chest while leading his men in an attack, only a few hours after the deaths at High Wood of Bert Bradley with his pipe, of young Alec Reader, still waiting for his release papers, and of Sidney Wheater, the hockey player from Scarborough. Unlike theirs, Asquith's response to being mortally wounded has gone down in history. Instead of seeking medical assistance, he lit a cigarette. Steel-hearted to the last, Asquith was determined to hide the seriousness of his injuries, to encourage his men to press home their attack. Afterwards, he was moved to a shell hole where there was an improvised dressing station and given morphia to ease the pain. He died an hour later, while being carried back to British lines. At Ginchy, too, Harry Farlam, the grocer's assistant who was so proud to be a Corporal, was killed the following day. The butcher's bill was rapidly increasing.

High Wood
Spring 2023

In the blazing heat of a peaceful spring day, I am struggling to imagine the chaos of battle which echoed in the trees and fields around me a century earlier. And having seen the devastation of modern warfare, it is near impossible to fully comprehend the carnage which unfolded. High Wood had been cleared of Germans by 1PM on Friday, 15 September, and the 47th (London) Division had succeeded in capturing the most heavily defended position on the Somme battlefield. But their victory – if the word victory can be used in such a context – had come at a colossal cost. As the Duke of Wellington had put it in 1815, after Waterloo, 'believe me, nothing except a battle lost can be half so melancholy as a battle won'.[41]

Some estimates suggest that beneath the soil of High Wood today, still lie the bodies of 8,000 nameless British and German soldiers, killed during the blood-soaked struggle for the innocent-looking patch of trees, brambles and grass where I stand.[42] So many Unknown Warriors, buried beneath my feet.

Unknown, yes, but only in death. I remind myself that these were real people who all had a mother and a father and a full life, long before they were reduced to soil and statistics. So many bereft parents, wives and children who would never know what really happened to their precious boy, who perhaps loved football and always remembered his mother's birthday; their beloved dad, who told the worst jokes but gave the best hugs; their devoted husband, with his cheeky grin and his awful snoring; their annoying big brother; their thoughtful fiancé, their roguish uncle, their wise young grandpa, their best friend from school. In the trees above my head, a bird breaks out into song and is answered by another. I shake my head, glad to have my thoughts interrupted.

* * *

In the whole Somme offensive, lasting from 1 July until 18 November 1916 – just a few months of the *four-and-a-quarter-year* war – the British Empire suffered 420,000 casualties and the French 200,000, for an advance of 8 miles. The German losses were at least 450,000 killed and wounded. 'You can no longer call it war, it is mere murder,' declared one Bavarian soldier at High Wood. 'All my previous experiences in this war are the purest child's play compared with this massacre, and that is much too mild a description.'[43]

In the cold, grey light of dawn on Saturday, 16 September, the survivors of the battle stared out over the stinking, pestilential rubbish heap, littered with mangled bodies, that had once been High Wood. Knowing that his work was only just beginning, Padre David Railton clutched his treasured Union Jack ready to move forward.

The task of rescuing the wounded had continued all night and was ongoing.

But the task of dealing with the dead had yet to begin.

CHAPTER TWO

THE GLORIOUS DEAD

HIGH WOOD, THE SOMME
SPRING 2023

Making my way up the gentle slope towards High Wood, I am dive-bombed by chattering skylarks. In the ridges of the landscape, I can just make out where deep-dug trenches once provided shelter for shattered men. Shell holes still leave faint shadows, like footprints in sand not quite erased by the tide. One of these shadows might have given fragile sanctuary to Anthony French, still dizzy from the death of his best pal, Bert Bradley. Coming to after being knocked unconscious by the exploding shell, French had spent several hours wondering if he would ever be found. That morning, this gentle meadow in northern France was a blood-spewing, bone-splitting hell of flying metal and flashing thunder. I must be very close to the spot where Bert and young Alec Reader gritted their teeth and forced themselves to clamber from the relative safety of their trenches into the murderous fire of the German guns. Somehow they managed to put one foot in front of the other, and did their best to climb this gentle incline in the face of the deadly onslaught. Here, too, is where Sidney Wheater, the hockey player from Scarborough, and Harry Farlam, proud to be a Corporal, must have shouted exhortations to their men.

Counting myself as a pilgrim, not a tourist, I slip through a gap in the hedge in order to venture just a few yards into the dense foliage of the wood and brambles. I don't want to go far, out of respect for the thousands of missing men still lying here, and also because of the ordnance that supposedly still lies around them. But I do want to see where so many made the ultimate sacrifice. I had an image of a wasteland of blasted stumps and desolation imprinted on my mind, from when Padre David Railton and his ilk fought and died here. However, now, looking around, I'm amazed at how densely *alive* the wood has become. So even on this dazzlingly bright day, when the sun on the headstones in the cemetery had made me squint a few moments earlier, the wood seems as dark as if dusk were falling; deep-green shadows draped languorously over the brambled humps and hollows of its depths.

After just a matter of seconds, the prickling sensation on the back of my neck makes me hesitate. I am an intensely practical person with no belief, or interest, in an afterlife. But now that I know the story of what took place here over one hundred years earlier, I have that feeling of ghosts again. The path that leads through the wood is clear in both directions. And yet I cannot ignore the slightly sinister feeling that this strange, dark landscape evokes. Looking down at my feet, I catch sight of something blood-red. A paper poppy trampled into the earth. Having read so much about Bert, Alec and their friends, I had been desperate to see where they fought and died. Now that I have done so, I find that I do not wish to be in this haunting location one moment longer.

Treading as lightly as I can, I creep quickly and quietly out of High Wood.

High Wood, The Somme
1916

The night of Friday, 15 September 1916 was not a peaceful one. The hours after any territorial gain, however minimal, never were. After all, the enemy knew exactly where the British soldiers were hunkered down in their captured trenches. Their heavy artillery pounded away with a well-aimed retaliatory barrage. Others, out in the open, had their own battles to fight. 'Amid the noise of the shells could often be heard the groans of the wounded who had not yet been brought in,' one officer recorded.[1] 'The shouts of the search party of stretcher bearers, and the curses of a ration or carrying party who had got lost.' Anthony French was one of these, trapped in a crater with a shattered leg, aware that death might well be close by. Bombardment from both sides was ceaseless, and French would have known that his chances of being found were limited. He comforted himself with the soldier's fond belief that two shells never fall in the same hole. Lost and unarmed, he wondered if another wave of infantry might come his way. 'Would it be ours or theirs?' he asked himself. 'If theirs, what? Should I feign death or fix them with a supercilious stare? I looked round for a hand grenade, any weapon. There was none.'[2]

Meanwhile, in makeshift trenches a few hundred yards away, filled with the stench of excrement, rotting flesh and smoke, the British battling for High Wood did their best to count their casualties. But how to be certain who was dead, and who was simply missing?

The grim roll calls lasted from teatime until well after dark.[3] One young Frenchman, working alongside them as an interpreter, watched haggard men standing around in their mud-soiled uniforms, waiting to announce that they had come back; listening for the names of friends who had not.

'Rifleman X?' the Major's voice would call.

No reply.

'Anyone know anything about him?'

'Yes, sir,' answered a voice from the crowd. 'He went over beside me. I last saw him as we got up to the German trench.'

Then silence. No one else knew anything more. Questions and answers went back and forth between the candle-lit table and the dark circle beyond it. Nor did anyone move until the work was completed.[4]

'Private Bradley?'

Silence. Had no one else seen Bert hit?

'Private Reader?'

Silence.

'Captain Wheater?'

Silence.

'Private French?'[5]

Now, perhaps, Anthony French and Bert Bradley's Corporal spoke up. Reporting how he had dragged French headfirst into a shell hole and poured a whole ampoule of iodine into the ragged wound above his knee. He could see the chalk-white bone, but French was still alive when he left him. 'Lie still,' the Corporal had told him before returning to the fight. 'Don't move the leg. We'll soon have you back in Blighty.'

The dead, like Bradley, still littered the area, but for now, they would have to wait their turn. It was the injured, like French, still lying exposed, who were taking priority.

* * *

Rupert Inglis, the army chaplain who had played rugby for England, was not present for roll call either. Instead, he was twelve hours into a twenty-four-hour stint at a primitive dressing station in a large crater near the vapourised village of Ginchy, doing his best to help patch up the wounded. 'It was awful getting them down, over a very rough country full of shell holes,' he wrote to his wife. 'Some of them must have been four or five hours on the journey. We had at least ten men hit bringing them down, and that means some pain for the wounded.'[6]

In a difficult situation, Inglis and fellow padre David Railton did what they could. And there could be no higher calling for them than to ease the suffering of a comrade. Another army chaplain confessed that, if he had to be on a battlefield, the more dead and wounded there were, the happier he was. Looking after others helped him forget his own fears. 'In going from one wounded man to another,' he said, 'I could often relieve the torment of thirst, perhaps by a drink from the man's own water bottle which he was unable to reach. I could take down a message from dying lips. I recall one lad lying in a shell hole, whose one thought was, "I don't know what my mother will do." I could at least write to that mother and tell her how her boy had forgotten his pain in his thought for her.'[7] Having been on the go for over twenty-four hours, Rupert Inglis, exhausted and soaked to the skin, collapsed in his dugout and composed a letter to his beloved wife. 'We are trying to clear a battlefield. Being very antique I always have a soft job. I was in charge of the stretcher bearers.'

They were the last words the padre would ever write. Two days later, his luck ran out. Leading a stretcher party at Ginchy, he was hit in the leg by shellfire. With one of his fellow bearers, he crawled into a crater for protection. But – flying in the face of the soldier's fondly held belief – another shell landed in the very same hole, killing them both. What remained of them was later collected and buried by their comrades.

What remained of them. I'd heard that phrase all too often to describe the dead of the First World War, but what did it really mean?

LONDON
SPRING 2023

It is difficult for me to truly picture the realities of the battlefields back then. The biblical devastation, destruction and desolation. Across the Somme and beyond, the dead and dying from one round of fighting would often be intermingled with the putrefying corpses of men, horses and mules yet to be collected from previous battles.

War films such as *1917* and *All Quiet on the Western Front* tend to represent bodies as largely intact. It is simpler to get actors to play dead rather than manufacture thousands of body parts – sometimes mere fragments – out of fibreglass or foam. Yet most of the deaths in the First World War were caused by artillery shells, then machine guns and rifle fire, with poison gas a distant third. And, in reality, soldiers hit by shells or shrapnel were often blasted apart.

'A booted foot and some bloody earth were all that were recovered to be placed in a sandbag and decently interred,' one soldier said after his officer was annihilated by a direct hit from a shell.[8] Unless the death was witnessed, and the witness survived long enough to report it, establishing who had lived and who had died, or trying to identify a person, or parts of a person in such circumstances, was often impossible.

Most of those who committed their experiences of the Great War to paper, 100 years and more ago, wrote sparingly of what they had seen and done. It was a time when the sensibilities of those back home were to be protected. Hearts were not worn on sleeves; terrible experiences were to be locked away.

As a former Tornado navigator, I was part of a vast military machine designed to deliver death and destruction to an enemy. But, sitting in the rear cockpit of a modern combat jet armed with lethal weapons, I was largely insulated from the carnage on the ground. Confronted now by the landscape of much earlier conflicts, I am beginning to realise I had thought little about what those young men in 1916 had really endured.

With the last First World War veterans long dead, how can I better understand what they went through? As part of my own journey of discovery, I needed to speak to people with personal, up-close experience of the effects of warfare – modern experts whose own stories could offer a limited insight into what their forebears had gone through 100 years earlier.

Andy Smith joined the Royal Air Force as a medic in 1987 and first saw active service as a young man in the Gulf War of 1991. Before this, as part of what he calls a 'Crash and Smash' team – a specially trained unit tasked with post-crash aircraft recovery – Smith had seen first-hand what happens to human beings on the receiving end of significant explosions. 'When a combat aircraft impacts the ground at high speed,' he says quietly, 'the effects are like a huge bomb blast. I went to one crash site where we found the pilot had somehow been blasted through some trees. He was in thousands of pieces. There was a set of lungs hanging from a branch and I had to climb the tree to collect the pieces of flesh. Then, a hundred yards away, I remember picking up a glove with the hand still inside. It wasn't a pleasant job but someone had to do it.'[9]

Smith subsequently saw action in both Gulf Wars, and in Bosnia during the mid-1990s. Now battle-hardened, he was still unprepared for the levels of trauma he saw in Afghanistan. 'A dead body hit by a bomb blast tends to adopt a very weird shape. Limbs at different angles, ragged flesh hanging off and jagged bones exposed. Most still had a look of shock and surprise on their face.'

Apart from the massive numbers of casualties involved, Smith's experiences would not have been so very different from those of the soldiers of the First World War – many of them recent civilians with little or no experience of battle – as they attempted to come to terms with the death of their friends, and wondered if they themselves would ever see their family again. 'In the first Gulf War I was sleeping in a tent and you could hear shelling, explosions going off in the background,' he says. 'But what still looms large in my memory is the sound of a man crying. It stood out above the noise of the battle. I knew who it was and I wanted to talk to him, but I thought he might be embarrassed, so you don't. You just try and ignore it.'

Smith's predecessors, the stretcher-bearers of the First World War, would have done more than their fair share of weeping, too, as they stumbled in pairs across the Somme mud trying to clear the battlefield of the injured and the dead as the shelling continued. Andy Smith and his fellow members of the Medical Emergency Response Team (MERT) now fly into the heart of battle in giant Chinook helicopters, bulked out with body armour, personal weapons and a heap of high-tech surgical equipment poking out from pouches attached to their desert camouflage gear – a world away from the muddy cotton uniforms, inadequate dressings and stained canvas stretchers of yesteryear – but they still have much in common.

Back in 1916, censorship, and a deep-seated aversion to revealing their emotions, would have prevented padres Rupert Inglis and

David Railton from telling their wives about the full savagery of what they witnessed when searching for the injured and dead. This part of the job has not got any easier with the passing of the years, and the scenes that live on in Andy Smith's memories paint a powerful picture of the battlefield experience a century earlier. 'I always noticed the Union Jack on their uniform as I felt for a pulse,' Smith says. 'Most just looked asleep. But some of the injuries were truly horrendous; I checked one body and was confronted by a young face, eyes open, looking straight at me. He looked as though he was still breathing. But it was just a reflex. Half his head was missing, so there was no way he could be alive. Another time I came across a torso which finished beneath the chest. I didn't need to check for a pulse then.

'I saw some truly terrible sights as a military medic, but if I think back to what my forebears would have seen during the First World War, I know that I have experienced just a fraction over the years of what they had to do every day.'

HIGH WOOD, THE SOMME
SEPTEMBER 1916

As the night of Friday, 15 September 1916 dragged on, a badly injured Anthony French managed to raise himself on his elbows and tried to drag himself back to the British lines. Suddenly he saw a shadowy figure passing to and fro across the battlefield, bending over each body he came to. Why?

He froze.

'My heart beat uncontrollably,' French remembered, when it was his turn. 'I stared, unbreathing. I saw a white collar and the familiar tin hat. He spoke in cultured English, his voice had a deep, rich timbre.' This must have been one of the regimental padres – perhaps David Railton himself – searching for the wounded among the dead. 'Better lie still,' the padre told him. 'You're some way off, but I'll try to send the stretcher bearers. They're all busy just now, but be patient and lie still.' French thanked him, then found himself alone once more. And while French's struggle to survive ground on, with many of the injured already being treated, the work to recover and bury the dead was now beginning.

Those involved had plenty of experience.

* * *

In the months before High Wood, the battlefield padres had already conducted countless burials, many using a Union Jack to cover a body during the brief service. Necessarily short because of the ongoing battles – and the numbers of dead – these quiet occasions exerted a power all their own. As soldiers gathered to say farewell to a comrade, they were deeply aware they might soon be lying beneath the 'padre's flag' themselves.

David Railton took great care of his personal Union Jack – acquired for him by his mother-in-law – treating it almost like a friend. The flag was a stirring symbol of home, of 'Dear Old England', as he put it.[10] It brought a flash of colour to the muted greys and khakis of their dun-coloured surroundings. And it was a Christian symbol, too: a blood-red cross which offered, perhaps, the possibility of resurrection for those upon whom it was softly laid. Railton described one of these rain-soaked ceremonies in a letter to his wife:

> *We carried our brave hero's mortal remains with the greatest difficulty over the rough ground, and buried him as reverently as we could. Indeed, it is wonderful to me to stand there with a group of soldiers at such a time; the picks and shovels are put aside. The Verey lights go up now and again, lighting our faces, and the guns keep up their usual squabbling with each other. And then all these men say the Lord's Prayer so firmly that you feel they really mean it. Then, they fill in the grave and go back to the firing-line.*[11]

The relentless threat of nearby fighting added immeasurably to the urgent solemnity of such occasions. Another army padre serving in

France, George Kendall, a working-class Yorkshire Methodist minister, described the bracing experience of burying three Welshmen after a spotter plane had alerted the enemy artillery to the whereabouts of his burial team. 'There was a terrific bombardment and I could see the flashes and hear the shells screaming through the air. The whole party rushed for a dugout just in time to see the high-explosive tear up the earth a few yards beyond. Then shrapnel burst overhead and we heard pieces falling around. During a lull we laid the boys to rest but owing to the exposed position, I was only able to repeat the opening sentences of the burial service, the committal and a short prayer. It is a solemn moment when engaged in such a task, for one never knew whether a chance shell would come and scatter further death.'[12]

On another occasion, Kendall was asked to take over the regimental duties of a colleague who barely survived the service. Having struggled through foot-deep mud and a fearsome artillery barrage, Kendall finally found the hapless cleric in a dugout. 'The chaplain had been conducting a burial party when the Germans opened fire on them. He jumped down into the grave, spraining his ankle in the process. For a long time he had to lie with the dead soldiers he had gone to bury.'

Under regular bombardment from enemy guns, Railton's battalion was tasked with providing a number of burial parties in an attempt to recover the dead in the aftermath of the battle at High Wood. Rescuing those who could still draw breath was bad enough. But risking their own lives to recover bodies lying alongside rotting corpses from previous assaults, or, even more horrendously, which had been buried and then exposed once more by further shelling, took the men into a whole new circle of hell. Especially when confronted by the crucial, though often impossible, task of identifying the bodies.

Burying a man with no name was to be avoided whenever possible.

* * *

Soldiers at the front would often be interred close to where they fell, individually or together in larger makeshift plots. Some, dealt with by colleagues, might be easier to identify. If they did not recognise a man, those collecting the dead would do their best to identify corpses from items they were wearing or carrying. Letters from home, photographs of loved ones, name labels sewn into uniforms. It was no simple task. Those mutilated or blown apart by shellfire posed the greatest challenge. Some had simply ceased to exist, with only fragments of scattered, intermingled remains to bury.

Identity disks helped. Since 1907, all British soldiers had been issued with at least one small tag – aluminium at first, and then red-brown vulcanised asbestos fibre – attached to a cord and worn like a necklace. Called 'dog tags' by my generation of military personnel, they were normally stamped with a man's name, number, religion and regiment. But they were supposed to be removed when a soldier was killed so the death could later be recorded, which left the interred body without any form of identification. Its owner could become anonymous in seconds, unless someone had managed to pencil his name onto a rough cross, jammed into the mud beside his head. Even then, further bombardment could take its toll, with the makeshift grave's occupant being blasted out, swiftly joining the already vast ranks of the anonymous. Some soldiers resorted to purchasing their own identity bracelets to remain on their body, and a second disc, a green octagonal lozenge, was introduced in late 1916. Though too late for the men killed at High Wood, this small but vital innovation meant that the new green disk could remain with a man's body after the red one was removed for registration.[13]

But the system remained far from flawless – why were so many First World War casualties listed as 'unknown', a body recovered but not identified? Or 'missing' – no trace of the person apparently ever found? There were countless possibilities.

Perhaps a comrade was buried in haste and under fire, with no time to record the essential details. Perhaps those carrying out a series of burials were then killed themselves, with any record of previous casualties lost with them. The horrific nature of industrial warfare could render the casualty unrecognisable. Or non-existent. The dead could be lost in collapsed trenches, or in the oceans of mud that swamped the battlefield. They could have lain in the open for months, on some occasions even years, decomposing and disintegrating all the while, or devoured by wild animals. And finally, as the war ground on and the same strips of field were fought over time and again, front lines ebbing and flowing, endless shelling churned up the earth and previously buried bodies could be blasted from their resting place to be scattered like confetti, any form of identity or registered location now gone. The ways a man could 'disappear', become 'unknown', cease to be, were endless.

And who knew when a recovered body, never identified, belonged to someone posted on the list of the 'missing' – those registered as never being found. If you didn't know *who* you had buried, it would be virtually impossible to reconcile those two groups – which is why so many headstones in the Great War cemeteries bear the sad inscription 'Known unto God'. And why the Thiepval Memorial, commemorating those with no *known* grave from the Somme *alone*, lists over 72,000 of 'the Missing'.

* * *

Although procedures varied, if a body had been identified, the responsibility for grave registration – attempting to list who was buried where and marking the spot – often fell to the army chaplains. The padres were expected to list the man's name, unit and so on, along with a map reference and other topographical details, before his closest relatives could receive the dreaded news:

It is my painful duty to inform you . . . then the words KILLED IN ACTION, or something equally stark, printed beneath the name. Unless the message that he was simply *MISSING* was the only one available.

Given the large numbers who died at High Wood, and the fighting that was still raging in the area, Railton and his comrades would have been able to do little more than the absolute minimum when it came to identifying and burying the bodies, and, if possible, collecting and returning any personal items to those who waited at home. Many casualties were simply deposited in graves unidentified. Heavy rain and enemy shellfire made burial duty a wretched task. 'No words can tell you how I feel, nor can words tell you of the horrors of the clearing of a battlefield,' Railton wrote to his wife. 'Several men went off with shell shock and two were wounded. I am certain the shell shock was caused not just by the explosion of a shell nearby, but by the sights and smell and horror of the battlefield in general. I felt dreadful, and had to do my best to keep the men up to the task.'[14]

It wasn't just the constant bombardment, or the intimacy of the experience – the pain of burying their friends – that made the job so tough for Railton and his team. It was the unimaginable, and ever increasing, quantity of the slaughtered.

Throughout the First World War, and during the Somme offensive in particular, death took place on a scale that few had anticipated, because the terrible lessons of mass slaughter experienced in the American Civil War had been largely ignored by the European military establishment. Technological advances like poison gas, long-range artillery and machine guns which could mow down row upon row of advancing troops in seconds offered an industrialised means of killing. How to begin the sheer logistical challenge of recovering the shattered bodies? Railton and his burial party managed to inter forty-seven members of their *own* unit in a large shell crater on the south-west side of High Wood. More of the dead were later buried around the site.[15] Throughout the conflict, bodies were often buried – either singly, or in groups – in shell holes, ruined trenches or shallow scrapes carved out of the battlefield. The men became experts with their shovels. It helped when the shell-blasted soil was as soft as a freshly ploughed field. Frozen winter earth was a good deal less forgiving.

Perhaps Railton and his team found the body of Anthony French's mate Bert Bradley still nestled in the shell hole where he fell, the new pipe sent by his sweetheart still lodged in his pocket.

Each time a fresh corpse was deposited, Railton would cover it with his Union Jack and say a few prayers before he and his men moved on. He did his best to identify the body if he possibly could, and – with a map reference – to keep a note of who had been buried where. During that first day at High Wood, Railton was searching on a patch of ground just forward of the trenches when he found the battalion's much-loved commanding officer, Colonel Hamilton. 'I found his body all alone,' Railton wrote to his wife. After searching it for any belongings or papers, he cut off the officer's rank badges and buttons, partly as proof of identity, and partly to provide precious keepsakes for Hamilton's next of kin. All that Railton left on the dead man's uniform was the ribbon of his Military Cross, awarded for bravery at the Battle of Loos the previous year. 'It is dreadful,' he wrote, despairingly, in another letter. 'Many men, who have stood it all, cannot stand this clearing of the battlefield. I don't know what to tell you, I expect it would be censored.' The work was clearly excruciating for them all. The fact that this was what Railton – like padres through the ages – had gone to France to do, made it no easier.[16]

LONDON
SPRING 2023

The sickening experience of standing over the body of a man you know is one that has haunted servicemen – and servicewomen – throughout history. It certainly troubled RAF paramedic Andy Smith. 'It brings it home to you when it's somebody you've actually known,' he says, recalling his work recovering remains after an aircraft accident. 'Perhaps you had done their aircrew medical a few days before. You've talked to them; you've chatted. Then, two weeks later, there's been a crash and you are literally picking up tennis ball-size bits of their body.' Listening to Andy relive his experiences of dealing with what is left of the dead, I am all too aware that he might, once upon a time, have been picking up bits and pieces of my friends – or, if my luck had failed, even me – from a crash site in Germany or a battlefield in Iraq. 'I put the various body parts we collected in clear plastic bags so they could be seen, and labelled them as best I could with what I thought each piece was. Often it was a guess, sometimes it was impossible to say.'

Although Padre Railton and his First World War burial teams clearly did not have the luxury of carrying out such time-consuming and intricate work when dealing with *their* dead, I was beginning to have an inkling of what they might have endured in the aftermath of each battle. Andy recognises the gruesome work he was required to do pales into insignificance alongside that undertaken by his predecessors. 'We were recovering one, sometimes two bodies from a crashed jet,' he says. 'We always *knew* who the crew was, because we *knew* a jet was missing and *knew* where it had come down. It is difficult, even for me, to imagine what those clearing the battlefields of the Somme, Passchendaele, Flanders and more had to cope with. Having to collect thousands of bodies, trying to identify the remains *and then* bury them. It must have been a truly horrendous job.'

THE SOMME
SPRING 2023

The extraordinary numbers of the dead, the missing, the unidentified, whirs around in my head as I drive the short distance from High Wood to Beaumont-Hamel. Six miles north of Albert, it is the largest preserved area of the Somme battlefield; a living memorial. I gaze in silence at the perfect, lush grass that coats the pockmarked meadows and eerily well-preserved trenches, with their deep-cut contours and their rusted barbed wire pickets still jutting from the ground like broken spears.

On the very first day of the Battle of the Somme in July 1916, the officers and men of the Newfoundland Regiment prepared to engage the enemy. The communication trenches through which they were supposed to advance were already clogged with the dead and wounded, so they were ordered to cross open ground instead.

Facing them was a battle-hardened German regiment, well dug-in, with prior warning of their attack. The result was heart-rendingly predictable. Of the 780 who took part, only 68 were available for roll call the next day; 324 men were killed, or listed as missing presumed dead, the rest wounded. The dead included fourteen sets of brothers. The battalion – and the community – had all but ceased to exist.[17] I examine the rusting supports which once carried the barbed wire that trapped them like flies in a web. A group of British schoolchildren, all around ten years old, are solemnly tramping through the preserved trenches wearing baseball caps and backpacks. Give them a wooden rifle each, and they would look like a platoon of little soldiers, marching off to war. I can tell from their excited chatter that the place has captured their imaginations. Their teacher and I give each other a friendly nod as we pass.

'Look, we're in a *real* trench,' exclaims one of the boys, much as he might announce that he was riding Space Mountain at Disney World. I am joyed by his excitement and grin at the teacher. He looks almost apologetic, as if the boy is taking too much pleasure in a place that should be sombre. But this stuff is *still* real, and these young people are learning so much about warfare. This landscape, studded with bullets and bones and undiscovered bodies, is rich with history and I am glad that the young have the chance to connect with it. I catch myself wishing that the forgotten, long-dead soldiers lying beneath our feet could somehow witness this peaceful scene and know that schoolchildren in Britain are still being taught about their sacrifice. I find myself thinking about Westminster Abbey again, and about the unknown man buried there. Was it here at Beaumont-Hamel that he lost his life?

There is a scattering of small cemeteries in the area, containing many, many hundreds of headstones, commemorating just a few of those who died in the summer of 1916. The graves in the Redan Ridge No. 1 Cemetery are grouped close together, in three long rows containing around 150 bodies. Nearly half are unidentified.

The nearby British Cemetery is home to ninety-seven identified and eighty-two not.

Just over 150 men lie in the Hawthorn Ridge No. 1 Cemetery, close to where the British front line was located. Only eighty-two are named.

There are over 250 occupants of the Redan Ridge No. 2 Cemetery. Only 150 who gave their lives have names.

Waggon Road Cemetery is located north-east of Beaumont-Hamel village. Little visited, 195 soldiers rest here in six rows. Thirty-six remain anonymous.[18]

This small handful of graveyards, telling the story of a fraction of the dead and missing, is mirrored across the Somme. And the plethora of other First World War battlefields. Many of the dead, never recovered and offered a permanent place to rest, still lie in the earth beneath my feet. So many Unknown Warriors. So many ghosts. Indeed, in the winter of 1916, months after the start of the Somme campaign, the ground here was still strewn with so many unburied corpses that, according to one army chaplain, it became a matter of real military importance that the work of burial should be completed. 'Nothing is more depressing to the living than to see unburied dead about them,' he wrote, lamenting the tragic vision that awaited him at Beaumont-Hamel, right where I am standing.[19]

In my mind's eye, this velvety grass morphs into a stinking quagmire, liberally scattered with corpses, shrapnel and gore. I can picture pale-faced, exhausted soldiers lining the dark trenches, sodden Woodbines trembling in frozen fingers, peering out through the pall of battle at the bodies of their friends and neighbours. I try to scribble some notes, but this place is too sad for words.

I cannot imagine the desolation of these young men, miles from home, their utter inability to fathom what the hell to do with so many bodies; so many precious fathers, sons and brothers. And as I walk among the graves that surround Beaumont-Hamel, reflecting on the Unknown Warrior beneath his black slab of Belgian marble in Westminster Abbey, I find myself haunted by the number of inscriptions which read so simply, and so heartbreakingly: 'A Soldier of the Great War. Known unto God.' I am haunted because these soldiers, buried in neat rows in France, were not known only unto

God. They were known unto their fathers and wives, sons, mothers and sisters. They were known unto their grandparents, their fellow factory workers, their mates in the pub and unto their chums in the village cricket team. They were real people, not just patriotic emblems, 'Known unto God'.

THE SOMME
1916

For David Railton and his comrades, still shattered from the battle, heaving yet more unidentified bodies into yet more earth must have been a dehumanising experience, the consequences of which, by the end of the war, were – at least by the Americans – becoming more fully understood. 'The effect upon the morale of combatant troops of being compelled to bury their own dead is very bad,' argued the Chief Surgeon of the US forces in France in 1918. 'During conditions where the bodies have become black, swollen, discoloured remnants of humanity, literally covered with maggots, the effect is of course tremendously bad.'[20] Because of the ebb and flow of the fighting, some corpses remained untended for weeks or even months. The smell of rotting flesh was a constant reminder of the need to be careful where one rested, and for the soil covering the deceased to be more than a superficial sprinkle. 'In the autumn heat the air is fouled with the smell of the innumerable dead,' complained one medical officer, 'so lightly covered that in unsuspected, though extensive places, one's tread disturbs the surface uncovers them, or swarms of maggots show what one is seated near.'[21]

Burying the escalating number of corpses on the battlefield was now a necessity, and threatening to become a national scandal. 'We are on the verge over here of serious trouble about the number of bodies lying out still unburied on the Somme battlefields,' wrote one medic in June 1917, nearly a full year after the start of the campaign. 'The soldiers returning wounded or on leave to England are complaining bitterly about it, and the War Office has already received letters on the matter.'[22]

Unrecovered, many of those fallen would become an integral part of the First World War landscape. Trenches could often be constructed around earlier burial sites and the men soon grew used to sharing their living space with the dead. 'In one deep, sandy trench, I saw a man who had been buried and could not be got out,' recalled one of the padres. 'Also, the blackened head of another man sticking out of the side of the trench, quite low. I was told nearly everybody stumbles and trips over it at night. They found him when digging the trench and did not like to interfere with him.'[23] And Anthony French had woken one morning to see a corpse entangled in the barbed wire that he had just helped set up. 'The gaping mouth and staring eyes depressed us all,' he wrote. 'There was no avoiding this horror. It hung in our line of vision. On two successive nights we had tried to bring it in, but Jerry, in anticipation, had sighted his machine guns on it.' The soldiers who had to live alongside these corpses could only take refuge in the fact that they had become ghoulish husks, no longer inhabited by the souls that had once animated them.

LONDON
SPRING 2023

Railton and the other padres offer limited recollections of their work as they slowly picked their way across the body-strewn battlefields of the Somme and beyond. It is difficult to imagine they were immune to the awfulness of the task, even with so much experience with the dead and dying. But theirs was not a generation to talk about personal vulnerabilities or trauma. So how did it *feel* to deal with the dead? With the 'unknown'?

As a young serviceman in 1982, I was glued to news reports from the Falklands War in the South Atlantic. I now realise I may have simply revelled in the headlines detailing the British victories there and had little understanding of what my colleagues were really going through.

Canon Alf Hayes, now a grizzled, twinkling 77-year-old, was a

Catholic priest serving in the British Army in Germany in 1982. He had been looking forward to seeing the Rolling Stones live on stage in Hanover when he got the call ordering him to deploy as a battle-field padre to the Falklands after Argentina invaded the islands in 1982. He was to sail south on the QE2, a luxury ocean liner that had been hurriedly converted into a troop carrier.

In 1915, Padre Railton had sailed to France from Southampton docks. In 1982, Hayes embarked from the very same place. The QE2 was a lot more comfortable than the *Golden Eagle*, the flat-bottomed Thames paddle steamer which took Railton and a lot of seasick soldiers to Le Havre in 1915. But the butterflies in the stomach will have felt much the same. Perhaps the send-off Hayes witnessed in 1982 was similar to that experienced some seventy years earlier. 'My lasting memory is of a young mother on the quay-side holding up her baby for her husband, somewhere among us, to see,' he told me. 'She must have been about nineteen and tears were streaming down her face. Amid all the celebration, flag-waving, perhaps jingoism, that young lady knew exactly what it all meant. Searching for the face of her loved one, knowing it might be the last time she saw him. Suddenly, I was hit with the realisation of what we were going to do. This was for real.'[24]

Just as Railton had, Hayes prepared his soldiers for battle know-ing some would die. 'In the same way as the clergy from the First World War, my role as a padre was to be where the troops were. Obviously I wouldn't be fighting trench to trench, but I needed to be near the battlefield in order to do my job. To offer comfort, perhaps counselling. A non-judgemental ear to listen to personal fears. To offer mass and absolution in preparation for fighting, and the very real possibility of dying. As a man of faith, I felt no conflict between my religion and the reality of war. My job was to minister to those in need, regardless of their religion, whether a friend or enemy.'

And, like Railton, it wasn't long before Hayes was required to deal with the aftermath of an early engagement, around Goose Green, when his team was tasked with recovering the Argentinian dead. 'One of the great acts of mercy is to bury the dead from battle until someone else can return later and do it properly. It's what padres have done through the ages,' he says. In time-honoured fashion, Hayes quickly became accustomed to the brusque realities of a so-called 'field burial' in the heat of battle. 'We were respectful but efficient. The war was still being fought and we could hear the guns continuing to fire elsewhere.'

The British dealt with their own dead after the battle at Goose Green and the iconic news footage of bodies being buried in a mass grave under the guidance of their own unit padre would be flashed around the world. Colleagues carried their fallen brothers in body bags, placing them gently at the bottom of a long trench, as the padre read each name from his list. Obviously, not only did every British serviceman carry identification, they were all well known to their distraught colleagues.

It was very different with their Argentinian counterparts.

The total numbers killed in the Falklands are a fraction of those killed in a single day on the Somme. But they still needed dealing with, and in the absence of the vast shell craters used at High Wood in 1916, a local farmer used his digger to create a mass grave. 'We collected around thirty-seven Argentinian dead . . .' Alf's words fade slightly at the memory. 'Unfortunately, although many were wear-ing one, two or even three sets of rosary beads, very few wore dog tags or carried identity cards. It was the first time I'd done anything like this, and I was struck by both the scale of what I was doing, and the sheer sorrow of my task. All these young men, all recently in their prime, now dead. Unidentified. Cold, wet, skin shrivelled like it does if you've been in the bath too long.'

Hayes's burial party was made up of Argentinian prisoners and he wrestled with what he was asking them to do. 'Many were young conscripts who knew little about their colleagues, and I felt truly sorry for them, silently sobbing as they retrieved their dead compatriots. As I searched the pockets of the deceased for any iden-tification, I looked into the faces and wondered who they were, who their families were, where they lived. I was laying someone's relative to rest; they would never see them again. This was the last thing I

could do for both the dead and the living – send their relatives to
their God.'

Hayes and his team laid the Argentinian dead side by side in
the mass grave, ready for a brief service. 'We were able to identify
very few. Most of them were simply unknown. But this was some
mother's son, and I wanted to be able to say that I gave them a
proper Christian burial. It was a sad, poignant, lonely experience.'
Later, echoing the First World War padres' experience, the rain
started to pour. 'The grave became half-filled with water, covering
many of the corpses. It was not a pleasant experience for any of us,
but we had to carry on with the service and move on to the next
battle. I couldn't allow myself to dwell, this was the reality of war.'

Listening to Alf relive his Falklands tour, I suddenly feel myself
sitting bolt upright. I'm back on my own tour on the islands, as a
Tornado navigator in 1994, twelve years after the war. I'm back in the
Argentine Cemetery, where most of their dead were relocated in the
aftermath of the war. I'm newly captivated by the walled enclosure
and the monument emblazoned with the image of Argentina's patron
saint, the Virgen de Luján. Each of the 236 graves is marked with a
simple white wooden cross, many carrying the name of the soldier,
but well over half of them bear the inscription with which I have
become increasingly familiar: '*Soldado Argentino Sólo Conocido
Por Dios*' – Argentinian Soldier Known Only By God.[25]

Back then, I couldn't really understand how soldiers from a relatively modern conflict could be 'unknown'. Now, listening to Alf,
the man responsible for some of those early burials, I have a better
grasp of what he – and the First World War padres – had endured.

I wondered if Railton and his comrades had experienced similar
emotions as they toiled beneath the rain and shellfire to get hundreds of broken bodies into the fetid earth, against the odds, in
1916? This was ever the reality of war, or at least it had been since
the Geneva Convention a decade earlier.[26] This ground-breaking
agreement had set a new precedent, requiring all nations involved
in a conflict to attempt to identify and bury their soldiers killed
on the battlefield, along with the dead of the enemy. Even though

conditions in the First World War clearly show this wasn't always possible, it was certainly attempted.

But the dead had not always been treated as tenderly as David Railton in 1916 and Alf Hayes in 1982 had striven to achieve.

* * *

A century before High Wood, one British officer described the battlefield at Waterloo, strewn with tens of thousands of bodies, as 'a sight too terrible to behold. The multitude of carcasses, the heaps of wounded men with mangled limbs unable to move and perishing from not having their wounds dressed, or from hunger.'[27] The survivors stripped the dead of their weapons, fine uniforms and other valuables, while locals scavenged whatever souvenirs they could: hats, leather belts, letters and even body parts. And they didn't stop there. Soldiers and locals armed with pliers often yanked the teeth from the gums of the deceased, for later sale to the highest bidder. Early dentists boiled these teeth and used them to fashion dentures for the rich. They were popular because of the youth of their original owners, and, according to the British Dental Association, 'Waterloo Teeth' appeared in supply catalogues well into the 1860s.[28]

Local peasants were hired to bury the corpses in mass graves, or to burn them on towering pyres. In the months that followed the battle, even the bodies that had been laid beneath the earth could not safely rest in peace. There were reports that many of the Waterloo burial pits may subsequently have been emptied, the bones shipped to Hull to be ground up and sold as bonemeal fertiliser.[29] Horrifying as this sounds, it appears to have been par for the course at the time. 'Many tons of human bone are sent every year to the North,' reported the *London Quarterly Review* in 1819, and 'bones of all descriptions are imported, with pieces of half-decayed coffin attire found among them'.[30]

This may have a certain bleak appeal to those who are attached to the circular connections between life and death, but it is quite a distance from the heroic conclusion so richly deserved by the fallen from one of Britain's greatest military victories, as the *Observer* of 1874 acknowledged, with grim pragmatism: 'It certainly seems hard on the great and mighty of past ages that their remains be utilised for commercial purposes, but business is business.'[31] This harsh desecration seems appalling to our modern sensibilities. Astonishingly, though, something similar was apparently suggested for the dead of the First World War. 'Surely it will be comforting for combatants to know that they have not died in vain,' one Australian bonemeal producer declared breezily in a series of letters to the *Cairns Post* in 1917. 'And that their bodies after death will still do good by helping to grow food for the living.' He went further: 'It should be a pleasant idea that their remains will help make explosives and assist in carrying on the war.'

His suggestion received short shrift from other readers.[32]

THE SOMME
WINTER 1916

On the Somme, it was the long-dead who were making the work of clearing the battlefield such a deeply unpleasant task. I imagine that Railton and the other padres did their best to prioritise the fresh bodies from the most recent engagement, but the constant shelling would have mingled and mangled the old and new together. 'Often have I picked up the remains of a fine brave man on a shovel,' wrote one young soldier involved with later burials. 'Just a little heap of bones and maggots to be carried to the common burial place. Numerous bodies were found lying submerged in the water in shell holes and mine craters; bodies that seemed quite whole, but which became like huge masses of white, slimy chalk when we handled them.' And then there was the grim ordeal of fishing around with their unprotected hands to locate an identity disc, a bracelet; anything that might identify the corpse. 'I shuddered as my hands, covered in soft flesh and slime, moved about in search of the disc,' he continued. 'And I have had to pull bodies to pieces in order that they should not be buried unknown. It was very painful to have to bury the unknown.'[33]

Anything – any wretched discomfort – was better than having to bury an unknown soldier. Anything was better than abandoning someone's son or father to perpetual anonymity. And this was even before the weary soldiers with shovels had considered the men's relatives sitting at home, staring out of the window at a cold grey sky, and wondering if the letter they were dreading would arrive today. Would they ever know if their son had a grave? And, if he did, would it be somewhere they could visit, in the endless months and years ahead?

* * *

On 18 November 1916, in the face of worsening weather, General Haig called a halt to the Somme offensive. The combined casualties of the British Empire, the French and the Germans numbered well over a million men.[34]

If High Wood was just a nod towards the horrors of the battle as a whole, then the Somme was just a snapshot of the all-encompassing brutality of the Great War. The battlefields of Ypres, Passchendaele, Loos, Verdun and countless other places – in Europe and around the world – would provide untold more millions of dead. The war itself would drag on for another two years. Of the many hundreds of thousands more who would be killed, some would be buried with names, some would be buried without. Many would never be found; simply logged as 'missing'. The exact total listed on the Thiepval Memorial, just a few miles from High Wood, to those with no known grave from the Somme *alone*, is over 72,000.

These things are, after all, quantifiable.

It is the suffering that goes with such a loss – with no body, no grave, no faint trace of a man's existence – that remains limitless.

CHAPTER THREE

THE YEARNING

SEPTEMBER 1916

Two years before the end of the war, John French had written a letter to check on his brother Anthony's welfare after the battle for High Wood. It had been returned unopened, stamped 'Missing. Location unknown'. That was the extent of the information. But what did those few stark words mean? Missing and alive? Or missing and dead? Fears deepened when the well-meaning father of another soldier in French's battalion wrote them a letter of condolence at their 'loss'. It transpired that French's friend had written home to tell his own dad that he had seen Anthony French 'blown sky high' at High Wood. This news dealt a final blow to the family's fragile sense of hope for a miracle. Their beloved son was surely dead?

In fact, after crawling across the battlefield for over twenty-four hours, badly injured and in searing pain, Anthony French had eventually been rescued by stretcher-bearers. Taken to a field hospital he had lain unconscious for nearly twelve days. Coming to, he struggled to comprehend all that had happened. 'The sounds are of the present and the scenes of the past and of home. Confused and overlapping. A face of exquisite oval symmetry is bent over mine. Hair fair and shining below a white linen crown.'[1] His initial pleasure diminished and he gritted his teeth as a doctor worked on the open wounds of his mangled leg with an instrument nicknamed 'the apple-corer'. His heart sank further when an orderly whispered: 'We found your home address and sent a field postcard.' There was something about that single word, *home* – the safe place every soldier dreamed of – which did for him in a way that the German bullets and shells had not. Anthony French, who had seen so much death and destruction, finally broke down in tears.

One imagines that a similar scene would have been played out in his West Country home when the field postcard announced – finally, miraculously – that French was, against all the odds, alive. His father immediately wrote to the young soldier who had wrongly believed he'd seen Anthony die at High Wood, to tell him the joyful news. In a tragic turn of fate, *that* letter was now returned to French Sr marked 'Missing. Believed killed'.

French's family were soon able to rejoice at the news that he was being shipped back to England in October 1916. But there was no similar miracle for his great friend Bert Bradley's family. They, too, had received the dreaded 'Missing' notice in the post, and were holding out the inevitable hope in response. French had witnessed Bert's death at first hand and he knew what he must do. He wrote to Bert's father as soon as he had the strength to do so.

From Tottenham in north London came the understated reply. 'I am thankful for your very kind letter,' wrote Mr Bradley with the quiet dignity of a man whose heart must have been torn to shreds. 'It is a great comfort to know that my son did not suffer long. He was a good boy and will be sadly missed. We are all very sorry for his young lady, for they were very much attached. Your letter will put her mind at rest, for she is still hoping he is alive and a prisoner.' The 'great comfort' that poor Mr Bradley would not have had, however, was the faintest idea if his dear son's body had been recovered and was buried. Or indeed, if there had been any remains to be recovered.

And as the war ground towards its inexorable, bloody conclusion, countless other families would join the Bradleys in wondering what had become of their loved ones.

ARMISTICE DAY
NOVEMBER 1918

Two years later, Anthony French struggled through the pouring
rain on 11 November to hand in his rifle at Wimbledon barracks.
His wounded leg was finally mended. He arrived to find the place
almost deserted. In the silence of the Corporals' Mess, French sat
at a table and wrote a letter to his dead friend:

> *This, my dear Bert, is your day, and I'm more than ever
> reminded of you and your gallant company. You have a full
> complement now in Valhalla. What on earth happened after
> I left you ...?*

French wrote page after page to Bert, relating his own story from
the two years since he had abandoned his lifeless body in a shell hole
in High Wood. 'Repeatedly I asked what had happened to him and
why he was never identified. As I wrote, a deep sadness afflicted me,
as when a loved one has departed and there are no longer any joys
because they cannot be shared.' This same scene was being played
out by the army of the bereaved. The war was over. The numbing
aftershocks had only just begun.

> *What happened to my beloved ...?*

* * *

Historians like to say that 'the guns fell silent' at 11AM on
11 November 1918, as if the guns themselves had been responsible
for the war. More intriguing to me, in my search for information
about that extraordinary day, is how silent the soldiers fell, too.

'The morning of 11th November came, and we did not speak
much,' recalled Padre George Kendall, who had been waiting for
the news alongside the officers of his brigade. 'The end of the titanic
struggle that had extended over so many weary months and years
was greeted by the same quiet stoicism that had characterised all our

most hazardous operations. If a single cheer was raised in the whole of the brigade I did not hear it. Probably our hearts were too full for words. In the hour of deliverance, we were not only thankful, but sorrowful. We thought of our pals who had gone West and were lying, as we left them, in some spot *forever England*.'[2]

For the soldiers, war had become such a habit that the idea of it stopping was hard to comprehend. Even the wise and empathetic Padre David Railton, who would be thirty-four in two days' time, found the sudden shift as challenging as everyone else. 'There was now a large void where before, every part of his being was focused on winning the war, making sure he did all he could for the fighting men,' says Railton's biographer, Andrew Richards. 'He was happy for it to be over, but he knew nothing would ever be the same again.'[3]

'Do you think it's real?' asked a young officer in the Royal Artillery, turning to the commander of his gun battery.

'Listen,' came the reply.

He listened. They all listened. And it was true. The only thing he could hear was the stamping and whinnying of the horses in a farm nearby. 'There had never been a night like this,' he wrote afterwards. 'We could hear the silence. It was a bit frightening. We had forgotten what silence was.'[4] The trouble with silence, of course, is that it gives you space to think. And with peace looming, the officer found himself consumed with thoughts of his dead comrades. 'Now we should become aware of their loss,' he realised. 'We had hardly done so until now, we had still been with them, in the same country, close to them, close to death ourselves. But soon we should have to go away and leave them, we should be going home, they would stay behind, their home was in the lonely desolation of the battlefield.'

Of course, people did rejoice at the end of the war, they danced, they drank, they sang, they hugged. They celebrated survival and the prospect of a bright new dawn, hopes of a better future. But, for many, it was too strange, too sad a time for celebration. Besides, it is easy to forget that this *was* merely an armistice – an agreed cessation of hostilities, akin to a truce – not some mighty victory over a humbled and remorseful enemy. Vera Brittain, a young volunteer nurse and feminist, would later recount her shattering wartime experiences in her memoir *Testament of Youth*: 'the men and women who looked incredulously into each other's faces did not cry jubilantly: "We've won the war!" They only said: "The War is over."' Elbows deep in the sink where she was cleaning the blood from hospital dressing bowls, she went on automatically with her work, 'like a sleeper who is determined to go on dreaming after being told to wake up'.[5]

Yes, the hated Kaiser had abdicated the day before. But the cost – in blood and treasure – of reaching this point had been so enormous, so impossible to grasp that the lack of any clear sense of triumph can only have deepened the sombre shadows clouding the shallow gaiety in the streets. A friend persuaded Vera to go out into the capital to witness the manic revelry. It was all too much for a young woman who had lost her brother and her fiancé in the conflict. 'Already this was a different world from the one that I had known during four life-long years. And in that brightly lit, alien world I should have no part. All those with whom I had really been intimate were gone; not one remained to share with me the heights and the depths of my memories. The War was over; a new age was beginning; but the dead were dead and would never return.'

With so many hundreds of thousands dead, Vera was not alone in mourning loss amid the revelry. Noel Evans, a Second Lieutenant in the Royal Artillery, died of his wounds at the same time the Armistice was being signed in a railway carriage at Compiègne. His parents, hurrying to France to be with him, only arrived in time to bury him. 'To think that we shall never see his dear smile again,' wrote Violet, Noel's stricken mother. 'It's all been so cruelly hard. All the horrible noise and crowds and rejoicing everywhere day and night, it has been a continuous nightmare and the journey back I thought never would come to an end. It was such an awful shock when we got there to be told he had already gone to the cemetery. I don't know how to face life without him.'[6]

Young Elsie Bennett found herself facing life without a father. He had enlisted in the army after a flaming row with his wife, who had goaded him into joining up. His family never forgave her after Bennett was killed, aged thirty-seven, in 1917. In Elsie's school, a thanksgiving service was organised on Armistice Day. But when the national anthem was played, Elsie refused to stand up. The headmaster demanded to know why. 'All the other little boys' and girls' [fathers] will be coming home now,' she explained. 'But my daddy will never come home again.'

She was caned for disobedience.[7]

LONDON
SPRING 2023

Professor Lucy Easthope is one of the UK's leading authorities on emergency planning and disaster recovery and has a lifetime of experience in helping communities rebuild their lives following a tragedy. In her book, *When the Dust Settles*, she describes what she has learned over the years, having worked in the aftermath of countless disasters including the 9/11 terrorist attack that destroyed the twin towers of New York's World Trade Center in 2001, the 2004 Indian Ocean tsunami which killed more than 230,000 people, and the 2017 fire that engulfed the Grenfell Tower in London. Lucy has witnessed the same heartbreaking process – this discovery of the bottomlessness of grief – time after time, across the world. 'One of the most painful similarities that I have encountered in the aftermath of disasters is that almost everyone, including the community and responders, is in denial about how long this will hurt for. They want to believe that life after disaster is a fleeting state. "But how long does it feel like this?" would be asked over and over.'[8]

The answer, for many, seems to be: *forever*.

In November 1918, alongside the tragic loss of so many relatives during the war, people now had to contend with a whole new sense of loss as they began to mourn the life they lived before the war. According to Easthope, the best way to describe this special feeling of loss is a word originating in Wales: *hiraeth*.

'*Hiraeth*,' she explains, 'is a longing for a place to which there is no return, an echo of something that can never be found, a heart-sickness for something that no longer exists and a time that can never be gone back to.'

Vera Brittain described her own *hiraeth* with characteristic acerbity: 'Only gradually did I realise that the War had condemned me to live to the end of my days in a world without confidence or security. In which love would seem threatened perpetually by death, and happiness appear a house without duration, built upon the shifting sands of chance.'

Looking back, it's clear what must have made this sense of loss so hard to bear in 1918. There were no funerals in villages up and down the land. No burials where communities could come together and families could lay their favourite sons to rest in familiar soil. There were no graves to visit in country churchyards. In modern parlance, they had no *closure*. Even for those with 'known' graves in France and beyond, it is easy to understand the desperation of families to have the bodies brought home. Perhaps, just *perhaps*, if they had a body to bury, a final resting place to visit, this awful gnawing ache that clutched at their hearts from morning till night might be eased.

Lucy Easthope has seen this process unfold, many times, at first hand. And the waiting game it involves is an excruciatingly painful one. 'There may be one collective death toll in a disaster,' she says, describing the lives lost in a helicopter crash in the North Sea in 2002, 'but the actual recovery of each of the deceased can take many weeks, months or never happen at all. Every new day can turn up another grim discovery. As a result, in the weeks and months following a disaster a hierarchy can emerge where those families who have a body are considered "lucky" compared to those who don't.'

* * *

As a forensic anthropologist, anatomist and academic, Professor Dame Sue Black is one of Britain's leading experts in the identification of corpses and in determining cause of death. Perhaps not surprisingly, her work often takes her to the same grim places as Lucy Easthope, and the two unstinting, inspiring women have become close friends.

A brisk and twinkling Scot, with a dry sense of humour underpinning her ferocious intelligence, Dame Sue has worked in warzones including Kosovo, Sierra Leone and Iraq. And, like Lucy Easthope, she has seen only too clearly the agony of families who do not have – who cannot find – a loved one to bury, so that the grieving process can truly begin. 'I absolutely understand that visceral need to have your relative's body,' she tells me during our discussion about loss, 'to know where they lie, and to have a grave to visit and to contemplate.' Time after time, in the aftermath of disasters, of wars, of court cases and investigations, Sue Black has witnessed people trapped in the awful limbo of not knowing whether someone dear to them is dead or alive. 'It hits them every morning on waking,' she says. 'It is their last thought at night before they fall asleep, and on occasion it strays into their dreams as well. While you are left replaying the same nightmare scenarios in your head in a continuous loop, you can never really begin to heal.'[9]

FRANCE
1915

One man who had, since early in the war, been thinking very carefully about the fate of the dead and their graves in France, while also seeking to identify the missing, was Fabian Ware. Born in 1869, Ware was a brilliant bundle of energies who had already achieved more success in several different careers than most people have in one. He had been a newspaper editor, and a teacher in South Africa, later working on educational reform. Ware was a natural fighter and persuader of men.

But when he offered his formidable abilities to the army, he was told he was too old to enlist. The same thing happened to many of his fellow members of London's Royal Automobile Club, including the likes of Clement Cazalet. The same age as Ware, he had won a bronze medal for tennis at the 1908 Olympic Games in London. Frustrated yet highly motivated, they responded to an appeal from the War Office for non-combatants to drive to France in their private cars. Not to act as a taxi service for Generals, but to look for wounded British soldiers and stragglers who had been separated from their units during the hurried retreat following the Battle of Mons in late August 1914.[10] They soon discovered that stragglers were very thin on the ground and the mission was a pointless one. Undaunted, Ware and his colleagues offered their services to the British Red Cross Society in Amiens and Paris and began ferrying the wounded to and from dressing stations behind the lines instead.

During this period as an ambulance officer for the Red Cross on the Western Front, Ware became increasingly conscious of – and concerned about – the many thousands of individual makeshift graves and burial sites that were springing up all over the battlefields. The task of finding a soldier's grave, even with precise co-ordinates, was already challenging enough; the churning mud of ongoing battles increased the task tenfold. He immediately recognised the vital importance of keeping tabs on who had been buried and where. And perhaps more importantly, the need for relatives to be able to find and visit the graves of their dead. And who would look after these shanty-cemeteries after the war was over and the return of the French farmers and landowners to whom the land belonged? Amid the chaotic maelstrom of trench warfare, all of this had been overlooked. Nobody, it appeared, had foreseen the staggering number of graves that would be created, or that somehow registering so many thousands would be a massive undertaking, particularly during shellfire. Thankfully for a nation's war dead, its grieving families and its debt to posterity, this one brave man decided, largely off his own bat, to take it on.

Before long, Ware's shoestring operation boasted a fleet of sixteen ambulances and a field hospital, as well as a motley collection of touring cars. It had gained a grand new title, too – the Graves

Registration Commission (GRC) – and was officially recognised by the War Office in March 1915.[11] Ware was given the rank of honorary Major, and Cazalet honorary Captain. Along with touring the rudimentary battlefield cemeteries that various regiments had created, Ware and his team of Red Cross officers would search out the growing numbers of burial sites in fields, woods and even private gardens. Some were marked with rough wooden crosses, often hurriedly knocked together from soapboxes and inscribed with pencil or scratched inscriptions which rarely survived the next fall of rain. So the GRC provided their own well-crafted crosses, with a painted inscription and a tarred base to prevent rotting.[12] Later, the inscriptions were stamped onto aluminium tags which were fixed to each soldier's wooden cross.[13]

It helped Ware that some of Britain's top Generals still remembered the chaos and distress caused by the neglect of graves in the Boer War. But his enduring success lay in his dogged determination and his skill at creating networks of informants. 'I have had considerable assistance from the local French priest,' declared one of his officers. 'But frequently I receive my best information from small French children who sometimes lead me for two or three miles across ploughed fields to a grave.'

Between May and October 1915, almost 27,000 graves were registered. That number would undoubtedly have been greater had Ware not felt so strongly that the work of the GRC did not justify risking people's lives. His team of men, some of whom had been deemed unfit for active service, were rarely deterred by danger, and often operated within range of the enemy's guns. But Ware himself was disturbed by reports of them working in exposed positions and under fire. One of his staff had already been killed in a cemetery at Ypres, and he was finding it impossible to recruit the extra men he needed. He therefore issued a directive forbidding them to take risks, and to concentrate their efforts in the safer areas behind the lines. Pragmatic as it was, this necessary decision would also have contributed to the heart-wrenchingly high proportion of unidentifiable graves being created – the sheer number of names without bodies, of bodies without names – that emerged in the final count of Unknown Warriors after the end of the war.

One of Ware's masterstrokes lay in the work he did to allow the Ministry of War to acquire land, granted by the French, for the burial of Allied soldiers. In early 1916, personnel had begun criss-crossing the battle sites to identify suitable locations for 'official' cemeteries. An additional headache was the arrangement for purchase or compulsory acquisition of the chosen land. With remarkable foresight, Ware was determined to avoid the creation of hundreds of tiny, isolated burial grounds. He wanted to facilitate the proper marking of graves, and to make them easy to find by relatives *after* the war. He also wanted, where possible, to reduce the likelihood of bodies having to be dug up, moved and buried elsewhere following the – hoped for – cessation of hostilities. Whenever that might come.

In practice, as I discovered at High Wood, the harsh realities of the ongoing conflict meant that there were still countless, isolated burials all over northern France and Flanders. And the process of identifying the dead and laying them to rest in larger cemeteries, both during and after the war, was a task that would take years to achieve. But at the very least, thanks to Ware's bold vision, machinery had been set in motion which would change the landscape of France forever, and which would still have the power to profoundly affect – and move to silence – even those with little knowledge of history over a century later.

* * *

Not everybody at home, however, both during and after the war, was on the same page. Many families were determined that their relative's remains would not rest in a foreign field and early in the war some soldiers killed in France had already been repatriated.

The officer grandson of the former Prime Minister, William Gladstone, killed in action on 13 April 1915, was disinterred under fire and buried in Britain nine days later, 'in obedience to pressure from a very high quarter'. A few days later, the first pilot to win the Victoria Cross in the war, William Rhodes-Moorhouse, was repatriated, too.[14]

Ware and the authorities quickly realised that it was both unfair and impractical to allow those few families who could afford it to bring their son's body home. An order was drafted that month to ban such exhumations for the duration of the war.

It made little difference to the fate of Alan Fowler, a grandson of the engineer-in-chief of the iconic Forth Road Bridge, designer of both Victoria Station and early components of the London Underground. Obliterated by a shell blast at Ypres in April 1915, his remains were never found. Inevitably, the young man's death weighed heavily upon his elder brother, Harrow- and Sandhurst-educated Sir John Fowler, a Captain in the Seaforth Highlanders. On his return to the front two months later, following an urgent trip home, he told his battalion chaplain, 'I think my days are numbered.'[15]

The morning after, he was enjoying a cup of tea with his Colonel in the trenches near Richebourg-l'Avoué, 20 miles west of Lille, when a shell landed on their dugout. The Colonel survived but, clambering to his feet, he discovered that his companion had not.

Fowler had written his last will and testament a week earlier, declaring with admirable clarity: 'I desire to be buried in the family burial ground, but if my mother decides that this is not a convenient arrangement, or that it entails undue expense, I leave her to decide where my burial shall be, and direct my trustees, in the event of my being buried elsewhere, to place a ship's anchor, weighing two hundredweight [100kg] or thereby, in the family burial ground, and to engrave thereon my name, date and place of birth, but no other memorial or stone shall be erected.'[16]

The April order to cease any repatriations notwithstanding, his body was afforded the treatment which would have been unavailable to the likes of a Bert Bradley or an Alec Reader. After a funeral service in France, a senior officer arranged for Fowler's remains to be returned to Scotland, accompanied by a military chaplain.

Though his family received only thirty-six hours' notice, they appear to have done Sir John proud. A local newspaper reported on the arrival of his remains at Inverness railway station: 'A handsome oak coffin covered with the Union Jack, on which were placed the dead soldier's sword and bonnet, were received by a guard of honour of 80 men at Fort George, and a firing party from the battalion, with pipers and buglers, was also waiting on the platform. A procession was formed to the station entrance, the pipers playing "The Flowers of the Forest".'

Later that day, several hundred mourners attended a ceremony on the lawn of the family estate – testament to the young baronet's popularity, the rarity of military funerals during the war and the fact that there had been no grand funeral for his younger sibling, who is commemorated on the Menin Gate at Ypres. He is just one of the 54,588 who still have no known grave, out of more than 150,000 Allied soldiers who lost their lives during the battles around Ypres over the course of the First World War.

Repatriations like Fowler's were extremely rare, extremely expensive and – by the summer of 1915 – extremely illegal. Now the wealthy, just like the less privileged families of dead or missing soldiers, could only sit at home, wringing their hands. 'As in wars of all times,' reflected Anthony French, looking back on his tumultuous experience, 'it was in the homes and hearts of the people that the full drama was staged.' They turned photographs to the wall. They waited. They prayed that one day, *their* family member might be brought home so that they could mourn them properly, at a graveside.

* * *

In the lead-up to the Armistice, bereaved families suffered a variety of excruciatingly painful experiences. A soldier might be reported as 'killed', with a letter from the Commanding Officer or the Battalion Padre to follow, assuring them that their boy was well liked, had died bravely and been laid to rest at a particular location which often proved impossible to identify, even if the body was relatively intact. But as I discovered, even with a marked grave, the reality of his burial place surviving the war undisturbed was a matter of chance. And mass graves were commonplace. The crater at High Wood, into which Railton and his burial party had committed the bodies of forty-seven soldiers, would turn out to be a relatively small one. Though its capacity was increased as the conflict wore on, it never came close to the mind-boggling scale of the burial site at Langemark, a village in Flanders just north of Ypres, where some 24,917 young German soldiers are interred. Even the troops themselves had become increasingly concerned about being lost in the mud. 'The men no longer fear death, we have made peace with the idea of our own demise,' wrote a German officer at Ypres. 'A much heavier burden is the fear of being forgotten on foreign soil – an infamous end for any soldier. Swallowed by the earth, far from home, with no sign of remembrance, separated from your comrades and family in your homeland. Forgotten – no one wants such a fate.'[17]

Worst of all for the waiting families were the fevered doubts, hopes, fears and uncertainties triggered by someone being reported as 'missing'. They knew something dreadful had happened. They just couldn't be sure exactly what. The Red Cross, Fabian Ware's Graves Registration Commission and a few other institutions did their best to fill the void. Acting as the eyes and ears of those at home, they endeavoured to support those left in limbo, and sought to replace red tape and impersonal forms with human warmth and clear statements of fact. But information became an elusive commodity, and, as ever, truth remained the first casualty of war.

The 'missing' label covered a variety of possibilities, most of which brought continuing heartbreak rather than comfort. Was their boy held captive in a German prison camp, and would he be released when the war was over? Might he be in hospital, perhaps with amnesia, while the authorities struggled to work out exactly who he was, and where he belonged? Or might there have been a case of mistaken identity, opening up the possibility that he was still alive, somehow, somewhere, separated from the mud-covered identity disc whose discovery had suggested his loss.

And all it took was a smidgen of possibility for tormented hope to take root; to allow the virtually impossible to blossom into the very likely indeed.

CHAPTER FOUR

CLOSURE?

FRANCE
1918

Just how desperate were people to find the missing? How far would
a family go to claim a person – living or dead – as their own?

Around a million and a half Frenchmen had died during the
war, of whom 400,000 were listed as 'missing'. These sons, lovers
and husbands had been lost on their own soil, in their own blood-
saturated mud, and their families' quest for closure and redemption
was made all the more intense by the focus of their grief being so
close to home. So, when sixty-four French unidentified former prisoners of war – all of whom had lost their minds or their memories
in the conflict – were released by the Germans at the end of the war,
there was no shortage of families desperate to claim them for their
own. Not exactly because they were willing to lie, but because they
yearned to believe this was the truth.

Perhaps the most celebrated of these prisoners, who had no idea
of their own identity but were expected to do their best to survive
after being shipped home, was a man who called himself Anthelme
Mangin. Or that's how it sounded. He had no recognisable marks
on his dirty uniform, and this was his sole, muttered response when
people asked his name. Two years after the war, he was one of only
six of the original sixty-four prisoners who remained unidentified,

so the authorities decided to publish the men's photographs in the national press, hoping that someone would come forward to claim them. Perhaps Mangin had one of those faces that somehow looks like lots of different people. Perhaps others felt especially sorry for him. For whatever reason, thousands of people immediately decided that he was their son, their husband, their brother or their uncle. Mangin became a celebrity overnight, and the queue of people wanting to visit him at his asylum in Rodez, a small city in the south of France, became a nightmare to manage.

According to Jean-Yves Le Naour, whose book *The Living Unknown Soldier* recounts Mangin's tragic story, the amnesiac prisoner accepted these visits with catatonic blankness, despite the tears and wailing of the families who were trying to hug and coax him into believing that he was theirs. The director of the asylum turned both crowd controller and grand inquisitor as he strove to unpick the truth of the various families' competing claims. The case dragged on for an incredible *ten* years, with families even taking the asylum administrators to court, accusing them of wrongful incarceration. By the 1930s, only two horses were left in the running. One, Lucie Lemay, was quite sure that Mangin was her missing husband, Marcel. The other, Pierre Manjoin, claimed that Mangin was his son, Octave. A bizarre experiment was devised in which 'Mangin' was dropped off at Pierre Manjoin's local train station and, with a detective following him, left to make his own way 'home'. He instinctively made his way to the house where he had – presumably – grown up, so it was finally established that Mangin was, in fact, Octave.

Bizarrely, the court cases rumbled on and Pierre Manjoin died in 1939 before things were settled. Sadder still, poor Octave/Mangin was never released from the asylum, where he appears to have died of starvation in 1942. It is a salutary tale, and one that reveals a great deal about the complex psychology of mourning and what Le Naour calls 'the drama of the missing', neither physically present nor officially dead. 'The truth is that Mangin really had no story of his own,' says Le Naour. 'His story was in the suffering of the families who claimed him.'[1]

And that 'drama of the missing', that suffering and lack of closure, was being echoed in homes across the globe.

* * *

Figures – understandably – vary, but according to the Commonwealth War Graves Commission 526,816 British and Commonwealth soldiers killed in the First World War have no known grave and are listed instead on monuments to 'the Missing'.[2] Yet the Victorian traditions in which the families of 1918 Britain were still steeped continued to require a grave where mourning could take place.

Fabian Ware was doing his best. By May 1916, his men had registered 50,000 of them. But everything had got a whole lot harder with the exponential cataclysm of the Somme, where thousands of bodies and hundreds of graves were obliterated on a regular basis. In his efforts to facilitate identification of the dead, it was Ware – among all his other endeavours – who had pushed for the introduction of that second identity disc; the one that could stay with the body after a man was killed. But even then, identification was often impossible, and he encouraged his burial officers to use every clue, no matter how small – a razor with a name on the handle; unit details engraved on a spoon; stencilled webbing; even the type of uniform which had been issued to a particular unit at a particular time.[3]

Like the combatants in the Falklands, or Iraq, or Afghanistan, the soldiers of the First World War had so little opportunity or space for personal possessions, that the few trinkets they did manage to keep mattered very deeply. A tiny Bible. A new pipe. A letter from a sweetheart.

Unfortunately, as Professor Dame Sue Black, the forensic anthropologist, explains, even clearly named items are not necessarily proof of identity. 'You have to be very careful indeed, as it's tragically easy to get it wrong,' she tells me. 'Suppose you find a body with a wallet carrying identification? Well, we have had bomb victims where a wallet has been blasted from one body and embedded into another. With decomposition, it's difficult to tell if that wallet was

being carried by that person or has been transferred by the blast.'
She points out, too, that soldiers might well have loaned items to
each other, as an act of kindness. 'So if that coat has a name on
it, does that mean the body we find it on is actually that named
person?'[4]

When a man was alive, all his material possessions were merely
'stuff'. But after his death these items really came alive. First, because an engraved cigarette case or a monogrammed Bible might be
the only way for Ware's team to identify a dead soldier whose face
and identity discs had been destroyed. And second, because – as
anyone who has ever loved another human being knows – something that has been carried close to the skin will be imbued, forever,
with a tantalising trace of the wearer's presence. They are still there,
somehow, in that wedding ring, that faded photograph, that notebook with a hole drilled right through it.

The soldiers knew this too. Many asked a pal or a padre to
promise that a treasured item would be returned to the family if 'the
worst happened', all too aware that these pitiful mementos might
soon be all that was left to send home; all that was left to show that
they had ever existed at all. Such objects might bring an ounce of
comfort to those at home, too. One bereft young widow kitted up
a dressmaker's dummy in the full Grenadier Guards uniform of her
dead husband, and slept with it beside her bed. The clothes smelled
of him and, when she was drowsy, she could almost imagine he had
come back to her.[5]

Lucy Easthope, the disaster expert who has a lifetime of experience recovering and returning the personal effects of victims of
catastrophes both national and international, has changed her relationship with the objects in her own life. 'I remember every disaster
by its personal effects. The aftermath of the 7/7 terrorist bombings
on London's transport network in 2005 was all about coats, bags
and office workers' lunchboxes. Tupperware filled with salad,
wallets, blown-off clothing and the thick paper wodge of a near-
to-submission PhD thesis, still being annotated up until the point
that the bomb exploded.' Whether to return these objects as they

were, or to clean them up and somehow sanitise them, was a fraught issue for the authorities. After the Hillsborough Stadium disaster in 1989, which resulted in the deaths of ninety-seven football fans, Easthope spoke to mothers of the dead. Many were distraught to learn that their son's lucky football shirt – which they had vowed to wear unlaundered for the whole season – had actually been cleaned. 'They did not want it washed until their team had won the cup, or the league,' says Easthope.

On the other hand, when Vera Brittain's fiancé, Roland, was killed in France in 1915, his mother and sister were appalled to receive a package including the outfit that their precious boy had been wearing when he was hit. 'I wondered why it was thought necessary to return such relics,' Brittain wrote. 'The tunic, torn back and front by the bullet, a khaki vest dark and stiff with blood, and a pair of blood-stained breeches slit open at the top by someone obviously in a violent hurry. Those gruesome rags made me realise, as I had never realised before, all that France really meant.'

She was overwhelmed by this vision of war stripped of its glory. 'For though he had only worn the things when living, the smell of those clothes was the smell of graveyards and the Dead. The mud of France which covered them was not ordinary mud; it had not the usual clean pure smell of earth, but it was as though it were saturated with dead bodies – dead that had been dead a long, long time.'

* * *

Fabian Ware's early work with the Graves Registration Commission to create more formal cemeteries for the growing numbers of dead had continued apace and General Haig, the Commander-in-Chief of the British forces, was quick to recognise its efforts. 'It has an extraordinary moral value to the Troops in the Field as well as to the relatives and friends of the dead, at home,' he said. 'The mere fact that these officers visit day after day, the cemeteries close behind the trenches, fully exposed to shell and rifle fire, accurately to record not only the names of the dead but also the exact place of burial, has a symbolical value to the men that it would be difficult to exaggerate.'[6] As a result, even while the fighting still raged, the GRC had registered 150,000 graves in France and Belgium by April 1917. Though they worked largely in areas well behind the lines, some of these sites would still be destroyed by later shellfire and fighting, especially in the spring offensives of 1918.

Some 12,000 photographs of graves had been sent to anxious relatives, and, even *during* the battles, seventy cemeteries had already been planted with trees and shrubs. This addition of plants was to become one of the hallmarks of Britain's war cemeteries. Initially the focus was upon the sites nearest the front, especially where there were large concentrations of troops. 'They help to brighten places often very barren and desolate,' observed Ware's horticultural expert, who had been sent out from the Royal Botanic Gardens at Kew. 'They cheer our men who are constant visitors to our cemeteries and who frequently pass these cemeteries when on the march.'[7]

As well as pushing the effort to make these final resting places beautiful, Ware was also working to establish a set of general principles for how the nation's dead were to be buried and memorialised *after* the war. A new heavyweight committee – which would soon become the Imperial War Graves Commission (IWGC) – was set up with the Prince of Wales as president. Rudyard Kipling, who had lost his beloved son, John, at the Battle of Loos in 1915, aged just eighteen, would become its literary adviser. Kipling wrote his iconic 1916 poem 'My Boy Jack' about Jack Cornwell, a 16-year-old sailor and the youngest recipient of the Victoria Cross. It is difficult to imagine that the emotions he expressed about someone else's son were not influenced by his own loss, echoing the grief of so many parents at that time. It was Kipling, too, who would coin many of the eloquent phrases carved into the gardens of stone in the cemeteries, including the line 'Their name liveth for evermore' from the book of Ecclesiastes. And, perhaps most poignantly, the phrase that adorns the white headstones of all the Unknown Warriors: 'A Soldier of the Great War. Known unto God.'

Ware's work, and the later deliberations of the Imperial War Graves Commission, were being examined both during and after the war. A report – *War Graves: How the Cemeteries Abroad Will Be Designed* – by Sir Frederic Kenyon, the highly respected director of the British Museum, was quietly published immediately after the Armistice and, in those pre-social media days, it took some time for its monumental implications to sink in.[8] Indeed, it was only when Rudyard Kipling wrote an article for *The Times* in early 1919, attempting to assuage a growing sense of unrest from those who still hoped for bodies to be returned and describing what the completed cemeteries in France would look like, that the protests began in earnest.[9]

Suddenly the truth was out there and fully understood: the wartime ban on repatriation was not about to be repealed. The bodies of British and Commonwealth soldiers who had died in France would not be coming home. Not now. Not ever.

The IWGC hastily followed up Kipling's article with an illustrated booklet, *Graves of the Fallen*, which was meant to soften the impact of Kenyon's report with its images of verdant beatific havens of peace.[10] But the public was now in full cry.

One of the fundamental principles laid out by Kenyon was 'equality of treatment'. There should be no distinction between the graves of the highest-ranking general and the lowliest private. Fabian Ware seems to have had an instinctive understanding, gained no doubt from his experiences as an ambulance officer working in the trenches, of the deep sense of comradeship that ran through the army. He also felt passionately that the war cemeteries should reflect this. He knew how the officers felt, too. 'In 99 cases out of 100, they will tell you that if they are killed, they would wish to be among their men.'[11] So far, so democratic and – given the spirit of the times, with the rise of the Labour movement and the shift towards universal suffrage – so uncontroversial. But it wasn't just balancing the differences between officers and other ranks, or between rich and poor, that made it important to bury the men where they fell, or at least in the new cemeteries nearby. It was also the fact that so many men had no known grave and to give the privilege of repatriation only to those who could lay their hands on an identified body would discriminate against a large section of the population.[12]

So equality also meant sticking to the wartime ban on exhumations and repatriations. No bodies were coming home. Many found the decision hard to accept. Not only had these soldiers volunteered to fight for their country and to die in its service but, now that they were dead, that same country was going to decide what happened to their remains. It was essentially taking ownership of their bodies. And *this* decision proved to be very controversial indeed. 'The dead are certainly not the property of the State or of any particular regiment,' declared Sir James Remnant, in Parliament. 'The dead belong to their own relations, who should have the right to erect what headstones they like.'[13] Meanwhile Lady Maud Selborne, the daughter of former Prime Minister Robert Cecil, deemed 'this conscription of bodies to be worthy of Lenin'.[14]

'The bereaved desire consolation from personal tributes to their dead,' she declared, in an impassioned letter to *The Times*, 'not from well-drilled, patterned uniformity.'[15] English law had never recognised ownership of a corpse. And, even if it had, try telling that to the mothers whose beloved sons' lifeless bodies were lying, lost and alone, in the mud of France. It didn't help that the US Secretary of War had recently reassured American families that *their* dead would be brought home.

* * *

'Sir,' wrote Sarah Smith to the *Yorkshire Evening Post* in the spring of 1919. 'As the mother of one of the heroes who will not return, I think it is time for mothers and widows of soldiers to protest against the attitude of the Government in robbing us of our beloved dead. They were taken from us, and have sacrificed their lives, and still we are not allowed to have their remains brought home. They are to be left in foreign lands, and they are only worthy of a paltry concrete cross. Exhumation would not appeal to everyone, but to the majority, where possible, it would; and what a comfort it would be to our aching hearts to have our dear ones placed in the family vault, and be enabled to tend their graves ourselves. Yours, etc. S. A. Smith.'[16]

A passionate woman of fifty-nine, whose 19-year-old son had died of his wounds in September 1918, Sarah would become a driving force behind the campaign to exhume bodies and bring them home at their families' own expense. Only then, she argued, could they exercise 'the right which has ever been the privilege of the bereaved'.[17] She organised a petition signed by nearly 1,400 families, begging the Prince of Wales to overturn the ban.[18] When this fell on deaf ears, she turned to the Belgian King, urging him to intervene on her behalf. When that failed, too, she wrote letter after letter. She made enquiry after enquiry. She lodged complaint after complaint.

Despite pleas from the indomitable Sarah Smith, Lady Selborne and other powerful establishment families who had lost sons, the IWGC stood firm.

* * *

At the same time, across the Channel, a gruesome process had already begun. Now that the war was over, countless bodies, spread across countless smaller burial plots all the way up the Western Front, still needed to be dealt with. The youth of Britain and France had sacrificed themselves with commendable zeal, or at least obedience to a cause. They needed to be recovered from their scattered graves and reburied in the official, neatly ordered plots.

So began the work of exhumation, with a plan to recruit 15,000 volunteers from the United Kingdom who would work for two shillings and sixpence a day. Search parties of thirty-two men carrying eight stretchers, each led by an officer, systematically worked over land marked out in grid squares on a map. Searching for bodies, with the aim of identifying them if possible, then relocating them to the more formal cemeteries described in Kenyon's report, designed by distinguished architects Edwin Lutyens, Herbert Baker and Reginald Blomfield, with inscriptions by Rudyard Kipling and planting devised by the Royal Botanic Gardens at Kew. By June 1919, even though only 4,347 men had been sent to France and Belgium, they had managed to locate, recover and rebury 130,000 bodies.

LONDON
SPRING 2023

Recover and rebury? Feeling both intrigued and repelled by the thought of this macabre work, I find myself wanting to question forensic anthropologist Dame Sue Black, who has spent much of her working life exhuming bodies at every stage of putrefaction. She has a wonderfully no-nonsense way of describing the process.

In war-torn Kosovo in 1999, for example, it was the mass graves that she and her team found which presented some of the biggest technical challenges. Three months after a massacre in which a Serbian special police unit had rounded up and machine-gunned or burned alive over forty men and boys, Dame Sue and her team were tasked with recovering, examining and identifying the bodies. 'I can still see that ramshackle building today; the doorway with a window on either side,' she tells me, her hands moving animatedly in front of her, elucidating various facets of the scene she is describing. 'The dead were all piled up in the corner. And they were under the rubble of the collapsed roof, so all you could see initially was a mound of debris with perhaps a hand or a leg bone protruding.'[19]

For the IWGC teams in France and Belgium exhuming similar sites, the experience must have been much the same. 'When dead bodies are crammed together this way, almost tangled up, trying to extract each body is a bit like human Jenga,' she tells me. 'You try to remove one, but a body part might come away, or another body might fall towards you from further back.' Listening to Dame Sue, I have the guilty feeling I am hearing someone describe what it's like to take part in a zombie movie. But it is all too real. 'Normally a body might be somewhat held together by its clothes,' she continues.

'But extremities can easily come away. So a head and upper verte-brae, hand or foot, will often fall away as you try to move it.'

I can feel myself grimace as I listen to her. And, of course, I want to know more, too. I want to know what those poor volunteers en-dured, as they tramped through France with their shovels and their doubts in 1919. What does it smell like when you dig up a body on a battlefield? Dame Sue nods, as if she knows exactly why I ask. 'The smell is truly horrendous,' she says, in a low voice. 'A body which has been rotting for months in the heat is rancid. There's a lot of fluid spreading around as body fat liquefies and fluids escape. You are crawling around in bodily mulch, maggots, flies and pupae. It is all deeply unpleasant.'

Given the horrific conditions in which the post-war volunteer burial teams in France worked, perhaps it is not surprising that drinking, insubordination and rowdiness were a problem. 'The men were constantly getting drunk, very drunk,' recalled one Private working with an Australian unit. 'The majority of the men were a bad lot and very inefficient. They were neither dependable nor re-liable.'[20] The area superintendent of the IWGC around Albert was reported to be 'incapacitated' following a motorcycle accident while drunk.[21] And some of those who weren't drinking were in an even worse state. Especially the ones who had been employed as ceme-tery gardeners but subsequently found themselves potting bodies rather than plants. 'The gardener here looks exceedingly gloomy, poor fellow,' reported a senior IWGC representative. 'He seems to spend his whole time in the wilderness.'[22] Another commander wrote, 'One of my section officers went to hospital with a nervous breakdown, and I have one or two others on their last legs.'[23] Even the bravest could succumb. One such man, who had been awarded both the Distinguished Service Order and Military Cross for his wartime service, prompted his senior officer to write, 'I have sent him away on leave, as if he did not get a couple of weeks' rest, he would crack up, and he has been showing signs of a breakdown for some weeks past.'[24]

These days, counselling would be the order of the day, in an attempt to help them to process and handle the emotional toll. Would this have helped? Dame Sue Black is not convinced. 'The counsellors asked us how we *felt*,' she recalls being asked in the wake of a heartbreaking experience collecting the remains of children. 'How the bloomin' heck did they think we felt? We were tired and we wanted to go home. We had just spent two months up to our elbows in the detritus of a war that had indiscriminately killed men, women and children and we didn't take kindly to outsiders poking around inside our heads and rattling those cages.'[25]

The Western Front
1920

The post-war task of identifying and relocating bodies carried on relentlessly: day by day, week by week, month by month. At home, the bereaved families of the missing wanted, more than anything, their son, husband or brother to be positively identified. If bodies had sometimes been difficult to identify the first time they were buried after a battle, the situation now, conceivably many years later, was considerably more challenging. Most were now too decomposed to be recognisable and could only be identified by accompanying effects, which, as Sue Black had made clear to me, were often impossible to find or might belong to someone else. A name on a compass, a photograph case, a key tab, a spoon or a pipe bowl might reveal the *owner's* name. But who was carrying it? Had 'Smith' loaned his engraved cigarette case to 'Jones', who had it in his pocket when he was shot? Had one man's named rifle strap been mixed up with another's during kit inspections? Had one soldier discarded his labelled uniform tunic when issued with a new one, only for it to be claimed by a friend in his unit and worn the day he was killed? The recovery teams were doing the best they could in terrible conditions, but in the pre-DNA era many of these later identifications were still impossible and others could not be truly regarded as definitive.

It was a tough, gruesome business and painstaking detective

work seems to have been sacrificed on the altar of speed, especially when several bodies had been churned together by the rage of battle, or a farmer's plough. And many were left behind, lost or mixed up with enemy remains. Some British units were even accused of chopping men in half in order to double their body count.[26]

* * *

Back home, emotions still ran high and, despite the edicts, occasionally, an individual mother or father who had lost a son felt obliged to take the law into their own hands.

Young Private Hopkins, who had joined the Canadian Light Infantry while still a university student in April 1917, had been in Flanders for less than a fortnight when he was killed by shrapnel at Passchendaele and given an impromptu burial close to the front line. His father, the former mayor of Saskatoon, was determined to be reunited with his only son. During his second, desperate visit from Saskatchewan to search the area, against all the odds and after considerable research, he finally tracked down the grave. His son's remains had been 'combined' in a plot with another soldier from his regiment, as sometimes happened when two bodies were too mangled to identify separately. Mr Hopkins underwent the grim task of identifying his boy's putrefying remains, largely on the basis of the shrapnel wound to his head, only for his request for repatriation to be refused. He was further dismayed to discover that, instead of accompanying him back to Canada, the body was to be relocated to Tyne Cot, today the largest Commonwealth War Graves Commission cemetery in the world with 11,961 graves, of which 8,373 belong to Unknown Warriors.

Undeterred, Hopkins Sr's next step was to approach army chaplain George Kendall and ask him to arrange the reburial of his son, along with the friend who had been killed alongside him. 'Mr Hopkins provided two coffins which he had had made,' recalled Kendall, 'and along with my men, we buried the two men next to each other in the cemetery. Incidentally, I know that he richly rewarded my men, but I turned a blind eye to this.' Was there, per-haps, something more than gratitude behind Hopkins' largesse? Accounts of what happened next vary, but it is clear that their benefactor was not happy with the idea of leaving his son to rot further at Tyne Cot. Determined to take the body back to Canada he appears to have paid an army officer to help him.

A secret exhumation took place by torchlight on the night of 17 May 1921, after which the officer hurried to the port of Antwerp. It must have been a hell of a journey, staggering under the weight of the young man's remains hidden in a suitcase which, almost certainly, was not hermetically sealed. Perhaps unsurprisingly, the authorities were already on to him and the hapless courier was stopped and the contents of his suitcase examined.

Private Hopkins was reburied, this time in a Belgian military cemetery in Antwerp. And Mr Hopkins Sr spent many more years writing angry letters to the IWGC.[27]

* * *

Several more such clandestine exhumations took place over the course of the 1920s, the most remarkable of which involved an-other Canadian, Anna Durie. When Arthur Durie enlisted in the Canadian Army and sailed to England in November 1915, his mother had followed, and when he was seriously wounded on 5 May 1916, she visited him daily in the hospital at Étaples where he was being treated, well behind the lines.

In other words, Anna Durie stuck to her son like glue. She had great ambitions for him. And clearly had great influence which she used to prevent his return to the front, somehow arranging a cushy staff job for him instead. How young Arthur felt about his loving mother's interference is not recorded, but when he recovered he chose to return to active service in December 1916, against her wishes. During 1917 he underwent a month's treatment for neuras-thenia – the First World War term for a nervous breakdown, often related to shell shock and/or PTSD – but managed to return to the front line once more, where, on 29 December 1917, he was killed by a mortar shell.[28] Arthur Durie's body was laid in Corkscrew Cemetery near the town of Loos in northern France, a place described as 'a desolate area' even by IWGC stalwarts. At first, Mrs Durie seems to have accepted his burial where she liked to imagine that 'with their comrades in arms our heroes sleep in enchanted ground'.[29]

But by 1920, as a regular visitor to her son's graveside, she had become fixated with the idea that he must return home. The staff at Corkscrew complained that she was becoming 'quite unreasonable' with the IWGC's officials. She responded by ramping up her case for repatriation; letters were sent to government ministers and, on one memorable occasion, she even ambushed the Canadian Prime Minister when he visited France to plead her case. In a later letter to him, Mrs Durie called Corkscrew Cemetery 'a spot of horror which baffles description: it is surrounded by five huge mines, in an arid plain torn by trenches with half a dozen narrow- or wide-gauge railways crossing it'. The formidable Anna Durie was having none of this. She had spent enough time at Corkscrew Cemetery to know that this was not the place where she wanted her precious boy to rest for all eternity. As in life, so in death: she wanted him close to her. Where was the sweet smell of home in this wretched industrial wasteland, in one of the ugliest corners of France?

And so, on the night of 30 July 1921, Mrs Durie and two French labourers travelled to Corkscrew in a horse and cart with an empty zinc coffin. Zinc was expensive and heavy, but it would safely seal the body, avoiding seepage and smells during the long voyage home. The three of them dug up whatever was left of her son and successfully transferred him to his new, extremely heavy casket, whereupon the poor horse – spooked to be out at all, let alone in the midst of such tense activity – took fright and bolted, smashing the springs of the cart in its headlong flight. All Mrs Durie could do was persuade her assistants to help her rebury the remains of her son. Finally, knowing that the authorities would not be far behind her, she pinned a notice to the grave, assuring them that the body had not been removed, despite the disturbed earth and the cart tracks.

But the story still wasn't over. After returning to Canada, Mrs Durie later protested against a plan to move her son from the cemetery she hated so much, to nearby Loos. Arthur Durie *was* moved, nevertheless. But not for long. If the authorities thought that they had finally seen the last of the indefatigable Mrs Durie, they were much mistaken. On 22 August 1925, two articles in the Canadian press announced that Captain Arthur Durie had just been buried in St James Cemetery in Ontario. How could this be possible, wondered the IWGC top brass, when he was still safely interred in their military cemetery at Loos?

A subsequent examination revealed that the zinc coffin was indeed still in place, but there was no longer a body inside. The job must have been done in a hurry. The casket had been broken open, and a few bone fragments and scraps of clothing had been left behind. But Captain Durie's mother had, finally, got her wish. Her son – or some of her son – was home at last.

THIEPVAL MEMORIAL, THE SOMME
SPRING 2023

I park some distance from the memorial to those who not only did not go home from the Somme, but whose bodies were never found, and I'm already too hot by the time I round an avenue of trees to be confronted by the spectacular stacked arches of Lutyens's great pink-and-white monument, dominating the landscape with silent insistence. It's my first visit and, as I climb the steps, I realise that almost every inch of every face of the monument's intricate tower of arches is carved with names. Each name is around an inch high. Over 72,000 of them from just this one battlefield. And just a few months of the war. I want to find Bert Bradley, Anthony French's pal who was killed at High Wood in 1916. Bert, who had such a lovely tenor voice that it made everyone who heard it want to sing along. Bert, whose dad died never knowing where his son's body lay.

Albert William Bradley: C13 Pier and Face declares the directory contained in an inscribed cabinet.

I wander around beneath the monumental arches. Here are A and B and D, but where is C? And here are 12 and 14 and 15, but where is 13? At last, on the very back of the monument – or is this the front? – facing the setting sun, I find the list of missing soldiers who died fighting with the Civil Service Rifles. And there, right near the top, is good old Bert.

'Hello, Bert,' I whisper, for reasons I cannot quite explain. I never knew him, and he is not even here. But each of the names chiselled perhaps 2 or 3 millimetres deep into the Thiepval Memorial are there for the duration. Unknown Warrior Bert is here, more than anywhere else. With the gentle warmth of the setting sun on my face, I wander down the steps beneath Bert's name, which lead to a cemetery created at the base of the monument: 300 French crosses on one side; 300 simple British headstones on the other.

The recovery and relocation teams had done their best over a century ago, and today, as I stand in one of the thousands of cemeteries in northern France, I find myself both amazed and deeply moved by the peaceful beauty of the scene. I cannot help but marvel at the serenity that Ware, Kenyon, Lutyens, Kipling and others managed to conjure up in these devastating places which are, on some level, monuments to human folly. Strolling down the ranks of perfectly ordered white Portland stone, the rows planted with neatly tended shrubs, I stop to look at the carved cap badges that indicate the regiment of each dead soldier. Many headstones bear no badge; they are simply engraved with a cross and inscription: 'A Soldier of the Great War. Known unto God.' I have read Kipling's words many times in countless other locations, but now, as I am beginning to truly understand how it all came about, what it all means, they seem more resonant. I ask myself: *Who is this grave for?* I don't mean whose grave is it? I mean, whose grief is it that this elegant white gravestone is intended to assuage? And how does this process work?

Having attended numerous funerals of friends and military colleagues over the years, I am convinced that graves, headstones, memorials, even the funeral itself, are for the living. Not for the dead. The dead are gone. They care not how we remember them.

The post-death rituals are essentially for we who remain. Honouring the dead lies at the heart of what makes us human. Helping us make sense of our loss, and of our own lives. So I contemplate the inextinguishable pain of all those parents in the aftermath of the First World War who couldn't emulate the achievement of the Fowlers and Anna Durie. What impact did this have on their lives? 'It is hard to imagine,' says Sue Black, 'the crippling, unresolved grief suffered by the bereaved who never have a body to mourn.'[30]

In theory, relatives *could* visit a loved one with a named grave, in a cemetery like the one where I now stand. If they were wealthy and intrepid enough to do so. Most were not. And unless they were as relentlessly determined as Mrs Durie, they could never, ever, bring him home. I find myself thinking, too, about those who had never been found. I am wondering if the thought of these massed ranks of gravestones, honouring soldiers 'Known unto God', gave the living any feeling of peace, or redemption, or that most modern of concepts, closure.

Did it help to think that these Unknown Warriors had found a resting place, somewhere? That their journey was therefore at an end? And if they had found their rest, might those waiting at home eventually find an end to the suffering they had endured every minute of every day since that letter, that telegram, arrived?

When would *their* closure come?

CHAPTER FIVE

THE NEED FOR A SYMBOL

NOVEMBER 1918

At the start of my search for the origins of the Unknown Warrior, I wanted to learn as much as I could about the day-to-day life of a First World War soldier caught up in the nightmare of industrialised warfare. To try to understand why almost half a million men from across the Empire who gave their lives for the cause have no known grave. But the more I discover, the more those personal, family stories of loss come to the fore. The realities of the emotional torture suffered by those at home; those who waved farewell to a loved one, never knowing if they would return.

The enduring agony of personal bereavement really seems to have sunk in after the Armistice in 1918. As I know only too clearly from my own – very limited – combat experience, it is not the cacophony of battle that sticks in the mind. It is the aftermath; the dawning reality of what one has done, and who has been lost. All over Britain, there had been an expectation that when the war was finally over, things would get back to normal. The living would come home. The dead would be honoured. The comfort of a lasting peace, hard won, would put a smile on the face of a war-weary nation.

On 24 November 1918, Prime Minister David Lloyd George (who succeeded Asquith in December 1916) stood on top of a

horse-drawn carriage in Wolverhampton and called upon his audience to work together to make Britain 'a country fit for heroes'.
This would become one of the great soundbites of the Armistice,
even if it would return to haunt him as the nation lurched through
a series of strikes and crises. Less well known is the way he framed
it, with his politician's knack for catching the spirit of the moment.
'What is our task?' the great orator asked the surrounding crowd,
some of whom had clambered onto the roof of a goods train for
a better view. A handful of women stood on the periphery, faces
shadowed by their wide-brimmed hats, listening intently to his
words.[1]

'To make Britain a fit country for heroes to live in. I am not using
the word "heroes" in any spirit of boastfulness, but in the spirit of
humble recognition of fact. I cannot think what these men have gone
through. I have been there at the door of the furnace and witnessed
it, but that is not being in it, and I saw them march into the furnace.
There are millions of men who will come back. Let us make this a
land fit for such men to live in. There is no time to lose. I want us
to take advantage of this new spirit. Don't let us waste this victory
merely in ringing joy-bells.'[2]

I am struck, especially after spending so much time in the war
cemeteries of northern France, by the strangeness of that line: *There
are millions of men who will come back*. Lloyd George understood
that many of his audience must have been thinking the exact opposite. Many of their friends and relatives were not coming home.
He needed to do his best to jolt them into thinking about the living,
not the dead.

It was going to be a very difficult task.

* * *

In Britain in 1919, there were 109 women for every 100 men.[3] Up
from 107 for every 100 six years earlier.[4] It didn't help that the
post-war process of demobilisation was a slow and chaotic affair
which caused considerable resentment and unrest among returning

soldiers. Unemployment was rife, especially for ex-servicemen. And almost no street or family in the country had been left untouched by tragedy or loss. A study in the 1930s concluded that there were only thirty-two of the 16,000 villages in England which could be called 'Thankful Villages'.[5] These were those rare, blessed communities where every man had returned from the First World War alive.

At Catwick in Yorkshire the local blacksmith nailed a horseshoe to the doorpost of his forge and fixed thirty coins around it to represent the thirty villagers who had left to serve their country. Remarkably, all had returned home, though not all completely intact. A notch in one of the coins acknowledged that one had 'left an arm behind' in France.[6] With an overall death toll of some 885,000 service personnel rocking the country, Catwick was a notable exception.[7]

And death had visited many families more than once.

With five precious sons in the army, William and Annie Souls of the Cotswold village of Great Rissington in Gloucestershire faced more tragedy than most.[8]

The first grim letter had dropped through their front door in March 1916, announcing that their youngest, Albert, had been killed in action at the age of twenty. Albert's brother Fred would die in battle four months afterwards. With no known grave, Fred's name is carved into Edwin Lutyens's great arched Memorial to the Missing at Thiepval, but Annie would keep a candle burning on her windowsill, night after night, ever hopeful that her personal Unknown Warrior might be found alive, or his remains identified.

She was already inconsolable when, less than a fortnight later, a third letter had arrived. When 24-year-old Walter's unit was hurled into the Battle of the Somme on 20 July, he probably wouldn't have known that a day earlier, Fred had gone over the top nearby, never to be seen again:

Dear Mrs Souls, I much regret to have to tell you that your son [Walter] died yesterday evening. He came to us with a

wound in the upper part of his left leg, and had to undergo
an operation, but he rallied from that all right. In fact he
was quite cheery, then the next day he quite suddenly
collapsed and died instantly from a clot of blood in the
heart. I am enclosing a postcard which he wrote on the day
he died. He will be buried in the little British cemetery just
outside Rouen where lie other brave lads who have fallen
in this dreadful war. This will be a dreadful blow to you
and you have our deepest sympathy in your great loss –
M. Phillips, Matron, 25 Stationary Hospital, BEF, Rouen.[9]

In response to her appalling threefold loss, the Prime Minister, Herbert Asquith – who would later lose his eldest son during the fighting near High Wood – wrote to convey the 'sympathy of the King and Queen for Mrs Souls in her great sorrow'.

Annie Souls's remaining boys both survived to see the Germans begin to drive back the Allies with their 1918 spring offensive. Tragically, 31-year-old Alfred Ernest Souls would be killed on 20 April 1918. Then, his twin brother Arthur, born an hour apart, would die on the battlefield just five days later. Arthur is among the 550 soldiers, half of them unidentified, buried in Hangard Communal Cemetery south-east of Amiens. Alfred would be awarded a Military Medal in recognition of his bravery, but this must have come as cold consolation for his mother. From that moment on, she refused to stand for the national anthem. And as if the pain of losing her beautiful boys was not enough, she also had to endure cruel local gossip about how well off she must be, now she was receiving a war pension of a shilling (5p) a week for each of them.

Walter Souls was eventually buried at St Sever Cemetery, Rouen, near another soldier who shares a tragic bond with his family; he, too, was one of five brothers to die in 'the war to end all wars'.

But Annie's torture was not yet at an end.

Alongside their three daughters, their youngest son, Percy, must have been terrifyingly precious to her and William. Sixteen when the war ended, he contracted meningitis and died after a short illness, aged just twenty-one. As her obituary recorded when she joined them, aged seventy-two, in 1935, Annie Souls had lived 'a tragic life'.[10]

* * *

Reverend David Railton and his already iconic flag had arrived home in Folkestone in January 1919. The padre's eyes were still smarting and bloodshot after a German gas attack in the final year of the war. His uniform had grown loose; his belt was now several notches tighter. And with the savagery he had witnessed over the preceding years still fresh, the concept of a way of memorialising the dead was still growing in his mind. Like many soldiers, he was struggling to adjust to the bland strangeness of peacetime life after the intensity and camaraderie of the battlefield. His thoughts were also still very much with the dead.

Despite his supposedly 'safer' role as a chaplain away from the fighting, Railton had won the Military Cross – one of the highest awards for courage in the face of the enemy – during the war. It wasn't in his nature to brag, especially in the company of men going 'over the top' into the jaws of hell. 'God alone knows how little I deserve it, compared to many of our combatant officers and men,' he later wrote to his wife. But deserve it he did.

On the afternoon of 2 October 1916, Captain Clark of Railton's battalion received a message that there was 'a wounded man reported to be lying somewhere in the forward area'.[11] Railton must have gone out into no-man's-land with several other men, presumably including Captain Clark, when they came under fire from a German sniper. Several of the British soldiers were hit, and – rather than keeping his head down – Railton then risked his own life helping to drag or carry them back to safety.

Never one for bravado, all he told his wife, however, was that 'Captain Clark was killed by my side, or strictly speaking, a few paces behind me, and four others were wounded. God alone knows how I was missed. Of course this kind of thing happens constantly among officers and men of the Army, but as a rule our Padre paths are freer of it. Will you send me an electric torch with a refill?'[12]

The official citation for his MC in the *London Gazette* gives a little more detail:

Rev David Railton, Temp Chapln to the Forces, 4th Class. For conspicuous gallantry in action. He rescued an officer and two men under heavy fire, displaying great courage and determination. He has on many occasions done very fine work.[13]

Much like Rupert Inglis, the rugby-playing vicar killed while searching for the wounded at Ginchy, or the padre who had found Anthony French lying stricken and bleeding in a shell hole at High Wood, the one useful thing that Railton had felt he could do on the battlefield was to help search for the injured in no-man's-land. These churchmen had no rifles, no grenades. Like the heroic stretcher-bearers, the bravest work they could do was to risk their lives in bringing the wounded back to the relative safety of their own lines. And perhaps it was this same instinct – this desire to bring people back from the brink – that prompted Railton to nurture the idea he had had for many years.

A way to commemorate those who would never return.

From all the letters he had received in response to his own describing the deaths of their relative, Railton knew that families cared deeply and passionately about what happened to the bodies of those they had lost. So how was he to tell these people that there was nothing left of their husband? That their son had been blasted into fragments? Or that, yes, indeed, there were hundreds of bodies which *could* be theirs. But they could, just as easily, be someone else's. Given the state of what was left, only God could possibly know.

Might it be possible to create a national symbol representing *all* the missing?

BERKSHIRE
SPRING 2023

What manner of man was David Railton? There are very few still living who remember him, but his daughter-in-law Margaret, now ninety-four, thinks often about the man who did such remarkable work during the war, and then pursued his single-minded mission to heal the country afterwards. On the eve of King Charles's coronation in early May 2023, Margaret and I talk about grand ceremonial occasions and the emotions they arouse. I describe the RAF service I attended in Westminster Abbey a few years earlier, the feelings prompted by my friend, the wheelchair-bound Second World War veteran, beside the Tomb of the Unknown Warrior, and my sudden need to more fully understand what it meant.

She nods, staring out of her living-room window at the splashes of colour in her sun-dappled garden, where the bluebells nod in the wind. Margaret has been unwell recently but is still determined to talk about her beloved father-in-law. 'His actions in the First World War were never mentioned at home, so it was only when I discovered all his papers in a bureau after my own husband died twenty-three years ago, that I really learned the details of his story. I certainly didn't know that he had won the Military Cross at the Somme.'[14]

'You never even *saw* the medal?' I'm astonished. I know from many years of interviewing veterans and their families that they rarely spoke of their awards. Any mention of courage would quickly be diverted onto their friends. But it is unusual that a medal for valour should remain totally hidden from view, never even acknowledged. Margaret shakes her head. 'It was never on display, never mentioned. Never. People just didn't talk about their war service back then. It wasn't the done thing. Perhaps seen as a little "off" to be talking about what you did during the war. So many hundreds of thousands of men had been involved – why would you talk about your own role? Nobody wanted to hear about that. But he really was a most remarkable man.' She nods in admiration. 'He was a wonderful person, admired by his men and a marvellous preacher.

I have a letter describing an event in 1916, when a lot of soldiers were waiting for him to turn up for a makeshift service. He arrived covered in mud and was thrilled to be given a wonderful reception by everyone waiting. There are also lots of letters describing how soldiers asked him if he would give them communion or confirm them before battles, knowing what their fate might be. Not all the padres gained such respect, but when you think of the conditions the brave ones were working under, my gosh, they deserved it.'

We talk about Westminster Abbey; about Railton's special connection with the place. 'No one in the family ever spoke about his involvement with the idea for an "unknown warrior". It was never mentioned.' Margaret takes a careful sip of water from the glass on the table beside her. 'Many years later, I must have been told something about his war service and his subsequent role; it was then that other memories of him began to make sense.' She rearranges her feet on the oatmeal-coloured cushion. 'Once, when he came to stay with us, I took him for a walk through the village. The trees around the church had all been pollarded; brutally pruned to within an inch of their lives. He was terribly, terribly upset when he saw it. This really struck me at the time. I now know it was because of all of the trees that he'd seen shattered and destroyed, blasted down to their stumps, during his time in battle.' Margaret thinks about this for a moment. 'And it got worse. Weedkiller had been sprayed along the church path so the flowers and greenery were all dying. He was terribly upset about that as well.' She peers out of the window at the grey-green fields in the distance. 'That image of him looking at the destruction still sits in my memory today. Thinking about that day many years later, I truly began to understand why he felt the dead deserved more formal recognition.'

FOLKESTONE
1919

Margaret has given me an intriguing insight into the intense empathy and compassion of the man whose story has begun to fascinate me so deeply. It becomes easier to picture how David Railton – fresh back from the war with a pack full of sad memories, jottings about grave locations and last letters to be passed on to bereaved relatives – must have ached to do something about the wretchedness and yearning so prevalent in post-Armistice Britain. Railton could clearly see that the nation needed to be healed. Needed some sort of symbol for the collective loss. He burned to help the families to whom he had written letter after difficult letter, bringing what meagre consolation he could with his descriptions of how and where their sons and husbands had died. 'Do you recall that dreadful year of reaction?' he would later write as he looked back on 1919 and struggled to piece together why he felt so strongly that he needed to act. 'Men and nations stumbled back like badly wounded and gassed warriors to their homes. The endless shedding of blood ceased but there was no real peace in the souls of men or nations. The mind of the world was in a fever.'[15]

If Railton's deep Christian faith had been tested by his experiences, where did that leave everyone else?

* * *

The battle at High Wood may have come as a shock to Railton and the other men of his battalion. But the aftermath presented them with an ever more extreme form of the horror they had been living with for months: the reality of so many unidentified bodies.

His grand idea for some sort of recognition of the 'unknowns' had initially formed in the early stages of the war, in 1916, when he was billeted in a small village about twenty minutes' drive from Lille, on the main road that leads to Dunkirk. Part of his cottage roof had been blown off by a shell, but the place was comfortable enough, despite the constant throb of bombardment. It even had a small back garden in which Railton could indulge his love of plants and take a few moments to reflect on the quiet family life he had left behind in Kent. And then another message would arrive, and he would once again be called to the front line, to bury a soldier who had put his head just a little too far above the parapet, or perhaps been blown into pieces by a German shell.

One particular incident in early 1916 was seared into his mind. As he later recalled, it was the spark which ignited a fire that would burn for years:

I came back from the line at dusk. We had just laid to rest the mortal remains of a comrade. I went to a billet in front of Erkingham [*sic*], near Armentieres. At the back of the billet was a small garden and a grave. At the head of the grave there stood a rough cross of white wood. On the cross was written in deep black pencilled letters 'An unknown British Soldier' and in brackets underneath 'of the Black Watch'. I remember how still it was. Even the guns seemed to be resting, as if to give the gunners a chance to have their tea.

How that grave caused me to think! How I wondered! How I longed to see his folk! But, who was he, and who were they? From which of the lonely mystic glens of old Scotia did he come? Was he just a laddie – newly joined – aged eighteen, the only son of a shepherd from the far away Highlands? There was no answer to those questions, nor has there ever been yet.

So I thought and thought and wrestled in thought. What can I do to ease the pain of father, mother, brother, sister, sweetheart, wife and friend? Quietly and gradually there came out of the mist of thought this answer clear and strong. Let this body – this symbol of him – be carried reverently over the sea to his native land. Then, quickly, the most common remark of those days came to my mind – There is a war on – so I thought this idea would never be an accomplished fact. I told nobody; yet I could not throw the idea away. Every Padre serving with infantry brigades was bombarded after each publication of casualties with at least this request: 'Where – exactly where – did you lay to rest the body of my son? Can you give me any further information? I have been officially notified that he is missing, believed killed.'

Oh, those letters of broken relatives and friends! They reinforced the idea, so that I could never let it drop.

Later on, I nearly wrote to Sir Douglas Haig, to ask if the body of an 'unknown comrade' might be sent home. But it was obvious that even if such a request had been granted, it could have had no personal meaning for those whose relatives fell after that date. So I held my peace with little hope.[16]

So were sown the early seeds of a concept that would eventually become an enduring national symbol: a tomb for a missing soldier with no known grave. Month after month, year after year, as the war rumbled on, Railton privately nurtured his idea. His letters to his wife make no specific reference to it; the thought of what it might achieve – in terms of the redemption and relief it could bring, to so many families – perhaps made it too precious to mention. What must have terrified Railton was the thought that, if he got it wrong – if he failed to persuade the right people at the first attempt – then the whole idea risked being blown clean out of the water as the crackpot sentimentality of an out-of-touch cleric. So even after returning home, and throughout 1919, Railton resolved to bide his time until the perfect opportunity arose to propose it.[17]

In the meantime, proposals for a different memorial, a different type of remembrance, were already underway.

England
1919

Across the land, individual communities had already begun erecting their own monuments to those who had given their lives during the war, especially those with no known resting place. On village greens, at roadsides and in churchyards, war memorials large and small were appearing in their thousands.

The country was doing its best to get back to normal, but it was taking time. At London's Covent Garden, the Royal Opera House announced the first season of performances since 1914, launched by

Dame Nellie Melba, the great Australian soprano. Melba was dismayed to see people wearing brown tweed coats in the stalls, which she viewed as quite a comedown after the white-tie glamour of the pre-war years.[18] County cricket grounds, which had not seen a ball bowled for five years, once more revelled in the sound of leather on willow. A young Frenchwoman, Suzanne Lenglen, won the ladies' singles title at Wimbledon in a sleeveless dress which, shocked observers noted, barely covered her ankles.[19]

At the same time in Paris, the ink was only just drying on the Treaty of Versailles. Signed on 28 June 1919, it finally enshrined the terms of the deal between the Allied powers and Germany which had begun with the Armistice on 11 November 1918.

Partly to celebrate the signing, but mostly in a desperate attempt to create a sense of unity in a nation that was both fractured and fractious, the Prime Minister threw all his weight behind the idea of the grand Victory Parade for July 1919. Like David Railton, Lloyd George understood the need for emotional recovery. Born at the height of Empire in 1863, he still clung to a touching faith in the power of marching bands, of well-pressed uniforms and miles of bunting to cure all ills.

The press were not so sure. Perhaps unimpressed by the Prime Minister's attempts to turn the yawning sense of confusion and dismay – almost of anticlimax – that marked the end of the war into a triumphal pageant, the event was quickly dubbed a 'Peace Parade' by the press. And, with caustic snobbery, it was dismissed as 'a servants' festival' by the novelist Virginia Woolf.[20] To Lloyd George's credit, the wily statesman did have a deep and empathetic understanding of the sacrifices that had been made by the British people. And he wasn't visualising any sort of celebration that didn't also take into account the sacrifices of the fallen. It was Lloyd George who proposed the construction of a temporary monument; a catafalque – a ceremonial structure upon which a body or effigy might traditionally be laid during a funeral or formal lying-in-state.[21] Built slap-bang in the middle of Whitehall, a few paces from 10 Downing Street and midway between Trafalgar Square to the north and Parliament Square to the south, it would give the soldiers a focal point to salute as they marched past on their 20-mile parade route.

Lloyd George was obviously trying his best to acknowledge the elephant in the room – nearly a million dead soldiers, almost none of whose bodies had been brought home, and many still missing beneath the shell-ploughed mud of France and Flanders. Other members of the Cabinet were unconvinced. Wasn't it all smoke and mirrors? Wasn't the idea of a fake funeral platform just a bit too theatrical for the British? Indeed, the Foreign Secretary, Lord Curzon, sneeringly dismissed the idea as 'rather foreign to the spirit of our people, however much it might be in harmony with the Latin temperament'.[22]

But Lloyd George stuck to his guns and pushed the idea through. A colleague had already discussed the possibility of a temporary catafalque with Sir Edwin Lutyens, the distinguished architect already heavily involved in the design of the Imperial War Graves Commission's cemeteries in France.[23] And Lutyens was excited enough about the idea to have sketched an initial design using black, blue and red chalks on the back of an old advertisement, which he showed to his mistress, Lady Sackville, that very same evening. Lady Sackville was, luckily, sufficiently enchanted by the idea that she asked to be allowed to keep the sketch.[24]

A couple of days later, Lloyd George invited Lutyens to Downing Street. Apologising for the short notice, the Prime Minister explained his urgent proposal. What was required, he said, was 'a point of homage to stand as a symbol of remembrance worthy of the reverent salute of an Empire mourning for its million dead'.[25] Despite opposition from the Church, Lloyd George wanted the memorial to be non-denominational. It should be decorated with no cross, nor any other Christian symbol that might exclude or alienate soldiers of other religions. There was also the matter of the date. Lutyens would have just two weeks in which to design and build it, ready for the Victory Parade on 19 July.

Not knowing that Lutyens's sketch was already pinned to the

green silk wallpaper of a bedroom in Mayfair, Lloyd George must have been pretty impressed when he rushed back that very afternoon with his design for a monument rolled up under his arm.

Lutyens called this structure a 'cenotaph', uniting the two Greek words *kenos* (empty) and *taphos* (tomb). It was indeed to be an empty tomb, as if awaiting the return of a missing soldier, and representing all the missing soldiers who were still out there somewhere, on the other side of the Channel. Though the structure resembled a solid, rectilinear cuboid, constructed of white stone, towering over Whitehall, it was to be merely a temporary focal point for the parade and had to be whisked up in the space of a few days. Built from wood and plaster, it was as flimsy as a stage set. But as it turned out, it was a work of pure magic. The success of Lutyens's vision lay in its simplicity and neutrality. A stark, monumental construction, it was effectively a blank canvas, upon which the viewer could project whatever thoughts, regrets, beliefs, memories and wishes they chose.

LONDON
19 JULY 1919

The day of the Victory Parade dawned grey and gloomy in London, and it cannot have been helped by the rain that fell at lunchtime. Other problems had grown out of the fact that the day was envisaged as a celebration of military victory, with very little time and space left for reflection and – despite the hasty construction of the Cenotaph as a useful saluting point – no special arrangements for the bereaved.

It was the country's 240,000 war widows[26] who fared worst. A discussion about whether they should be included in the ceremony ended with the abrupt conclusion that they would not be interested in attending. Besides, as His Majesty's Officer of Works briskly explained, the Organising Committee 'did not consider it necessary to reserve anything for war widows, as they said the bulk of them had remarried'.[27] How he deduced this is not recorded. But then the

Queen got involved. On 8 July 1919, she instructed her secretary to write to the committee, urging them not to 'forget the mothers and widows of the dead in making arrangements for the day's events'.[28] Thanks to her intervention, places were reserved to give the widows a better view. But still not such a good spot as the ones reserved for veterans and Members of Parliament. Others expressed anger at ongoing slights. One ex-soldier wrote to the *Manchester Evening News*: 'I am sure the title Peace Day will send a cold shiver through the bodies of thousands of "demobbed" men who are walking about the streets looking for a job.' He went on to lambast the 'many Manchester businessmen [who] refuse to employ the ex-soldier on the grounds that he has lost four years' experience through being in the Army.'[29]

Despite such injustices, the day was a popular success, with large crowds attending. London's hotels and boarding houses were fully booked, and many had camped overnight in the streets around Trafalgar Square. Some estimates suggested that the throng was so dense that only 5 per cent of the people lining the streets could actually have caught a glimpse of the parade itself. Some 20,000 Allied soldiers took part in the march-past.[30] With elements led by General Pershing from America, Field Marshal Haig from Britain and Maréchal Foch from France, the whole parade was described by King George V as 'the most impressive sight I ever saw'.[31] As the columns passed down Whitehall, 'men's eyes turned instinctively to the simple white cenotaph, with a silent bowed sentry at each corner, and they remembered those other soldiers who will march no more'.[32] It was estimated that if all the dead soldiers represented by the temporary Cenotaph were lined up for their own parade, it would take three and a half days for the column to march past in salute.[33]

The British Army is not known for its displays of naked emotion, so those close enough to the soldiers as they marched by in silence were surprised to see how many of their faces, shaded beneath peaked caps as they turned towards the temporary wooden monument, were wet with tears.

Having attended parades and services at the Cenotaph on many occasions, I am certainly acquainted with the rollercoaster of emotions they inspire. I still remember the Second World War Bomber Command veteran I was pushing in his wheelchair insisting I come to a halt during a march-past, holding up many thousands in the parade behind us. He struggled to his feet to give a formal salute to the monument and to the friends he had lost, before flopping back down, eyes glistening.

In 1919, people had begun to lay wreaths and flowers around the monument's base that morning and were still doing so long after nightfall. Within a couple of days, over a million people had visited the site.[34] We have seen this same instinct, this tradition, time and again in modern Britain at moments of intense public grief. After the death of Diana, Princess of Wales, in 1997, crowds flooded the approach to Kensington Palace with floral tributes. And we saw the acres of bouquets laid in Green Park to form an impromptu memorial following the death of Her Majesty Queen Elizabeth II in 2022.

* * *

The supposedly temporary plaster and wooden structure – a tribute to *all* the missing – made a deep impression on those gathered there. 'You could scarce see the Cenotaph for the *aura*, the halo, the throbbing air that encompassed it,' waxed the reporter from the *Daily Mail*,[35] while the *Manchester Guardian* declared that 'a light was shining in the daylight like a light on an altar'.[36]

Lutyens's understated monolith had responded perfectly to the prevailing spirit of grief and loss. It was as if the pinched, stiff-upper-lipped restraint of Edwardian England was finally being given licence, by the purity and simplicity of this flimsy structure, to let itself go. To bask in the emotional intensity of the day. One reporter at the Cenotaph claimed to have witnessed 'moments of silence when the dead seemed very near, when one almost heard the passage of countless wings – were not the fallen gathering in their hosts to receive their comrades' salute and take their share in the triumph they had died to win?'[37] Poetic as these observations were, I suspect they say as much about the desperate mood of the times, people clawing for something to soothe their emotional pain, as they do about Lutyens's architectural genius.

Two days after the parade, *The Times* observed, 'The Cenotaph is only a temporary structure made to look like stone, but Sir Edwin Lutyens' design is so grave, severe and beautiful that one might well wish it were indeed of stone and permanent.'[38] The idea caught on and plans were quickly put in place for a permanent version of the catafalque on the same spot in Whitehall. Some argued that the din of motor vehicles in the area was not the right ambience for so solemn a memorial, but, as the *Daily Mail* pointed out, the site had already been 'consecrated by the tears of many mothers'.[39] And the fact that the day-to-day traffic in both directions would have to deviate from its normal path to drive around the monument would be a fitting way of making sure that, for all time, the sacrifice it immortalised could never be forgotten or ignored.

For now, the temporary structure was kept in place to stand as a focus for the commemorations on the upcoming Armistice Day, when even bigger crowds were expected to gather.

November 1919

The first anniversary of the Armistice saw the introduction of a transcendent ritual that has since become a national tradition. The concept of a two-minute silence had originated in Cape Town, South Africa, in 1918. Lloyd George had initially argued for five minutes. The King, perhaps having a better grasp of the attention span of his subjects, especially of the children, felt that even three minutes would be too long for them. He was concerned that insisting upon any silence at all might be a challenge and his obsession with punctuality filled him with doubts as to how it could be synchronised for a whole city, let alone a nation. But Lloyd

George carried the day, calming the King with his proposal that exploding rockets could be fired high into the sky to announce the start and finish. Mollified, the King released a personal statement to the press, with clear instructions for how the silence was to be observed:

> Tuesday next, November 11, is the first anniversary of the Armistice which stayed the worldwide carnage of the four preceding years and marked the victory of Right and Freedom. I believe that my people in every part of the Empire fervently wish to perpetuate the memory of the Great Deliverance and of those who have laid down their lives to achieve it. To afford an opportunity for the universal expression of this feeling it is my desire and hope that at the hour when the Armistice came into force, the 11th hour of the 11th day of the 11th month, there may be for the brief space of two minutes a complete suspension of all our normal activities. No elaborate organisation appears to be required. At a given signal, which can be easily arranged to suit the circumstances of the locality, I believe that we shall interrupt our business and pleasure, whatever it may be, and unite in this simple service of Silence and Remembrance.[40]

On the day, shops, factories and businesses found their own ways to signal the silence. A murder trial at the Old Bailey was stopped. Trading on the stock market ceased. All over the country, passenger trains and goods trains came to a clanking, clattering halt. In the Channel, steamships stopped their engines and bobbed as if becalmed. At Harrods in Knightsbridge, they set off the fire alarms at 11AM. At Selfridges, a bugler marched out onto a balcony overlooking Oxford Street and sounded the Last Post. At Lloyd's of London, the great Lutine Bell was rung.[41]

Not everyone thought the silence was golden. Each, then as now, responded in their own personal way. Thus a young Evelyn Waugh, who would go on to write *Brideshead Revisited* and *Decline and Fall*, dismissed the two-minute silence as a 'disgusting idea of artificial nonsense and sentimentality. If people have lost sons and fathers, they should think of them whenever the grass is green or Shaftesbury Avenue is brightly lighted, not for two minutes on the anniversary of a disgraceful day of national hysteria. No one thought of the dead last year. Why should they now?'[42]

But Waugh was wrong. People were constantly thinking of their dead. The dead were inescapable. Their shadows stood on every street corner, sat at every bar, travelled on every bus. Given their ultimate sacrifice, was it not reasonable to allow them at least two minutes in which to monopolise a nation's grief?

* * *

London's winter weather had taken its toll on the wood and plaster of Lutyens's temporary creation and, in January 1920, the Office of Works announced that it would be demolished. All hell broke loose. There was a public outcry, and one newspaper denounced whoever had taken this decision as 'utterly without soul or sentiment or understanding'. Nevertheless, the demolition went ahead behind screens to spare the feelings of those for whom so heinous an act might prove too shocking to witness.

It had already been decided that the finer, permanent memorial, commissioned again from Lutyens, was to be unveiled by King George V on 11 November 1920 – the second anniversary of the Armistice. The great architect set to work at once and while Lutyens was busying himself with calculations of stone weights and geometry, the Reverend David Railton was having a similarly industrious start to 1920.

In April 1920, at the age of thirty-five, he was appointed vicar of Margate in Kent, around the same time as his wife Ruby was pregnant with twins. Andrew and Freda were born on 1 August 1920.[43] With two children already clamouring for his attention, these must have been chaotically happy times for the war-weary cleric.

He knew that the time to propose his grand idea was close at hand. Yet still he hesitated. Was his wish to exhume the body of an anonymous British soldier, and bring him back to London to be buried where umpteen kings and queens had been crowned and buried, realistic? He must have wondered what gave him, a minor cleric just settling into an unfashionable seaside town, the right to thrust himself into the great affairs of state? To offer an idea that might lead the country out of its grief-stricken post-war torpor? How on earth was he going to get his unique project off the ground? Whom should he consult to avoid it getting rejected as unrealistic by the pen-pushers? He knew that he needed a champion, someone to grab his idea and run with it. Many years later, Railton would recall this highly charged period:

Who of the 'great' men would be likely to heed the request of an ordinary Padre at such a time? They were all busy. A failure to get the idea accepted might be final. What of the Prime Minister – Mr Lloyd George? He would act quickly if he approved of it. But if he did not? – and he was very powerful in those days.

I could surely go to the noble Haig, most brotherly of men? But I knew something of the strained relationship between soldiers and politicians and he probably would have to ask the Cabinet for leave, assuming he himself agreed. Then there was the Archbishop of Canterbury – wisest and most calm of all 'moderns'. But the politicians always lagged behind him, and they might debate it in a hurry and argue it away.

Why not His Majesty the King? After all, there had been no nobler or wiser King in this land. He would, I felt somehow sure, agree, because he understands the hearts of the people. But I feared His Majesty's advisers might suggest an open space like Trafalgar Square, Hyde Park, or the Horse Guards for the tomb of the Unknown Comrade. There could be only one true Shrine for this purpose. The Unknown Comrade's body should rest, if it were possible, in Westminster Abbey – the Parish Church of the Empire.[44]

Eventually, on 13 August 1920, less than a fortnight after the birth of his twins, Railton asked Ruby the question he had been asking himself since 1916:

Was now a good time?

Still recovering from the births, and snowed under caring for their other children, Ruby must have been fed up with her husband's endless agonising. But the clock was ticking. Armistice Day 1920 was approaching fast.

'It's now or never,' she told him wearily.[45]

That night, he sat in front of his typewriter and composed the letter he had been wondering how to write for nearly four years.

The target Railton finally chose was the Right Reverend Bishop Herbert Ryle, Dean of Westminster. Most importantly, he had the ear of both the King and the Prime Minister. But Railton had never written or spoken to him before.

Now, distilling all his experience, fervour and powers of persuasion into a single, typewritten missive, he asked the Dean to consider the possibility of burying in the abbey the body of 'one of our unknown comrades', to represent the hundreds of thousands of fallen who had no identifiable grave. Railton also dared to suggest that a battle-stained war flag in his possession might be used at such a burial, rather than a new flag that had never seen active service. But, even as he posted the letter, Railton very much doubted that his great scheme would ever be carried out.[46] He had good cause, as Ryle's biographer later noted: 'Of all the questions with which a Dean of Westminster may be called upon to deal, none can be more troublesome than those connected with a demand for the burial of some distinguished person in the Abbey. Such demand is apt to be presented with little warning. It will probably be taken up by the press, ever eager to agitate the public mind.'[47]

However, on this occasion, and only three days later, Ryle wrote back:

At a distance from the Abbey and in the middle of a needed
holiday, I am perhaps not altogether in a position to give
you a final decision on either of your two suggestions. But
they make a strong appeal to me. On first consideration of
them I find myself warmly inclined to favour them.

The suggestion of commemorating the Unknown Dead
has indeed been made in different quarters. But your
suggestion strikes me as the best I have received. If I could
obtain the War Office permission, I think I could carry out
the rest of the proposal – the interment, etc. And the idea
occurs to me that it would be appropriate as a wonderful
way of commemorating the Armistice. However, I must
not move, or talk, too fast. The idea shall germinate. On
my return at the beginning of September or beginning of
October, I would see you if possible; discuss it with my
chapter; approach the government; and try and find a
vacant and suitable spot on the floor of the nave. These
ideas of which you have spoken to me had better not
be talked about; or they may get prematurely into the
newspapers and do harm instead of good.[48]

After such a positive response, everything went quiet for poor
Railton. 'August went by and September,' he lamented. 'No further
news! The first two weeks in October brought nothing.'[49] At the
same time, the national preparations for Armistice Day 1920 were
already well underway and being discussed in the national press.
Lutyens's new permanent Cenotaph was to be unveiled that day.
Was Railton's idea too late? Or too far ahead of its time? Perhaps it
had been decided that the tens of thousands of war memorials being
erected in villages across the country were enough?

Unknown to Railton, Dean Ryle was clearly giving the matter
serious thought and it is easy to see how seductive the idea must have
been for him; offering the possibility of carrying the actual physical
remains of a British serviceman – and, with him, the attention of an
entire nation – into the very heart of the Anglican establishment.

Back from his holiday in Harrogate, Ryle wrote to the King's private secretary in early October, asking him to discuss the project with the King and, seemingly, claiming the idea of burying an unknown soldier in the abbey as his own: 'There are thousands of graves, I am told, of English "Tommies" who fell at the front – names not known. My idea is that one such body (name not known), should be exhumed and interred in Westminster Abbey in the Nave.'[50]

Initially, the King was less than enthusiastic:

For the moment the King is doubtful about the proposal contained in your letter of the 4th. His Majesty is inclined to think that nearly two years after the last shot fired on the battlefields of France and Flanders is so long ago that a funeral now might be regarded as belated, and almost, as it were, reopen the war wound, which time is gradually healing . . . His Majesty would like you to speak to the Prime Minister on the subject, and then let him know how Mr Lloyd George regards the suggestion.[51]

Ryle was already on the case and the idea had gained traction in high places. Lloyd George and the new head of the Armed Forces, Field Marshal Sir Henry Hughes Wilson – who would be assassinated by the IRA eighteen months later – managed to change the King's mind. Surely this new idea for a national symbol of loss might be exactly what was needed to bring the nation together? After some obviously very rapid governmental discussions, the Cabinet Secretary replied to Dean Ryle the same day he officially proposed the idea:

I am directed by the Prime Minister to inform you that your memorandum of the 15th of October, suggesting that the remains of one of the unknown men who fell and were buried in France should be exhumed and buried in Westminster Abbey, was considered this afternoon by the Cabinet, and adopted in principle.[52]

On 19 October 1920 – a mere *three weeks* before the 11 November services – Ryle finally wrote to Padre Railton with the good news:

> *The idea which you suggested to me in August I have*
> *kept steadily in view ever since. I have been occupied*
> *actively upon it for the last 2 or 3 weeks. It necessitated*
> *communications with the War Office, Prime Minister,*
> *Cabinet and Buckingham Palace. The announcement which*
> *the Prime Minister will, or intends to, make this afternoon*
> *will show how the government is ready to co-operate. Once*
> *more I express my warm acknowledgement and thanks for*
> *your letter.*[53]

One can picture even the habitually restrained Railton punching the air with excitement on seeing Ryle's words. There was nothing, for now, about his precious flag. Yet as he read and reread the letter clutched tightly in his shaking hand, he was, he confessed, 'overwhelmed with joy'.[54] And later recorded, 'it is to this most noble Dean that we owe the carrying out of the whole idea. To this day I do not know what difficulties he had to overcome. Bishop Ryle was a great man and a humble man.'[55]

Behind the scenes, things were – by necessity – now moving quickly. On 22 October, *The Times* ran a small column entitled 'Cenotaph' revealing – with underwhelming fanfare – the new plans:

> We understand that all the arrangements made for the unveiling of the Cenotaph on Armistice Day are now in abeyance. They were to have been finally settled yesterday, but Lord Curzon's Committee, which is now considering the details of the ceremony of re-interring the body of an unknown warrior in the Abbey, will also be responsible for the arrangements in connexion with the Cenotaph, the two ceremonies being interdependent.[56]

When I visited the Westminster Abbey archives, I was surprised at how little information existed about what must have been a frenetic few weeks for those now charged with organising those two 'interdependent' parts of the day. As Dr Tony Trowles, Head of the Abbey Collection and Librarian, explained: 'Planning for the unveiling of the Cenotaph was already well underway, and the concept of including the burial of an unknown warrior was included, almost at the last minute. There must have been a real sense of urgency, but there is no definitive answer as there is very little documentation about the event in our archives. One problem is that the Deanery was bombed in 1941, and many of our records were destroyed, so we shall never know if anything relevant was ever there. And, secondly, it was barely a century ago, and although we like to think that we can find out all we want to know about such a comparatively recent event, even today there are many uncertainties. And that is part of the wonder of the whole project.'[57]

On 25 October, many newspapers carried the following statement from Dean Ryle:

It is stated that the Dean of Westminster, with whom the proposal originated, desires that no one shall ever know to which branch of the services the Unknown Warrior belonged. The intention is to preserve a profound secrecy with regard to every detail of the man's identity, so that a mother who has lost a son, or a widow who has lost a husband in the war may, when pausing before the tomb, be encouraged to imagine that it is her own sacred dead upon whom this great honour has been bestowed.[58]

Though Padre Railton may have choked on his porridge when he saw this announcement and that the Dean was apparently taking credit for his idea, a personal letter from Ryle arrived the very same day containing yet more good news. He was responding to the padre's proposal that his own flag be used in the ceremony. The very flag that had accompanied him throughout the battles of the Somme and beyond. Which had done sacred duty at the burials of hundreds of British soldiers. Upon which Railton had celebrated countless Holy Communions, in the dim light of a shell-battered trench. His treasured flag might make a fitting ceremonial pall for the coffin of an 'unknown comrade'. Depending on its condition.

'The War Office will be quite willing to accept the Flag for use at the service on the 11th November, provided that it is in a condition not unsuitable for the occasion,' wrote Ryle. He and the abbey staff were no doubt concerned that Railton was going to produce a blood-stained and mud-caked pile of rags like the ones that had been returned to many distraught relatives. 'Perhaps you may be able to bring it up to Town in the course of the next week or so? In any case, if it is used, I should like to have a short description of it, so that I could let the press have full information. It would add further interest (not that such is needed) to the ceremony.'

Ryle had also added his own small contribution to Railton's proposal: 'The grave at my request is to be filled in with French earth which the War Office consents to have brought over.'[59] Already, in this one tiny detail dreamed up by Ryle – the substituting of battle-hallowed French soil for plain old London grit – one can see that Railton was not alone in grasping the opportunity for high theatricality and dramatic symbolism that the burial of an unknown soldier offered.

This was not going to be just another Anglican funeral. Like Railton, Dean Ryle clearly recognised that here was an opening for a sacramental moment of deep and resounding national significance. This one was right up there with a coronation or state funeral. And, like the coronation ceremony, with its orb and its sceptre and other timeless props, each imbued with mythic and mysterious significance, the burial of this Unknown Warrior demanded all the pomp and circumstance that the powers that be could bestow. Interestingly, Ryle's biographer would write in 1928 – with no mention of Padre Railton's role in the process – that 'it is not possible to say to whom the credit is due for the original idea of such a service. But it was Dean Ryle who took up the suggestion, and after consultation with a few of his colleagues and with powerful support, won for it, approval.'[60]

To be fair, Railton was not the only person in the world to have come up with the idea of burying the body of an unknown soldier as a symbol of national loss. The French were gearing up for something similar at the Arc de Triomphe on Armistice Day 1920. Two newspapers – the *Daily Express*[61] and the *Comrades' Journal*[62] – had both put forward early proposals for some form of burial of a soldier with no name. But the way they presented the idea failed to catch on, perhaps partly because of the success of the temporary Cenotaph, whose symbolic power and popular appeal initially made it seem as if no other memorial or commemoration could possibly match it. But there can be no doubt that it was David Railton's initial concept which ignited the process and was to become the focus of the nation on the second anniversary of the end of the war. And his flag, the friend he had carried through the toughest of times, was to play a starring role in the ceremony.

* * *

Even if people could agree on the merits of Railton's idea in principle, the details of how to carry it out in practice were fraught with difficulty. Especially considering Dean Ryle's edict that 'no one shall ever know to which branch of the services the Unknown Warrior belonged'. If the person being buried was to be genuinely anonymous and unidentified, considerable secrecy would be required. And yet surely, any corpse would presumably need to be sufficiently *identifiable* to ensure that the King and the British people were not interring a blown-up French civilian or, perish the thought, a German, by mistake? Worse still, the timeframe within which an appropriate corpse must be found, dug up and transported with due ceremony to London was now perilously short.

To help organise proceedings, Ryle had been invited to join the Memorial Services Committee, set up by the government to plan the event and headed by the Foreign Secretary Lord Curzon, who also happened to have a genius for arranging grand state occasions. It had already accepted and adopted the word 'warrior' to describe the fighting man who would be buried, even if 'soldier' was probably the obvious choice, and despite the fact that Railton had argued strongly for the body to be described as an 'unknown comrade'. The problem with 'soldier' was that it threatened to exclude both the navy and the air force. And the problem with 'comrade' was that it smacked of the Bolshevism that lay at the heart of the Russian Revolution of 1917, and which the government feared might soon gain a foothold in Britain.

The committee also began to hammer out the most fundamental – and tricky – questions.

Should he be an officer, or a humble private?

From which battlefield should he be exhumed, and how could this be kept secret?

What about the navy and the air force?

Must the soldier be British, or should the dominions and colonies be included, too?

What level of decomposition was acceptable?

To add to the committee's anxiety, rumours were already beginning to circulate in the press; and some were woefully inaccurate. The fallibility of journalists is not a recent phenomenon after all.

A press report published on 26 October stated that, 'Whether he was a sailor, soldier, or airman, and whether he had belonged to the forces of Britain or the Dominions, will be unknown.'[63] But how accurate might that statement be?

Historians still argue, and many thousands of words have been written, about how those hurried deliberations in 1920 might have had a bearing on the service and background of whichever deceased warrior would eventually be selected. But as Justin Saddington, curator at the National Army Museum in London and acknowledged expert on the Unknown Warrior, writes:

This event holds a special allure both because it took the form of a macabre ritual and because the story presents an intriguing and intractable historical puzzle. The root cause of this conundrum is the shroud of secrecy that surrounded the process. Anonymity was of course fundamental to the concept and the government was therefore scrupulously secretive in all its planning. No official account of how it was done was ever issued and historians have been forced to fall back on divergent and less reliable later accounts. While there have been many spirited attempts to get to the bottom of this story, it has remained stubbornly mired in mystery and many of its details are still disputed.[64]

Which is exactly what those planning the event wanted.

If one knew which battlefield cemeteries the body *might* be recovered from, or roughly when he fell, could one make a stab at a military unit? You could certainly make some *assumptions* about which service he might have belonged to. And if you do a lot of research and investigation, some possibilities and exclusions could certainly – indeed have been – posited.

But for me, the detective work and arguments are rather meaningless; it was the *concept* which was important.

It really didn't matter who he was, his colour, service or religion; the person to be buried would be an Everyman. As many experts have pointed out, there were some obvious anomalies in the proposals for how the final selection be carried out. Moreover, was every order formulated subsequently followed *to the letter*? I know from personal experience that when military orders come down from on high, there can often be an element of personal interpretation in their execution. And, of course, the vagaries of the early, chaotic, wartime burial processes, then the constant disruption of bodies and graves as the fighting continued, and the post-war recovery and reinterring of many bodies in formal cemeteries, meant that nothing could be *certain*.

I suppose I like to think that the man they eventually selected – as we will see later – could, just *could* have been anyone. Which was the whole point of Railton's initial idea. And, more importantly, was what the mothers and fathers of Britain needed to *believe* in November 1920.

He *could* have been a young volunteer, conscript or officer, from any branch of the forces, from any corner of the Empire, and could have died in any year of the war.

He just *could* have been Anthony French's pal, Bert Bradley, who had such a lovely tenor voice. Or the brilliant intellectual, Tom Kettle, who never did get to read his last poem to his tiny daughter, Betty.

He *could* have been Padre Rupert Inglis, who played rugby for England. Or Sidney Wheater, who played hockey for Yorkshire. Or Alec Reader, who gave up his job at the post office to enlist when he was only seventeen.

Grieving mothers needed to believe that the Unknown Warrior who was to be buried in Westminster Abbey could be – *really* could be – *their* son.

Widows had to be able to cling to the hope that this could be *their* husband.

Children had to be given the chance to make the leap of faith that the man in that box could be – in fact, probably *was* – their father.

Whether or not this daring idea succeeded would depend entirely on the way it was stage-managed. The pressure on Lord Curzon and his organising committee was intense.

And the first thing they had to do was to select a body.

Somebody who was nobody to represent *all* the missing.

CHAPTER SIX

MISSING – FATE UNKNOWN

THE SOMME
SPRING 2023

I knew that my visit to High Wood and the battlefield cemeteries of the Somme would be sobering. But the quiet individuality of each grave strikes a positive note which takes me by surprise. The headstones may look the same, yet – like Guardsmen on parade – each face is slightly different, and the varied plantings of roses, carnations and shrubs add a personal touch. Most bear the cap badge of the soldier's regiment, originally chiselled by hand, along with his rank, name, date of death – his age when the clock stopped, when he sacrificed his life for his country. And there are some moving personal inscriptions – an option offered to families who could choose their own tribute, subject to approval, with a maximum permitted length of sixty-six characters, including spaces, for a fee of 3½ pence per letter (about £2.30 in today's money).[1]

Many of the sentiments expressed are touchingly simple: 'No lad more tender, no lad more true. Dearly loved by mother, father and family.' There is something that moves me, too, about the inscription on the headstone of Private Harry Pickup, buried in the military cemetery at Étaples: 'He gave his life for me. In ever loving memory of my dead husband.'

One epitaph, of course, is repeated all too often: 'A Soldier of the Great War.' Followed by Rudyard Kipling's haunting words: 'Known unto God.' And as I wander quietly among the rows of graves across the Somme, I find myself reading Kipling time and time again. Every single one of these stones, I remind myself, marks a family bereft and wondering what happened to their boy. And where, in the shell-ploughed hell of the battlefield, he might lie.

Because of my own combat experiences, the loss of close friends and the lasting mental scars war leaves, I try not to dwell on my past. But these feelings creep up on me now and then. Images of loss flickering at the back of my mind. And, to my surprise, I begin to recognise the fact that my journey to trace the origins of the Unknown Warrior has elements which are far more personal than I could possibly have imagined.

I had begun researching a story about a man who died more than a century ago. But now I realise he's still right here, among us. The Unknown Warrior is a kind of Everyman, and Everywoman too. And I have met him once or twice, myself. I *know* these people. I know the widows and children robbed of a husband or a father killed in service, whose body has never been recovered. I have attended the funerals of many friends. Watched as families stand around a polished oak coffin in an English country church, feeling close, for one last time, to the man or woman they loved in life, and to whom, in death, they are now bidding farewell. But, I now remember, I also know some relatives of the modern-day missing, who never had the option of saying that final goodbye.

LONDON
NOVEMBER 2022

In the centre of the Royal Albert Hall's vast arena stands a petite fifty-something lady in a black dress. Her shoulders shake as she struggles to contain her grief. Alone, beneath the brilliant spot-lights, with a vast image of her father projected onto the floor beside her amid swirling clouds, she has been doing her best to read aloud from the sheet of paper she's clinging to. The last letter her dad ever wrote to her. She composes herself as the band of His Majesty's Royal Marines launches into a plaintive lament. I hold my breath.

'Dear Mary,' she begins. 'By the time you get this letter . . .'

But it is too much. Not just for Mary. For all of us. Tears stream down my face as I am confronted by the harsh reality of loss.

Mary Fowler never had a chance to say goodbye to her father, Michael 'Foxy' Fowler, killed when his ship was bombed during the Falklands conflict in 1982. His body was never recovered. There was no funeral, no burial or cremation. Foxy Fowler, alongside many of his comrades, went down with his ship; a modern Unknown Warrior. And forty years on, his daughter is still bereft. Watching her hurting on stage, it feels as if her father could have been killed yesterday.

Few events in British public life draw attention to the sacrifices of the fallen more effectively than the Royal British Legion's annual Festival of Remembrance at the Royal Albert Hall. And there is a lot riding on it this year, just a few months after the death of Queen Elizabeth II. This will also be the first Festival of Remembrance attended by the new King. I am truly honoured, and delighted, to have been invited to say a few words from the stage as part of a tribute to the late Queen.

Although the rehearsal for my part is over, several of us have stayed to watch some of the other segments, including renowned Italian tenor Andrea Bocelli and a host of other stars. There is a lengthy sequence commemorating the fortieth anniversary of the Falklands War – those who survived, and those who never came home. Watching Mary Fowler talk about her loss amid projections of smoke, clouds and the distant ocean where her father still lies ratchets our emotion to a new level. Later that day, just before the live performance, I chat to Mary over tea and sandwiches in a side room we share with other bereaved families. She admits that she is still worried that she may not get through the letter without bursting into tears. I murmur something about how proud her dad would be. She gives me a rueful smile and nods her thanks.

That night, in front of the King, most of the royal family,

thousands in the hall and millions more watching on TV at home, she reads her father's last letter with a steadfastness and loving care that is only heightened by the hint of a tremor in her voice. She quietly composes herself each time her enduring pain threatens to burst through. For me, Mary's tribute to her missing father is perhaps the most moving moment in an evening crammed with moving moments. And exactly what this story, and my journey in search of the Unknown Warrior, is all about.

Petty Officer Michael 'Foxy' Fowler, respected sailor, loving husband and much-adored father, who died in battle in 1982, is from the same mould as those 'unknowns' from 1916. It is Mary's solitary, lasting grief that helps me to understand more deeply the extraordinary sense of loss felt by so many in the face of those hundreds of thousands of the missing at the end of the First World War. More than this, the way Mary's story touches all of us as we sit in the shadows of the Royal Albert Hall, biting back the tears, gives me an insight into the way a single death can affect an entire community and continue to touch those left behind many decades later.

THE SOUTH ATLANTIC
APRIL 1982

The Round Tower on Broad Street, just outside the docks at Portsmouth, was the best place to watch the big ships come in. Wives, children, mothers, fathers could stare across the Solent to Gosport and the Isle of Wight and see the approaching silhouettes from miles away. Mary Fowler went there often. Aged thirteen, she would hurry over from her secondary school in Southsea, just in case. Her dad was a sailor on HMS *Coventry* and he was due home from Gibraltar any day now. Michael was a wonderful father: patient, loving and always joking around. So the sense of excitement at home was palpable. The Fowlers were an incredibly close family and having him home after a long absence brought joy into their lives. 'We did so much together and he was always full of fun,' recalls Mary, or 'Cuddly Head' as her father called her. Her parents were both very sociable and her father and his navy friends lived their lives to the full, but he always had time for her. 'I remember him explaining how light bulbs worked, and taking apart and fixing my hairdryer, showing me how the different parts functioned.' Mary falters. 'I still remember that to this day.'[2]

Mary is dyslexic and he devoted himself to helping her with reading and spelling. 'He was so patient and understanding. But also loved doing daft stuff, like throwing a wet flannel down the stairs at my head. He was always joking around. There was always laughter in the house.' Just a few months earlier, he had surprised her with his choice of Christmas presents. 'Instead of the usual toys, he had bought me make-up and some of the beauty books all my teenage friends were so keen on.' She smiles at the memory. 'It made me realise that I was finally growing up, and that he recognised I was no longer a little girl.' But a telegram arrived that April with bad news. In the wake of Argentina's invasion of the Falkland Islands, Mary's family would have to wait a while longer for the laughter to resume. Rather than returning to dock at Portsmouth, HMS *Coventry* had joined the vast naval Task Force already steaming to the South Atlantic.

Her dad was going to war. Whatever that might mean.

* * *

On board *Coventry*, the sailors knew almost as little as their families. The ship's skipper, Captain David Hart Dyke, had been looking forward to getting back to his wife and two daughters, 10-year-old Miranda (who would later become a famous comedian and TV actor) and 7-year-old Alice. A specialist navigator with a knack for diplomacy, Hart Dyke had been surprised to be given the command of the guided-missile destroyer. A very different challenge after his stint as the Commander of the Royal Yacht *Britannia*. Hart Dyke had been leading *Coventry* through a series of exercises in the Mediterranean when his flotilla was ordered to rearm, reprovision and sail south. 'It was quite traumatic when we knew where we were going,' he says. 'Anxious letters from home increased our concerns as well. It was a very unsettling time.'[3] Michael Fowler and the rest of the ship's company shared his unease. 'We were just getting ready to return home to our families,' says Chief Petty Officer Russell Ellis, who shared quarters with Mary's father. Responsible for the ship's Sea Dart anti-aircraft missiles, Ellis would be at the forefront of any action. 'We had stopped off in Gibraltar for a few beers and to phone our families, letting them know we would be home in a few days.'[4]

That phone call turned out to be the last time Russell Ellis would speak to his wife for months. For some of his fellow sailors, it would be the last time their families heard their voice. HMS *Coventry*'s job would be to defend the other ships with her Sea Dart missiles. Argentina had more than 200 aircraft. It was clear that the ship's company were going to be extremely busy.[5] There was no turning back.

Foxy Fowler was regarded as a father figure and was highly respected by all who knew him, especially the younger sailors – many still in their teens – who worked with him in the ship's Sonar Control Room. 'His team knew they could always go to him for advice,' says Russell Ellis. 'He was lithe, fit as a fiddle and sociable. Foxy was a commanding presence on board. As the "Damage Control Petty Officer", he had to prepare the entire crew how best to respond if the worst happened. Instructing the ship's firefighters and first-aid parties, training the crew to repair battle damage, and perhaps most importantly of all, preparation for an event every sailor fears – abandoning ship.' This meant training the crew in the use of life jackets and their twenty-man inflatable life rafts. 'Launching and boarding a life raft in the heaving, freezing waters of the South Atlantic, possibly while still under air attack, was a fearsome challenge we never really believed would happen.'

Fowler's skill at counselling the younger men was put to the test early on after a visiting Admiral put the wind up the crew. 'Make no mistake, this is going to be a tough war,' he told them. 'And we

John Nichol at the cemetery opposite High Wood.

Soldiers resting during a break in the fighting on the Somme in 1916.

British stretcher bearers carry a wounded soldier through the clinging mud of Passchendaele

RAF paramedic Andy Smith (centre) treats a seriously injured casualty on board a Chinook helicopter during the war in Afghanistan in 2007.

British soldiers awaiting burial in a cemetery near Monchy-le-Preux on the Western Front in France in August 1918.

High Wood in 1919. Skeletal remains from the battle in 1916 still lie in the open awaiting recovery and burial. A cross marking another temporary grave can be seen in the top left of the photo.

Professor Dame Sue Black, the lead forensic anthropologist to the British Forensic Team, in Kosovo in 1999, where she was responsible for the recovery of bodies from mass graves.

Members of the Graves Registration Commission (*c.1918*) recover a body for later reburial in one of the newly created cemeteries.

John Nichol in Westminster Abbey at the Tomb of the Unknown Warrior.

Padre David Railton, the man who conceived the idea for an Unknown Warrior, pictured just before leaving for France in 1916.

John Nichol with Railton's daughter-in-law Margaret during a visit to her home in 2023.

Canon Alf Hayes (second left, wearing the stole) buries unidentified Argentine soldiers during the Falklands War in 1982.

Mary Fowler with her father Michael 'Foxy' Fowler in 1972. Michael died on board HMS *Coventry* when it was sunk during the war in the Falklands in 1982. His body was never recovered.

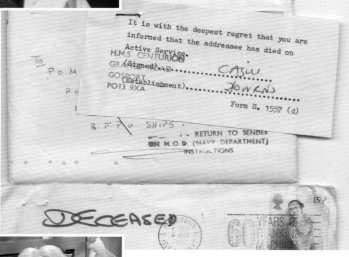

Undelivered letters returned to Michael Fowler's family after he died.

Mary Fowler and Canon Alf Hayes at the Royal British Legion's Festival of Remembrance in 2020, where they would both recall their experiences of the Falklands War.

Lieutenant Cecil Smith (second from left), who carried out a midnight mission to rebury the remains of those not selected to be the Unknown Warrior. The padre who accompanied him, Reverend George Standing, is on the left. Joining the group on what are probably the steps to the temporary chapel at Saint-Pol-sur-Ternoise is Major Ernest Fitzsimon (far right), who was involved in the selection process.

Brigadier General Louis Wyatt, the officer who made the final choice of the Unknown Warrior.

Staff from the Directorate of Graves Registration and Enquiries at Saint-Pol. Vere Brodie is sitting in the middle with a dog on her lap.

The Unknown Warrior's coffin during the photo shoot in Westminster Abbey in November 1920, just before it was transported to France.

can expect ship losses. We might as well face that now, as well as the fact that some of you may not be returning home.'

'I *think* the Admiral's intention was to come and give us a pep talk,' one young sailor said. 'But in my view, he singularly failed. I just stood there and thought: "Some bloody pep talk *this* is." And with that, off he went. Everybody's chin was just hitting the deck. It was extremely busy in the engineers' workshop after that. Everybody was stamping their name, their service number and their blood group onto dog tags. They all thought they were going to die.'[6]

Russell Ellis and his friend Foxy would privately discuss their concerns about what lay ahead. '*Coventry* was a close-knit family and as Senior Ratings we had to show confidence to all our troops and boost their morale as best we could. We had to ensure we showed no apprehension about the task before us. Foxy was confident in our abilities and a great leader in the way he prepared us for war.' As news of Argentinian air attacks on other elements of the Task Force began to reach them, Fowler would lead the men through various scenarios – evacuating the injured, damage control, firefighting, shoring up breaches and more. The two friends would have long conversations about how to react, both as individuals and as a ship's company. 'What if we were hit by a bomb? What if we were holed beneath the water line?' says Ellis. 'You go through everything in the hope that you are prepared if the worst happens. Foxy would orchestrate it all. He would brief us on the drills for abandoning ship and getting into the life rafts, again and again. Of course, we never thought it would happen. But in the military, you always hope for the best while preparing for the worst.'

* * *

Back in Portsmouth, Mary Fowler's family were hoping for the best too. Night after night, they would watch the news unfolding on TV. 'I can still see the image of the government spokesman, as he gave his press statements.' She shakes her head. 'Still see his heavy-rimmed glasses and hear his steady, almost musical, tones as he spoke about what was happening and, as the conflict developed, which ships had been attacked.'

Most of the family's information came from the news. They had hushed conversations – especially after the sinking of the Argentinian ship, the *General Belgrano*, in which 323 men died on 2 May 1982. And then again, two days later, after HMS *Coventry*'s sister ship, HMS *Sheffield*, was hit by an Exocet missile and twenty members of the crew lost their lives. Even though her mother and older brother tried to explain, it was difficult for the young teen-ager to make sense of what it all really meant. 'We would sit at the kitchen table late at night, discussing what was happening,' she says. 'There was no doubt that thousands of miles away, my dad was in great danger. It was quite disconcerting.'

* * *

Fowler and Ellis had watched *Sheffield* burning in the distance. They both had friends on the doomed ship, but their job was to rally their own troops now that the gloves were off. To focus on their own survival. 'Of course, *Sheffield* was the only topic of conversation that night in the Mess,' says Ellis. 'We had a minute's silence and raised a small glass of rum to lost comrades. Then Foxy began to discuss how we would react if *we* were hit, how *we* might prepare for a similar missile strike. It was clear that the war had been brought home to us in a very personal way. We knew that people had died; gone down with their ship, but nobody said the words out loud. And although there was certainly more dying to do, you just didn't think about what it actually meant, you didn't think about people never going home; there was a war to be fought and that was our reality.'

Though he kept his own fears as far as he could beneath the surface, they would come back to him when he was alone in his bunk. 'I had a wife and three young kids. What would happen to them if I died? We were embarking on a journey into the unknown. And I think we were all trying to work out how we would react when the time came for us to "go over the top" and face the enemy for the first time. With friends already dead, it was not a comfortable prospect.'

Russell Ellis echoes the feelings of those young Tommies waiting in the trenches in 1916. That same, queasy sensation of wondering if you might survive the next few hours. Or even the next few minutes. The men heading south aboard HMS *Coventry* would have been more than aware of the catastrophic loss of life in both world wars and the ease with which soldiers, sailors and airmen can be turned from individuals into statistics in the blink of an eye. The technology may have changed, but the nagging fear of approaching battle had not. And, as on the Western Front, waiting was the hardest part. 'It was hard knowing an attack was inevitable; it certainly plays on your mind,' says Ellis. 'War can be boring when you're not fighting – just staring at the radar screen, knowing there's going to be nothing there until the next morning. But deep down, you know that danger will eventually come.'

His words make me think of the description of a British Army sentry written by Tom Kettle, the Irish poet-statesman whose body was never found after he was killed at Ginchy, close to High Wood, in September 1916:

A figure in khaki stands with his steel helmet forming a bulge over the parapet as he peers through the night towards the German lines. Over there, in No Man's Land, there are shell-holes and unburied men. There are two sinister fences of barbed wire, on the barbs of which blood-stained strips of uniform and fragments more sinister have been known to hang uncollected for a long time. Strange things issue from No Man's Land, and the eyes of the army never close or flinch. And so, strained, tense and immovable, he leans and looks forward into the night of menace.[7]

That feeling of menace – understood by all who prepare for battle – pervaded the atmosphere as the Falklands conflict steadily unfolded.

'I think most people were thinking, *Are we going to survive this?* And, *How will my family survive if I don't make it home?*' recalls Russell Ellis. 'You never say it out loud, but I'm fairly sure everybody must have been thinking it at some point. I certainly was. But the harsh reality of war means you just carry on. And as the days ground on, we became more confident in our capabilities. More steely, too. Put simply, we had to try to kill the enemy before they killed us.'

Back in England, Russell's family were doing their best to celebrate his birthday when British landings on the Falklands began in the early hours of 21 May 1982. In response, Argentinian air attacks came in thick and fast. But Captain Hart Dyke still managed to find a moment to send Russell Ellis a chocolate egg as a gift. Though the crew's hearty rendition of 'Happy Birthday' was interrupted by the incoming hostiles.

Coventry had already fired her Sea Dart missiles in anger in the previous days, shooting down a number of enemy aircraft. But now the Argentinian Air Force began to attack the British fleet with increased ferocity. 'Every now and then, between raids, I remember Foxy would pop his head into the ops room and check how we were all doing, and if we needed anything,' Russell recollects. 'And in quiet periods, when we were not at action stations, he would sit near my position, and we'd discuss how the war was going. When might it end? We'd crack the odd joke and then get back to work. We never actually said the words, but the unspoken question was: *What is tomorrow going to bring?*'

'We knew 25 May would be a bad day,' says Russell, looking back. The Argentinian national day was equivalent to the Fourth of July for Americans. 'There was a feeling that they would do all they could to win back a bit of glory for their "motherland". I felt very apprehensive; we knew they would be throwing everything against us. And, stuck so close to the land, we were effectively acting as bait to draw the enemy. Like pawns on a chessboard.'

'Things were hotting up,' recalls Captain Hart Dyke. 'I personally felt that if we survived the 25th, we would survive the war. It was going to be a difficult day.'[8] In the Operations Room, three decks below the bridge, he was mindful of the gathering storm. Intercepted Argentinian radio signals gave the Intelligence Officers a good idea of what was coming. It wasn't pretty. 'We knew exactly what they were doing; how many fighters were taking off, and who they were going for,' he says. 'We detected the enemy flying straight for us, clearly determined to destroy us.'[9]

* * *

In Portsmouth, 25 May was a warm, slightly muggy day, with a stiff south-westerly breeze making the white horses dance on the Solent. Just a few scattered clouds scudded across the sky.[10] But it was far from 'business as usual' in the town. Hundreds of local sailors had sailed south and the fate of too many families was wrapped up in the conflict unfolding in the South Atlantic. And they had all seen that morning's searing headline in the local paper:

FIREBALL DEATH OF WARSHIP: ANTELOPE EXPLODES

On the buses and in the streets the sense of foreboding was palpable. What would today's news bring?

Apart from the butterflies dancing in the pit of her stomach, Mary Fowler's Tuesday at school had been much like any other. Studying a map of the world during a geography class, she searched for the tiny red pinprick representing the Falkland Islands. None of her schoolfriends had fathers on the Task Force, so they were not really aware of what she was going through. The war seemed so distant. But Mary thought about her dad every day. And every day he was away, was a day closer to the moment he would come home.

That evening, while her mother prepared supper, Mary got stuck into her homework. Across the world, 7,862 miles away, four Argentinian A-4 Skyhawk jets were screaming fast and low across

Falkland Sound. Two sinister pairs: *Vulcano* flight, closely followed by *Zeus* flight.

* * *

Russell Ellis was jolted awake as 'HANDS TO ACTION STATIONS!' blasted over the ship's loudspeakers. 'There was no time for fear,' he says quietly. 'I dressed quickly and scrabbled around trying to find my life jacket. In the initial rush, I forgot to zip up my bunk and secure it. You don't want any of your gear flying around if the ship is hit, so I turned back to sort it out, but Foxy was already there. "No problem, Eli," he said to me. "I'll do your bunk, mate. Just make sure you take out a few more of those A-4s."' Ellis still has a clear picture of Fowler in the momentary calm before the storm. 'He was smiling, carrying his own life jacket and wearing his uniform jacket along with his flash hood and gloves.' He pauses. 'I still remember being distracted by the brass buttons on his jacket. Things were happening very fast, but with a strange clarity. I said, "Thanks, shipmate. I owe you one . . ."'

Ellis's voice trails off again. While he raced to his Sea Dart station to prepare for the incoming attack, Fowler hurried to his own action station in the Junior Rates Dining Hall, along with his highly trained Damage Control Team.

In the Operations Room, Hart Dyke and his men knew the aircraft were coming for them, but where the hell were they?[11] Nearby, HMS *Broadsword* had managed to pick up the hostiles on radar, but with the landmass of Pebble Island cluttering *Coventry*'s radar picture, there was nothing visible on their own screens. At the last moment, one of the lookouts spotted them. Two glinting pinpricks on the horizon.

At the missile desk in the Operations Room, Russell Ellis and his team had been scanning their screens for a while, hammering their fists in frustration, fighting to achieve a missile-lock. Why wouldn't their Sea Dart bloody lock on? Ellis knew the answer. The ragged contours of Pebble Island were interfering with their radar picture, playing havoc with its ability to identify the attackers. At last, Sea Dart had achieved a successful lock. With the sound of an express train racing through a tunnel, the whole ship shook as a missile hammered into the sky, dragging a dazzling rope of white smoke behind it. But even as the solid-fuel booster was accelerating the 14-foot Sea Dart off its launcher, Ellis knew it had been wasted. The radar lock had almost immediately been lost.

Vulcano flight were first in to attack.

Coventry and *Broadsword*'s crews opened fire with everything they had; the main 4.5-inch gun with its sleek anti-aircraft shells, and the starboard 20mm Oerlikon cannon, a Second World War weapon designed well before the era of fast jets. Machine guns clattered away from the flight deck. Then there was the frantic *pop-pop-pop* of those armed with their personal rifles taking potshots at the deadly intruders.

Initially, it was HMS *Broadsword*'s turn. The frigate looked the softer target, compared with the more concentrated fire and smoke coming from *Coventry*. Her Sea Wolf short-range missile had managed to achieve a missile-lock, but a split second later a computer glitch caused the system to reset. The crew battled frantically to bring the system back online. Too late.

The two aircraft released their weapons then howled over the ship. One bomb tore through *Broadsword*, sliced up through her flight deck, tearing the nose off the ship's Lynx helicopter. Fire broke out, but miraculously the bomb carried on, exploding harmlessly in the sea beyond.[12]

Now it was HMS *Coventry*'s turn. Her time as a pawn on the battlefield chessboard was almost up as *Zeus* flight launched their low-level attack. As shells and bullets continued to ravage their approach, the Argentinian pilots pressed on, one later admitting that he'd closed his eyes, telling himself, 'I've had it, but I'll get this ship before I die.'[13]

'BRACE! BRACE! BRACE!' echoed over *Coventry*'s PA system.

Then a strangled shout of 'Take cover!'

'I've never been so scared in my whole life,' recalled one sailor, who can still vividly picture the incoming aircraft skimming low over the water. 'And I hope to God I'm never that scared again.'

Chris Howe, the ship's communications and electronic warfare specialist, remembers turning to Captain Hart Dyke. 'We're about to get attacked by ...' he began, as three bombs struck the ship. 'I'm not sure if I had actually finished my sentence when there was a thud. My life just slowed down completely, as though I was living in a slow-motion film.'[14]

Russell Ellis could hear the jets screaming overhead. 'There was a couple of dull thumps. I thought, *That really doesn't sound good*. Then there was silence. I still remember those quiet few seconds every night.' The 1,000-pound bombs, armed with delay-action fuses, had penetrated the ship.

'I remember this terrible hush in the Ops Room,' says Hart Dyke. 'It seemed to last a very long time.'

'The bomb exploded in a computer room,' says Chris Howe. 'There was a flash. And then a fireball was rolling around the Operations Room, searching for the oxygen.' Unable to dodge it, Howe became tinder for the rampaging fire. 'My arm was burning,' he grimaces. 'My skin was literally alight and I was trying to slap out the flames with my left hand.'[15] As the thick, searing smoke enveloped him, Chris remembers wanting to lie down, desperate for it all to stop. Then, an image of his wife and children flashed into his mind. Something was forcing him onward. *You are not ending your life here. Not like this.*

'I didn't hear any explosion or feel any blast,' says Russell Ellis. 'I just remember the Ops Room implode and the screen in front of me beginning to melt and fold before my eyes. All in total silence. I was blown off my chair and lying on the deck, breathing in black, toxic, horrific smoke. I tasted the rubber and the wire going down into my lungs as I sucked in the remnants of the burning equipment.' He passed out.

'The first thing I remember was a terrific blast,' says Captain Hart Dyke. 'Then heat. Searing heat. Total chaos and devastation. People on fire.'

Others were desperately trying to find enough air to stay alive. 'I could hear the guys in the computer room burning to death,' remembered another survivor. 'One was trying to get out and I crawled over to try to help pull him up.' He fell back through the hatch into the flames. 'Those screams will never leave me.'[16]

A few seconds later, Ellis came round. 'I couldn't see anything. I could just hear screaming. At that instant, I thought I would die.'

Hart Dyke, too, was preparing for the end. 'The smoke was thickening in the Ops Room. I was suffocating, I was trapped, but completely rational. I saw no alternative but to die. I was surprised by how calm I was. Actually, I felt quite concerned about who was going to mow the lawn at home in my absence.' Moments later, he was bemused to find himself in the starboard passage with no idea how he had got there. He was alive, could breathe, but then, 'I felt the whole ship lurch to port. I knew that it was doomed, that it was the death throes of my ship.'

Chris Howe, too, was making his way in the same direction. 'I realised then that I only had a pair of boots on, along with my underwear and a piece of shirt collar. Everything else, my anti-flash hood and all, had been blown clean off me. All that was left was my wedding ring and my St Christopher. Which I still wear today.'

Russell Ellis had spotted a flicker of light through the acrid smoke, and, despite being badly burned, managed to crawl towards it. *Coventry* was heeling badly and water was lapping into the lower decks. 'It was all happening in slow motion. I staggered up some stairs where a young sailor helped me, saying, "Chief, you've got no clothes on!" All my clothes had been blasted and burned off, apart from my boots, belt and underpants. That was it. I was burned from head to foot.' Ellis remembered Foxy Fowler's survival training and was helped into a hi-vis survival suit before sliding down the side of the ship. The shock of the icy Atlantic hit him hard. His comrade had forgotten to do up the suit's collar, and it filled with water. 'In reality, it was actually a good thing.' His eyes light up. 'It doused and blanched my burns, soothing and cooling them.' A life raft materialised among the other lumps of bright orange flotsam, and he was hauled aboard.

Chris Howe, also assisted by a friend, had staggered zombie-like onto an upper deck. When he finally felt fresh air on his skin, the pain made its mark. 'I could feel I was badly burned,' he says. 'Adrenaline kicks in, and it's utter agony. My back was stripped of skin, down through several layers.' He was also hitched into a survival suit and tumbled down the side of the ship like a sack of coal.

Captain Hart Dyke had watched the unfolding drama, almost spellbound. 'I never actually gave the order to abandon ship. I was in no position to give orders. But it was the only thing to do, so the younger members of the crew took the initiative, launching the life rafts, and so on. Everyone was calm, helping each other. It was remarkable.'

A total of 280 crewmen escaped the conflagration. Behind them, HMS *Coventry* sank in twenty-five minutes. 'In the life raft, someone gave me a shot of morphine,' says Russell Ellis. 'I remember peering out and watching *Coventry* turn over. It was an unreal, devastating sight. This is your home, your life, your world, dying in front of your eyes. And you know that some of your mates are going down with it. Everything had gone, every personal possession, every letter, every photograph. All I had left was my underwear, boots and a belt. Many of my colleagues had made the ultimate sacrifice, and they were gone too.'

The men had been trained to wait twenty-four hours before opening the life raft's emergency canisters containing survival equipment, water, chocolate and other rations. But the rescue was already underway, and they had just come within an inch of being burned alive, then drowning. Within minutes, the canisters were cracked open. 'And, fuck me,' says one survivor, with a broad grin. 'There's fags in the ration packs! Sod the fact that I'd given up for the past three months. I started again.'[17]

* * *

Next morning in Portsmouth, the local newspaper began to drop through letterboxes. Another bald headline screaming from the front page. For many, this was the first they had heard of the tragedy:

HMS COVENTRY SUNK: HUGE LOSS OF LIFE

'It was a terrible time for the families,' says Ellis, looking back on the experience forty years later. 'I think that our loved ones waiting at home had a worse time than us in battle. Not knowing if we were alive or dead.' Which families were going to be among the lucky ones? Which were about to be overcome by a sense of loss that would be lodged in their hearts forever?

Blissfully unaware of the events taking place thousands of miles away, Mary Fowler walked to school that morning wondering when she would see her dad again. When she got home later, a crowd was gathered outside. 'Mum and Dad were heavily involved in the Scout movement and one of the other leaders was coming out of the front door,' she remembers sadly. 'Why was he there? What had happened so that the house was full of my parents' friends and colleagues? What did it all mean?'

It meant that, in the aftermath of the attack, and the crew abandoning ship, her father was missing, fate unknown.

'It was a terrible few days. All we could do was wait, and hope, and pray. I remember us joking that Dad would probably be in a life raft, furious that his tobacco had got wet. That he'd be keeping everyone's spirits up. He was always meticulous and very tidy, so we knew he'd be really annoyed at all the mess caused by the ship sinking. That was our way of keeping our spirits up, I suppose. We never thought for one minute that he wouldn't come home to us.'

One of the Argentinian bombs had exploded inside the aft engine room, the blast totally destroying the dining room above, where Michael 'Foxy' Fowler and his Damage Control Party were based. He and his team had no chance. Seventeen of the crew died in the ship; two more were killed in the process of trying to abandon her.[18]

'After a couple of days, we were told the news that Dad was now listed as missing ... presumed dead ...' Mary's voice breaks. 'We were later told that he had gone down with the ship, that his remains would not be coming back to the UK.'

Weeks later, as the Task Force began to head home, Mary and her family would watch the news with its images of joyous celebration and happy reunions. As the bands played, families welcomed back husbands, fathers, brothers. News footage from the time shows cheering HMS *Coventry* survivors aboard the *QE2*, waving banners and flags. 'My whole school was given a day off to go down to the port and be part of the welcome,' says Mary. 'I didn't go.' She would turn away from the screen when the evening news was on the TV. 'I didn't want to be part of the story. There were no celebrations in our house. We remained hunkered down behind closed doors.'

* * *

Recovering in hospital as the news filtered through, Russell Ellis gradually learned the fate of his shipmates. 'I still give thanks that I'm alive. But my personal survival was tinged by deep, heart-rending sadness that so many friends had gone. Nineteen members of my naval family.' Ellis sits in silence for a moment, reflecting on the enormity of the experience through which he had lived more than four decades earlier. 'It is all, even now, still excruciatingly fresh. We have a reunion every year where we raise a glass of rum and make a toast to our friends "still on patrol" in the South Atlantic.' It is their personal tribute to lost friends with no 'normal' burial place. 'The families of the missing don't have graves at home to visit,' he says quietly. 'Their final resting place is thousands of miles away, on the ship where they fought and died. But even then, you can't see it, can't visit it. You can stand next to the memorial on Pebble Island and look out towards the spot they went down. But that's all.'

His words take me back to the trenches at Beaumont-Hamel, and the tens of thousands of people who have made their own journeys to the battlefields of the Somme, seeking to find closure and perhaps even closeness to the father, uncle, grandfather or husband – to the Unknown Warrior they had lost. 'I used to have a lot of silent periods,' admits Ellis. 'I don't know where I went. I suppose I was thinking of what happened. I mean, why was *I* lucky? Why did *I* survive when nineteen friends did not? Why did *I* make it home?'

It is a question many of us who have survived the vagaries of war regularly ask ourselves.

Mary Fowler still wonders why it was *her* father who didn't come home. She treasures the last letter he sent her. The same letter, jotted with a biro on 17 April 1982, that she read at the Royal Albert Hall forty years later:

Dear Mary,

I hope you received your birthday card all right? I'm sorry it was a bit babyish. It was the only one left in the canteen on board.

We are all very warm in the sun but as we go south I suppose that will change.

By the time you get this letter, your birthday will have come and gone, but I do hope you have a good happy one. I'm sorry I can't be with you, but I shall be thinking of you.

I suppose your mum is a little upset and maybe a bit short-tempered. So I would like you to look after her, and make things as easy as you can for her.

I'm afraid I do not know when I shall be home again. But let's hope it's not too far away.

Well love, that is about all for now, so till next time, God bless and take care of yourself.

Love,
Dad xxx[19]

As it was for the families of the soldiers who had marched off to war in 1914, at first, Mary says, it was very hard to square in her mind the difference between the very-much-alive funny and devoted dad who had sent her this letter, and the missing-in-action dad who was never going to come home. How could both be possible? And where *exactly* was he now? 'It took a while,' she says, 'but eventually we accepted that he wasn't coming home. And nor was a body. There would be no coffin. No funeral. There weren't even any possessions to return. No photographs. No clothes. No letters. Not even a pen or comb. Everything had disappeared at the same time he did.' Mary gives a shrug of weary surrender. 'He'd just *gone*. And that was the end of our story.'

That summer, the Fowler family held a memorial service at the Trinity Church in Southsea. Everyone came: her father's pals from the navy and from the Scouts, family, neighbours, old friends. The congregation wore either uniform or else funereal black. There were flowers, hymns and readings. 'But one thing was missing,' says Mary, sadly. 'A coffin. There was *nothing* physical. We had nothing to look at, nothing to touch. No grave to stand beside and talk about him. Or to him. We had nothing. It hit my family hard, made it much more difficult fully to understand what had happened. To accept his death.'

She lapses into silence and I wonder if I should not have asked so much about her missing father; encouraged her to revisit such pain. But the experience of those not granted the blessed closure of being able to bury a body has not changed over the years. Mary's tragedy sheds further light on how Padre Railton's concept for the Unknown Warrior was such powerful medicine for a country in mourning in 1920.

NORFOLK
AUGUST 1990

I was nineteen years old and had been in the RAF for just over a year when HMS *Coventry* went down. Like everyone in Britain, I followed the war closely, and, as a new serviceman, those Falklands deaths hit me pretty hard. Some of the dead were younger than me. It was a real wake-up call. Perhaps one day my life too could be on the line.

Nearly nine years later, after Iraq's invasion of Kuwait and with

war brewing in the Gulf, these thoughts came to the surface once
again. As an RAF navigator on Tornados in 1990, many of us were
preparing to deploy to the region to evict the invaders. Having heard
Mary's story, I have a far better appreciation of how my own family
must have felt, mentally preparing for the day when we would head
off to war. A war from which some of us would not return.

* * *

Jenny Green, now an elegant matriarch in her seventies, was going
through that process in August 1990. Her husband, Bill, was a
popular Squadron Commander at a Tornado base in Norfolk. He
would shortly be leading his personnel to the Gulf and Jenny was
steeling herself for his departure. Like all military spouses, she was
never totally comfortable with the risks involved in fast-jet flying,
but she did her best to remain philosophical. 'Everyone had lost
many friends killed in training, but as your husband heads out of the
door, you never really think that you might never see them again.'
She gives me a wry smile. 'If you thought that way, you would never
let them go.'[20]

It had been a warm, dry summer. Prince, New Kids on the Block
and Madonna were in the top ten. Bill and Jenny's teenage children,
Jeremy and Philippa, were both home from boarding school and the
four of them were looking forward to spending a few days together
as a family in Northumberland. A brief lull before the storm; there
would be long walks on the beach. Plenty of time for goodbyes.

On Thursday, 16 August, the night before the trip north, Bill had
one last training sortie to complete. Jenny hadn't mentioned the
strange dream she'd had, two nights earlier. 'It was totally ridiculous
and bizarre and had never happened before,' she says now, almost
apologetically. 'I suppose it was something to do with the fact that
he was about to be deployed to the warzone, and that some of our
friends and colleagues had been killed in crashes over the previous
few weeks.' Jenny had dreamed she was at Bill's funeral, looking at
his coffin in a church. 'Do you really have to fly tonight?' she asked

him. 'He did. That was that. And the events of the next twenty-four hours are indelibly imprinted on my brain, even though it was over thirty years ago. However much you think you know what it *might* be like, because you have seen others go through it, it is very different when it happens to you. When it is *your* life.'

She remembers the doorbell jangling her awake at 1AM. Assuming Bill had forgotten his keys, she headed downstairs. A cursory check through the blurry spyhole revealed a figure in full dress uniform; gold braid on a polished peaked cap.

It was Bill's Station Commander.

'As soon as I saw him, I knew that my life had changed forever,' she says. 'He didn't even have to say the words.' Bill's Tornado had not returned from the training sortie over the North Sea. He and his navigator were both missing, presumed dead. It would later emerge that during a bombing manoeuvre, they had hit the sea at nearly 600mph. No attempt had been made to eject. Both of them had been killed instantly.

'They told me he was missing, and that there was no hope of him, or his navigator, being found alive ...' While Jenny immediately accepted her husband was dead, she didn't fully comprehend that his body would never be found. And she certainly had no concept of how this would impact her family. 'In almost every other aviation accident, some human remains are normally recovered,' she says, with the melancholy benefit of her years of experience as an RAF wife, 'so there is conclusive proof that someone has died.' Initially, that absence of a body was not uppermost in her mind. She was too wrapped up in the shock of Bill's death, how to talk to her children about it, and how they were all going to cope with their life-changing loss. 'At that immediate moment, I didn't really understand what "missing" would mean to me over the coming days, weeks and months.'

But the lack of proof soon began to niggle and rankle. Her 15-year-old daughter, Philippa, wondered if perhaps the crash was a cover. 'At first she refused to believe he was dead. She thought he had been spirited away on a secret mission, something important

for the war effort, and that he would eventually return home to us.'
Even Jenny herself, a bright and pragmatic woman who had met Bill
when they were both studying at Oxford University, began to have
her doubts. 'I suppose there was a tiny bit of me that wondered if
this could be true. He had been attached to the Special Air Service
as a liaison officer on an earlier tour and was never allowed to talk,
even to his family, about some of the tasks he'd been involved with.
Perhaps he really was off on some secret mission? I knew in my heart
that it couldn't be true. But it does play on your mind.'

She is not alone in allowing her mind to stray into the realms of
the incredible. Another widow, who also lost her pilot husband in a
crash at sea, tells the same story. 'Without a body, it was difficult to
draw a line under the situation. For many years after the accident I
would dream that there would be a knock at the door and my husband would be standing there. Perhaps he had been on some sort
of secret mission and couldn't contact anyone? Now it was over he
had returned. It was silly. But without his body there was always a
thread of hope.'[21]

Jenny pauses as she takes stock of her own willingness, albeit
momentary, to believe the impossible. 'I think that when someone
dies and there is no body to bury, it is always difficult fully to accept
they have truly gone. With no Bill, and no body, it was terrible that
I couldn't say a final goodbye. There was no proof, which was difficult for us all.'

The precision with which she is able to anatomise her loss is
deeply touching. And I am fascinated by the way her words echo
Mary Fowler's. Going back to school after her first summer holiday
without her father was difficult. 'I was overwhelmed by the whole
situation and trying to come to terms with what it all meant,' she
says. 'There was no counselling or professional help in those days.
You just had to cope on your own. As a teenage girl, it was a very
tough time.' She hesitates. 'It still is. Grief becomes your friend; you
are always sad about that personal loss and it becomes part of you.'

Like Mary's family, the Greens held a memorial service for Bill. 'It
was a full military "funeral", all the pomp and ceremony expected,

including a Tornado flypast,' says Jenny. 'Although, obviously, there was no coffin. Bill's cap, with his Group Captain's gold braid on the peak, was on a stand alongside a large photograph of him in uniform at the front of the church – as representative of my husband as any coffin might have been.' As at Foxy Fowler's memorial service, the church was packed with a congregation in mourning black or military uniform. Jenny remembers it as a very sombre occasion, and one with a certain edge too. 'After the ceremony, the vicar told me that some people had felt very disturbed during the service. In the absence of any coffin, they felt that Bill was there as a physical presence.' She pauses, then adds briskly, 'Personally, I didn't have any of those feelings or emotions.'

On the other hand, she made sure that, for many years after Bill's death, the service cap which represented him at his memorial still sat on a table in the hall, exactly where he would leave it when he came home. As a journalist from the *Sydney Morning Herald* eloquently put it, when reflecting on the missing of the Great War, 'there are few things more expressive than a dead soldier's empty cap, the last remnant of him above earth'.[22]

Thinking of Mary Fowler, and her profound sadness at what little her family was left with by which to remember her father, I can see how valuable these mementos can be. 'One friend told me that they thought it was rather macabre to have Bill's hat sitting there as a memory,' says Jenny. 'But, tragically, a little while later, one of her children died. And the next time we spoke, she told me that she absolutely understood the need to have a memory, a symbol that a person is no longer with us.'

Mary Fowler says that before she read her father's letter at the Royal Albert Hall, she went through her mother's small box of memorabilia: the letters written but never delivered, returned unopened after his death, a couple of telegrams and a few photos. 'It's all we have left of Dad,' she says. 'Everything else went down on the ship with him and his friends.'

Such valuable keepsakes make me think of Alec Reader and his copy of *Treasure Island*, and of David Railton doing his best to return wedding rings, taken from the knuckles of dead soldiers, to their widows. 'I do have empathy with all of those hundreds of thousands of people who didn't get back the body of a relative after the First World War,' says Jenny Green. 'With so many men missing, and the fate of so many men unknown, the nation needed some way to come together, to commemorate, to acknowledge those losses and events.' She pauses. 'Sometimes you have to experience death, loss and tragedy in order to fully understand what it means to those who are left behind.'

Mary Fowler agrees. 'Shopping last Christmas, I was in a lift with a man and his daughter. They were chatting and joking about Christmas presents and the upcoming holiday. I suddenly realised how much life I had missed with my own father. Forty years on, I still wonder what might have been. I still wonder where *my* dad is ...'

CHAPTER SEVEN

THE CHOSEN ONE

SAINT-POL-SUR-TERNOISE, NORTHERN FRANCE
SPRING 2023

'Where is *my* dad . . . ?'

'Where is *my* husband . . . ?'

The questions Mary Fowler and Jenny Green still ask would have echoed across the world at the end of the Great War. And now, examining the names of dead Frenchmen on an unusually stark memorial in northern France, I find it difficult to comprehend the numbers involved. In Britain alone, hundreds of thousands of families were touched by the loss of a missing soldier, sailor or airman.[1] And everyone wanted to know the same thing: Where were they? Even those who could answer the question were still denied the solace and closure of bringing their loved one's body back home.

The dream of healing this numbing, national heartache had driven the Reverend David Railton relentlessly to create a permanent memorial to the missing, with the burial of an Unknown Warrior in Westminster Abbey, the nation's parish church.

To Railton's relief, by late October 1920 the King and Prime Minister were both on board and Lord Curzon's Memorial Services Committee, set up by the government to implement the scheme, were immersed in its planning. Curzon had already been tasked with organising the grand ceremonial parade on Armistice Day and the unveiling of Lutyens's permanent Cenotaph in Whitehall. Now he was instructed to conjure up a state funeral for the Unknown Warrior, as monumental as if the man in the coffin had been a garlanded national leader, not an anonymous soldier.

But time was short. And with only three weeks to go before the ceremony many doubts still remained.

Could one man, one body, really represent half a million missing?

Who should this Warrior be?

Who was going to make the choice?

And how could the process be kept secret for all eternity?

* * *

These questions – and the urgent search for Somebody who was Nobody – have brought me, on yet another punishingly hot day, to the boxy little town of Saint-Pol-sur-Ternoise, 50 miles south of Calais. While Lord Curzon was planning the white-gloved rituals and precision-choreographed parades that would transform the burial of an anonymous bag of bones into a profoundly resonant national spectacle, this is where the process would begin.

Twinned with the town of Hebden Bridge in West Yorkshire, Saint-Pol is a hilly commune with fewer than 5,000 inhabitants. A few miles away lurk the concrete remnants of one of the massive bunkers that once housed elements of Hitler's V1 flying-bomb programme. Saint-Pol became an important transit stop for the German goods trains, and an obvious target for the Allied bombers which destroyed much of the town, and its original 1922 war memorial, during the Second World War.[2] At the end of the First World War, it had become the headquarters of the Directorate of Graves Registration and Enquiries (DGR&E). A place where people were doing their absolute damnedest to identify where the missing were buried. Brigadier General Louis Wyatt, who had been wounded in the Boer War, was now the officer in charge of all British troops in France and Flanders. Under his direction, it was from here that the ongoing campaign to exhume, identify and formally rebury the dead was conducted.

Although Saint-Pol had been preoccupied with the business of death, it was a thriving community, too. The men arranged hockey matches and the camp even had its own mascot, Old Bill, a venerable fox terrier.[3] Vere Brodie described Saint-Pol as 'a very happy home to everyone'. An aristocratic volunteer nurse from the Highlands of Scotland, Vere had been drafted in to lead the thirty-one members of the Women's Army Auxiliary Corps (WAAC), who worked alongside the men. 'The camp was mainly engaged in searching the battlefields for the fallen, who were each given a service in the new cemetery, whether they had been identified or not.' They must have provided a welcome contrast to the all-male regimentation of Saint-Pol when they emerged from their own quarters, popularly known as the 'Waackery'. 'We had been well spoiled, from the General to the Privates, but it was appreciated,' said Vere. 'And, I think, we all did some spoiling in return.'[4]

I scan the bleak, grassless space opposite the town's railway station. Three French flags flutter in the breeze. I know it must be here somewhere. Not the Waackery, which is long gone, along with the army hospital, military buildings, even the divisional baths where grubby soldiers could once have had a restorative soak. My gaze is drawn to a stone cross surrounded by dead flowers. It turns out to be a monument to Charles de Gaulle, the leader of the Free French in the Second World War, and still a patriotic hero for many. Then, a few yards away from the cross, set in the midst of a bed of desiccated rosebushes, I glimpse a small white headstone. It doesn't look like much, considering what it commemorates. But here, on the slab of grey slate attached to the front, is the inscription I have been searching for:

THE BODY OF THE BRITISH UNKNOWN
WARRIOR WAS SELECTED AT ST POL ON THE
NIGHT OF THE 7TH–8TH NOVEMBER 1920. TAKEN
TO WESTMINSTER ABBEY AND INTERNED
THERE ON THE 11TH NOVEMBER 1920[5]

Surrounded by soulless concrete buildings, and the roar of traffic speeding along the road behind me, I take in these words. Turning away, something at its base catches my eye. A child's cuddly toy? I bend down. Half-hidden in the dry earth is a sun-bleached, woollen commemorative wreath, the size and shape of a deck-quoit. A printed card tells me it was left by the Royal British Legion Cyclists' Branch during a recent commemorative cycle ride through the battlefields. The faded, rain-blurred scrawl in royal blue ink, more than 100 years after the event this stone commemorates, makes me pause once more:

We shall not forget.

LONDON
20 OCTOBER 1920

On an autumnal evening in Westminster Abbey, footsteps echoed in the nave. The Dean, The Right Reverend Herbert Ryle, was engaged in hushed conversation with a representative of Lord Curzon's committee as they contemplated the final resting place of the Unknown Warrior.[6] The approach to the Great West Door had already been selected as the most public and accessible location. But there was still the question of whether the grave should be sited right in front of the entrance, or further away, near David Livingstone, the legendary explorer and anti-slavery campaigner.

Outside the Westminster bubble there was no shortage of attention-grabbing newspaper stories vying for prominence. The *Daily Mirror* reported that Britain's railwaymen and miners were threatening a general strike, that anti-British violence continued in Ireland, and detailed the case unfolding at Battersea magistrates' court concerning two schoolgirls who had each been paid fifteen shillings to bunk off school and spend two hours dolled-up as mannequins at Arding & Hobbs department store in Clapham Junction.[7] Elsewhere, the fire brigade was still fighting to extinguish a vast blaze at London's Hop Exchange. And King Alexander of Greece was gravely ill after being bitten by his pet monkey.[8] But countless snippets surrounding the upcoming ceremony and burial were now appearing almost daily. Even though the full details of the Unknown Warrior's funeral were still under discussion, the *Nottingham Evening Post* confidently declared it would be 'without doubt the most impressive and the most inspiring service the great Abbey has ever seen'.[9]

SAINT-POL-SUR-TERNOISE
22 OCTOBER 1920

The heavy weather over France was finally beginning to lift when a messenger, clutching an envelope marked 'SECRET' from Lieutenant General Sir George Macdonogh, the Adjutant General and one of the most senior officers in the army, was admitted to General Wyatt's[10] headquarters at Saint-Pol:

UNKNOWN WARRIOR

The following provisional instructions have been issued by the AG in connection with the interment of 'An Unknown Warrior' in Westminster Abbey on Armistice Day:-

The Director of the Graves Registration service will exercise his discretion as to location from which the body is to be exhumed.

Date of original burial should be as far back as possible.

Under instructions to be issued later, the body will be conveyed to Calais and there placed in a full-sized coffin, which will be sent out from England.

Sufficient soil is to be sent with the body to cover the coffin and fill a full-sized grave.

War Office
33–38 Baker Street
22nd October 1920.[11]

The pressure was on. The process had begun, and General Louis Wyatt became its main driver.

Quiet and highly principled, he loved the natural world, and birdlife in particular. 'He always walked with his dog beside him,' his daughter remembered. 'He was emphatic you should finish a job if you started it. He hated boasting, and he made lifelong friends.'[12] That insistence on finishing a job properly was going to come in handy. The bird-loving General had a little over a fortnight in which to ensure a body that fitted the bill was selected and prepared for transport across the Channel in time for Armistice Day.

Many years later, he outlined his initial thoughts upon receiving his instructions:

(a) The Body must be a British Soldier, and that there could be no means of him being identified.
(b) A Body should be chosen from each of the four Big Battle Areas.

> *Aisne*
> *Somme*
> *Arras*
> *Ypres*

(c) The Bodies should be brought to my Headquarters at St Pol and placed in the Chapel on 8th November 1920.
(d) The parties bringing the Body should at once return to their Areas.[13]

The emphasis on secrecy was so great, the importance of the chosen Warrior remaining absolutely unknown so essential, that for days the General opted to hold his fire before ordering his shortlisted candidates to be brought for final selection. And he was fortunate in having many resourceful officers on his staff.

Foremost among them was the remarkable Lieutenant Colonel Edward Gell. The Cambridge-educated ordained vicar had enjoyed remarkable success as an amateur heavyweight boxer during the

Boer War, then declared at the start of the First World War that he would be more useful as a fighting officer than as a chaplain.[14] Wounded at Beaumont-Hamel in 1915, the former padre had been awarded the Distinguished Service Order and the Military Cross for leadership and bravery in action.[15] It may well have been Gell to whom Wyatt had entrusted the job of arranging working parties to bring the bodies to Saint-Pol from four different battlefields.[16] He was certainly instructed to report to Wyatt at HQ when the task was complete.[17]

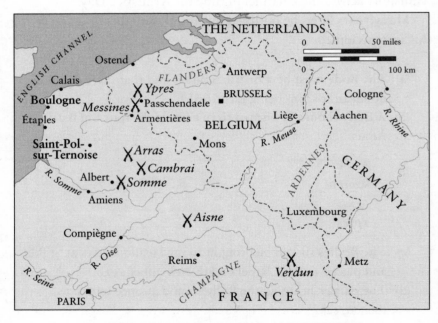

FIRST WORLD WAR MAJOR BATTLEFIELDS

LONDON
27 OCTOBER 1920

As part of the planning for the Armistice Day ceremony, David Railton had received the letter from Dean Ryle, informing him that his beloved flag – which had served as the final covering for so many warriors throughout the war – would indeed play a role at the funeral of the Unknown Warrior. Providing, of course, it was in a condition 'not unsuitable for the occasion'.[18] Ryle did not elaborate on his concerns about the state of the flag, and while Railton prepared it for action and General Wyatt finalised his plans for the selection of an appropriate corpse, other key elements of the proceedings were set in motion.

John Sowerbutts, secretary of the London Centre of the British Undertakers' Association (BUA), was working in his office when the phone rang.

'Hello?'

'Is that Victoria 946?'

'It is indeed.'

'Is Mr Sowerbutts there?'

'Speaking.'

'Good afternoon, sir; we are HM Office of Works, and we have to arrange the burial of the Unknown Warrior. Can your Association undertake the making of the casket for the remains? It has to be made to special designs yet to be got out, and it has all to be done in a very short time. Can you do it?'

'Yes, sir, of course we can, nothing is impossible to my Association!'[19]

At 10:30AM the following day, Sowerbutts and Kirtley Nodes, the association's president, gathered with a delegation of their fellow undertakers to be presented with the desired template for the Unknown Warrior's coffin. It was a bit of a blow. 'I well remember that some of the deputation had come armed with the most elaborate designs,' Nodes lamented. 'But we were soon informed they were not wanted. No, what was wanted was the cost of supplying the casket, as in the drawing by the architect of the Office of Works. We were asked to go over to a corner of the room and talk the matter over.'[20]

Their challenge became immediately obvious. 'The casket was to the design of a sixteenth-century treasure casket, made of a two-inch English oak, with slightly rounded sides and lid,' Nodes recalled. 'It was mounted with four pairs of hammered wrought-iron handles and iron bands from head to foot, and across the shoulders.' Distinctive and original with its unique iron furniture, it was unlike anything in their inventory. 'But still,' Sowerbutts said proudly, 'your humble servant was confident that the Association could do the work.' Kirtley Nodes stepped forward from the gaggle and cleared his throat. There could be no question of a fee, he said. He and his fellow members wished to build the casket as a gift to the nation; their tribute to the Unknown Warrior. In appreciation of their generosity, Nodes and Sowerbutts were invited to accompany the finished casket to and from France, and to make the necessary arrangements to lay the Unknown Warrior's body inside it when the time came. 'It was felt that by placing the matter in civilian hands, no jealousy should arise between the various sections of the Forces,' Nodes said. 'At the same time,' he added, a trifle undiplomatically, 'we were asked to be diplomatic.'

That afternoon, the Memorial Services Committee was meeting to give final approval for the construction, and Sowerbutts was asked to remain in his office until it was delivered. 'It was 7:30PM when the architect brought the design to the office,' he said, 'and that same night, the work was put in hand.' An inner shell of 1-inch-thick English pine, which would fit inside the grand casket, was commissioned simultaneously. It was to be sent directly to Saint-Pol in order to receive the body for the initial part of its journey to the French coast.

* * *

At his home in Margate, David Railton – like most of the public – knew almost nothing of the complex arrangements now underway. As late as 27 October, the newspapers were still presenting the event as a military occasion. 'Within the Abbey, around the open grave, it will be wholly a soldier's funeral,' trumpeted the *Daily Telegraph*. 'It is the intention to fill the Nave with massed troops. No civilian, save those few among the mourners – members of the Cabinet, and public representatives, a mere handful – will witness the actual interment. The Abbey will echo to the strains of martial music, the tramp of armed men.'[21]

Given Railton's deep feelings for the comrades alongside whom he had served, he must have known at once that Lord Curzon and the Memorial Services Committee were horribly out of step with the spirit of his idea. It was as if the government wanted to create a fierce tribute to the Armed Forces, with plenty of crisp marching and rifle spinning, along the lines of that lavished upon Admiral Horatio Nelson and the Duke of Wellington. It was only gradually that those in charge of the process began to understand what Railton had grasped from the outset. If organised correctly, this very public burial could heal the pain of the nation's bereaved, rather than glorifying the cause of their loss.

Exasperation was evident in a grouchy editorial in the *Daily Mirror* on 29 October:

The same indecision which has characterised the official arrangements for [Armistice] Day is now evident in the preparations for the Abbey funeral of the Unknown Warrior. Although we are within a fortnight of November 11th, practically nothing has been decided. Relatives of the fallen are impatient at the official delay.[22]

The newspaper had discovered that letters from heartbroken families begging for a seat at the abbey now ran into the thousands. Indeed, by this date – just a day after undertakers Nodes and Sowerbutts had agreed to build the coffin – applications had already reached 15,000.[23] Yet only a scant 250 spaces had been allocated to the bereaved, as the military and assorted dignitaries were still to take precedence. 'All this unnecessary correspondence, reflecting the anxiety of thousands of homes, could be avoided if the committee would only come to some swift and definite decision as to the allocation of seats,' the editor thundered. Railton must have been heartened to see the extent to which the great British public, undaunted by any plans for civilian exclusion, were scrambling for tickets.

Meanwhile, Curzon's press officer made sure that a small announcement appeared in *The Times* on the very same day, announcing that the number of available places in the abbey had risen to 2,500, and that the committee was 'now considering the lines to be followed in regard to the allotment of seats to relatives of those who died in the war'.[24] The Memorial Services Committee had been forced into a U-turn, brought about by the sheer weight of public opinion. The number of applications had reached 19,000 by the following day, with many more in the post.[25]

At the same time, tantalising glimpses were emerging about how the Unknown Warrior might be chosen:

> Bodies of unidentified soldiers will be exhumed from the various battlefields that were the scenes of actions at different periods of the war, and assembled at one centre. The responsible officer will then remove every badge or mark that could convey any indication of regiment or rank, and his choice will then be made, without the exhumation party gaining any clue.[26]

Then, as now, the press did not get everything right. But this particular bulletin was surprisingly close to the mark.

CAERNARFON, NORTH-WEST WALES
1 NOVEMBER 1920

David 'DJ' Williams was hard at work in his one-shed ironworks when the telegram arrived from the Office of Works. His presence was requested in London, it said, in block capitals, on a 'MATTER MOST URGENT'.[27] Williams wiped his hands, hung up his leather apron and caught the next available train. He was no stranger to the railways, having travelled to Liverpool at the age of fourteen to spend five years as an apprentice, then another five at an 'arts metalworks' in Manchester.[28] Even so, the journey to the capital was long and tedious.

Arriving at King Charles Street in Westminster, the mystery of his summons was revealed. The Prime Minister himself – for whose private residence Williams had fashioned a number of lamps – had decided he would be the best man for the task of creating the metal-work for the Unknown Warrior's coffin. Williams was shown one of the solid iron rings, resembling an ancient door knocker, which had already been produced. It quickly emerged that the frowning officials from the Office of Works were dissatisfied with the quality of the ironwork. It was solid enough, but lacked the period styling to match the casket. Could Williams find a way to improve on it? And provide a new sample in twenty-four hours? Taking the handle as a model, Williams clambered wearily on to the return train and set to work the moment he arrived in Caernarfon, heating, hammering and twisting metal through the night.

Next morning, he hurried back to the station clutching a canvas bag. After yet another interminable journey, Williams presented its contents to the Men from the Ministry. Williams's handles were exactly what was required. The race was on.

Besides making lamps for Lloyd George's London residence, Williams's enterprise had also made railings for the Tower of London's Raleigh's Walk and for the Houses of Parliament. Prison officials had once forced him, against his wishes, to manufacture metal scaffold parts for the execution of a murderer in Caernarfon. He was clearly a remarkable and dependable craftsman. But this challenge was something else again. It was already Tuesday evening. And Williams would have to make seven more handles, as well as the iron straps which would bind the casket, before Sunday, when the Unknown Warrior's empty coffin was due to be examined and photographed inside Westminster Abbey prior to its departure for France. He and his team worked long days on the Wednesday and Thursday. But it wasn't enough. As the deadline approached, they toiled continuously for two full days and nights – forty-eight hours of hot, hard, noisy labour – to complete the precious job in time.[29]

SAINT-POL-SUR-TERNOISE
3 NOVEMBER 1920

Like David Railton, who had felt he must wait until the very last minute before daring to share his idea for the Unknown Warrior with the Dean of Westminster, at Saint-Pol, General Wyatt was also biding his time. He knew that selection of a body at the last possible moment was the key to maintaining secrecy. The choice would be made on the night of Monday, 8 November, which would leave just enough time for it to be transported to Boulogne and placed in its ceremonial coffin on Tuesday. Then, next morning, it would be sailed across the Channel and taken by rail to London, ready for the Warrior's great moment in Westminster Abbey on Thursday, 11 November.

Following General Macdonogh's order of 22 October, to 'exercise his discretion',[30] Wyatt had already decided that four different bodies of unidentifiable British soldiers would be required. One from each of four major battle areas of the war: the Somme and Arras – both fairly close to Saint-Pol – as well as the Aisne to the south, near Rheims, and Ypres in Flanders, to the north. Once they were in front of him at Saint-Pol, he would make his final choice. The fate of the remaining three unknowns – for whom there would be no triumphant homecoming – had yet to be decided, but Wyatt had had enough experience of invasive war journalists, desperate for a scoop, to know that keeping their whereabouts secret was going to be almost as important as guarding the anonymity of the Warrior himself.

* * *

Preparing for his trip to London, David Railton carefully folded his precious flag into the army pack he had carried in the trenches, to High Wood and beyond. After considerable hesitation, he had finally decided to have the holy relic cleaned, ready for Dean Ryle's inspection.[31] His wife, Ruby, had done a beautiful job of patching the holes, as well as unstitching the '141 Inf Brig' from one corner.[32]

He climbed aboard his train at Margate railway station and was soon steaming through the Kent countryside. There were plenty of stories about the Unknown Warrior in the papers to keep him occupied.

'His Majesty's torpedo boat destroyer *Verdun* has been selected to convey the body of the Unknown Warrior to England,' declared one.[33]

'Replying to Earl Beauchamp in the House of Lords,' began another, 'Earl Curzon said he had no doubt that peers would be willing to waive their right to attend the ceremonies on Armistice Day in favour of bereaved relatives.'[34]

Curzon and his committee were now bending over backwards to accommodate the families of the fallen.

*　*　*

Although David Railton rarely spoke of his wartime activities, he would later write a short memoir, *The Story of a Padre's Flag, Told by the Flag*, in which he used the 'voice' of his flag to recount – and yet distance himself from – his memories. Here, his flag describes its journey from Margate to London:

> A week before Armistice Day 1920, I was once more put into the same dear old pack to go to London to be inspected. During the journey to London the Padre was scribbling away all the time, writing a summary of my history for the Dean of Westminster. When we got to the Deanery they spread me out for measurement. The Dean and Mrs Ryle were delighted to find that I should suffice for the purpose of the burial of the Unknown.[35]

Railton's account of his flag's war subsequently appeared in *The Times* during the run-up to the funeral. It offers a powerful insight into the flag's history, and the hard-fought experiences of its resourceful owner:

As no regimental colours were allowed in France at that time with the infantry, 'the Padre's Flag' gradually became in great demand, both in the line and behind the line. Its influence was a constant inspiration to officers and men in religious, ceremonial, and even social events. In the dead of night or at early dawn it enshrouded the bodies of our gallant men as they were carried down a trench to the little cemeteries and other places. This is not to mention the numerous occasions when it was dipped in the single grave of 'an unknown British soldier'. The officers and men reverenced this flag in a remarkable way. And no wonder, especially when it is borne in mind that in thousands of cases there was not even a blanket or any other covering available. In such cases the flag lay immediately next to the khaki-clad figure on the stretcher.

For these reasons it is, in a very special sense, a sacred flag. It is literally tinged with the blood of the men of London and of every part of England, Scotland, Wales, and Ireland – infantrymen, sappers, gunners, airmen, dismounted cavalry, tunnellers, and of many other units. Once, at least, it lay on the grass floor of a tent, with the Cup of Salvation and the Bread of Communion resting upon it, for the strengthening of one who underwent sentence of death at dawn.[36]

This last event, one of the darkest of Railton's life, had taken place on 9 July 1917. From the way he singled it out at the end of his narrative for Dean Ryle in November three years later, it is clear it stayed with him for the rest of his days. An entry in one of his private notebooks reads: 'Monday – Private Denis Blakemore. Spent all night with him until 4.30AM – when sentence of death was carried out – God help his people.'[37]

KEMMEL HILL, FLANDERS
9 JULY 1917

A 28-year-old conscript from Shrewsbury, one of four brothers and four sisters, Private Denis Blakemore had already been court-martialled for an earlier desertion in November 1916. Sentenced to death, his punishment had been commuted to fifteen years' penal servitude, which was then suspended by General Haig. Later, in June 1917, poor Blakemore went missing again and was found hiding in a shell hole behind the assembly trenches, just as his battalion was due to advance during the battles at Messines Ridge, during which around 25,000 of his comrades would become casualties. Blakemore's platoon sergeant brought him forward, putting him back with his section as they prepared to attack. But he absconded again, to be arrested in Boulogne eighteen days later.[38]

He told the subsequent court martial, 'I was too upset to go on with my section. I knew the attack was coming on that morning.' His testimony cut no ice, and a guilty verdict was passed. A sentence of death by firing squad was ordered, and later signed by Haig himself.[39] David Railton never openly discussed his involvement with Blakemore's execution. But he did commit his thoughts to paper – again, choosing to separate himself from the scene using the trusted voice of his flag. His description of the hours he spent with the young soldier before his death is shot through with uncharacteristic anger and passion:

Indeed, as long as I rest in the Abbey I shall always remember how in the dead of a certain night the Padre got up and took me in his pack into the wood. In the wood was a little tent and, inside the tent, three men. Two of them got up and, after speaking with the Padre for a few moments, went outside. The Padre laid me down on the grass and talked with the third man. Then he came to me and spread me over the grass and laid upon me the chalice and paten that he always used in the central part of that wonderful communion service. Soon after the service the light of the day seemed to be coming, and I heard voices of other men. A doctor came into the tent and soon after that the Padre left me and took the arm of his friend and went into the wood.

The next thing that I can remember is that there was a startling report of rifles and presently I heard footsteps rushing through the wood and all the twigs crackling and the Padre snatched me off the ground in a way he had never done before.

He did not fold me up. He just crushed me into his pack and ran through the wood and up a hill to a little dugout. He flung me on the floor and stamped up and down. I do not know all he said but the words 'devilment' and 'blood' and 'misery' kept on coming.[40]

Obviously devastated by the execution, Railton wrote to Blakemore's parents, telling them he had carried out the funeral, while trying to spare them the pain of knowing their son had been shot for cowardice. But Blakemore's father needed more information, writing back: 'I should be further thankful if you could kindly inform me what action he was in, and when and how he was wounded before coming into your charge.' However, before the padre could reply, the family were given the devastating – official – notification that, 'with great regret, Denis Jetson Blakemore was sentenced after trial by Court Martial to be shot for desertion. The sentence was duly executed.'

Railton then received another letter, marked 'Private', from Mr Blakemore:

Rev'd and Dear Sir,

I felt it my bounded duty to write again to you this evening, and inform you that it is only this morning that I received official word from the War Office, notifying me of the sad death of my son, Denis. It is, as you will readily understand, a terrible shock to us, and the very last thing in the world which we expected to happen to him. There is one great consolation in it nevertheless, which we shall always be grateful for, that through your sympathetic feeling, and holy administrations, he died, at all events, a good Christian soldier in the faith where he was always brought up.

One of 306 men shot for cowardice, desertion or other serious offences during the war, Denis Blakemore, who had previously fought through the ghastly first days of the Battle of the Somme, lies alongside his comrades at the Commonwealth War Graves Locre Hospice Cemetery in Belgium.

Along with the yellowing documents from Denis Blakemore's court martial held by the National Archives is a much newer one, signed by the Secretary of State for Defence in 2006: 'This document records that Private D. Blakemore who was executed for desertion on July 9th 1917 is pardoned under Section 359 of the Armed Forces Act 2006. The pardon stands as recognition that he was one of many victims of the First World War and that execution was not a fate he deserved.'[41]

LONDON
5 NOVEMBER 1920

To the extreme relief of undertakers Nodes and Sowerbutts, the great 'Treasure Chest', as they had taken to calling it, was finished. 'A little more than seven days and the task was complete,' John Sowerbutts declared proudly, and a trifle wearily. Just to keep them on their toes, the Office of Works, at the last minute, asked for the second coffin they had commissioned, the 'shell', to be sent out to Saint-Pol immediately. It needed to fit as snugly as a Russian doll inside the Treasure Chest. 'The shell was provided in a few hours,' said Sowerbutts, 'and despatched to France.'

Though it would be seen by few people, it would soon play a more intimate and personal role in the Unknown Warrior's journey than the grand one in which he would be ceremonially displayed.

WESTMINSTER ABBEY
7 NOVEMBER 1920

An extraordinary scene was taking place after the last visitors had left Westminster Abbey. The pews had already been removed from the nave during the day. Now only the memorial tablets of distinguished Britons populated the vast stone floor.

Messrs Nodes and Sowerbutts, assisted by two strong helpers, heaved the zinc-lined coffin out of their Rolls-Royce hearse and staggered through the cloisters, en route to the western end of the nave. Grey-haired Horace Nicholls also shuffled through the deserted abbey behind them, carrying his box camera on a wooden tripod. Chief photographer of the newly inaugurated Imperial War Museum, Nicholls had worked as a freelancer in the early years of the war and been appointed the first Home Front Official Photographer in 1917. A date which tragically coincided with the death of his eldest son, George, in the Battle of Arras. Back in 1914, George had been among the first to enlist. Starting as a 19-year-old Private in the Honourable Artillery Company, by early 1917 he was serving as a Second Lieutenant. His early letters home were full of youthful enthusiasm and pride. 'Great news!' he wrote in April that year. 'I am going up to the guns tomorrow morning. I feel so relieved, as life at wagon line is very tedious and uninteresting.'[42] Three days later, on Easter Sunday, he put pen to paper again. 'I am now with the battery. I have no news for you except that I am well and very cheerful. My love to everyone.'

George was killed the next day, a few miles from Saint-Pol, and buried at the nearby Ronville British Cemetery. He was twenty-two.

Since 1905, Horace Nicholls had always assembled a photograph album as a Christmas gift for his wife. The first few showed George growing from a little boy into a handsome young man. The opening page of the one dated Christmas 1917 showed four portraits of him in uniform. Beneath them, Nicholls had written, simply: 'Our dear son George, who fell for his country.' Although devastated, Horace was one of the 'lucky ones' never in doubt about the exact location of his son's resting place. Now he had to photograph an empty casket in an empty church, hoping to provide some similar comfort to the many thousands of families who would never know the precise fate of their relative.

Electric light from on high gave the wax-coated English oak, hewn from a tree growing in the grounds of Hampton Court, a spectral glow. Mounted with the four stout pairs of wrought-iron handles, two sets of hammered iron bands ran from head to foot and across its shoulders, meeting at a grand sixteenth-century crusader's sword, reportedly donated by the King from his private collection.[43] A hammered iron shield was bolted to the sword, bearing, in Gothic script, the inscription:

A BRITISH WARRIOR WHO

FELL IN THE GREAT WAR

1914–1918

FOR KING AND COUNTRY

If Horace Nicholls pondered the anonymity of its future incumbent, perhaps he could comfort himself with the thought that at least his son George's name appeared on his own headstone. A photograph of the cemetery would appear in the 1920 Christmas album, which he would assemble for his wife a few weeks later. Of its 331 graves, twenty-three are still unidentified, and there are special memorials to fourteen casualties whose burial plots had later been destroyed by shellfire.

Nicholls and the two undertakers tried various ways of positioning the coffin for the camera and their challenge can be seen in the surviving pictures. In some, it is placed on a Union Flag. In others, on the embroidered silk brocade of the Actors' Church Union pall, presented to the abbey in memory of their members who had died during the war.[44] They tried it on the floor (too lonely and forlorn), and then on a raised platform (better). Then they stood it almost vertically, like a soldier leaning against a wall.

Finally satisfied, they moved the coffin into the abbey's Jerusalem Chamber, where it would spend the night before heading across the Channel to receive its charge.

SAINT-POL-SUR-TERNOISE
8 NOVEMBER 1920

On the day for which General Wyatt had been meticulously preparing, four field ambulances clattered to a halt outside four cemeteries dotted across the Western Front: the Somme, Arras, the Aisne and Ypres. Each vehicle was accompanied by an officer and soldiers equipped with shovels and sacks.

Padre George Kendall, the Methodist priest who had once had to bury three Welshmen during an artillery bombardment, had been tasked with assisting one of the exhumation parties. They were instructed, he said, to dig up a body from a grave marked 'Unknown British Soldier'. Wyatt had – presumably – also passed on General Macdonogh's directive that the selected corpse was to be from 'as far back as possible',[45] as well as his further instruction, in a handwritten note, that the body was to be 'only bones'.[46] Significantly, however, even today there is remarkably little information about what orders Wyatt himself sent to his exhumation teams regarding the selection, nor communications from his subordinates back up the chain of command, requesting clarification. The blanket of secrecy seems to have been immaculate.

Kendall understood that need for secrecy, even regarding the general area of the exhumations. 'No one, and this is very important,' he declared later, 'was to know from which district a body had been taken. The graves which were opened in all the theatres of war were marked only by a cross stating that an unknown warrior lay there. If the regiment or division in which the man had served were specified, the grave remained untouched.'[47]

With little other personal testimony available, I can only imagine the scenes unfolding across the former battlefields. It must have been a very strange exercise for all concerned. The exhumation parties, trained to identify bodies, were now doing the exact opposite. They were digging up the long-dead, decomposed – or still decomposing – remains of former colleagues. Their job, presumably, was to double-check boots, uniform, insignia and personal effects in the quest for a corpse that absolutely could *not* be identified in *any* way. It can't have been an easy, or pleasant task.

* * *

The day wore on, and at last the first field ambulance drove through the gates at Saint-Pol. The others would follow at intervals. Wyatt had ordered their arrivals to be carefully separated, so that the crews could have no chance to see or talk to each other, to discuss from where they had come, let alone who or what they thought they had brought in.

Hour by hour, they came and went.

Vere Brodie, busy looking after her group of female personnel at Saint-Pol, was very much aware of the process. The arrival of one vehicle marked with a scarlet cross on a white roundel would have attracted mild curiosity. But three in a row must certainly have raised eyebrows and I assume she could sense that something was up. 'On the night of November 8th, three remains of unknown soldiers were brought in separately by ambulance from three different battle areas and laid in our small camp chapel,' she said.[48] As in so many personal accounts of this time, it is not clear if Vere was an actual eyewitness, or simply relating a story she heard later. And many writers and historians have disputed exactly how many bodies were brought for selection. Vere Brodie said three. Padre George Kendall was convinced it was six.[49] Major Ernest Fitzsimon, one of Wyatt's staff, told his son that it was five.[50]

For nineteen years, General Wyatt – the man who organised and ran the whole selection process – maintained a dignified silence about exactly what had happened that November night in 1920. 'My view is that he regarded it as a sacred trust that had been committed to him,' his daughter said. 'And that some things are just too sacred to ever be discussed.'[51] However, with the Second World War bringing new focus to the grave of the Unknown Warrior and questions still being asked whether someone in high office perhaps knew more about his identity than they were letting on, Wyatt provided his own impressively clear version of events to the *Daily Telegraph* on Armistice Day 1939.

He was quite clear: there were four bodies, brought from four different battlefields. That letter, widely regarded as definitive (although it included a mix-up in dates), forms the basis for the narrative that follows.[52]

CHARING CROSS STATION, LONDON
8 NOVEMBER, 10AM

After carefully lifting the precious empty casket back into the hearse, Kirtley Nodes and John Sowerbutts drove the short distance from Westminster Abbey to Charing Cross Station, where it was transferred into the special goods wagon chosen for its homecoming. Beautifully decorated though it was, it contained no proper seats, so the two undertakers sat on the floor. At eleven o'clock precisely, the driver released his brakes and the locomotive headed towards the coast. At Folkestone Junction, an extra coach was attached to the casket-wagon, and as they were shunted to Folkestone Harbour, Nodes and Sowerbutts were finally able to take their seats. Moving from the train to the boat seems to have been a lengthy process. Sowerbutts recalled, 'It was 6:30PM before we got the Treasure Chest aboard the *Invicta*.'[53]

The 300-foot-long, twin-funnelled steamship, which had been used for ferrying troops and supplies from Folkestone to France throughout the war, was now tasked with the first part of a journey to bring one of them home. 'At 7PM, we were away. It was a delightful passage across the sea,' Sowerbutts reported. 'All that could be desired. Fog was run into off the French coast, but all was well, and soon we were alongside the jetty at Boulogne.' French officials might have watched them with some suspicion as they escorted their crusader's casket down the gangplank. Fortunately, the Office of Works in King Charles Street had provided them with a document Sowerbutts described as an 'open sesame' to ease their way across the border:

HM Office of Works
Thursday 4th November, 1920

TO ALL WHOM IT MAY CONCERN:-

The bearer of this letter, Mr John W. H. Sowerbutts, and his colleague, Mr H. K. Nodes, have been authorised to accompany the casket to contain the remains of the 'Unknown Warrior' to France, and having sealed it, to accompany it back from France to this country, and hand it over to the Military upon its arrival at Victoria.

Lionel Earle
Secretary[54]

Once through customs, and with their cargo safely under military guard for the night, Nodes and Sowerbutts checked into the Hôtel de Londres on the harbourfront.

Presumably, they were unaware that 60 miles to the south-east, in Saint-Pol-sur-Ternoise, their companion for the return journey was about to be chosen.

SAINT-POL-SUR-TERNOISE
8 NOVEMBER, 11:45PM

Lieutenant Colonel Gell knocked on the door of General Wyatt's office. The four candidates his boss had requested were ready.[55] The two men made their way quietly towards the 'chapel', a draughty, corrugated iron Nissen hut, a glorified garden shed, 'very plain inside, with a rough wooden floor'.[56] An officer stood on guard at the door – I picture him silhouetted by a paraffin lamp on the exterior wall as footsteps and muffled voices in the darkness announced the arrival of the selection party.

General Wyatt and Lieutenant Colonel Gell climbed the rickety wooden steps. 'The men who had brought the bodies had gone,' Wyatt said many years later. 'With Colonel Gell, passing the guard which had been specially mounted, I thereupon entered the chapel. The four bodies lay on stretchers, each covered by a Union Jack.'[57] This image must have stayed with him for the rest of his life. The exhumation parties had clearly performed their duties to the letter. They were confronted by 'nothing but a collection of bones, placed in sacks'.[58] Though 'shell-torn and unrecognisable' was how Padre George Kendall described them in a magazine article ten years later.[59] As in much of the story, recollections varied. 'It was a skeleton and no more,' Nodes, the undertaker, confirmed when he lifted the coffin next day. 'It might have been a baby in the shell, for the weight.'[60]

'In front of the altar was the shell of the coffin which had been sent from England to receive the remains,' Wyatt continued. The scent of the freshly cut timber must have lent a welcome hint of the forest to the chapel's fetid atmosphere. One can imagine the two men standing there for a moment, allowing their eyes to become accustomed to the darkness, and their noses to the smell. The exhumation parties might well have succeeded in finding four sets of bones. But even bones have a distinct odour after years of burial in the pestilential mud of Belgium and northern France.

Though Gell wore his religion more lightly than most, Wyatt must have been conscious that he was in the presence of a man of the cloth. But he does not report, in his tantalisingly brief description of the event, whether he asked Gell to say a prayer, or indeed if any conversation took place. There was to be a service in the chapel next morning; perhaps that would suffice? Gell must have watched in silence as the shadow of General Wyatt fell across the row of Union Jack-shrouded stretchers. No words could adequately express the resonance of the moment. Years later, Padre George Kendall would write that Wyatt wore a blindfold for the selection process, but Wyatt himself mentions nothing of this. 'I selected one [body],' he said simply, without expanding upon how he did so.

Now the two officers worked quietly and efficiently, carrying out the plan they must have earlier discussed, gently lifting the chosen body, presumably still in its sack, off its stretcher and placing it inside the simple pine shell which waited by the altar.

'We screwed down the lid,' Wyatt added, bluntly.

It was done.

* * *

Who was he? An officer or an enlisted man? Which regiment? From where did he hail? Was he rich or poor? Was someone still searching for him? Little is known about this initial aspect of the story. Which is exactly what David Railton, Dean Ryle, Lord Curzon and his committee and General Wyatt had intended.

This truly was an Unknown Warrior.

And his final, epic journey was about to begin.

CHAPTER EIGHT

THE BURNING CHAPEL

SAINT-POL-SUR-TERNOISE
8 NOVEMBER 1920, MIDNIGHT

Lying in the darkness of the deserted chapel in northern France, the four sets of remains – carried in as equals – awaited their destiny. General Wyatt's selection lay in a fresh pine coffin before the altar. The others remained in their sacks, on stretchers, each covered with a Union Jack. Alive, these four men had almost certainly never met. Now, exhumed from four different battlefields, they were bound together in the same unlikely story.

Across Britain, countless bereaved families were lying in the darkness too. What comfort might they feel to believe *their* son, *their* father, *their* brother was in that coffin, in the cool simplicity of a silent chapel, no longer lost to the thick mud of no-man's-land?

The four were about to embark on very different journeys. One was to be guarded overnight, transported in state to London to be buried among poets, artists and monarchs. His final resting place already awaited him, prepared that very day behind barriers set up in the nave, in the dry, sandy soil that had lain below the abbey floor for perhaps a thousand years.[1] The other three would soon be returned to the earth. But the secrecy surrounding the Unknown Warrior's selection – and the whereabouts of the three 'unused' bodies – had to remain sacrosanct.

General Wyatt was admirably concise when later chronicling those events, in 1939: 'The other bodies were removed and reburied in the military cemetery outside my headquarters at St Pol.'[2] But an examination of the graves of unknown soldiers in the Saint-Pol cemetery renders it unlikely that any were buried there at that time. Had the General misremembered this detail, or, nineteen years after the event, was he still conjuring up red herrings to throw people off the scent? Perhaps a fellow officer was responsible for this part of the process?

In some ways, the final journey of those bodies may not seem terribly important when viewed alongside what was in store for the Unknown Warrior himself. But then consider the upset caused by the clumsy conclusion to a newspaper article in November 2008. 'Amid all the public anguish, no one thought to wonder what had become of the other three bodies that had been disinterred from their unmarked graves. A rather less exalted fate awaited them. After Wyatt had made his choice, the Union Flags were folded away. Then the three bodies were loaded onto the back of a truck, tipped into a shell hole beside the road near the town of Albert – and promptly forgotten.'[3] This unlikely scenario, loosely based on an alternative account, bears little relation to most of the existing evidence, especially with regard to the devotion to duty and meticulous commitment of the staff at Saint-Pol who registered and honoured the graves of the fallen.

The eventual fate of those three bodies remains shrouded in mystery, yet still arouses considerable passion. The available evidence tells a variety of stories.

DUISANS CAMP, NEAR ARRAS
6 NOVEMBER 1920

Two days before Wyatt made his selection, it must have come as a surprise for Captain Jack Fisher – a chiselled 29-year-old who had begun the war as a humble Private in 1914 – to be suddenly handed an 'On His Majesty's Service' envelope labelled 'SECRET'.

Organised and straight-thinking, Fisher had recently been appointed Officer-in-Charge of one of the Graves Registration units at Duisans army camp, north-west of Arras.[4] While discretion and privacy had always been central to his work, secrecy had not. Written in fine, well-spaced, italic handwriting, the mysterious letter headed 'CAGNICOURT BRITISH Cemetery' was also marked 'SECRET':

1. *Please arrange for a party of 4 French civilians, equipped with shovels for exhumation work, and an ambulance (capable of proceeding to St. Pol and back) to be at the above-named cemetery at 15:15hrs Nov 8th. Having done this, you will return to your camp and stand by in case you are needed. The ambulance driver should be a French man also.*

2. *At 22.00hrs the same date you will again return to the cemetery with the French labour, equipped as before plus lanterns, and reinter in the cemetery three bodies (graves having been dug in the meantime). For this work again you will not be needed but will be required to stand by in your camp.*

3. *The contents of this document will not be communicated to anyone and you will arrange for the civilian labour yourself.*[5]

It must have been quite a set of orders for Fisher to digest. He was to enlist four French navvies, ready to dig three graves in the nearby military cemetery. And an ambulance was required, ready to complete a round trip to Saint-Pol and back. Then, late at night, he and the navvies were to return to the cemetery with their lanterns. And there, they were to bury three bodies which – presumably – had been collected from Saint-Pol around the same time General Wyatt had chosen the Unknown Warrior. The order was sufficiently unusual for Fisher to have kept it tucked away among his private documents, where it remained until after the death of his son in 2007.

One cannot be sure exactly what transpired that day. Perhaps deliberately, the paper trail is disjointed and many theories abound. But – as Mark Scott asks in his examination of Fisher's role in his book *Among the Kings* – why preserve that particular missive?[6] Was he concerned that he might later be called to account for his actions that night? After extensive research into the matter, Scott certainly believes that the three 'unchosen' candidates for the Unknown Warrior were given a proper burial in Cagnicourt British Cemetery by Captain Jack Fisher and his team.

* * *

In later years multiple contradictory accounts emerged by those claiming to have taken some part in the selection and transport of the Unknown Warrior. One newspaper related the story of an officer claiming to have been involved in the process, who dug up some bodies in Flanders before finding one with no identification, other than the remains being in a private's uniform. 'The body was stripped of its clothing, wrapped in canvas, then placed in a coffin ... and shipped to London.'[7]

General Macdonogh, the Adjutant General, responded brusquely to this account, 'Captain White is an unmitigated liar.'[8]

Yet another version of what supposedly happened to the remaining candidates lay dormant for many decades until an article by the Chaplain of Westminster in a November 1980 edition of *The Times* repeating Wyatt's now familiar account of their reburial in the military cemetery at Saint-Pol prompted a rapid response from an officer of the DGR&E who had served under the General.

Sir Cecil Smith, a young officer at Saint-Pol in 1920, but by then a retired Major General aged eighty-four, wrote two letters correcting the chaplain for following Wyatt's 1939 claim:

Dear Padre, I have read with interest your excellent article. I notice, however, that you inadvertently perpetuated an error which has occurred in other accounts, about the disposal of the three surplus bodies, in stating that they were buried in

*the Military cemetery at St Pol. This is incorrect. The sudden
appearance of three unknown graves in St Pol military cemetery, which was a cemetery of a military hospital (by that
time closed) where all the dead were probably known, might
have caused undesirable speculation.*[9]

Smith went on to describe his mission to move the three sets of remains to a location where they would hopefully later be discovered
by the teams still searching for the dead:

*At midnight, when the selected body had been removed,
I drove an ambulance to the hut where the three bodies
lay. You will appreciate that by November 1920 the
majority of the bodies of soldiers buried were little more
than skeletons with perhaps a few rags of clothing. This
applied particularly to unknown bodies, many of which
had probably been blown to pieces in the first instance
and none of which, including the Unknown Warrior and
his companions, would be more than a bag (sand bag) full
of the approximate bones, including a skull to make up a
complete body. We had little of substance to carry.*

Smith recalled that the sacks were placed in the back of a Daimler
ambulance alongside a chaplain and two fellow officers. No one
volunteered to ride up front with him, perhaps because the cab
provided little shelter. 'It had a canvas apron and two canvas
sheets where one would now find doors. Very draughty indeed.'
They drove through the frosty moonlit night to a 'previously
reconnoitred and carefully map-referenced' spot on the Albert–
Bapaume road, around 40 miles south of Saint-Pol, where they
knew groups of 'searchers' were still locating and reinterring
bodies. 'All did not go entirely well. I stopped once to run up and
down the road to get warm. My living passengers were all right,
they had blankets and a flask of rum! They sang hymns, too – well,
not always hymns.'

When he drove on, the Daimler's carburettor began popping and the journey with three sacks of body parts took an even more surreal turn:

It could only be one thing – water in the petrol. There was only one cure: take off the top of the carburettor float chamber, remove the float, mop up the petrol/water mixture with a rag (having turned off the petrol), and turn the petrol on again in the hope that there would be no more water. I had a flash lamp and the necessary tools but I found that the float chamber was under the inlet manifold and a nut had to be slackened to allow the carburettor to swing out from under the manifold as there was not room otherwise to lift the cover. But the nut was seized and all my efforts could not move it.

Continuing at a much-reduced speed, they finally reached their destination after six hours on the road. The journey of the 'spare' Unknown Warriors was nearly over. 'On arrival the bodies were placed in an old trench which was filled in. The Padre held a short service.' This was all they had time to achieve, as they then spotted a team of searchers coming over the horizon:

They were spread out and I was reminded of an enemy attack on our trenches. We sped off down the road to Albert. What the searchers, who must have heard us and probably saw us, made of the party of four men and an ambulance at 6 or 7 o'clock in the morning I can't think; however, scrutiny of the records subsequently showed that three unknown bodies were recovered from the map reference at which we had deposited them. We got back to St Pol about midday, a weary party.

It must indeed have been a draining twelve hours and, according to Smith at least, those 'surplus' bodies were later discovered as planned, and given a decent burial. No connection with the three extra Warriors at Saint-Pol was ever suspected.

How, then, to square Sir Cecil Smith's version of the story with Fisher's secret orders and the other available accounts? Are they all red herrings, including Wyatt's – part of a complex smokescreen to cover exactly what happened on the night of 8 November 1920? Perhaps this was the plan all along? General Wyatt will have been no stranger to the creation of diversionary tactics in the theatre of war, so the apparent contradictions between these different accounts – How many bodies were brought to the chapel? From which battlefields? What was the fate of the remaining corpses? – may simply demonstrate how effectively Wyatt did his job. As Vere Brodie, the lady in charge of the female staff at Saint-Pol, put it: 'Very few people knew what was going on.'[10]

Or is it simply a case – yet again – of recollections varying?

Saint-Pol-sur-Ternoise
9 November 1920, 9am

Dawn must have come as a relief for the officers guarding the chapel at Saint-Pol. The mercury had dropped below freezing point in the overnight thermometer and the camp's corrugated tin huts must have felt almost as cheerless as Cecil Smith's Daimler ambulance.[11] That morning in Britain, the *Penrith Observer* carried this stirring request to its readers:

> Sir, Will you kindly assist me through your columns by publish-
> ing the following extract from a letter received this week from
> an officer doing duty on the Imperial War Graves Commission
> in France? – *Life here is rather miserable now on these dark
> nights, with little comfort for the men. Can you help us with
> some games, cards, etc., something to pass the dull hours
> away?* – This appeal is from an officer in charge of men who are
> searching for our fallen, for 'the Unknown Warrior', and working
> on cemeteries out there. I know the officer well; a kind-hearted

north-countryman who takes a keen interest in his men, and one
who does a great deal to assist anyone in search of the graves of
the fallen. Any tobacco or cigarettes, games, cards, or literature
suitable for men that your readers care to send to my office will
be forwarded at once.[12]

It was clear that the plans for the Unknown Warrior had already
begun to capture the nation's imagination. At Saint-Pol, meanwhile, as the staff of the Graves Registration Commission began to
surface, there must have been some speculation about the previous
day's comings and goings. Vere Brodie will not have been alone in
noticing, perhaps, a hint of tension in the air.

* * *

Major Ernest 'Fitz' Fitzsimon, a compact, handsome Irishman with
an aquiline nose, deep-set eyes and a fierce parting in his thick jet-
black hair, would have been keeping a close eye on his watch. Years
after these events, as a barrister in Dublin in 1942, he would declare
in his CV: 'Submitted and carried out the scheme for the selection
of and removal of the remains of "The Unknown Warrior" from
the "field" to the destroyer *Verdun* at Boulogne.'[13] From the photographs and documents available, the evidence is compelling that Fitz
played a significant role in the Unknown Warrior's journey, so he
must have been facing a stressful day.

A service was to be held over the body that morning, by Anglican,
Roman Catholic and Non-Conformist chaplains. Fitz would then
drive north to Boulogne with the pine coffin-shell and its precious
contents, ensuring every element of the plan was carried out with
dignity and precision. Perhaps it all came easily to the young
Irishman, who had been quickly promoted at the start of his army
career. On the eve of the Battle of the Somme, Fitz had been in the
thick of the action at Thiepval Wood, in the high-pressure role of
Brigade Intelligence Officer – attempting to piece together what
was happening from the constant, chaotic barrage of messages,

signals and eyewitness reports landing on his desk. In the eye of the storm, Fitz had proved equal to the challenge. Now, the Unknown Warrior wasn't just a logistical challenge for Fitz. It was personal. His younger brother, James, had been awarded the Military Medal for gallantry on the first and bloodiest day of the battle. And there was an even younger brother there, too.

Jack Fitzsimon, a draper's assistant in Belfast, was just twenty-one when he went 'over the top' on the first day of the Somme. It was his first taste of action. Working in staff headquarters with the artillery bombardments in full swing, Fitz would have been painfully aware of the nightmare unfolding to his north. Jack was initially recorded as 'Wounded' that day. Then 'Now Missing' was added. And at some point, the final, blunt correction: 'Now Killed. 1/7/16.' A picture of James and Jack appeared in the *Belfast Telegraph* a few days later. The caption beneath it perfectly expressed the capriciousness of fortune: 'The former has been awarded the Military Medal, and the latter is wounded and missing.'[14]

Their mother, Jeannie, who had borne four boys and four girls, would not, could not, accept that her son was dead. After all, where was his body? In her mind, Jack was still missing. Like the many thousands of confused, almost-bereaved parents and siblings across the Empire, Jeannie chose to believe that perhaps, just perhaps, he was still out there. Somewhere. And he would eventually come home. When she later received Jack's three campaign medals, she promptly returned them to the authorities. Jeannie Fitzsimon didn't want any bloody medals. She wanted her son.[15]

Perhaps Major Ernest Fitzsimon was thinking of his missing brother when the neatly typed notice appeared on the camp notice-board at Saint-Pol: 'The Camp Chapel will be open from 10:30 to 11:30 hours in order that all ranks who wish to do so may view the coffin containing the remains of The Unknown British Warrior.'[16] According to Vere Brodie, the magic had already begun. 'The hushed thrill in the camp all that day was marvellous,' she remembered with a hint of rapture. 'The beginning, so simple and sincere, was wonderful.' Later adding, 'We of St Pol can never forget the

simple dignity in which the representative of all those of British nations who had lain down their lives came to existence in our camp
chapel and the proud sorrow that we felt.'[17]

Vere Brodie's proud sorrow will have run deeper than that of many.
Her experience of being so close to the magical symbol of the
Unknown Warrior seems to have ignited a host of carefully buried
emotions. Her brother Douglas had been killed at High Wood in
August 1916, during one of the preliminary attacks that would cul-
minate in the massive blood-letting on 15 September, when Anthony
French's friend Bert was lost on the battlefield, along with Alec
Reader, the boy who never did return his copy of *Treasure Island*
to the school library, and Sidney Wheater, the hockey player from
Scarborough.

All still missing.

At least Douglas Brodie had a grave.

Vere's relative, Ewan, had not been so fortunate. Killed at Ypres,
his body had been recovered and buried, but his resting place was
later destroyed in ongoing fighting. Thus, much like the names of
the missing from the Somme recorded at Thiepval, Ewan Brodie's
name is carved on the Menin Gate in Ypres. He is in good company.
Alongside Ewan's name appear those of 55,000 of his comrades still
out there, buried in the rich mud of Flanders' fields. Vere would have
known many others, too, who would never be coming back to the
wild beauty of the Brodie Castle estate. In 1917, William Cheyne,
one of the family's ghillies, had died in an ill-planned attack on the
German Hindenburg Line in which 432 soldiers from his regiment
marched against well-dug-in machine-gunners. Unsurprisingly, only
fifty-seven of them returned. The gamekeeper was reported missing
and still has no known grave. He was one of five brothers, three of
whom gave their lives in the Great War.

Headkeeper of their estate was father of five John Morrison.
One of his sons, George, was cited for a Military Cross the day he
died from his wounds in April 1918. Another, John, had been killed
in January 1915, while, despite being badly wounded himself, he

attempted to come to the aid of an injured officer. He died a hero's death, his body – presumably – lost forever. It seemed everyone had a connection with the simple pine coffin currently resting at Saint-Pol.

In Boulogne, undertakers Kirtley Nodes and John Sowerbutts had spent a comfortable night at the Hôtel de Londres, and, after lunch, found themselves awaiting transport to convey them and their precious Treasure Chest the short distance to where the Unknown Warrior was due to arrive that afternoon.

'The car has just come,' noted Sowerbutts. 'And with the casket following in an ambulance, we are off to the hills at the back of the town, and to the grim Château.'[18]

With the short, interdenominational service at Saint-Pol completed, the Warrior was lifted into motor ambulance number 63638, ready to be driven under military escort to Boulogne. Vere Brodie recorded 'a bodyguard of eight sergeants' escorting the 'simple little wooden coffin'.[19] Presumably, the six barrels of French soil which would be required at Westminster Abbey must have been loaded too.[20]

The little convoy took more than three hours to make its draughty way the 60 miles to the coast.

BOULOGNE
9 NOVEMBER 1920, 3:30PM

The roads approaching the port were lined with soldiers, British and French, as if for visiting royalty.

It must have been a strange experience for Wyatt and his team after working so hard to keep their activities under wraps. Now, following weeks in the shadows, here they were in their run-down cavalcade, blinking in the glare of an impressive military turnout and the wooden cameras of umpteen photographers, all eager to get the first shot of the Unknown Warrior's cortège. But this next stage had, once again, to be conducted behind closed doors. The Warrior was still in his naked pine coffin-shell, unfit for public display. There was still some work to be done before he was ready to face the press.

Nodes and Sowerbutts were already waiting at the thirteenth-century Château, the Boulogne headquarters of the French Army. 'Just picture the quadrangle of an old French fortress,' wrote Sowerbutts. 'We pass into it through two low archways; on the left, through a low doorway we enter a small room draped with bunting and dressed with greenery. The floor is strewn with laurels and chrysanthemum blossoms; this is the Chapel of Repose. Outside is drawn up a guard of honour of *poilus* [French soldiers]. And so we await the coming of "our boy".'[21]

Eventually, the escort vehicles from Saint-Pol swung into the quadrangle followed by the battle-scarred ambulance. A bearer party of British and dominion soldiers was waiting to carry the Union Jack-wrapped coffin up to the Château's library. The men had been carefully selected to represent all branches of the army: the Royal Army Service Corps, the Royal Engineers, the Royal Garrison Artillery, the Australian Light Horse, the Canadian Infantry, the 21st London Regiment, the Machine Gun Corps and the Royal Army Medical Corps.[22] 'And before we can realise,' Sowerbutts said, 'it is borne on eight shoulders, the simple shell covered with England's flag and, within it, the Unknown Warrior.'

The Château's library had been commandeered for the Officers' Mess; a place to relax, eat and drink. And perhaps to forget the haunting memories of war. But, today, for their extra-special guest, about to spend his very last night on French soil, the officers were giving up their library-cum-bar. It had been converted into a *chapelle ardente* – a so-called 'burning chapel', specially prepared and lit with countless candles to receive and honour the body of a great personage. With shields stuck with French and British flags, decorative palm trees suggesting the outer reaches of the Empire, and the floor scattered with flowers, the setting was perfect. A hallowed place to honour the memory of a British warrior representing all those who had shed their blood on French soil.

'It is a touching scene,' wrote Sowerbutts, recalling the moment the Unknown Warrior was finally transferred into the great coffin in which he would be buried for all time. 'Gently we lay him in the Treasure Chest. The lid is on, the bolts are driven home, and we step forward wondering, "Whose is this image and superscription?" And there, on a shield of hammered iron, we read: "A British Warrior who died in the Great War, 1914–1918, for King and Country". Bound round the waist and from head to foot in bands of hammered iron, with a crusader's sword thrust under the shield, we leave him in the guard of France for the night, but in the casket of England's heart, bound round with the bands of grateful love. Tomorrow we will bring him home on a destroyer, when the French have done him their *devoir*.'[23] The Treasure Chest was then gently placed on two Union Jack-draped trestles in the centre of the room. French soldiers in long tunics and steel helmets stood smartly to attention, the long barrels of their rifles pointing at the ceiling, rather than reversed in the British manner signifying mourning.

That night marked the only point in the Unknown Warrior's journey when he was not under the strict care and protection of British troops. The *poilus* – 'hairies' as the French soldiers were affectionately known – now chosen to guard him had earned that honour in battle. All were from the 8th Regiment, which had recently been awarded the Légion d'Honneur en masse, for its bravery in the war.[24]

PORTLAND HARBOUR
9 NOVEMBER 1920, 11PM

On the south coast between Exeter and Bournemouth, HMS *Verdun* slipped her moorings, made steam and moved quietly away from Portland, through the harbour walls and out into Weymouth Bay. The 110 sailors on board were relieved to be finally underway. Even by naval standards, preparations for the short voyage across the Channel had been meticulous, with every surface of the Admiralty V-class destroyer either freshly painted or polished.

Once in open water and having made contact with her escort of six destroyers, *Verdun* made a sweeping turn east and, with her running lights twinkling in the darkness, set her course for Boulogne.[25]

HÔTEL DE LONDRES, BOULOGNE
9 NOVEMBER 1920, MIDNIGHT

At the Hôtel de Londres it seems John Sowerbutts was rather enjoying being in the middle of a full-scale military operation. 'The hotel has become temporary Staff Headquarters,' he recorded, with some excitement. 'There is a field telephone on the table; the lounge is full of staff officers. Soldiers and officers are coming and going, all busily preparing for tomorrow's function. All the chiefs are staying here tonight. The French mean to make a big show. We have just learned that the Destroyer is timed to arrive at 10AM, and to leave at noon.'

CHÂTEAU DE BOULOGNE
10 NOVEMBER 1920, 9:30AM

Just as the Château's library made the perfect resting place for the Unknown Warrior's final night in France, so Boulogne was the ideal port from which to sail home. As one newspaper said, it was the 'Soldier's Port':

> Calais was sacred to the staff. Le Havre and other centres were dedicated largely to stores and munitions. But Boulogne saw the arrival and departure of some 8.5 million British fighting men. It saw them come full of high hope. And it saw nearly three-quarters of a million sick and wounded go back to hospitals across the water. It was right and fitting, therefore, that Boulogne should be the embarkation point of that unknown lad who represents his comrades sleeping by Ypres and Amiens, and in all the battlefields from the Flanders coast to the Somme and beyond.[26]

In the streets of Boulogne, crowds had already been waiting for hours by the time the Adjutant General of the British Army, General Macdonogh, gave the order for the coffin to be carried down from the makeshift chapel. A line of French soldiers with fixed bayonets stood to attention and the assembled officers saluted as the eight pallbearers appeared with the oaken Treasure Chest. Each held his cap in one hand as they made their way gingerly down the stone steps, before the struggle to lift their charge onto the wagon the French authorities had provided.

It was certainly not the gun carriage they had been expecting. If anything, it looked more like a large farm cart, and two of the soldiers had to mount it in order to help steer the coffin into place. The outline of the King's sword – reportedly George V's personal tribute – was visible beneath its Union Jack. At least one newspaper claimed that there was also a handwritten card bearing the inscription 'A soldier's gift to a soldier', though this is not visible in the news footage of the procession.[27]

With a French soldier at the reins and six black artillery horses already harnessed, the wagon was ready to go. The eight soldiers marched in two ranks, four on either side. Seven wore their peaked caps, the lone Australian standing out in his distinctive slouch hat. They joined the main procession already formed up on the wide shopping street in the shadow of the cathedral. From there they would pass along the Grande Rue, past the Place Dalton, into Rue Victor Hugo and over the Pont Marguet to the quay. The previous night this route, newly decorated with flags and bunting, had had a whiff of celebration about it. Now, beneath a sombre sky, an atmosphere of deep mourning had settled on the silent streets.[28]

At 10:30AM, all the bells of Boulogne began to toll, and after a blazing salute from the trumpets of the French cavalry, the great bass drums of the massed band began to thump out the sombre rhythm of Chopin's *marche funèbre* (funeral march). The deep booms echoed through the town like heavy artillery as the mile-long procession set off. The fire service in their polished brass helmets and a detachment of disabled French soldiers, their chests jingling with medals, led a thousand local schoolchildren followed by an entire division of 15,000 French troops carrying their regimental colours aloft.[29] Here was a squadron of French cavalry; four batteries of French artillery and three battalions of infantry, all in their blue-grey service uniforms and rounded steel helmets.[30] It was a dazzling, almost stupefying sight. A detachment of French lancers, four horses abreast, escorted the Unknown Warrior's wagon. Its great wheels clattered over the cobbled streets and raised tram tracks.[31]

It was a precious moment for the people of Boulogne, who had come out in their thousands to pay their respects. They had watched the millions of bright-eyed Tommies passing through on their way to the front. Then watched the countless injured returning. They had their own dead to mourn too; France had lost more than 1.3 million men in the war, most of them on the Western Front.[32] So this haunting symbol of each and every man who had paid the ultimate price for their freedom being carried through their streets was something which obviously mattered very deeply.

It clearly mattered deeply to Maréchal Ferdinand Foch, too. The Supreme Allied Commander must have been powerfully aware of the intense human suffering that had resulted from his part in the wartime decision-making. So, somewhat unexpectedly, the 70-year-old Foch had travelled here on his own initiative to march beneath the iron-grey sky and show his profound gratitude and respect.[33]

Foch and Macdonogh walked side by side, just behind the wreath-bearing soldiers who staggered in the wake of the Unknown Warrior's wagon. Some of their grand flower displays were almost twice as big as the cart's thundering wheels, one was so heavy it took four men to carry it. Behind the two military leaders came yet more French troops, marines and cavalrymen, marching along the route decorated with striped Venetian masts topped with the red, white and blue flags of both nations. The crowds were so dense that some took to the dock's warehouse roofs for a better view.

QUAI GAMBETTA, BOULOGNE
10 NOVEMBER 1920, 11AM

Arriving at the quay ahead of the main procession, Major Ernest Fitzsimon waited with a party of French dignitaries, British officers, press reporters and the swarming public. He was keen to witness the arrival of the ceremonial gun carriage he had arranged to bear the coffin to HMS *Verdun*, so what finally appeared in the distance must have come as a bitter shock. Looking at the black-and-white news footage, instead of a grand military carriage at the heart of the procession there is something resembling a nineteenth-century hay-cart.

At last the harbour hove into view, and there, lying alongside the jetty, was the hulking, 300-foot-long HMS *Verdun*, waiting to receive its unusual cargo. On her afterdeck the ship's proud motto gleamed: *On ne passe pas* – 'They shall not pass' – the battle cry given by Maréchal Pétain to his hard-pressed troops at the Battle of Verdun in 1916. The ship had been chosen for this historic mission in homage to the catastrophic French losses during the fighting. With the destroyer's crew standing stiffly to attention, a circle of French buglers sounded the Last Post as General Macdonogh stepped forward. The polished leather on his uniform belt glinted faintly beneath the pale sky. A black armband was clasped around his left sleeve. After a short pause, the trumpets sounded again, this time with the brighter rhythms of 'Aux Champs', as the stately figure of Maréchal Foch moved into position. A great walrus moustache drooping towards his chin, his deep, mournful eyes swept the crowds as he saluted the awaiting officers. And then, noted one British reporter, 'the great Marshal walked all alone to the coffin and raised his hand to his *képi*, keeping it there for what appeared to be a very long moment'.[34]

Voice trembling with emotion, Foch spoke eloquently and from the heart. 'I express the profound feelings of France for the invincible heroism of the British Army, and I regard the body of this hero as a souvenir of the future and as a reminder to work in common to cement the victories we have gained by Eternal Union.'

Macdonogh responded in French, thanking the Maréchal on behalf of the King and the British government, and reminding the crowds of the undying significance of the ceremony.[35] The band then played 'La Marseillaise' and 'God Save the King' and it was time for General Macdonogh to receive the body of the Unknown Warrior on behalf of the British nation.

While the bearer party of British and dominion soldiers carefully eased the coffin off its cart, HMS *Verdun*'s crew prepared for the next stage of the carefully choreographed ceremony. The orders from the Admiralty to the ship's Captain four days earlier had been admirably clear:

> The coffin is to be received on board HMS *Verdun* by a seaman guard of about 20 men under an officer, and placed on a bier in a suitable position. A large Union Jack is to be taken to cover the coffin from Boulogne to London. Colours to be half-masted as the coffin arrives on board. The ship's company is to be fallen in. After arrival on board, sentries with arms reversed are to be posted round the bier.[36]

While the eight-strong bearer party slowly made its way up *Verdun*'s narrow gangplank, the boatswain's mate piped the body on board with his shrill whistle, an honour generally accorded only to Admirals and Captains.[37] At the same moment, the ship's white ensign was lowered to half-mast, while the massed bands on shore broke into 'La Marseillaise' once more.[38] General Macdonogh and his aide-de-camp boarded the ship next, and the wreath-carrying soldiers laid their flowers around the coffin, now guarded on the quarterdeck. At 11:45AM precisely, Macdonogh took up position facing the Unknown Warrior, and the band struck up 'God Save the King' one last time. Maréchal Foch, visibly moved, stepped forward, almost to the water's edge, and stood alone, saluting his dead comrade as HMS *Verdun* unmoored and withdrew from the pier.[39] 'I shall never forget the scene or the thrill,' recorded undertaker John Sowerbutts. 'It would take a volume to describe it all.

Here, the Unknown Warrior rested on the quarter-deck abaft two grim torpedo tubes bowered in flowers and veiled in a battle-stained gown of three crosses intermingled [the Union Jack]. We cast off, and out into the "glory mist" we glide.'[40]

Beyond the harbour wall, *Verdun* was joined by the dark silhouettes of her escort – six destroyers of the British Atlantic fleet, line abreast, three on each side. A minute or two later, the first booming explosions of a nineteen-gun salute echoed across the water as an escort of French ships fired their volley. The great cannons of the fortress at Boulogne responded with their own salvo.

As the echoes faded, HMS *Verdun* and Britain's most precious soldier slipped silently into the fog.

CHAPTER NINE

THE WARSHIP OF THE DEAD

DOVER
10 NOVEMBER 1920, 1PM

It was just a pinpoint of light, flashing across the lead-grey seas.[1] But for the crowds ranged along the clifftops it was everything. Some had been standing there for hours, scanning the horizon for the looming shape of HMS *Verdun*.

Amelia Bromley, dressed head to toe in black, was among them. Her son Cecil had become obsessed with aviation in 1909 when – just six years after the Wright brothers' first powered flight – daredevil French aviator Louis Blériot crossed the English Channel in his box-girder and wooden aircraft, landing near where Amelia now stood. When war broke out, Cecil had volunteered to become an engineer in the Royal Flying Corps, but the shortage of flyers meant that he was quickly chosen to train as a pilot.[2] The odds were not in his favour. On the Western Front at that time, average life expectancy for aircrew was around eleven days.[3]

In November 1916, Cecil and his co-pilot were on an artillery-spotting mission at 2,500 feet, a few miles north of High Wood, when a German fighter pounced on them from the clouds. Cecil's comrade was severely wounded in the engagement, but, despite one arm being shattered, managed to bring the aircraft down. Cecil had been shot in the head, and later died of his wounds in a dressing station.[4] After his burial, his parents were sent a photograph of the grave, so at least had the comfort of seeing his final resting place, and perhaps the hope of visiting it when the war was over. But even this crumb of solace was quickly swept away. Cecil's grave was destroyed in subsequent fighting, and he became one of the Unknowns.

Four years on, Amelia Bromley squinted out to sea, perhaps hoping her son was finally coming home.

* * *

HMS *Vendetta*, another V-class Admiralty destroyer, had already steamed out of Dover to meet her sister ship mid-Channel. She was armed to the teeth with journalists, ready to witness the Unknown Warrior's arrival upon home shores. Around 7 miles off the Kent coast, *Vendetta* spotted the approaching flotilla and her Captain ordered a message to be sent across the water.

'WHO ARE YOU?' flashed the signal lamp on the bridge, its louvred shutters drumming.

A short pause. Then a response flashed back through the mist.

'*VERDUN* ... AND ESCORT ... WITH UNKNOWN WARRIOR.'

'There was scarcely a ripple on the Channel,' recorded the special correspondent of the *Daily Telegraph*, 'not a break in the canopy above us. Grey, grey – the whole picture was grey, and the ships in it – but with a curious, intense serenity. No wash could be detected on the prows of the oncoming flotilla but as we mutually sighted each other, the point of a flash-lamp on the leading destroyer of the funereal escort answered our challenge. Even as the signal and others were exchanged, the tiny blue-grey specks on a grey expanse of flat waters grew into their own big, battle-grey shapes. In the centre of the convoy was the Warship of the Dead with six destroyers acting as a screen about her.'[5]

Three of the escorts carved a delicate wake ahead of *Verdun*, three followed in line astern. Each ship's Union Jack and White Ensign flew at half-mast.

'Tenderly and without haste, the ships stole through the last few miles,' observed the reporter from *The Times*, leaning on the deck-rails of HMS *Vendetta* as she came alongside the *Verdun*. 'So silently and solemnly that one could compare their measured progress only to the slow march of troops in a funeral procession. Waters which are often turbulent seemed strangely gentle. There was no wind to stir the folds of the Union Jack from Ypres which covered the coffin, as it lay on the deck of the *Verdun*. In this impressive silence, sailors seemed for a time to have taken into their special keeping the remains symbolical of the glorious dead.'[6]

The *Daily Telegraph*'s man found himself wondering if he was on a ghost ship, not powered by machinery at all. 'Destroyers usually strain and shake and whine like some weird hounds of the sea,' he noted. Whereas today's silent, mournful pace, 'equivalent to the Dead March on some noiseless pavement, had reduced these fighting ships almost to the sense of "painted ships upon a painted ocean".'[7]

The calm sea had put the convoy well ahead of schedule. 'About 2PM, we sight Blighty,' said undertaker John Sowerbutts aboard HMS *Verdun*, 'and a wireless message is received, asking us to cruise in the Channel, arriving at Dover at 3:30PM.'[8]

Most of the shops in the seaside town had already wound away their awnings and rattled down their shutters for the day. The police brought road traffic to a standstill an hour before the landing. HMS *Vendetta* disembarked her party of journalists so they could file their copy for the evening editions.

Tantalisingly, *Verdun* and her escort remained in sight of the crowds on the clifftops as she waited to make her grand entrance.

THE CITADEL, VERDUN, FRANCE
10 NOVEMBER 1920, 3PM

As the Unknown Warrior was poised to sail into Dover Harbour, the French Minister of Pensions entered a small, candle-lit chamber beneath Verdun's citadel in northern France in preparation to select their own Soldat Inconnu.[9] André Maginot had been wounded in the Battle of Verdun, one of the longest and bloodiest of the war, during which the Germans fired 2 million artillery shells in their attempt to make the French Army 'bleed to death'[10] in their defence of the ancient city.[11] The French somehow managed to hold off the invaders, at a cost that made their action a hallowed, almost mythical emblem for patriotic self-sacrifice. 'I arrived there with 175 men,' wrote one officer, following a German artillery bombardment. 'I left with 34, several half mad, not replying anymore when I spoke to them.'

Some 162,000 Frenchmen were killed, with a further 230,000 wounded. Too mangled to identify, many of the human remains were placed in the Douaumont Ossuary within the battlefield, which contains the mingled bones of at least 130,000 friend and foe.[12] Now the same motto etched on the quarterdeck of HMS *Verdun* – *On ne passe pas* – was emblazoned on one of the banners confronting André Maginot as he blinked in the half-light of the chamber. Pine fronds, floral wreaths and flags decorated the stone walls, much like Boulogne's *chapelle ardente* where the Unknown Warrior had spent his last night on French soil. Eight identical coffins, each adorned with a *tricolore* flag, stood before him. Maginot had chosen 21-year-old Auguste Thin of the 132nd Infantry Regiment to select the one that would become the representative of their own missing.

Private Thin had enlisted in 1918 after his father was killed in action, and, despite joining the war so late, he had been both wounded and gassed before its conclusion. 'Monsieur Maginot handed me a bouquet of carnations,' he recalled. 'He said, "Whichever coffin you lay this bouquet upon, that one will go to the Arc de Triomphe to immortalise all the dead of the war."' After considering the options, 'I placed my bouquet on the sixth coffin. This was because the three digits of my regiment – the 132nd – added up to six. And we were part of the army's 6th Corps, too. So I chose the sixth body.'[13]

The French Unknown Warrior began his journey to Paris almost at once, ready to be honoured there the following day as his brother-in-arms was being buried at Westminster Abbey.

DOVER
10 NOVEMBER 1920, 3:30PM

The stillness was shattered by the measured boom of Dover's coastal battery's nineteen-gun salute. White puffs of smoke blossomed from the gunports in the stone walls. The sharp crack of a blank round followed a split second later, then the thump as it echoed off the cliffs. To this accompaniment, HMS *Verdun* glided into port, 'a majestic, almost supernatural mien, as if she too – a ship – had come from the Unknown'.[14] Dover Castle lay to her left, its stark, blue-grey outline already beginning to lose itself in the rapidly encroaching dusk. To her right, the busy harbour seemed frozen in time and, at that very moment, a partial eclipse of the sun – the moon shadowing one side – added to the spectral magic.[15]

The fishermen, sailors and townspeople gathered near the Admiralty Pier had not been allowed onto the quay. A few dockside staff stood dotted among the navy boys, almost hidden behind the long rank of soldiers standing with their backs to the ship, rifles reversed. Docker William Chandler was there, ready to help with the lines and hawsers flung from above. Many of those assembled had their own experiences of loss.

As the *Verdun* drew closer to her mooring, stern first, there was a muffled roll of drums from the band of the Royal Irish Fusiliers, and then the majestic opening chords of 'Land of Hope and Glory' filled the air. 'Played softly, almost caressingly, the proud music of the Motherland brought a thrill of emotion to every spectator,' declared the *Daily Mirror*, 'it was an impressive moment.'[16] John Sowerbutts was certainly transported. 'Never can one forget the scene, we just glide in and, as we get close to the jetty, the bands sing softly.' His colleague Kirtley Nodes was similarly moved. 'The thrill of it sent shivers down my back and I was proud to be British.'[17] At each corner of the Unknown Warrior's coffin stood a sailor, head bowed, rifle reversed. Behind them, at the head of the bier, stood the stern, moustached figure of General Macdonogh. *Verdun*'s crew stood silently to attention along the deck as William Chandler and his fellow dockhands ensured she was made fast.

'An order rapped out from the bridge and the bluff old seamen on the harbour doffed their caps, and ran out the gangway gently and noiselessly,' one correspondent noted:

> There was a rattling of capstans, a straining of hawsers, and HMS *Verdun* was still. The air was still. The waters of the harbour, and of the Channel beyond, were still. Not a flag fluttered. Not a seagull flapped its wings. A diffused pearly-grey sky lay motionless above us. I do not ever remember a scene so static, except the Two Minutes' Silence last year. No doubt the Commander of the *Verdun* gave his orders as usual. But it was in undertones that reached no ear among the onlookers. There was not a sound and not a movement. This, for many seconds that seemed like an hour, so tense were those moments of waiting. It was with this wonderful vigilant, inviolable silence that Dover today first received back on English earth its Unknown Warrior.[18]

A few moments later, the wreaths and flowers were being removed, and the shrouded Treasure Chest was borne ashore and passed to six senior officers of the army, navy, marines and air force who had all seen active service in the war.[19] General Macdonogh, local dignitaries, officers from Dover Garrison followed – not to mention undertakers Nodes and Sowerbutts – along the short route to Dover Marine railway station, which was densely lined with soldiers from several different regiments. 'Soon he is borne aloft on his comrades' shoulders,' rhapsodised Sowerbutts, 'and we follow him ashore to the garden of repose.'

It was an impressive sight, and the grainy Pathé newsreel of the arrival captures its bleak solemnity. But something is missing. Where were the thousands of bereaved relatives who had come to greet the Unknown Warrior? Unlike the citizens of Boulogne, the Dover locals had been held back from paying their respects at the Admiralty Pier, which caused considerable upset. 'Not even those widows from Dover who mourn their husbands who have no known grave were allowed entry,' fumed the *Dover Express*.[20] The 'Today's Gossip' section of the *Daily Mirror* went further. 'I hear from Dover that there was much dissatisfaction regarding the arrangements in connection with the landing of the Unknown Warrior there. Townspeople had no opportunity of seeing the coffin. It was early closing day, and thousands waited in vain around the Marine Station.'[21]

They might have been kept at a distance, but even the briefest glimpse of the Unknown Warrior's coffin still exerted a powerful spell. 'I saw a woman, older-looking, much older-looking than her years,' wrote one reporter, 'with two children at her side who have grown up since the terrible war began. She swooned. Did she think that the body in that oaken casket covered with a battle-scorched [Union] Jack and followed by fighting men, all of whom have seen battle service, might be that of the husband and father whom they must wait and wait to meet again? *God help her!*'[22]

THE CENOTAPH, LONDON
10 NOVEMBER 1920, 4PM

Workers were busy enveloping Lutyens's memorial to the dead of the Great War in Whitehall in two vast Union Jacks.[23] It was a complex operation – an intricate system of levers, wires and behind-the-scenes trickery would be required to allow the flags to drop simultaneously to the ground at the very moment the King pressed a button during the unveiling ceremony. What could possibly go wrong?

A 'people's pilgrimage' to the monument had already begun. A steady stream of visitors passed along Whitehall, pausing at the

Cenotaph in silent reflection.[24] Many carried bouquets and wreaths, in keeping with the tradition of placing flowers around the original, temporary monument, as a memorial to the glorious dead. But the police were now discouraging such tributes, so that the base of the monument would not encumber the following day's parade. The thousands of soldiers, sailors and airmen, marching and mounted, would require the full width of Whitehall.

DOVER
10 NOVEMBER 1920, 4:45PM

Dockworker William Chandler had watched the procession pass along Admiralty Pier, the sight of gleaming rifles and sound of marching boots transporting him back to the war years, when he had witnessed so many young soldiers heading in the opposite direction. And perhaps he was also remembering his young great-nephew's face, when the news came through that the boy's father had been killed at Ypres in October 1914. Private Sidney Aldin's body was never found, his name yet another addition carved on the Menin Gate memorial.[25] Harold was six when his father was killed. He must have struggled to understand what it all meant. Why wasn't Daddy coming home? Where *was* he? Tragically, the one person who might have been able to answer some of his questions, his mother Fanny, succumbed to the Spanish flu epidemic four years later. Aged just ten, Harold was an orphan.

William Chandler will not have been the only man wondering where a missing relative was, staring at the now empty space on HMS *Verdun*'s quarterdeck where the Unknown Warrior's coffin had lain, surrounded with flowers. When he spotted a rosebud, its stem still wrapped with florist's wire, which had fallen off one of the huge wreaths, he carefully put it in his pocket, not yet sure what he would do with it.

DOVER MARINE RAILWAY STATION
10 NOVEMBER 1920, 5PM

From a tin-hut chapel in northern France, via a battered military ambulance, a night in the library of a thirteenth-century château, a procession through the crowded streets of a seaside town, and a Channel crossing aboard a torpedo-equipped destroyer, the Unknown Warrior's coffin was now carried reverently into the soft light of Dover Marine railway station. Dover itself had been the principal evacuation point for an estimated 1,260,000 wartime casualties. Eventually closed in 1994, the railway station is now a P&O ferry terminal with its appropriately understated memorial plaque mounted on an office wall, commemorating the arrival of the Unknown Warrior in 1920. It had been a hushed and peaceful affair.

The Reverend David Railton stayed well away from the lime-light, never wanting to take undue recognition for the gathering momentum of his idea. Perhaps this is why he appears to have made no record of his perspective on this phase of the odyssey. But I can imagine him keeping a close eye on proceedings as the Unknown Warrior finally arrived in his beloved Kent. The padre's old parish at Folkestone was only a short hop up the coast. And his new one at Margate was little more than 20 miles away. He may not have felt the need to pay his respects at Dover Harbour. He would be seeing the Unknown Warrior – and his flag – in Westminster Abbey the following day.

* * *

Though its white roof had been freshly painted to make it easier to spot as it rattled through the rain and darkness, passenger luggage van No. 132 of the South Eastern and Chatham Railway Company didn't look like much from the outside: a small goods wagon of varnished oak planks fitted to an iron frame, with two double doors on each side and four small windows protected by a steel grid. But it had been chosen for the next section of the Unknown Warrior's

journey for a reason. Built in 1919, it had already carried the bodies
of two dead heroes to the nation's capital – Nurse Edith Cavell and
Captain Charles Fryatt.

Edith Cavell's arrest and execution by a German firing squad in
October 1915 had been met by outrage around the world. Well-
known even before her death, this pioneer of modern nursing had
treated both Allied and German soldiers at a Red Cross hospital in
occupied Belgium. 'I can't stop,' she said, 'when there are lives to be
saved.'[26] Cavell's 'crime' was to have helped around 200 wounded
British and Allied prisoners being treated in her hospital to escape
into neutral Holland.[27] As she waited for the firing squad, she instructed the German prison chaplain to, 'Tell my loved ones that my
soul, as I believe, is safe, and that I am glad to die for my country.'[28]
   'Edith' soared in popularity as a girl's name after her martyrdom,
Edith Piaf, the legendary *chanteuse*, among the recipients.[29] After
the war, a special case was made for Cavell's body to be repatriated, honoured with a state funeral and reburied at her birthplace
in Norwich.

Captain Charles Algernon Fryatt was an unusually fearless and
pugnacious merchant seaman, who – with his unarmed ships,
owned by the Great Eastern Railway Company – seems to have
had a knack for making the lives of German U-boat captains very
uncomfortable. In early March 1915, his SS *Wrexham* survived a
hair-raising game of cat-and-mouse after being attacked by a U-boat
in the North Sea and was pursued for 40 nautical miles as Fryatt
urged his deckhands to work alongside the stokers, shovelling extra
coal into the ship's roaring fireboxes. After a remarkable display of
seamanship and sheer brute force – for which he was presented with
a gold watch by his employer – the *Wrexham* arrived at Rotterdam
with scorched funnels. It proved to be just the beginning of Captain
Fryatt's U-boat-baiting career.[30]
   Less than a month later, his new vessel, the SS *Brussels*, was ordered to hove to by a surfaced U-boat off the Dutch coast. Seeing

that it was preparing to torpedo them, Fryatt ordered full-steam-ahead and attempted to ram the submarine, forcing it to crash-dive, and allowing his unarmed ship to escape. Praised for his actions in the House of Commons, Fryatt's collection of congratulatory timepieces was further increased, this one inscribed: 'Presented by the Lords Commissioners of the Admiralty to Charles Algernon Fryatt, Master of the S.S. *Brussels*, in recognition of the example set by that vessel when attacked by a German submarine on March 28th, 1915.'

The following year, the watch would sign his death warrant.

In June 1916, a week before the start of the Battle of the Somme, the SS *Brussels* was captured by the enemy. Fryatt and his crew were arrested and their valuables requisitioned. Though sent to an internment camp near Berlin, the British sailors probably felt quite confident of their release – until a Dutch newspaper reported that Fryatt had been charged with attacking a German submarine.[31] The Germans had found his commemorative watch. At 7PM on Thursday, 27 July, Fryatt was executed as a *franc-tireur* – a civilian who breached the rules of warfare by taking up arms – by a naval firing squad at Bruges; an act denounced by the *New York Times* as 'a deliberate murder'.[32]

His body was also repatriated to Britain after the war and honoured with a state funeral. Like Edith Cavell, he had been conveyed from Dover to London in passenger luggage van No. 132.

* * *

Now, on 10 November 1920, the carriage was about to see its finest hour. Converted into a travelling *chapelle ardente*, it had been adorned with purple and gold trappings, a trellis of bay leaves – the traditional garland of victory, bouquets of sweet-smelling chrysanthemums for mourning, and evergreens to signify everlasting life. 'Beautifully draped and garlanded, it is just a paradise,' sighed John Sowerbutts as they loaded the coffin. 'We lay him down, and until the train starts, the doors are left open for the public to view.'

In fact, only a select few dignitaries were allowed anywhere near the carriage. The public had been kept at a distance yet again – except for those who realised that buying a train ticket would grant them access to the station for a closer look.[33]

'Solemnly,' recorded one journalist, 'and with the utmost reverence, the remains were laid to rest for the train journey.' Inside the wagon, two tiny electric lights shed a purple glow over the coffin. 'The giant wreaths were almost too large to be put through the doors of the brake, they required four and five soldiers to lift them.'[34]

DOVER MARINE RAILWAY STATION
10 NOVEMBER 1920, 5:20PM

With the coffin safely stowed, there was now a silent hiatus before the train could start its journey. 'One bluejacket [naval rating], one marine, one soldier and one airman stood sentinel over the glories of their unknown comrade,' recorded the special correspondent of the *Daily Telegraph*.[35] At 5:20PM, the remaining troops finally marched out of the station, swivelling their heads in an 'eyes left' salute as they passed the Warrior's wagon. Wisps of steam hissed from the darkness as the 58-tonne E-class locomotive, still in its wartime grey livery, prepared to depart.[36] The remaining honour guard of soldiers stood to attention, heads bowed, muzzles of their rifles pressed onto their polished toecaps. 'It was,' as the man from the *Daily Mirror* put it, 'an impressive ending to a wonderful ceremony.'[37] In a brightly lit separate passenger carriage, a travelling guard party of one officer and fifteen men of the Connaught Rangers had quietly taken their places. Having closed and padlocked the 'Cavell Van', Messrs Nodes and Sowerbutts also took their seats. Leaving nothing to chance, General Macdonogh boarded too. At 5.30PM, the train clanked out of the station and into the darkness.[38]

In Dover, many of the townsfolk made their way to churches for special evening prayers, where 'pathetic scenes were witnessed among the women of the congregations who have lost their dear ones in the war'.[39] In Margate, David Railton preached a sermon to his congregation, even though it wasn't a Sunday. His heart must have felt unusually full that night.[40]

* * *

'The train thundered through the dark, wet, moonless night,' reported the *Daily Mail*. 'At the platforms by which it rushed could be seen groups of women watching and silent, many dressed in deep mourning. Many an upper window was open, and against the golden square of light was silhouetted, clear cut and black, the head and shoulders of some faithful watcher.'[41] The *Daily Mirror* told a similar story:

> Station platforms of towns between Dover and Victoria were crowded with people who stood in reverent silence while the train halted for a few moments. The crowds included many thousands of women, and between the stations every street corner and road running parallel with the lines held groups of watchers, some of whom had waited patiently in the rain, if only for a fleeting glimpse of the train containing the dead Warrior.[42]

Nodes and Sowerbutts marvelled at the sights they beheld through the windows of their passenger carriage. 'All the way up, at every station, are crowds; by the crossings, on the bridges out of the darkness, white faces peer as we speed with our treasure to London. The rest the papers will tell you.'[43]

Local reporters certainly did their best.

At Sittingbourne in Kent, the train stopped for almost five minutes. The station was thronged with people, some of whom had travelled for miles, 'to render reverent homage to the remains of one who will symbolise for ever in the hearts of many their own lost ones'.[44] At Faversham, veterans completely filled the platform, carrying at their head a Union Jack surmounted by a wreath of bay leaves, a tribute to their dead comrade. Movingly, it was a detachment of Boy Scouts in short trousers who sounded the Last

Post.[45] At Gillingham, a team of bluejackets formed an impromptu guard of honour, bowing their heads and reversing their rifles as the gleaming train slowed through the station.[46]

And on into the London suburbs and 'scores of homes with back doors flung wide, light flooding out, and in the garden, figures of men, women and children gazing at the great lighted train rushing past'.[47]

Victoria Station, London
10 November 1920, 8:30pm

The lights still burned at London's Victoria railway station as the evening rush cleared and commuters hurried home. Theatregoers were already chortling in the stalls or swooning at the tenor voice of a Welsh coalminer who was halfway through his recital at Steinway Hall.[48] After a couple of drinks, many must have been doing their best to feel a little happier about the world.

On the rain-slicked pavements outside the station, temporary barriers had been erected and the crowd – now several rows deep – was silent but restive. Thousands had already gathered, and the police were doing their best to control the unexpected numbers.[49] One journalist noted that these were the same people, nearly all women, who had gathered here in the war, bidding their menfolk farewell, or waiting, hoping, for their safe return. 'Men had gone out with their last memories of England from here,' he wrote. 'The ladies in the buffet used to tell the men that Victoria meant victory. And so they shouldered their heavy pack, and headed to their train and went out to France.'[50]

Whispers came from behind the barriers, then a wave of emotion swept through the assembled crowd beyond the gates. The soldiers on the platform stiffened.[51]

The train pulling the Cavell Van and the passenger carriage waited outside the station for a new locomotive to transfer them to their allotted platform, closest to Buckingham Palace Road on the western side of the station.[52] Though they could still see nothing, the throng surged forward. 'A wild rush was made past the barriers and some of the crowd mounted the footplates,' said one observer, although other newspapers reported that the arrival took place in an atmosphere of silent reverence.[53] The *Daily Mirror* hedged its bets and claimed both that the police had succeeded in holding back the crowds, and that the same crowds had 'climbed over the engine and the carriage'.[54]

Whatever the case, any chaos, such as it was, was quelled as quickly as it had begun.

Again they waited.

At 8:32PM precisely, the red tail-lamp of the small shunting engine and its two carriages could be seen slowly approaching platform 8.[55] The few civilians allowed onto the platform removed their hats and the small detachment of sixteen Grenadier Guardsmen saluted. From behind the barriers came the smothered sound of weeping.[56] The pain and longing were visible 'in many a woman's eyes'.[57]

It may be . . . came one whisper.

Oh, I wonder . . . came another.[58]

With a gentle groan, the ghost train glided to a halt.

* * *

While the Unknown Warrior rested in London, Dover dockworker William Chandler returned home that night and placed the rosebud he had salvaged from one of the giant wreaths in a cup of water, determined to keep the bloom as fresh as possible while he decided what to do with it. A few days later, he composed a letter to his young great-nephew Harold Aldin, whose father Sidney was one of the Unknowns. On a sheet of cream paper, neatly folded three times, he wrote in beautiful and florid copperplate script:

Dear Nephew,
    In Loving memory of your Dear Dad who arrived at Dover Nov 10th 1920 in the Destroyer 'Verdun'.
    Buried in Westminster Abbey Nov 11th 1920.

The Unknown Warrior.
The enclosed is a part of a rose which fell from a large
wreath given by the British Army. I hope you will keep
it & in years to come, you will be able to show it, in
remembrance of your Dad.
From your Affectionate Uncle,
W Chandler

* * *

At Victoria Station, the Unknown Warrior's wagon was clearly opened at some point – a famous photograph of the time shows it guarded by sombre-faced young soldiers and an ancient, white-haired railwayman. The end of the coffin is visible on the floor of the carriage, still draped in its flag. 'Men wept as they saw the double railway carriage,' noted *The Times*. 'They knew not why they wept. But the great gloomy arches of the station, and the rows on rows of white faces pressed to the barriers were a setting which might not be denied.'[59]

One last time, Nodes and Sowerbutts checked that all was in order before shuttering the carriage windows and padlocking the doors. A brief tête-à-tête, and then the keys were handed to the Guard Commander on the platform. The officer, in return, signed and held out a slip of paper: 'Received from Mr Sowerbutts, two keys of Van no. 132, South Eastern and Chatham Railway. November 10th, 1920.' Finally, it was time for the two undertakers to head home. It had been, as an exhausted Sowerbutts put it, 'a labour of love we would never forget'.[60]

The Unknown Warrior – perhaps it just *might* have been young Harold Aldin's dad? – was home, safe, and under the watchful guard of comrades-in-arms alongside whom he may have fought and fallen. On the platform at each end of the carriage, a young Grenadier Guardsman took his ceremonial place, reversed his weapon and stood with his head bowed. Every half-hour, two new

Guardsmen would march into position, salute the coffin and their comrade, and take their turn. For some, the image conjured a vivid memory of Edward VII's lying-in-state at Westminster Hall in 1910, where four sentinel Grenadiers had stood in similar positions, at each corner of his coffin on its high catafalque, draped with the royal standard.[61]

And it would be echoed just over a century later at the great lying-in-state of Queen Elizabeth II in 2022, when four soldiers would take their turn, standing at the four corners of Her Majesty's catafalque, heads bowed, swords reversed, one hand folded over the other, later being joined by princes and princesses, senior military officers and government ministers too.

Many thousands had waited to see the Unknown Warrior's arrival at Victoria in 1920, and perhaps a quarter of a million queued for hours simply to stand beside the late Queen's coffin for a few seconds over one hundred years later – what is it about this acknowledgement of sacrifice, this ceremony of death, that compels people to be part of the occasion?

CHAPTER TEN

WELCOME HOME, BOYS

VICTORIA STATION, LONDON
AUGUST 2023

For most – older – military personnel, railway stations touch the heart. Places to say goodbye, places to be welcomed home. Places of beginning and sometimes, sadly, of ending. I well remember standing in Newcastle Central train station as a 17-year-old boy in 1981 alongside two holdalls crammed with almost all my earthly possessions. Another dozen fresh-faced, wide-eyed teenagers were saying their goodbyes to tearful parents, or, if they were lucky, tearful girlfriends. We were all leaving home for the first time, heading south to start recruit training and a new life in the Royal Air Force. At the time, I'm sure none of us even contemplated the possibility of any future danger, or that some of our friends might spill their blood on foreign fields. We were simply excited to be embarking on a new shared adventure.

London's Victoria Station, a gateway to the trenches of the First World War, has seen more 'goodbyes' than most, and I wonder if those equally fresh-faced youngsters in 1916 felt the surge of awe and excitement that I did when they embarked on their own 'adventure'? I wonder if they had even an inkling of how many friends would never return? How many would never be seen or heard of again? The layout of the current station and platforms is very different; the old Grill Room, with its chandeliers and starched napkins folded into neat cones, is long gone. So, too, the Refectory Room with its clerestory windows, bar and polished beer taps, not to mention the ladies' first-class waiting room. But the place remains steeped in echoes of the past. These soaring glass canopies are a reminder of the days when steam trains blackened the air with wet soot and the stench of burning coal.

Even today, with tourists and commuters hurtling past me, buried in their mobile phones, there is a tinge of ancient-and-modern melancholy about the place; a faint whiff of *Brief Encounter* in the scrolled stonework and the empty faces. That same milky glow filtering through the roof lights that must have fallen on the Unknown Warrior's coffin on the evening of 10 November 1920, as, behind the barriers, heaving crowds of hollow-eyed men and women tried to catch a glimpse of the train standing at platform 8. Many would have had one terrible thing in common – a letter or telegram which they could hardly bear to open, knowing that the contents would smash their world into bitter fragments. Now, two years after the end of the war, they were still trying to find a way to put their personal jigsaw back together, even though the most precious piece was still missing. Was it on that train?

I have attended many funerals of friends killed in action or during training, and attended countless memorial services and Remembrance Day parades over the years. The heartbreaking loss experienced by the bereaved during the First World War is part of a continuum. Warfare, and the technological means of waging it, may well have changed over the last 100 years. But death, loss and grief forge unbreakable, and unbearable, links across the generations, which intimately connect them – and us – with the broken hearts and inspirational resilience of thousands of families, friends and comrades living today who have also received the modern equivalent of that telegram or letter – the 'knock at the door' by someone wearing military uniform.

I think of young Mary Fowler, seeing a crowd of people outside her house on her way home from school and somehow knowing that her dad must be missing at sea. Or Jenny Green being woken at IAM and finding herself unable to open the front door, because she had glimpsed the gold braid on the polished peak cap on the other side of it.

* * *

Nikki Scott knows all about that fateful knock at the door. Her husband, Lee, was killed in Afghanistan little more than a year after their marriage. A warm-spirited woman with soulful brown eyes and a ready laugh, Nikki had first met Lee when working at a pub in King's Lynn, Norfolk. He wasn't yet a soldier. Just a bit of a Jack-the-lad, who didn't seem to take life too seriously. 'He used to come into the bar with his mates. Always getting drunk and messing around, he seemed quite immature to me. He kept asking me out on a date, but I told my friend: "There's no *way* that I'm ever going out with him!"' she recalls, with a wistful smile. 'I could never have imagined the journey that lay ahead.' Lee proved to be as spirited as she was. Determined, too. 'He just said to me, "One day you'll be Mrs Scott." I told him in no uncertain terms that never in a million years would that happen!'[1]

The couple were married in February 2008.

In the meantime, Lee had joined the army. He was a fast-rising star of the 2nd Royal Tank Regiment and proved himself during operations in both Kosovo and Iraq. Known as a 'soldier's soldier', Lee had also managed to find the time to become a qualified free-fall parachutist and coastal day skipper. And now, above all else, a quintessential family man.

Nikki had one of those rare military marriages which seemed to work perfectly on every front. Lee was not just an instinctive soldier with a keen and canny tactical brain who was 'usually at the centre of any mischief', according to his Commanding Officer,[2] he was also a wonderful husband and enthusiastically hands-on dad. 'Ask anyone who was lucky enough to have met him and they'd all tell you the same thing,' she says. 'He was the most loving, kindest, thoughtful person you could ever meet. He was so full of life. He permanently had a cheeky grin on his face.'

Nikki thinks about this for a moment, visibly brightening at the thought of him, even though she is speaking in the past tense. She, too, is one of those people who seems to glow from within. And then, switching defiantly to the present tense, she adds: 'I am so proud to be his wife.' Sitting in the Corporals' Mess of Lee's tank regiment at Tidworth in Wiltshire, Nikki gazes around the room with a mixture of familiarity and wonder. I can see that she is recognising old friends among the furnishings and in the portraits on the walls of square-jawed soldiers in camouflage uniform, one of whom is her husband. With a deep breath, Nikki returns to long-banished memories of the morning of Friday, 10 July 2009, and her personal knock on the door.

Whether it occurred during the First World War, the Falklands or Afghanistan, it is a story told again and again by those whose loved ones head to war.

'Saying goodbye to Lee when he deployed to Afghanistan had been simply heartbreaking,' she says. 'It was so hard to let him go. He'd been on operations before so I was used to him being away, but there had already been a *lot* of casualties in Afghanistan. I was worried, but we didn't really talk about that aspect as it wouldn't have helped. Whatever was going to happen, was going to happen. He even joked, "I have just filled out my will form and if I snuff it you'll be minted." He recorded some bedtime stories I could play to the kids when he had gone, so they could hear his voice and remember who their daddy was while he was away over those long months. The day he left, I was trying to be so strong. We hugged and said that we loved each other. He said goodbye and I shut the door as he walked down the path. Then I broke down in tears; I couldn't believe that I wouldn't be seeing him for six months. Of course, I didn't know that it would be the last time I would ever set eyes on him.'

Early in July, one of Lee's friends was killed in an explosion. 'It was truly devastating, and really brought home the reality of what our loved ones were facing,' she says. 'I remember thinking that the war was really coming close to home. I felt very lonely and insecure; it was a massive wake-up call for all the wives and girlfriends waiting at home. I still remember looking out of the window into the cul-de-sac, wondering when the official car might pull up outside my house to tell me that my husband had been killed. It was a truly, truly terrible time.'

Tracing lines in the air with the fingers of one hand, Nikki looks intently at the far wall as she speaks, as if the memories are being projected in front of her, and she is swiping through them as she describes the events of fourteen years earlier. 'The children and I had had a really disturbed night – both Brooke and Kai had been awake and unsettled. At one point we were all sitting together in my bed. It was all really unusual. Looking back now, I think I must have sensed that something was wrong.

'I felt really low when I woke up the next morning, really flat, but we continued as normal. Kai went to a friend's house and I was on the way back from the park with my daughter when two cars drove past me. That image is still seared in my mind. One driver was wearing a suit, the other was in combat uniform. I instantly knew they were coming to give me bad news.' She blinks, creases her brow, swallows hard. 'The cars stopped outside my house and I vividly remember crying as I walked towards them. As the men were getting out, I said, "Are you looking for me?" One simply replied, "Are you Corporal Lee Scott's wife?" That's when I knew.'

Nikki speaks quickly now, the words tumbling out. 'I just kept saying, "What happened? What happened? Just tell me, just *tell* me." I don't remember how, but we were standing in the hallway of the house, and I must have been fumbling to get Brooke out of her buggy. One of the men said, "Can you please just hand your baby to my colleague?" I kept saying, almost shouting now, "Tell me! Just tell me! Has Lee been hurt?" And that's when they told me. My husband had been killed by an improvised explosive device [IED] – a bomb – during operations that morning. They didn't really have any

more information. That was it. Lee was dead.' His young widow
pauses to gather her emotions. 'I don't really remember much after
that.' She almost smiles at the thought. 'Sorry,' she says, under her
breath, wiping away a tear with the tip of her thumb. She takes a
breath, blinks at the ceiling, eyes shining. 'Sorry ... it's just really
hard ...' Another glance around the room. A helpless flick of her
wrist at her husband's portrait on the wall.

Nikki is one of hundreds to have had to come to terms with her
life being turned upside down during the recent actions in Iraq and
Afghanistan, and this one moment, for just one bereaved wife, captures the intensity of their sacrifice and loss. As an officer, I had to
'knock on the door' on two occasions. Both are over thirty years ago
now, but still clear in my mind. The blind panic when the occupant
registers the formal dress uniform, then the dreadful realisation of
what is to come. A wife collapsing on the stairs, children appearing
from bedrooms to stare uncomprehendingly at the drama unfolding
below. It is almost impossible to imagine the scale of this scenario
being played out during the First World War, the millions of homes
affected.

'You never, *ever* think it will happen to you, to your husband,'
Nikki says, voicing the highly charged response to 'the knock'
which has echoed across the ages. 'Yet here we were. I had known
how bad it was out there. A friend had already been killed. But you
just don't think the war will ever come into your own home.' She
uses her fingertips to carefully brush away the tears from beneath
her lashes, before her mascara starts to run. But the dam begins to
crumble. Her shoulders begin to shake. She lowers her head, as if to
hide her quiet sobs. I wonder if my questions have been too searching, too personal. I ask if she'd rather stop, but she is determined
to go on, to relive her pain so that those who have never – thankfully – known it might try to understand the grief military families
experience. Whether it comes via a telegram or letter in 1916, or a
personal notification in 2009.

'I wasn't stupid,' she says firmly. 'I had always tried to prepare
myself for something you never imagine will happen.' She raises

her head, eyes wide, as if registering the shock and amazement for
the first time that fate had chosen her. 'The most painful thing was
knowing that our two precious children would now have to face life
without their father. Brooke was just seven months old. She would
have no memories of him. But Kai was five and adored Lee. How
was I going to tell our gorgeous little boy that his daddy wasn't
coming home?'

Nikki's recollections make me think of young Harold Aldin
and his great-uncle William Chandler, rescuing a precious rosebud
fallen from the Unknown Warrior's wreath in Dover as a gift for his
orphaned nephew: *In Loving memory of your Dear Dad*. Harold
was almost the same age as Kai when his father was killed at Ypres
in 1914. What was it like for his mother to give the child the news?
What was it like for the hundreds of thousands of other mothers
to go through the same traumatic process? 'Without a shadow of
a doubt, it was the toughest thing I've ever had to do in my life,'
Nikki says, as if reading my mind. 'I was dreading it, but I knew that
I had to be straight, to the point, and not give him any confusing
messages.'

When Kai arrived home a little later, Nikki took him upstairs.
'We were sitting on the bed together, and I said, "Kai, do you remember where Daddy is?"

'"Yes, in Afghan."'

She smiles at his five-year-old's use of the military diminutive.
'We had explained the good work that Lee was doing out there,
and that there were "baddies" out there, trying to stop him and his
friends.' Nikki takes a deep breath. 'I told him that I'd always said
that Daddy was going to come home, but something has happened:
*Daddy has been killed by the baddies. And he won't ever be able
to come home*.' Tears begin to stream down my own face as Nikki
stares into the distance, repeating those words, imprinted on her
heart, fourteen years later. 'Then, I simply burst into tears. Kai just
put his arm around me. It was so . . .' She puts her hand to her chest.
'And then he began crying too. Very, very quietly. I don't think he
really understood what was going on. How can a child possibly

understand these things? But this was just the start of it all. There were so many other people to tell.'

I hadn't really considered this aspect of bereavement. Before deploying on active service I had certainly written a couple of 'last letters' to my closest family, only to be opened in the event of my death. But there are so many more people than immediate family who need to be told. An intricate web of siblings, cousins, in-laws, comrades and colleagues, neighbours and friends. It is a long, complex list and someone has to make those calls.

Nikki had to ring Lee's father. It was almost too much. 'How do you tell a grown man that his beloved son has been killed? And then to hear that man break down . . .' She shakes her head at the memory. 'Then I had to telephone my own parents, to give them the same news. It was a devastating experience. I was lost. My world had fallen apart. Even though I had amazing friends and family around me, I just felt completely alone. I didn't know how I was going to carry on without Lee in my life.'

Nikki's experiences of dealing with Lee's death shed new light on the less well-recorded feelings and emotions of families 100 years earlier. Then there was the process of bringing Lee home: a rare and precious crumb of comfort not available to many widows of the First World War.

RAF LYNEHAM, WILTSHIRE
14 JULY 2009

Seven other soldiers were killed in Afghanistan on the same day as Lee Scott, including three eighteen-year-olds. Age really shouldn't matter, but there's a particular poignancy when service personnel are slaughtered before their life has really begun. It was one of the worst days of the war and the amount of British blood shed made newspaper headlines across the country. The repatriation of the bodies a few days later was covered by every major news channel.

It clearly matters how these things are done; how we humans

learn to let go of each other, and the ritual and recognition which help to make the process even fractionally more bearable.

The eight soldiers were flown home to RAF Lyneham, where their families waited in an open marquee directly in front of the main terminal building, muted sobs punctuating the silence. They heard the aircraft before they could see it: the unmistakable howl of four jet engines overhead. Before it landed, the vast transport aircraft made a low pass across the airfield, dipping one wing in salute to the bereaved relatives below. Nikki remembers the occasion with agonising clarity; how one of the fathers struggled to hold his emotions in check as the aircraft roared past. And yet, in his intensely private grief, he recognised that this was a shared moment. His son had not died alone.

'We heard him say very quietly: *Welcome home, boys.*' She looks down at her hands. 'Then the weeping got even louder.'

Nikki had been preparing for, anticipating, her husband's return from war since the day he had deployed. But not like this. 'I was going to get my hair done, buy a new outfit, get my make-up done, get the house and the kids ready for his glorious, joyful homecoming. Now I was wearing black on a windswept airfield waiting for his coffin.' Gritting her teeth, she watched as a hand-picked bearer party marched up the aircraft's rear ramp to carry her young husband's body back onto British soil. Unlike the eight men who carried the Unknown Warrior reverently from the château in Boulogne, these pallbearers were Lee's friends; carefully chosen from his regiment, they had all served alongside him. But there is much that links this scene with that exit from Boulogne: the sense of deep respect and timeless ritual; the cautious, achingly slow gait of the escort. The clenched jaws and fixed expressions. The struggle to hold emotions in check, to remain professional and composed as you carry a comrade's body, knowing that their next of kin are watching nearby, and the world watches from afar.

'Seeing his coffin being carried off the aircraft was possibly tougher than the funeral, which came later,' Nikki says. 'I find it very difficult to talk about his repatriation. But a short time later, as each coffin was carried down the aircraft ramp, the next family in line would begin crying as *their* loved one came home for the final time. It was just awful to hear other people's grief.' She wipes her eyes again at the memory. But there was some comfort in the ceremony. 'All the guys who carried Lee were his mates,' she says, pronouncing each word very carefully, for emphasis. 'I love that it was really important to *them*. I knew everyone who carried him off that aircraft. And so did he.' She pauses. 'I thought that was wonderful.'

Each family had been allocated eight places for the repatriation ceremony on base. A congregation of sixty-four bereft souls, alongside the senior officers and dignitaries representing the military and other organisations. 'I had always been very private when I cried.' Nikki gives an almost imperceptible shake of her head. 'And now my grief was on public display.' Nikki's reflection on 'public' grief takes me back once more to the emotional outpourings of 1920, and the importance of public recognition of private suffering, particularly in a cultural environment unused to such lack of restraint.

WOOTTON BASSETT, NEAR RAF LYNEHAM 14 JULY 2009

Two years before Lee Scott's death, RAF Lyneham had been tasked with handling all repatriation flights of Britain's war dead from Afghanistan and Iraq. As a community policeman attached to the base, PC Jarra Brown's job was to ensure the safe passage of the coffin-laden vehicles as they began their journey to Oxford's John Radcliffe Hospital for the post-mortem formalities. An ex-soldier himself, he was deeply conscious of the responsibility. He will never forget the first rehearsal. 'Many people talk about the hairs on the back of their neck standing up. Well, this was one of those moments. Talk about honour, dignity and respect, this was overwhelming. And I really do mean *overwhelming*. I had never witnessed anything that displayed so much mixed emotion, deep sincere sadness, yet with chest-swelling pride, in knowing this is what our country does when bringing our fallen home.'[3]

So Brown had been touched by what happened a few minutes after the cortège set off during the very first repatriation in 2007. Five miles into their journey, their solemn cavalcade was abruptly forced to stop and wait in the middle of the market town of Wootton Bassett by – of all things – a lorry winching a rusty skip into position, painfully slowly, en route to the local rubbish dump. By pure coincidence, the cortège had been halted alongside the war memorial on the High Street: a bronze globe, held aloft by four outstretched hands, just beside a pelican crossing. 'The lights changed allowing people to get to the other side of the road,' he recalls. 'But instead, all the pedestrians chose to remain where they were, standing in silence. Some even bowed their heads. They stayed there for the next minute or so, until we went on our way.'

That small demonstration of silent remembrance, spontaneously paid, marked the start of an extraordinary journey for both Jarra Brown and the place that is now known as Royal Wootton Bassett.

Soon afterwards, he noticed that ex-military men and women were beginning to congregate around the town's war memorial whenever a repatriation was expected. Many wore their old berets and freshly polished medals, regimental ties and blazers. Then the mayor and several members of the town council announced that they too intended to stand at the war memorial when a cortège came through.[4] Sure enough, when the next one appeared, there they stood, 'giving a brief but significant bow of their heads as we slowly drove past'. As time went by, the number of townspeople and military veterans who assembled to pay their respects increased. The local branch of the Royal British Legion began to alert their members and other veterans' groups when a ceremony was to take place. Then a request was made for the cortège to pause for a moment by the memorial in order for those gathered to properly offer a formal salute. A moment of silence in the presence of a warrior who had made the ultimate sacrifice. The sense of occasion was heightened when the great tenor bell of St Bartholomew's Church, cast in 1663, began to toll for each repatriation, lending an impression of timeless gravity to the proceedings.

Word spread. Police officers began to volunteer to help escort the convoys. The local press cottoned on, too. 'I think they knew they were starting to witness something completely different,' says Brown. 'Something which had not been seen before.' And the British military had its own reasons to be grateful to the town, as the Commanding Officer of one of the repatriated soldiers declared: 'I know the family will be touched by the compassion of the people of Wootton Bassett who stood in the cold winter weather to show their sincerest respects to Sergeant Johnson. He will be greatly missed, but it is a comfort for those who knew him to know that his repatriation didn't go unnoticed. We are honoured by the people of Wootton Bassett, and their actions shall not be forgotten.'[5]

The mother of a Royal Marine killed in Afghanistan in January 2009 spoke for many when she stated: 'I stepped off the bus at Wootton Bassett to be completely overwhelmed as I saw hundreds of people who had taken the time out from their busy daily lives to line the streets in order to pay their respects to Travis. I could see lots of familiar, frozen-looking, distraught faces amid the crowds. Although our visit was traumatic, it was humbling, too. I wouldn't have wanted Travis's repatriation to have taken place anywhere else.'[6]

It had not always been this way. Early recognition of the sacrifice in the 'controversial' wars in Iraq and Afghanistan was muted, to say the least. I well remember that in the aftermath of the 2003 Iraq War, the deaths of British service personnel barely warranted a few inches of type on page two of the *Daily Telegraph*. There was rarely a single mention of the return of the dead. And the return of the catastrophically injured living received no coverage at all in those early days. But as time went on, and the cost in blood and treasure increased, deaths became 'breaking news' and homecomings were covered live on TV. Thank goodness, then, for Wootton Bassett and a media, for various reasons, hungry for images of flag-swathed coffins being driven through throngs of silent well-wishers. Footage of flowers being thrown onto hearses was a graphic acknowledgement of the latest deaths in foreign fields. And people began to travel from all over Britain to pay their respects to these fallen warriors.

In total, the coffins of 345 service personnel would pass slowly down that High Street between 2007 and 2011. Perhaps its most heart-rending moment came when Nikki Scott's husband, Lee, arrived home from Afghanistan.

PC Jarra Brown had been detailed to escort the unprecedented convoy of eight hearses, lined up one behind the other, each with its coffin carefully wrapped in a Union Jack, illuminated in the vehicle's glassy interior like a precious treasure chest. 'It was a devastating sight,' he recalls of what greeted him in the rear-view mirror of his police car. But the ovation of the local schoolchildren was what absolutely demolished him. 'It really caught me off-guard, and the tears were blurring my vision,' he says. 'I had to remind myself that inside those coffins behind me were some lads only seven years older than these children in primary-school uniform.' He had been warned that there would be thousands lining the route, but the reality still made his scalp prickle. 'Ten deep, I counted. People on rooftops, looking out of windows, all wanting to share compassion and sympathy towards those families who were hurting with so much pain.'

News footage from the day shows the silent crowds nearly twenty deep in places, shielding their eyes from the brilliant sunshine as the glittering black hearses rolled slowly past. At their head strode the funeral director, slow-marching the route in his Edwardian garb, top hat, cane and all, his every fourth step matching the mournful toll of St Bartholomew's tenor bell. Ghostly expressions and cascading tears marked out the relatives as they launched their floral tributes. The silence was broken by the family of one soldier, killed by a roadside bomb as he tried to rescue his comrades from an earlier blast. His relatives and friends ran out to his stationary hearse, flinging red roses onto its roof as one called out, 'Love you, man.'[7] Further back in the column, someone hurled a football shirt towards a hearse.

After the brief pause alongside the war memorial, the wheels of the cortège slowly began to turn again, and a spontaneous wave of applause rippled through the vast gathering. 'It really was emotional,' said Jarra Brown, leading the procession. 'I looked around and saw many people openly caught up in their own emotions, not ashamed to shed their tears.' In all, it took three hours for the eight hearses to travel the 46 miles to Oxford, slowed by the thousands lining the route. 'Our country was hurting, not in a manner that can be anything near the trauma the young men's family and friends were suffering, but the genuine compassion was overwhelming.'

Lee Scott's coffin had been borne through vast crowds of devoted well-wishers, mourners, veterans and supporters, many of them carrying British flags and bouquets of flowers, all patiently lining the streets of a town that had somehow become synonymous with the uniquely painful duty of honouring the nation's war dead. It was not unlike the crowd standing ten deep outside Victoria Station in 1920, pressing against the barriers, desperate for a glimpse of the coffin of an anonymous man, because this was the closest they could get to the event of which they had so often dreamed over the previous years.

Nikki Scott had not been able to witness the procession in person. 'We were told not to go to Wootton Bassett,' she says, still saddened by her absence from this visceral moment of shared grief and respect. 'There were real security concerns because of the large numbers involved and all the press in attendance. I had really wanted to go and be part of that welcome home, that recognition of sacrifice. But I had to watch it on TV back at RAF Lyneham.' She shrugs her acceptance. 'My mum was there, with Lee's stepmum, and the rest of his family and friends. She told me that it was incredibly emotional to be part of it all. Tragic, of course. But, in a strange way, somewhat uplifting to see so many thousands of people gathered to show their respect; to show their gratitude for the sacrifice of those eight young men.'

Later that day, Nikki finally made it into Wootton Bassett herself.

'I was desperate to see what it was like, to be part of that shared experience,' she says. 'The pubs were all filled; there were still people wandering around the streets wearing their blazers and berets and medals; there were wreaths and flowers scattered on the tarmac and the pavements, from where families had been throwing them towards the cortège. I met my mum in one of the crowded pubs and sat with loads of other veterans for the rest of the day, drinking and chatting about *their* wartime experiences. It was incredibly emotional to be part of that military family again. To have that connection with people who understood what I had been through, what I had lost.'

Later, after Lee's post-mortem in Oxford, Nikki began to arrange his funeral. 'I wanted him to be close to me,' she says, of the decision to bury her husband in King's Lynn in west Norfolk. Yet again, her words spirit me back to all those bereaved families in the First World War who wanted the bodies of their sons and husbands exhumed from war cemeteries and reburied in their local graveyard.

This urge to remain physically close to the dead is clearly a strong impulse in Western culture and Nikki's words highlight how tough it must have been for British families a century ago never to be given this option. Nikki's only scrap of comfort, if you can call it that, was to have had a body to bury. Unlike Mary Fowler and Jenny Green, compelled to take it entirely on trust that the men they had adored really had died, the presence of Lee's body offered – on some level – physical proof that he was dead.

But even this, it turned out, was not quite enough for his widow.

* * *

Because of the injuries caused by the catastrophic explosion, Nikki was strongly advised *not* to look at Lee's body before he was buried.

'I could have done if I had insisted,' she says now, 'but I chose not to.'

It is a decision she still regrets today. 'I wish I had had the courage to look at his remains; to *prove* that he was dead,' she says. 'I needed to know that he had gone; that he was not coming home. I needed that confirmation; that final closure. I sat with his coffin when it returned, but I do regret not choosing to have that proof.'

The testimony of friends who witnessed the final moments of someone's relative in the First World War was often crucial to a family's understanding, and sometimes acceptance, of the death. When Padre David Railton wrote to bereaved families explaining the circumstances of the death, they were profoundly grateful for the information. That hasn't changed today, however much established so-called wisdom suggests that we should remember the version of the dead that existed prior to the traumatic event which killed them, and Nikki wanted to know every detail about what had happened to her husband. So when Lee's colleagues finally came home from Afghanistan that December, they offered to answer every question she had. 'I wanted to know exactly how and where he died, and the full story of that day, however horrendous.'

She pauses to consider this for a moment, perhaps concerned I might find her quest for such information ghoulish. But having spoken to other families who have lost someone in a catastrophic aircraft crash, I fully understand the need for some to be furnished with all the information. However graphic and upsetting. 'I was so angry that I hadn't been with him when he died,' she says at last, 'that I wanted to know *everything*, every single detail, however distressing. I wanted to know who was first to him after the explosion. What condition was he in? Was he already dead? Had he said anything? I got them to describe his injuries and what the scene looked like. Even the smallest detail, like was he lying face down, or face up? They were brutally honest with me and it was difficult, but I needed to hear it all.'

She looks at me intently, to check if I understand.

I nod.

'I just needed to know,' she says quietly. 'I needed *proof* that he died that day.' Then she adds: 'That need to know continues today.'

We both sit in silence for a while.

Taking a deep breath, Nikki continues, her words coming quickly and with urgency. 'I still need to reassure myself he has gone, is really dead. I still need to know that somebody was with him in his final moments. I need to know somebody was by his side, all the way through from dying, until he was returned home and buried. That's incredibly important to me. And I can't imagine the pain and the suffering of those who could not have that final satisfaction. That final knowledge. That final comfort.'

I think about those families who secretly exhumed and brought home their dead during, or just after, the First World War. Nikki's words seem to shine a new and unflinching light on this enterprise, which only a few weeks earlier had seemed so strange to me. 'Even today, I still have dreams where I wonder if Lee is actually alive somewhere,' she says. 'I didn't have that final proof, that very *final* closure. So, curiously, deep in the recesses of my mind, there is a tiny inkling of doubt.' She eyes me carefully. 'It's ludicrous of course. But it's there, so I sometimes call one of Lee's friends who was with him that day, fourteen years ago, and I'll ask them once more: "He's *definitely dead*, isn't he? You *definitely* saw him dead?" And they will repeat what they have told me over the years. *Lee is dead, Nikki. He's gone.*

'Those occasions can be horrible, but I can't help it. I still wonder. But then, I'll just crack on with my day.'

Unlike the families of the First World War missing, Nikki has a physical grave to visit. 'It's so important for us to have somewhere we can go and sit. To remember Lee; his sacrifice, the person, the soldier he was. I tell the kids that they can think about him wherever they want, but when they visit his grave, he can probably hear them chatting more clearly. This is their daddy's place, and they can talk to him, laugh or cry with him, tell him their hopes and their dreams and their fears. He will always be waiting for them at his grave. For me, it's a place of peace and tranquillity. Of certainty.

'When I think of the missing from the First World War, the families who never knew what happened to their husband or son, who never had the body returned, I find it incredibly upsetting. I simply can't comprehend the emotions of people who were either not allowed to have their loved one home, or couldn't have them home because nobody knew where they were. I think that you need that special place to go, somewhere to contemplate, somewhere just to chat to your husband, your father or your son, to connect with them. I can't imagine not having that, and it upsets me to think about other people not having the comfort that I have. I know that I would be absolutely furious if I hadn't had the opportunity to say that proper goodbye, to finish Lee's and my journey together.'

Victoria Station, London
August 2023

The ghosts of the past remain elusive amid Victoria Station's modern, brightly lit fast-food joints and convenience stores. But they are here. The bronze plaque that commemorates the Unknown Warrior's arrival here – and the outpouring of public grief that attended it – is bolted to the wall between platforms 8 and 9, close to the left-luggage office:

> THE BODY OF THE BRITISH UNKNOWN
> WARRIOR ARRIVED AT PLATFORM 8 AT 8.32PM
> ON THE 10TH NOVEMBER 1920 AND LAY
> HERE OVERNIGHT BEFORE INTERMENT AT
> WESTMINSTER ABBEY ON 11TH NOVEMBER 1920.

I look around. This forbidding grey brick barrier also marks the dividing line between the two separate termini which once jostled for position, which time and frequent rebuilds have now blurred into one. The platforms of the old 'Chatham' concourse, with its wide-arched roofing and a glassy coffee shop striving to lure the passengers arriving on this new platform 8 – 'YOUR COSTA, just the way you like it' – would have been to the left of the plaque near where the Unknown Warrior's train first arrived in 1920, before being shunted across to the posher side of the station. On the adjoining concourse to my right – where an exclusive entrance had been created on Buckingham Palace Road for the royal family when the station was rebuilt in 1908[8] – are the shadows under which the carriage containing the Warrior's coffin spent the night. Behind me, beyond the main entrance, is where the crowds stood behind the barricades in their thousands, watching and waiting. So many shattered lives. Like Nikki Scott, they never expected it to turn out this way. Perhaps they, too, were still looking for proof.

I think back to all the men I have encountered on my journey retracing the footsteps of the Unknown Warrior. Those who fell and whose bodies were never found in the earth I trod around High Wood. Did Bert Bradley's father travel the 10 miles south to Victoria from Tottenham, four years after writing his letter to thank Anthony French for the 'great comfort' of telling him that his son, who had such a beautiful tenor voice, did not suffer long when he fell at High Wood, never to be seen again? We know that David Railton was preaching at Margate on the night of 10 November, and would not make the journey up to London until the next morning. But he must have been intensely aware that the precious casket would, finally, have arrived. That his idea to commemorate the missing was finally coming to fruition, just as he had imagined. I think back to Lucy Easthope, the expert in disaster recovery, evoking that feeling of *hiraeth* which survivors experience in the aftermath of a disaster: 'That longing for a place to which there is no return, an echo of something that can never be found, a heart-sickness for something that no longer exists and a time that can never be gone back to.'[9]

Like the memorials at Saint-Pol and Dover Harbour, the plaque here at Victoria Station, placed by the Western Front Association, attests to the almost mythical significance of the stopping points on the Unknown Warrior's final journey towards burial. So I was delighted to discover that 101-year-old Chelsea Pensioner and First World War veteran Frank Sumpter had been enlisted to unveil it in 1998.

It was reported that Sumpter, aged just twenty-three, had been one of the original pallbearers during the Unknown Warrior's sojourn at Boulogne on the night of 9 November 1920.[10] Born in 1897, two years before the start of the Boer War, he had fought at the battles of the Somme, Passchendaele, Ypres, the Marne and Messines Ridge. He outlived three wives, before dying at the Royal Hospital Chelsea just five months short of the millennium, at the age of 101.[11]

He had even been present at the Christmas Truce of 1914, when British and German troops along the Western Front took a pause from the killing, laid down their weapons and greeted each other in no-man's-land for a rare moment of soft-hearted kinship.[12] 'We heard the Germans singing, and then they put up a notice that said "Merry Christmas",' the old soldier recalled years later. 'Next, they started singing "Silent Night". Our boys said: "We'll join in with a song." And when we started our singing, they stopped. So we sang on. And then we stopped, and they sang.'[13] It was a moment of pure magic as, besides singing carols, the troops had a kickabout and exchanged gifts. The brief spell of festive spirit was soon broken, and the killing began again. 'The worst thing was being hit by shells – people with their stomachs hanging out – but I don't dream about it,' he said a few years before his death, when recalling later events. 'They used gas on us. We had no masks, so you urinated on a field dressing, bunged it on your face. The Germans used to drop like wheat when they were being machine-gunned, and so did we. I went out with one platoon and I was the only one who came back. But it was just a job of work.'[14] At five-foot-four, Sumpter had his own larky explanation for his survival. 'The reason why I didn't get it through the head is because I wasn't tall enough.'[15]

The closest he ever came to death was when a lone German lobbed a grenade into a trench full of sleeping soldiers, then began bayoneting the survivors. On seeing the 18-year-old Sumpter, he said, 'No, not you,' before running off into the night. 'I looked very young in those days,' said Sumpter, 'and was very short. He must have thought I was a boy.'[16] He never forgot the comrades with whom he had served, or the terrors they endured. 'I remember all our chums. And I remember the trenches, when they were filling with water and blood. How could I ever forget them?'[17]

It seems a miracle that Frank was still alive to unveil the Victoria Station plaque representing his missing 'chums' eight decades after the guns fell silent. 'I'm lucky,' he said. 'I should have died seventy years ago, with the rest of those poor souls.'[18]

As I trace the words on the plaque with my finger, I wonder how Frank Sumpter would have viewed the scenes at Wootton Bassett and the way his modern comrades are honoured. I'm sure he'd be pleased to hear that every year, on 10 November, members of the Western Front Association, which continues to highlight the sacrifice of the First World War generation, gathers at this spot to remember the moment when the Unknown Warrior's carriage arrived. They are surrounded year on year by a growing number of commuters, tourists and Londoners keen to pay their respects. At 8:30PM, a bugler sounds the Last Post. A two-minute silence follows, then finally, at 8:32PM – the exact moment the train arrived here – there is a presentation of wreaths.

The ceremony of death and remembrance goes on.

People need to remember. They need to acknowledge sacrifice and loss – personal, national and international. Just like the silent crowds who lined the streets of Wootton Bassett, and like the crowds who waited here at Victoria Station in 1920, hoping for a glimpse of their missing loved one.

CHAPTER ELEVEN

DAWN AT LAST

VICTORIA STATION, LONDON
11 NOVEMBER 1920, 6:40AM

As dawn broke over London, the two weary Grenadier Guardsmen stood steady on Victoria Station's platform 8. The pale glow creeping through the vast canopy above their heads offered the first inkling that their vigil was almost at an end.

Three miles away in south-east London, it had also been a long night for 8-year-old Donald Overall and his little brother Cecil, snuggled in their shared bed. Their mum was determined to find a good spot on the pavement close to the Cenotaph when the barricades were opened to a limited number of the public at 8:15AM. The two boys had barely slept. Now, with the foggy streets slowly brightening, they were rushing, with a tide of other Londoners, towards the centre of town.[1] There was an air of hushed anticipation, even reverence, as the crowds hurried along the Embankment that frosty morning. 'Streams of women of all ages and conditions in deep mourning and in working dress, but nearly all with a floral tribute to the one Unknown,' was how one reporter saw it.[2]

It was a gilt-edged business opportunity for the flower stalls at Covent Garden market. And, dispensing with their usual apples and cabbages, the costermongers were also arriving, barrows loaded with white chrysanthemums, purple violets and green laurel leaves for those who had come unprepared. The war's survivors – the 'lucky ones', as the newspapers liked to call them[3] – were lining the pavements too, determined to honour their dead comrade. To remember the pals they last saw enjoying a mug of tea in a trench, or face down at the bottom of a shell hole at High Wood. They wore an eclectic mix of clothing, from full dress uniform to labourer's corduroys, ribbons and medals pinned to their chest.[4]

Donald didn't really understand where they were going. All he knew was that his dad had been killed in France in 1917 and his mum hadn't been the same since. He missed his dad badly, so when she said they had to get ready for him, his heart fluttered just as vigorously as it had done on the rare occasions he saw him. 'I was five when he came home on leave,' he recalled. 'He sat me on the instep of his foot and I used to hold his hands and he would rock me up and down. He was in his army uniform and I remember my father carrying me upstairs on his left shoulder. My head was against his face, and I can remember seeing his ears and smelling his jacket and tobacco.'

It was the last time he would ever see him. Just like the day Nikki Scott watched two men get out of their car and knew that the worst had happened to her husband in Afghanistan, Donald would never forget the moment his childhood came to an abrupt end.

'I remember the day very distinctly,' he said. 'We lived in a flat just off the Old Kent Road. Mother and I were downstairs when the doorbell rang, I was hiding behind her as she was handed an envelope. She opened the letter at once. I didn't know what it said, but she screamed. Then she collapsed on the floor. I tried to wake her up; I didn't know what was wrong. I was holding onto her skirts, I called out for help and an elderly couple who lived in a lower flat came out and comforted both of us. Mother came round slowly and they eventually got her upstairs into the bedroom. She was there for about ten days and it was while she was getting better that she turned onto her side and said to me, "Your father's dead, he won't come back. Now you are the man of the house, you must do things as best you can." I was five years old.'

Donald was the same age as Nikki Scott's son Kai had been when his dad was killed in 2009. In the aftermath of the tragedy, Nikki set up a charity, Scotty's Little Soldiers, to support bereaved military children. But there was no help for Donald in 1920; he just had to get on with it. 'That changed my life; it had to,' he said. 'I'd look after my brother and I'd look after my mother. I accepted it all. Obviously I lost my childhood. But I never felt I had, because I had to look after my family. And I felt 10 feet tall.' Now, with Donald in the lead, they were nearing the end of their hour-long walk to Whitehall. As they reached the Embankment, the faint glow in the sky was growing and at last, after an hour and a half huddled together for warmth among the crowds, a policeman nodded them through a gap in the great, diamond-shaped wooden barricades. They were in.

It was a perfect late-autumn day. Dry leaves rustled in the gutters and in the first rays of sunlight the Cenotaph was still shrouded in its two vast Union Jacks, and a thin veil of mist. In the streets around Westminster Abbey, the pedestrians, many of them clad in mourning black, whispered to each other as if they were already in church. The smoke from London's thousands of chimneys rose straight up into the blue mist, past the few flags which hung limply at half-mast. 'There seemed something appropriate in the utter stillness of the air,' declared *The Times*. 'The Unknown Warrior, in his daydreams in France, may have pictured his homecoming to himself, fancying how England would look on the day that he came back to it. If he did so – and who did not? – he never could have imagined a more lovely English day than the day of his homecoming. If he was a Londoner, he could not have wished to see his city looking more beautiful.'[5]

* * *

In Grosvenor Gardens and Buckingham Palace Road, the crowds had begun to form outside the tall iron gates of Victoria Station, and by 8AM, in the echoing concourse itself, hundreds of soldiers and veterans had started to arrive, ready to be registered and ranked for the great procession. In nearby Chelsea Barracks, an exalted honour guard of almost 100 holders of the Victoria Cross and other awards for bravery – perhaps the greatest parade of living war heroes ever assembled – was also gathering.[6] Lining up on the parade ground in a mix of uniform and civvies, they would be heading straight for Westminster Abbey, arriving an hour before the two-minute silence at the Cenotaph was due to take place. By the King's wish, the VCs and their ilk would be organised according to their height and not their rank, so there was a considerable amount of standing on tiptoes and craning of necks as a pecking order was established. The official instructions stated that, 'Service dress is to be worn by all who have it in their possession, but plain clothes may be worn by demobilised officers and other ranks who have no uniform. Medals and decorations will be worn. All officers will wear crepe mourning bands.'[7]

The buzz of muted anticipation spread across Victoria Station as the adjutants checked in the troops. Servicemen from all over Britain mingled, muttered and wondered aloud if they might once have served together at Passchendaele or Arras or that godforsaken High Wood back in September 1916. *You knew Jack too? Yes, he was quite a character, wasn't he?*

There would be nearly 1,500 men of all ranks on parade, as the comprehensive orders for the Coldstream Guards in 1920 reveal:

A Funeral Procession will be formed at Victoria Station on the morning of November 11th and will conduct the Coffin in slow time by way of Grosvenor Gardens, Grosvenor Place, Wellington Arch, Constitution Hill, The Mall, Admiralty Arch, Charing Cross to the Cenotaph in Whitehall. Length of route – 3,960 yards (2¼ miles).

The Procession will be formed by:

1. Firing Party – 1 Serjeant, 1 Corporal and 12 Guardsmen of 3rd Battalion Coldstream Guards.

2. Gun Carriage with a team of 6 horses, together with 3 Limber Gunners on foot, will be furnished by 'N' Battery Royal Horse Artillery.

3. Bearers – 1 Serjeant and 8 Guardsmen of 3rd Battalion Coldstream Guards.

4. Pall Bearers – 12 Distinguished Officers of the Royal Navy, Army and Royal Air Force.

5. The Massed Bands, Pipes and Drums. The Band and Drums of the Coldstream, Scots, Irish and Welsh Guards, the Pipes of the Scots Guards – total of 4 Officers and 209 other ranks including 1 Director of Music and 1 Serjeant Drummer of each of the 4 regiments.

6. The Mourners
Royal Navy – 76 Officers, 150 other ranks
Army – 174 Officers, 307 other ranks
Royal Air Force – 31 Officers, 60 other ranks

7. Representatives of various ex-servicemen's organisations – 400 in total.[8]

The main body of troops was to form up with a private, a sergeant or corporal and an officer representing a different regiment, ship or squadron in every row.[9] So three men from the Cheshire Regiment were to stand alongside three from the Royal Welch Fusiliers, with three from the South Wales Borderers and three from the King's Own Scottish Borderers lined up behind them. Behind these would come three from the Royal Inniskilling Fusiliers and three from the Scottish Rifles. On – and on – it went with endless military units. The procession was essentially a map of loss.

The architect of the day's events, Lord Curzon, had decided it was to be nothing like the grand Victory Parade of 1919 that he had also co-ordinated. It was a funeral, not a celebration. 'The ceremony of bringing into the Abbey an unknown soldier, whose remains should be borne in honour through London, and then interred in the Nave,' Curzon had said to his colleagues, while outlining his plans for the occasion, 'had not merely its emotional, sentimental and dramatic aspect, but would offer a worthy and highly esteemed tribute to those who fell in the war, and strike a chord of deep feeling in the hearts of the nation.'[10]

Instead of a grand march-past bristling with power and discipline, *this* military parade was to be a more sombre occasion, its tone reflecting that vast absence which stretched the length and breadth of the country.

And, in the crowds, there would be many hoping for a glimpse of *their* regiment's distinctive cap badges and insignia, as a remembrance of dad, or some long-suffering husband or darling boy. Almost every regiment was represented, including – in the rear – the Indian Army, along with men from Canada, Australia, New Zealand, South Africa and even three of the few Newfoundlanders who had survived the massacre at Beaumont-Hamel on the first day of the Battle of the Somme in 1916.

Having attended similar parades myself, I could imagine that each of them would have been unable to resist stealing a surreptitious glance at the white-roofed wagon standing at platform 8. Here was their comrade, back in Blighty at last. I suspect some also wondered, as so many of us who have seen death in battle do, 'How come *he* is the poor blighter lying there in a box, and not *me*?' The soldiers must have exchanged glances, too, at the rare, close-up view of some of the great Generals and Field Marshals – Earl Haig, Earl Beatty, Viscount French, Air Marshal Sir Hugh Trenchard and others – arriving with their batmen. These distant, exalted beings, their faces familiar from the newspapers, would act as the Unknown Warrior's twelve honorary pallbearers, even though in life they were personages 'so great, so far above him, that when he was alive they were like figures in mythology to him'.[11] Although officially described as 'pallbearers', the role of the '12 Great Men', as many newspaper articles referred to them, would be purely ceremonial, limited to marching on either side of the Warrior's gun carriage in the procession. A team of highly trained Guardsmen – the bearer party – would do the actual lifting and carrying of the cumbersome zinc-lined coffin. 'It was a bit like the war,' one or two soldiers might have muttered drily.

The press did not report whether Lord Curzon was at Victoria to see his great procession beginning to pull itself together, but he had been there the night before to witness the Unknown Warrior's coffin arrive. Perhaps this was enough for the brilliant organiser, moonlighting from his day job as Foreign Secretary. It is to the lasting credit of the statesman, often mocked for his pomposity and tendency to grandiosity, not just that he devised an event that displayed a common touch and captured a deeply felt mood, but that at this moment, when the story was all about an unknown dead soldier – a humble Tommy, a heroic nobody – Curzon himself had the grace and wisdom to fade into the background.[12]

Bathed in the milky light filtering through the station's soot-coated glass roof, it must have been an other-worldly scene. How different this send-off must have felt to the uniformed participants compared with the excitement at Victoria witnessed by one London restaurant owner in 1915 when soldiers were heading out to the Western Front, even though some of the men 'hardly dared to look' at the brave women waving them off. 'I never saw such a sight as it was when the khaki arms were waving out of the windows,' he recalled, 'to those dear ones who were left standing on the platform as long as the train was in sight.'[13] Now, on 11 November 1920, many of those same 'dear ones' may have been standing again, just outside the station, waiting for 'their man' to be gently carried from his homecoming train.

* * *

The key roles of the Unknown Warrior's bearer party and firing party had been bestowed upon the 3rd Battalion of the Coldstream Guards. The bearer party would carry his coffin onto the gun carriage and, later that morning, into Westminster Abbey. The ceremonial firing party, carrying rifles at the head of the procession, would normally fire a volley of shots into the air over the grave, though that wouldn't be happening in Westminster Abbey today.[14]

All of the men involved had seen action during the war.

Guardsman Jimmy Dunn from Clitheroe was wearing the Albert Medal for 'conspicuous bravery' attached by its red-and-white-striped ribbon. He had been decorated in 1918 for rescuing – despite the risk of imminent explosion – several men trapped beneath a burning ammunition train. His brothers had not been so lucky. One had been gassed in the trenches and later discharged from the army with shell shock. The youngest, 18-year-old Freddy, had been killed in action just before the end of the war, his body never recovered. Freddy is still one of the missing, his name etched on the Thiepval Memorial.[15] Jimmy's mind must have been churning as he watched his fellow Coldstream Guardsmen form up in front of the white-roofed luggage wagon. If poor young Freddy's body was anywhere, might it not be lying in there?

Trusted to lead the bearer party beneath the gaze of history was Sergeant Harry Ivey. Like Jimmy, Harry was also wearing an award for gallantry: the Distinguished Conduct Medal, one of the highest awards for courage in the face of the enemy. He, too, had fought alongside his own brother in France. But the Ivey boys were among the 'lucky ones'. They had both come home, albeit with wounds to show for their service. Harry had won his exalted place on platform 8 the hard way, having fought through almost the entire war, beginning with the retreat from Mons in 1914, and only ending when he was wounded near Ypres in October 1917.[16] He had even been at the dreaded village of Ginchy – or at least the rubble it had become – close to High Wood, on 15 September 1916. The fateful day when tanks went into battle for the first time, when Anthony French's friend Bert Bradley was shot dead, never to be seen again. The same day the Prime Minister's son, Raymond Asquith, had been killed, and the day before humble Harry Farlam, still waiting for his notebook from home, would also lose his life.

So many men lost. So many bodies missing. So many Unknown Warriors created.

Harry Ivey had been there, pinned down by shellfire and machine guns. Seeing that his company's officers had all been killed or wounded, he 'sprang forward and led the unit's attack with the greatest coolness and bravery',[17] for which he had been awarded the Distinguished Conduct Medal, now pinned to his chest on its distinctive crimson ribbon with a dark blue central stripe. Under Harry's supervision, the bearer party was about to enter the Cavell Van with the symbolic items Lord Curzon had selected for the Unknown Warrior's coffin: a steel helmet, and a set of webbing soldiers had worn for carrying ammunition, rations and rifle-cleaning kit into battle.[18] Perhaps they were also armed with Padre Railton's hallowed Union Jack.[19]

Harry took a deep breath, then the silence was split with his barked command.

VICTORIA STATION
9:15AM

The jingle of harnesses and the hollow clop of hooves announced that 'N' Battery of the Royal Horse Artillery had arrived in the concourse.[20] A gleaming gun carriage, drawn by six gloss-black warhorses, turned a wide half-circle and rumbled into its allotted space alongside the Cavell Van. As it did so, the massed bands of the Guards Division took up their positions just inside the station entrance. At the same time, the troops of the bearer party would have been reverently unfolding Railton's flag and spreading it over the coffin in the shadows of the van, then mounting the webbing and helmet.

At Wootton Bassett, almost a century later, PC Jarra Brown would comment on the way the Union Jacks were folded around the coffins repatriated from Afghanistan as neatly and tightly as wrapping paper. But this was the Padre's Flag: a historic artefact, imbued with the blood of sacrifice. So it was to be draped like a precious counterpane upon the bed of a king, not crisply tucked in, like a bedsheet ready for a barracks inspection.

It must have been quite something for the young soldiers to come face to face at last with the medieval-style coffin, banded with strips of wrought iron, its ceremonial sword and shield bolted to the lid.

* * *

King George's sword? When the Unknown Warrior's coffin was first paraded at Boulogne, the newspapers had announced that the sword had been presented by the King himself, some adding that it had been personally selected from his private collection, 'a gift from a soldier to a soldier'.[21] The story of that 'King's sword' has become the accepted version over the years. When the Royal Armouries Museum was contacted for further information about the 'sixteenth-century crusader-type sword' that George V donated, I was surprised to learn that the King himself, apparently, had nothing to do with it.

On 29 October 1920, Charles ffoulkes,[22] a medieval expert and Curator of the Armouries at the Tower of London, had written to the Office of Works, presumably having already sent over a selection of symbolic weaponry which he was proposing might be used for the Unknown Warrior's casket:

1. I sincerely trust that the rifle and bayonet will be used on the coffin of the 'Unknown Soldier', either as part of the integral design, or placed on the Union Jack. I certainly think that on sentimental grounds it should be buried with the coffin.
2. If it is definitely decided that a cross-hilted sword must be used, *I am sending you two swords of my own, of modern make. The one with the brass hilt I made myself, many years ago.*[23]

    My only stipulation would be that their origin should be kept confidential, and no notice of them sent to the press. As I understand that the coffin is the gift of a trade organisation, I think HM Government might accept the sword as from the successor to the Armourers of the Tower.[24]

The coffin of the Unknown Warrior is carried out of
Boulogne Castle, ready to begin the journey home.

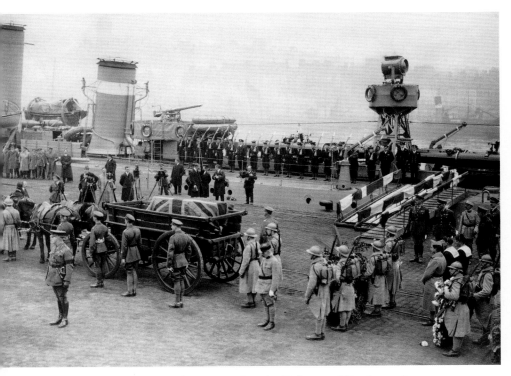

The procession and cart carrying the Unknown Warrior arrives
at Boulogne harbour alongside HMS *Verdun*.

The Unknown Warrior's coffin can be seen in the carriage after its arrival at Victoria Station on 10 November 1920.

Dean Herbert Ryle (standing centre, bearded) looks on as the Unknown Warrior's grave is dug in Westminster Abbey in November 1920.

Corporal Lee Scott with wife Nikki and children Kai and Brooke during a family holiday at Disneyland in April 2009. Lee would be killed in Afghanistan just a few months later.

Nikki Scott with some of the bereaved military children her charity, Scotty's Little Soldiers – set up after the death of her husband Lee – supports. They are waiting on Horse Guards Parade before taking part in the annual Service of Remembrance at the Cenotaph in 2023.

Crowds wait at the Cenotaph, still shrouded in the Union Jacks, after the arrival of the Unknown Warrior's procession in November 1920.

Donald Overall, aged five, with his brother Cecil at the time of his father's death in 1917, when he was told he was now the man of the house. Donald and Cecil would witness the unveiling of the Cenotaph with their mother in 1920.

Donald finally manages to visit his father's grave in 2007, ninety years after his death.

John Nichol at the Beaumont-Hamel memorial site. A party of visiting schoolchildren can be seen walking through the trench system towards the Newfoundland memorial.

Swede and Hannah Williams at the Tomb of the Unknown Warrior in 2020, at the end of their journey to commemorate the centenary of the burial.

The Unknown Warrior's procession arrives at Westminster Abbey in preparation for the burial on 11 November 1920.

John Nichol with Garrison Sergeant Major Andrew 'Vern' Stokes in his office on Horse Guards Parade. Stokes is responsible for the planning and delivery of all state ceremonial events.

GSM Stokes leads the royal family during the late Queen's funeral in 2022.

The King places his wreath on the Unknown Warrior's coffin
during the Cenotaph unveiling ceremony.

Crowds file past the Unknown Warrior's grave in November 1920.
The Padre's Flag can be seen resting on top of the Actors' Pall.

The Padre's Flag, which Reverend David Railton had used throughout the First World War, is paraded over the Tomb of the Unknown Warrior during the centenary service in 2020.

To his disappointment, ffoulkes's rifle was rejected. Although one can certainly see the logic of his proposal, perhaps the weapon was deemed to be too obvious a sign of the Warrior's role as a killer of men. An official at the Office of Works had replied, 'I do not think that the inclusion of a rifle and bayonet on the coffin of the Unknown Soldier will be possible, but I certainly think that the sword with the longer blade of the two which you kindly submitted to me is admirably suited to place on the coffin. I accept this gift from you on behalf of His Majesty's Government, and on the conditions stipulated by you, with deep gratitude and thanks, and I will take the earliest opportunity to inform Lord Curzon and the Cabinet Committee over which he presides, of your kind assistance and generosity in this particular question.'

A member of the Worshipful Company of Armourers and Brasiers, Mr ffoulkes clearly took great pride in his skills as a metalsmith. His homemade sword, 'single handed, possibly double-edged, with hollow ground fuller, slightly upturned flattened and flared quillons, barrelled handle, and with what is probably an ovular pommel with a tang button', clearly passed muster with the authorities.[25] It seems that it was this sword that DJ Williams of Caernarfon had bolted to the Unknown Warrior's coffin.

It was perhaps ffoulkes's modest request for confidentiality, and – just possibly – the press's desire to embellish a story, which meant that this fact took years to establish, even though he had written to Dean Ryle at Westminster Abbey at some point – presumably including the previous correspondence or photographs of the swords – clarifying that they had actually come from him. Clearly dismayed that the newspapers had been incorrectly describing them as from the 'King's personal collection', apparently without any official correction, ffoulkes had noted: 'My only reason for sending them to you is that should any question arise as to the date and workmanship of the sword in after years, your records may have the true facts. You will see that I pressed very strongly for the rifle and bayonet to be placed in the Coffin but the Cabinet decided otherwise and accepted the Sword, the hilt of which was made by myself as

curator of the armouries in the Tower of London and Freeman of
the Company of Armourers and Brasiers.'[26] The photograph of the
two swords, shot by Horace Nicholls – the war-bereaved photographer who had taken the atmospheric pictures of the empty coffin
in the abbey with undertakers Nodes and Sowerbutts – remains
in the keeping of the Imperial War Museum.[27] What happened to
ffoulkes's second sword remains a mystery.

VICTORIA STATION
9:20AM

Harry Ivey's pulse must have been racing as the bearer party
dressed the coffin. They placed the steel helmet above the spot
where the Warrior's head might lie. Next, the webbing belt
was spread around his imaginary waist, with a bayonet in its
scabbard pointing towards his toes. Then, he and his comrades
hoisted the heavy coffin onto their shoulders and carried it from
the Cavell Van, 'their feet moving', according to one eyewitness,
'with the unanimous shuffle of a many-legged insect'.[28] Turning
to face inwards, they slid it gently onto the raised platform of the
gun carriage from which the first British shot of the First World
War had been fired. Eight years later, it would be used for Earl
Haig's funeral.[29] A bearer party from Queen's Company, 1st
Battalion Grenadier Guards, flown home from operational duty
in Iraq, would perform an almost identical ritual during Queen
Elizabeth II's funeral in 2022.

A mile or so north, pungent white smoke billowed across Hyde
Park to mingle with the lifting fog as nineteen guns from 'N' Battery
of the Royal Horse Artillery let loose the first salvo of a thunder-
ous barrage in honour of the dead hero. Such a salute was usually
reserved for the death of a grand Field Marshal, not some soldier
nobody knew. But the day was to be remembered for a hundred
years, and more. 'There has never been another funeral on this
scale,' says the writer and historian, Neil Hanson. 'The great
state funerals of Queen Victoria and Winston Churchill and the

public outpouring of grief for Princess Diana don't even begin to compare.'[30]

Alongside platform 8, the bearer party took a step back and slowly marched to their position at the rear of the bier. The light was becoming more dazzling now and the polished steel and brass of the carriage and its traces shone like burnished gold. In the yawning space around the empty station, the vast bodyguard, representing innumerable regiments, ships and squadrons of the Armed Forces, was arranging itself in two great, serpentine columns. They assembled on each side of the concourse in their half-ranks of three, leaving space between them for the gun carriage and bearer party to advance. By 9:20AM, the Royal Air Force was in place.[31] The Army had formed up by 9:23AM, with the Royal Navy joining the procession at 9:25AM. By the time they had all formed up, the massed ranks stretched the whole length of the platforms and back again.[32]

Into the silent concourse, the '12 Great Men' of the army, navy and air force now emerged from the first-class saloon to take their places on either side of the gun carriage. Like all officers on the day, each wore a black band on his left arm. 'It would have been a fine thing if a Private had been allowed to walk with them, too,' noted the *Guardian* coldly.[33] But here was Field Marshal Earl Haig alongside General Lord Byng, the popular commander who had brilliantly led the Canadians to victory at Vimy Ridge in 1917. Admiral of the Fleet Earl Beatty strode a few paces behind them. The diminutive figure of Viscount French, who had been in charge of the army prior to Haig, was among the last to take his place, in the penultimate spot on the left-hand side.[34] 'Then a sharp command,' recorded the *Daily Telegraph*, 'and simultaneously everyone was presenting arms. In that one moment, I realised more than words can tell, the tremendous significance of that very simple coffin.'[35]

On the station's platform, sprinkled with sand to avoid both boots and metal hooves slipping, the parade readied itself, and, at the barked order to 'slow-march', stepped forward as one to the fearsome roll of muffled drums. Raising their cold instruments to their lips, the wind and brass players launched into the sombre opening of Chopin's *marche funèbre* as the sleek, well-drilled horses moved slowly towards the station's western arch.

From the far sides of the concourse, lined up at the very back of the procession – behind the massed bands, behind the gun carriage and pallbearers, behind the neatly serried bodyguard of the Armed Forces – advanced another group of 400 men. If they looked almost like an afterthought, it is because that is exactly what they were.

The original plan for the ceremony had not included any veterans. But following a strenuous request from the four main ex-servicemen's clubs, not to mention a suggestion of civil unrest if they were excluded,[36] 'Top-hatted, pot-hatted men, some in soft hats, some in caps, some tall, some short, some maimed, some sturdy, some pale and ill, some with many ribbons on their coats, some with only a badge,' as one eyewitness described them, were integrated into the proceedings. It was important to make these discharged soldiers visible as they tried to scrape by in the harsh conditions of post-war Britain. 'In different ways – in dislocated lives, in shell-shock and injuries, in nerve-strain and lost opportunities – they, too, have paid. They offered their lives; other things were taken from them instead.'[37]

HORSE GUARDS PARADE, LONDON
SEPTEMBER 2023

The detail of the day's organisation appears to have been mindbog-gling in its complexity. An official statement declared that it would take fully twenty minutes for the procession, proceeding at slow march, just to clear the station platform.[38] In an attempt to under-stand the logistical challenge of such a grand ceremonial event, I visit an old friend, Garrison Sergeant Major Andrew 'Vern' Stokes.

A Coldstream Guardsman since the age of sixteen, Vern is responsible for the planning and delivery of all state ceremonial events. He played the leading role in designing and running the funeral arrangements for both HM the Queen and the Duke of

Edinburgh, and organised Her Majesty's Platinum Jubilee. His remit also includes the annual Trooping the Colour and the Festival of Remembrance – grand state occasions which have drawn plaudits from around the world for their combination of dazzling precision, emotive power and sense of profound significance.

'You have to keep a complete overview of the event,' he tells me, when I ask how it's done, 'from the smallest detail of where a single Guardsman might stand, all the way to the great logistical issues of how you transport and house maybe five or six thousand troops so that they can all be ready for the start of a parade when arriving from countless different locations.'[39] Sitting in the Garrison Sergeant Major's office, which looks out over Horse Guards parade ground near the Cenotaph, we can hear the rhythmic crunch of military boots on gravel. On the wall, alongside a photograph of Vern with Her Majesty the Queen, are images from his thirty-five-year military service in Northern Ireland, Iraq and Afghanistan, as well as countless ceremonial occasions featuring kings, queens and presidents from around the world. His glossy bearskin hangs from a hatstand, with his ceremonial sword glittering beneath.

As an example of how challenging great state parades can be, he talks about the complex business of the Queen's funeral in 2022, not least the task of extracting 3,000 troops from Wellington Barracks, next door to Buckingham Palace, for the procession. 'With just one narrow exit point, you could only have a frontage of a column three personnel wide. It presented a serious logistical issue to get thousands of people through the gap and required second-by-second planning.'

I am beginning to think that getting the Unknown Warrior's funeral parade out of the concourse at Victoria and onto Buckingham Palace Road must have presented a similar challenge. Vern nods. 'Most importantly, once the plan is executed, once those 3,000 troops start marching off, it's like a long train, and it simply isn't going to stop. It *has* to keep moving, regardless of what happens along the route.' Organising grand ceremonial events is, clearly, a

demanding and stressful business, and one that requires a combination of meticulous attention to detail and exceptional foresight.
Fortunately, such pressure does have its rewards. 'Her Majesty's
funeral and the ceremonials surrounding it clearly galvanised the
nation,' says Vern, echoing the sentiments of 1920. 'The common
theme is pride. Pride in Her Majesty's life and her legacy; pride in
our Armed Forces and the role they played; pride, above all, in the
feeling of what it is to be British. Her Majesty's funeral seems to
have ignited a renewed sense of patriotism for so many people.'

We watch the grainy newsreel footage of the Unknown Warrior's
funeral procession. As one might expect, the Garrison Sergeant
Major has studied it many times. 'Most of the decisions I have to
take are based on precedents and experiences from previous parades
and events,' he explains. 'I examine old documents and orders,
along with ancient Pathé news clips, to see how events were planned
and unfolded many years ago. I am lucky to have that great heritage
of experience from my predecessors on which to build.'

So what does he think of the funeral procession on the day, back
in 1920? Was there anything remarkable about it, apart from the
presence of the Unknown Warrior himself? 'When I watch that old
black-and-white film and look back to 1920, it's difficult for me to
comprehend how they managed to put such a large and incredibly
complex procession like that together in a matter of weeks,' he says,
shaking his head. 'The parade from Victoria Station, all the way
round Hyde Park Corner, Constitution Hill and The Mall, and
then stopping and regrouping for the unveiling of the Cenotaph,
before moving on to Westminster Abbey: all this was a *massive*
logistical feat. It must have taken incredible forensic planning and
preparation.' Coming from a soldier with a fearsome – even ruthless – attention to detail, it is an enlightening point. On the other
hand, Vern is perhaps more aware than many of how Britain – and
the military – have changed over the century or more that separates
those two events. It was, as he reminds me, a very different environment back then. 'The military operated in a totally different way
with a *very* different mindset,' he says. 'We had an army which,

although it had recently gone through an almost unimaginable campaign of death, destruction and suffering, were used to carrying out orders. Without question.'

We both smile. In the ten years I have known him, 'the Garrison', as he is referred to by most, has never shied from voicing his spiky criticism of my lax, RAF-style drill at various veterans' events. 'A lot of the troops on parade that day must have been battle-hardened and almost certainly *not* used to being involved in large ceremonial occasions,' he says. 'But, again, I think that the environment of the time – and the fact that many of them had fought together in battle, shoulder to shoulder – must have meant that they could more easily come together to deliver such an impressive and complex parade. There was a sense of honour, too: that they were doing all this, not for King and country, but for their dead comrade; for the Unknown Warrior. For the countless friends they had lost.'

I nod, we have both lost friends in war. And I well remember sitting alongside Vern during rehearsals for the Royal British Legion's Festival of Remembrance at the Royal Albert Hall the previous year. 'You and I both watched Mary Fowler trying to read the words from her father's last letter to her, before he was lost on HMS *Coventry*,' he reminds me. 'Mary's struggle with her emotions – that personal battle to read her beloved father's words in front of a vast audience – spoke to me so much about sacrifice and loss.' We both think about this for a while. 'Her father has been absent from most of her life,' he continues quietly. 'And she has no grave to visit; nowhere to commemorate his loss; no place to say goodbye. It brings everything into sharp focus, doesn't it, John?'

It does. And I was pleased that Vern didn't appear to have noticed the tears running down my face as we witnessed Mary's struggle. Or if he had, he was kind enough not to say. Outside on the parade ground, the soldiers are still marching. We – and they – are more than aware that, while training for future ceremonials, they are also fully prepared for future wars, from which some of them may not return.

Buckingham Palace Road, London
11 November 1920, 9:40am

A ripple of emotion passed through the crowds waiting outside
Victoria Station when the first slow double-thumps of the great
bass drums, their skins muffled with black felt, punched through
the stillness of the November air. Then came the bleak, repetitive
harmonies of Chopin's searing funeral march evoking images of
war-weary soldiers foot-slogging over duckboards close to Ypres.

Elsewhere across London, no fewer than 35,000 soldiers and
policemen had been called up for duty. Four police officers on
horseback, tasked with making sure the route was clear, advanced,
and behind them, from the western arch of the station, marched the
procession 'into the kindly sunshine of a mellow day'.[40] The great
train had been set in motion. There would be no stopping it now,
as it rumbled, crunched and trumpeted its way towards the King,
the Cenotaph, and eternity.

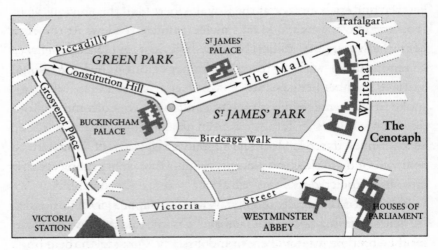

UNKNOWN WARRIOR PARADE ROUTE, 11 NOVEMBER 1920

For the tens of thousands of people who had failed to squeeze
into Whitehall before the barricades were shut, the procession's
2-mile zigzag route to the Cenotaph was now their one and only

chance to see the Unknown Warrior before he was lowered into his grave. 'This is the occasion for the ticketless multitude to pay its tribute,' declared the *Guardian*.[41] The crowds had come from across the land – England, Scotland, Wales and Ireland, and from every other country in the Empire. And from the Allied nations too; from Belgium, France and the United States. It had truly been a world war, with worldwide repercussions. 'He's a Knight of the Empire,' declared one American onlooker as the great cavalcade approached.[42] The German ambassador, Herr Sthamer, and his wife discreetly watched the parade from the terrace of the German embassy overlooking The Mall.[43]

Meanwhile, Admiral Lord Beatty, the First Sea Lord, had generously offered the windows of his offices in the Admiralty buildings to relatives of the dead of the 'Lower Deck', an informal, representative organisation formed by naval ratings to protest against harsh discipline and low pay.[44] The Lower Deck had gained considerable influence in 1920, so it was magnanimous of Beatty to recognise its sacrifices in such a way.[45]

Of course not everyone had such a privileged view. At the back of the crowds, many utilised old trench periscopes – previously used to spot snipers, without the risk of a bullet through the skull – to watch the cavalcade pass by.

And there were some, too, who could not bear to come at all.

In a deprived street in Hornsey, 6 miles to the north of Whitehall, 5-year-old George Musgrave was peering down from a grubby upstairs window, wondering why so many people were dressed in black today. George still didn't really understand what had happened to his dad. 'When he was wounded at Cambrai in 1917, my father wrote to my mother, sending his fondest love and kisses "to you and the dear boy". Mother went to see him,' he recalled. It had been a terrible journey, she told her son. Louisa had travelled to the hospital at Rouen with a pass and a ticket supplied by the War Office. 'It was herself and another woman who went from Newhaven, and they crossed in rough seas. She could hardly talk about what she saw going into the hospital, but she told me that the men were crying out seeing an English woman, a civilian, who wasn't staff. I suppose it was a little bit of home, but she found it harrowing. Dad had gangrene by then and he'd lost fingers as well as having serious problems with his legs. He was still alive when she saw him. I don't know if my dad understood the seriousness of his condition.'[46]

When her husband died a few days later, George's mother received a letter from the War Office, sending the remainder of his possessions. 'They came in a little brown paper parcel and included his gold watch, the chain of which was hanging out of the brown paper,' said George, looking back. 'It had come through the post and nobody had stolen it. That was a vivid memory she had.' But George had been just two years old when his father died and he had no memory of him. All he had was a sketch of a train that he had drawn for him in the trenches, lovingly inscribed, 'To little George for his birthday, from Daddy.' It meant everything. 'The one tangible thing I had from my father was this picture; this train that he drew for me while he was under fire.'

Today, for Armistice Day, George's mother had dressed in black – as she had the previous year – and was wearing her husband's medals. But there was no question of going out. She had internalised her pain and loss. George had learned to do the same. 'I didn't want other children to know my difficulties, and for that reason I went into my shell,' he said. 'I didn't want to be seen. I didn't feel I had anyone to talk to, so I had to fend for myself.' Shell-shocked by the cards fate had dealt them, George and his mother stayed in their little Hornsey garret. Sitting in silence, they waited for eleven o'clock.

For those who had made it into the centre of town for the procession, the *Daily Mirror* helpfully published the anticipated schedule, which resembled a railway timetable:

Victoria Station	9:40AM
Grosvenor Place	9:45AM
Hyde Park Corner	10:00AM
Wellington Arch	10:05AM

Constitution Hill	10:10 AM
The Mall	10:20 AM
Admiralty Arch	10:30 AM
Whitehall	10:35 AM
Parliament Street (The Cenotaph)	10:45 AM

GROSVENOR PLACE, LONDON
9:45 AM

The parade passed into Grosvenor Place between the vast crowds crammed onto the pavements. In their wake came the firing party, the silver and brass of the massed bands, the pipers and then the thudding drums. The Unknown Warrior himself, high on his gun carriage drawn by six black horses, followed by the '12 Great Men' marching in two columns of six on either side. Then Harry Ivey and his bearer party. The 800-strong bodyguard of 'mourners', all ranks from the army, Royal Navy and Royal Air Force, marching in lines of six abreast, followed. Then the 400 veterans, some in uniform, some in mufti, some on crutches, all of them heroes. It was quite a sight.

As were the crowds on the pavements and roofs and hanging out of windows, colonising every inch of space. Some sobbed, hoping that today might help to make the hurt go away. 'Who is it who lies there under the flag, with Field Marshals and Admirals for his pallbearers?' demanded one eyewitness, speaking for many. 'Each member of this huge, quiet crowd gives him a name, each a different face. He is husband, lover, brother, son to each, and many a woman here would give all her income from dreamland for a touch of his hand on her cheek.'[47] At Hyde Park Corner the numbers were even greater. The silent masses peered across the wide empty avenue sprinkled with sand and lined with troops. Their silence was broken only by the muted cries of the programme sellers, and the mounted police marshalling the crowd.[48] So many people were wearing black that, in spite of the watery sunshine, the entire parade route gave a strange impression of darkness, like an old oil painting covered in varnish.

Despite the hush, they were probably all too far away to register the great crash that suddenly echoed across Westminster Bridge around 10AM. One of the giant cranes perched on the top of the new City Hall being built for London City Council had toppled over without warning. 'The fall created a noise like a gun,' said one witness, 'and one of the spectators on Westminster Bridge (a woman) fell in a dead faint.'[49]

THE MALL, LONDON
10:20AM

'Golden rays of an autumn sun filtered through the treetops in the Mall,' noted the *Sunday People*, 'and gilded the shrapnel helmet lying on the coffin.'[50] What a sight it was; simple, sombre, serene.

In 1920, the road surface of The Mall was black, not the ceremonial red of today, but fringing it on either side towered the same great plane trees (leafless on that November day) that do so now. On the north side, near the Victoria Memorial, stood a fleet of charabancs – open motor coaches – containing blinded and wounded soldiers.[51] They may not have been able to see the procession, but in their mind's eye they could see their dead friends, clear as day. And they might not be able to salute – a number were missing their arms – but they would offer the appropriate greeting to the Unknown Warrior in their hearts.

He was one of them, and they were him.

As the distant throb of the drums approached, the first sections of troops lining the Buckingham Palace end of The Mall lifted their rifles, spun them upside down, and stood with their heads bowed. Then the waiting mourners heard the music of the massed bands. There was a wave of movement as each man and woman respectfully bared their head, despite the November chill.

For Coldstream Guardsman Jimmy Dunn, perhaps the silent beauty of London was too much for him.[52] Why wasn't his brother here to see all this? I can imagine Jimmy standing there, perhaps gritting his teeth, wondering why he was on parade and his missing brother was not. Did he try to block out the pomp and ceremony of the day, believing he didn't deserve to be alive to witness it? Trying *not* to picture the name carved on the monument at Thiepval. Trying *not* to think about his poor dear brother lying in the coffin on the gun carriage. Did his cheeks glisten as he waited?[53] 'It was as if his watching countrymen relaxed at last his hold upon their tears, as the Warrior was borne away to burial,' declared *The Times*. 'It was the simplest, but equally the most impressive, procession ever seen in London,' declared one Yorkshireman.[54] 'There were no trappings of state ceremonial; no panoply of gorgeous uniforms, nor cavalcade of horsemen richly clad. There were no waving flags or banners. No, the only flag in the long procession was the soiled and war-worn Union Jack which covered simply the unknown hero's coffin.'

Ahead, in Trafalgar Square, a whisper began to spread through the crowd of perhaps 50,000 people who had gathered there. *He is coming.*

And now the crowd sobbed in genuine grief, without shame or restraint.

'Behind the coffin was a long river of men that changed in colour from dark blue to turbid yellow and brown, and then to slate, and last of all was flecked with greys and blacks,' wrote *The Times*, describing the blue uniforms of the navy and the khaki of the army, the RAF in their grey-blue, followed by the veterans in their salt-and-pepper mix of uniforms and civvies.[55]

Perhaps the most impressive figures in the procession were those limping with walking sticks or holding the arms of comrades for support. But the crowd must have wondered why a young girl was marching among the veterans. Dressed as a gunner in the Royal Field Artillery, a row of war ribbons on her chest, she did so without a hat and in a uniform a few sizes too big for her. With her flaxen hair falling to her shoulders, they could see she was doing her very best to march in step, and to keep her head held high.[56]

It emerged in the newspapers the following day that she was 12-year-old Jennie Jackson from Burnley, where she had become known as 'Little Kitchener' after managing to raise £4,000 (an astonishing £175,000 in today's money) for war charities.[57] Wearing the uniform in memory of her brother William, killed in September 1917, Jennie had been regularly photographed alongside wounded soldiers and heroes.[58] One of her greatest achievements was raising the money to buy a motor ambulance, which she presented to Queen Alexandra. One small consolation was the fact that, after the war, she was able to visit her brother's grave in France, and to pose for a photograph beside the flower-strewn spot.[59]

Little Kitchener died in 1997, aged eighty-nine.

WHITEHALL, LONDON
10:35AM

Donald Overall, along with his mother and his younger brother Cecil, must have felt as if they had been waiting for hours. Thanks to his weaving a skilful path through the crowds, with only the very *slightest* bit of jostling and barging and treading on toes, they had managed to inveigle themselves close to the Cenotaph, standing almost opposite the ghostly monolith wrapped in its gigantic pair of Union Jacks.[60] This, despite the fact that the crowds, 'packed close and orderly, like slates on a roof', filled every inch of the pavement.[61] 'It was,' said *The Times,* 'a silent, strange, orderly crowd, chiefly composed of women in mourning, and one woman in every five or six carrying a great bunch or wreath or cross of white chrysanthemums in her arms.'[62]

There was little class distinction. 'The charwoman rubbed shoulders with the delicately nurtured lady of the West End mansion; the youthful hospital nurse with the pallid worker of the slums; the faded mothers from mean streets with prosperous suburban wives. All were brought together in bonds of sorrow and pride and sympathy.'[63] The waiting was almost over. Above the long ranks of soldiers and policemen, the hands of Big Ben's clock tower were climbing slowly towards 11AM.

Philip Gibbs, the celebrated war correspondent, must have been standing quite close to Donald Overall and his family, notebook in hand, witnessing the very same sights. 'The tower of Big Ben was dim through the mist like the tower of Albert Church until it fell into a heap of dust under the fury of gunfire,' he wrote. 'Presently the sun shone brighter, so that the picture of Whitehall was etched with deeper lines. On all the buildings, flags were flying at half-mast.'[64]

Gliding out from the Home Office, His Majesty the King appeared, dressed in the uniform of a Field Marshal. For young Donald, his mind teeming with images of his father, it was hard to take it all in. 'There was the normal hubbub,' is how he would remember those moments years later. But now that the King was here, it was the eerie silence that struck him. 'Even the wind in the trees made a noise,' he said. 'I remember that, as King George V stepped forward. Nobody dared move; nobody wanted to move.' The King stood in front of his three uniformed sons, looking down Whitehall towards Trafalgar Square. The King, apparently deep in thought, stared hard at the paving at his feet.

The Prime Minister was there too, along with the Archbishop of Canterbury, the Bishop of London, and dignitaries from all over the Empire, including multiple maharajahs and a white-bearded old man in a matching turban, whose face reminded Philip Gibbs of an Eastern prophet.[65] The King glanced at his watch. The man Queen Elizabeth II used to lovingly call 'Grandpa England' was fastidious about punctuality. So concerned with being on time, he had all the clocks in his royal residences set forward, so that no one was ever late.[66]

At last the dark shape of the procession loomed out of the haze, coming down Whitehall from Trafalgar Square. The King allowed himself a brief glance skywards as the resonant throb of the drums approached. The concentration was visible on the horsemen's faces as they guided the Unknown Warrior's gun carriage in a wide semi-circle, bringing it to rest directly in front of the flag-shrouded Cenotaph. Facing the coffin, the King stood with his arm raised in a protracted salute as faint sobs found their way from the crowd.

Now the King stepped forward, holding a beautiful wreath of bay leaves and blood-red roses, with a handwritten note tucked

into the deep-green foliage. 'In proud memory of those who died
unknown in the Great War,' the King had written. 'As unknown
and yet well-known; as dying, and behold they live' – a quotation
from an epistle of St Paul in the New Testament. After a moment's
pause, he reached up, and with one hand slid the wreath onto the
lid of the Unknown Warrior's coffin, before giving it an extra nudge
to push it perfectly into place. A brief salute, after which he turned
and walked away.

'Then all was still,' Philip Gibbs scribbled in his notebook, 'and
the picture was complete, framing that coffin, where the steel hat
and the King's sword lay upon the flag which draped it. The soul of
the nation at its best, purified at this moment by this emotion, was
there, in silence, about the dust of that Unknown.' It was still a few
minutes before eleven o'clock and the massed bands launched into
the opening chords of the hymn 'O God, Our Help in Ages Past',
and the choirs stationed outside the Home Office began to sing.
One newspaper wondered if everyone else was too overcome with
emotion to sing. Or was it that they didn't know the words? Or that
they simply could not agree with them?[67]

> Time, like an ever-rolling stream,
> Bears all its sons away;
> They fly forgotten, as a dream
> Dies at the opening day.

For the bereft mothers standing there in Whitehall, the suggestion
that the memory of their dead sons would simply fly away, forgotten
as easily as a waking dream, must have felt somewhat hollow.

The Archbishop of Canterbury stepped forward, into the pregnant silence that followed. 'Let us pray,' he said. 'Our Father . . .'

His voice clear and resonant, he began to recite the Lord's Prayer.
But again, nobody except the choir seemed to have the heart to
join in.

Again they waited. Some gazing up at the great clock tower,
willing the minute hand to advance to the vertical. Some peering

blankly at the enormous flags enveloping the Cenotaph. Most stared at the coffin on the gun carriage, their eyes at once swimming and ablaze.

Waiting ...

CHAPTER TWELVE

THE GREAT SILENCE

THE CENOTAPH, LONDON
SEPTEMBER 2023

Traffic thunders down Whitehall as London grinds about its business. At its centre, the Cenotaph feels like an inconvenient traffic island, obstructing cabbies, commuters and Deliveroo riders dicing with death on two wheels.

During my time in the military, I used to watch the Remembrance Sunday parade at the Cenotaph with some detachment. Back then, it seemed to be primarily for old people. But since leaving the RAF, the annual service at the Cenotaph has become an important part of my calendar. Gathered together with old friends and comrades, it is a sobering but always uplifting occasion. When I joined up, as a naive seventeen-year-old in 1981, I never truly expected to go into battle in the traditional sense. We trained hard and prepared for conflict, but in a Cold War mindset. The massive military might of NATO and the West faced overwhelming numbers of Soviet troops and weaponry across a divided Europe. We all knew that if the Cold War ever turned hot, it would almost certainly trigger a nuclear exchange, destroying much of the world we inhabited. And neither side, we believed, would ever want that. Even the sabre-rattling that punctuated our never less than uneasy stand-off seemed to confirm our conviction that an all-out war was unthinkable. Those early assumptions were, of course, seriously flawed. During my mere sixteen years in the RAF, I saw service in the Falklands, Bosnia and the Gulf, where, despite my deeply unpleasant experiences of capture and torture as a prisoner of war after being shot down over Iraq, I think of myself as one of the 'lucky ones'. I survived and returned home to my friends and family. Many of my friends did not; they tended to be the ones in my mind at the Cenotaph.

As they were in 1920, the Whitehall pavements are packed with large crowds on Remembrance Sunday. But there is a more celebratory air to proceedings, once the sombre service and two-minute silence are over, with much cheering and clapping as the veterans take part in the traditional march-past. I remember one year pushing a veteran of RAF Bomber Command – a friend and fellow prisoner of war, but from the Second World War – in a wheelchair at the heart of the 10,000-strong parade. A young girl in the crowd – aged around six – smiled at us and waved a large, homemade placard on which she had painted the words 'Thank You'. Seeing her bright, innocent face and her enthusiasm for the veterans made tears well in my eyes.

So I have *seen* the Cenotaph many times. But standing next to it now, alone, I realise I have never properly *looked* at Lutyens's masterpiece before. Stark and severe as it is, the monument turns out to be strangely beautiful, too. Amid the less than pristine city streets, its delicate whiteness feels like a symbol of purity and hope. The Portland stone is now a vivid reminder of my recent visit to the French battlefields and the white headstones dotting the landscape at High Wood and Beaumont-Hamel. So many of them commemorating the lasting heartache of families and friends of the missing: 'A Soldier of the Great War. Known unto God.' Standing with my toes almost touching the low stone step that frames the structure, my attention is drawn inexorably upwards, past the flags, past the carved inscription: 'THE GLORIOUS DEAD'. This is the brilliance of Lutyens's design, with its almost invisible curves, echoing the Parthenon, softening hard edges and tricking the mind into following the lines skyward.

Until I embarked on this journey, retracing the steps of the Unknown Warrior, I had always thought the Cenotaph was simply a great, white, solid block of stone. A regal monument, like a menhir or an obelisk. A grander, vertical incarnation of the Stones of Remembrance that Lutyens had designed, like great altars, for the largest war cemeteries in France. I simply hadn't understood the masterstroke that gave the Cenotaph its name – the combination of two Greek words, *kenos* (empty) and *taphos* (tomb). But the focal point is right here, in plain sight: *an empty coffin* lying on the very summit of the tapering structure. This hallowed monument is a mighty pedestal for the grave of missing heroes.

THE CENOTAPH
11 NOVEMBER 1920, 10:58AM

Standing on tiptoes and squinting through the microscopic gap between the two ladies in front of him, 8-year-old Donald Overall, there to witness the unveiling and to honour his beloved father killed in 1917, could just make out the severe, bearded figure facing the Cenotaph. He had never seen a king before. He looked rather normal. A man in uniform, just like everyone else. A man like his dear father?

The King, looking straight ahead, touched his moustache. In front of him stood a low grey plinth, which looked as if it might have been borrowed from one of the nearby gentlemen's clubs. On top of it was a single, highly polished brass button, glittering in the gauzy sunlight, drawing his attention away from the array of wires and pulleys running from the plinth to the two great flags draping the memorial. To his left, the brilliant white surplices of the choir made the black garb of the mourners appear all the more bleak, just as the two great Union Jacks enveloping the Cenotaph seemed to make the structure loom larger, much larger, than the wooden version that had stood here for the Victory Parade the previous year. At 35 feet, it was almost as high as three B-type London buses piled on top of one another. The same rickety thirty-four-seaters which were, even now, groaning to a halt in Piccadilly Circus, Oxford Street, Whitechapel Road and across the City. The Great Silence was only moments away.

In front of the choir stood the white-haired figure of Prime Minister Lloyd George, with his predecessor, Herbert Asquith. One onlooker noted that the ex-premier was doing his best to conceal surging emotion, 'which at times threatened to overcome him'.[1] It was four years since his first-born son, the brilliant Raymond Asquith, had been killed near High Wood. It might as well have been yesterday. Lord Curzon was there too, the master of ceremonies, desperately hoping that his forensically planned day would unfold without a hitch. On the King's right stood the Archbishop of Canterbury, looking rather more regal in his robes than George V in his khaki uniform. The King shook the archbishop's hand. Was he thanking him for some previous service? Or seeking reassurance from a trusted associate?

The King had initially expressed misgivings about the day. Reluctant to get involved, fearing ostentation, only agreeing to unveil the monument under pressure. Was it not sentimental to bury the bones of an unknown soldier with so much pomp and palaver? Might not a funeral simply reopen old wounds across the nation, only just beginning to heal? But now, just look at all these people, united in grief and loss.

Waiting.

His people.

The monarch must have been profoundly moved by the sight of these tens of thousands of mourners; silent, focused, reverential. He knew that *he* was a symbol for which many of their men had volunteered, fought and died. More than 500 members of the royal household had joined up. Three had been killed in the first months of the war.[2] And two of the King's sons had served: the future Edward VIII as a staff officer on the Western Front; the future George VI as a naval officer at the Battle of Jutland.[3] With his wife, he had visited the Western Front numerous times, in an attempt to bolster morale. The whole country knew how much Queen Mary had cared about the men who went to war. How much she had done to try to ease their suffering with visits to the wounded and the dying. 'You can't conceive what I suffered going round those hospitals in the war,' the King had told a courtier.[4] And the Queen had made so many more visits than he had.

So the royal couple must have had more than an inkling of the chaos and the carnage, of how bloody the slaughter. And the experience had left him with lasting pain. Following a visit to the Royal Flying Corps in 1915, the men on parade had given their King – with particular zeal – a traditional 'three cheers'. 'Unfortunately my horse took fright, reared straight up and fell back on top of me,' His Majesty recalled. 'It completely knocked the wind out of me. They picked me up and took me back in the motor car as quickly as possible. I suffered great agonies all the way.' The King had sustained a fractured pelvis, which caused him serious discomfort for the rest of his life.[5] But what was his pain compared to theirs, he must have wondered, surrounded by the hushed crowds, listening to their weeping. 'It was an overwhelming thought,' as one eyewitness observed, 'that all those thousands of people, rent and strained and overwrought, had gone through the pangs of great bereavement.'[6]

11AM, THE 11TH DAY OF THE 11TH MONTH, 1920

Like the opening shot of the nineteen-gun salute in Hyde Park, like the thumping drums of the massed bands at Victoria, the first resounding stroke of Big Ben at 11AM caused many in the crowd to flinch. At that same moment, a patch of clear sky suddenly opened in the mist, and the sun came blazing through, sharpening the reds and blues of the flags on the Cenotaph and casting fresh shadows across Whitehall.[7]

King George V took a deep breath. And then, with his leather-gloved hand, he pushed the button on the pedestal in front of him. For half a second, nothing happened.

Then one of the great flags draping the Cenotaph fell to earth. Unfortunately, the other stuck fast, refusing to budge. The crowd held its breath as the strokes of Big Ben echoed around them. A man in a suit eventually hurried forward to the base of the monument, gave the second flag a hefty tug, and sent it tumbling to the ground.

'And there was the Cenotaph,' said Donald Overall, remembering, decades later, the awe of his bereaved family. 'Resplendent, far better than it is today, because it was brand new; spotlessly clean.'[8] Then, once the last boom of the great bell had ceased to quiver in the air, the Great Silence could begin. For young Donald, his mum and his little brother Cecil, it was almost too much. 'My mother stood there with her arms round us two kids and she cried and I just stood there dumbfounded.'

It wasn't simply the Cenotaph and the silence and the sobbing that made the experience so overwhelming. It was the physical presence of the coffin lying just in front of them: a palpable reminder of what had been lost. Everyone's warrior, home at last. His casket being publicly transported from the French battlefields was the 1920 equivalent of the giant RAF transport aircraft touching down at RAF Lyneham, returning their flag-wrapped coffins from the tail-ramp, watched by weeping families on a windswept airfield.

Welcome home, son.

For Philip Gibbs, the war correspondent, as for so many that day, it wasn't the coffin alone that touched them. 'It was a steel helmet, an old "tin hat", lying there on the crimson of the flag, which revealed him instantly,' he wrote. 'Not as a mythical warrior, aloof from common humanity, a shadowy type of national pride and martial glory, but as one of those fellows, dressed in the drab of khaki, stained by mud and grease, who went into dirty ditches with this steel hat on his head, and in his heart unspoken things which made him one of us in courage and in fear.'[9]

* * *

The Union Jack. That morning, *The Times* had printed the story of Reverend David Railton's flag, using the very words he had written for Dean Ryle on the train from Margate a week earlier, while travelling up to London to present it for approval at Westminster Abbey. After Railton's description of its morale-boosting role in ceremonial and social events, the article in *The Times* had cut to the heart of the matter:

> And, at last, in the dead of night or at early dawn it enshrouded the bodies of our gallant men as they were carried down a trench to the little cemeteries and other places. This is not to mention the numerous occasions when it was dipped in the single grave of "an unknown British soldier". It is literally tinged with the blood of the men of London and of every part of England, Scotland, Wales and Ireland; infantry men, sappers, gunners, airmen, dismounted cavalry, tunnellers and of many other units.[10]

How many people standing there in Whitehall must have stared at Railton's battle-scarred Union Jack and wondered if it was dipped in the blood of *their* father, *their* husband, *their* son? And *The Times* had not held back from including the bitter note Railton had included at the end of his account, when he recalled the harrowing nightmare of young Denis Blakemore's execution for desertion: 'Once, at least, it lay on the grass floor of a tent, with the Cup of Salvation and the Bread of Communion resting upon it, for the strengthening of one who underwent sentence of death at dawn'. This was the moment which had left Railton, a man who had seen too much death and destruction through the war, feeling so disgusted that he had thrown the pack containing his precious flag into the dirt and vowed to abandon the army and return home. His recollections must have caused eyes to widen and a few people to choke on their toast and marmalade that morning.

Cowardice and desertion were, even in 1920, realities still too painful to face.

* * *

In the silence that morning, Gertrude Harris's mother was mourning an Unknown Warrior of her own. She hadn't wanted to go to the Cenotaph. She couldn't even face going downstairs. Instead, from the window of their tiny servants' quarters on the fourth floor of a smart townhouse in Hampstead, Gertrude and her mother were watching the motionless traffic below them. For 7-year-old Gertrude it must have been a bizarre sight. Cars and carts halted in the middle of the road, pointing in all directions. On the pavements, men wearing medals stood to attention.[11]

'Harry should be there with them,' whispered Gertrude's mother.

Gertrude knew nothing about her father, except that he had been killed in action, like all the others who hadn't come back. He was rarely mentioned at home, and certainly never by the wider family. Then there was the curious mantra her mother often repeated: 'My Harry was not a coward. He was a brave soldier.' Young Gertrude didn't understand what it all meant, and there had been other mysterious events too. In 1916, her mother's pension and child allowance had suddenly stopped. She remembered the trip to the post office, and the postmistress telling her mother: 'I am ever so sorry, Mrs Farr, but there is nothing for you.' And she remembered, all too well, the hot flush of shame with which her mother read the letter of explanation the postmistress handed her. How she tucked the letter down her blouse and dragged Gertrude home by the wrist, heads down, shrinking from what they imagined were the accusatory glances of passers-by.

Her mother was just twenty-one, barely out of her teenage years. Gertrude was three. They were near-destitute. 'Eventually, my mother got a job at a home in Hampstead and they were willing to take me,' Gertrude said, 'which in that era was a wonderful thing, as it was unheard of for a child to go into service.' But it was not a comfortable childhood. 'Whenever I hurt myself, Mother used to say, "Now don't you cry. Don't you let Cook hear you." She was so afraid that if I made a fuss we'd have to go. If I was ill, I used to be isolated in the bedroom. If I got mumps or measles I would be left up there with a sheet dipped in Lysol draped across the door, to keep the germs away from the rest of the family. I would be shut away for hours and hours as Mum worked as a skivvy, carrying the coal, taking the water up, cleaning. As an adult I find it very, very hard to cry, I think that was something that was suppressed in me when I was little.'

Gertrude would not find out the truth about her father, until, at a family gathering forty years later, an aunt had asked, 'Is this true what I hear about how Harry died?' The room fell silent. There was some uncomfortable shuffling of feet and clearing of throats. 'We don't talk about Harry,' someone said, quietly but firmly. But when they were alone later, Gertrude insisted her mother explain what had happened. 'Your father was shot for cowardice in 1916,' she said, wringing her hands. 'You were three years old. The family disowned him.' Harry's father would never say his son's name again; the family shame was all-encompassing.

Two days after the battle of High Wood on 15 September 1916, Private Harry Farr and his fellow soldiers in the West Yorkshire Regiment were to attack a formidable German defensive position east of Ginchy. Harry had already been hospitalised twice for shell shock, including a five-month stint in 1915. 'He shook all the time. He couldn't stand the noise of the guns,' his widow remembered. 'We got a letter from him, but it was in a stranger's handwriting. He could write perfectly well, but couldn't hold the pen because his hand was shaking.' The day before his company was due to attack, and in the midst of a deafening artillery bombardment, he reported to the medical officer complaining he was unwell. Unsympathetic, the medic sent him forward to the trenches as he had no visible injuries. Harry refused.

'I can't stand it,' he explained to his Regimental Sergeant Major.

'You are a fucking coward and you will go to the trenches,' the RSM reportedly replied. 'I give fuck all for my life. I give fuck all for yours. And I'll get you fucking well shot.' As he was being escorted back to the front line a struggle ensued. It seems Harry was disorientated and unable to understand what was happening, but he was arrested and charged with 'misbehaving before the enemy in such a manner as to show cowardice'. A month later, near Albert, Harry Farr was executed for cowardice. He is said to have refused a blindfold when facing the firing squad. At some point, Harry's grave must have been lost, as his name is listed on the Memorial to the Missing at Thiepval. The army chaplain who attended Harry's execution later said that he had died with dignity, writing to his widow that, 'A finer soldier never lived.'

In 2006, alongside many of those executed, shot at dawn, Harry was pardoned. 'I was so astonished that when the solicitor said, "We've got it", I didn't know what he meant,' said Gertrude. 'It took quite a while for it to sink in.' It had taken almost all of Harry's 93-year-old daughter's life. But it changed everything. 'To me now, Harry is a real person, whereas before I didn't know him. Now I feel I do. He's not just Harry any more. He's my dad.'

The father she could not mourn properly during the Great Silence in 1920 had finally come back.

* * *

In their shared room in Hornsey, a few miles across north London, 5-year-old George Musgrave and his mother were already standing – ready and waiting – when the church clock struck eleven. There were no crowds around them. No massed bands. No Field Marshals. No King in uniform, black armband on his sleeve. But George's and his mother's pain was as great as anyone's. She was wearing a smart white blouse, with her husband's medals pinned to her chest. Together, they were having their own ceremony. George had got out his father's drawing of a train, lovingly inscribed in flowing handwriting, 'To little George for his birthday from Daddy'.

'We could see all the vehicles come to a stop,' he recalled. 'And all the horses and carts, and all the people were just standing there.' In the silence, the clock ticked away the seconds. It seemed a *very* long time since his father had died of his wounds in 1917. 'The two of us looked down from our room, onto the trams and the tram-wires, and I could hear my mother crying beside me.'[12]

Then the silence was over, and the trams clanked back into life.

George's mother clutched him tightly. 'You are all I have,' she murmured.

* * *

Across London, and all over Britain, the Great Silence had brought people to a respectful and reverent standstill.

Later, the Post Office would announce that the country had, for two minutes, been completely cut off from the world. Every instrument in the Central Telegraph Office was silent, and throughout the nation's telephone exchanges, work was completely suspended.[13] The London Stock Exchange ceased trading. Fire alarms sounded in Harrods to announce the start of the silence, while Selfridges went one better and engaged a group of buglers to trumpet the Last Post.[14] On the railways, the Cornish Riviera Express paused near Taplow and the *Irish Mail* train squealed to a halt near Crewe.[15] Ocean-going liners and warships stopped their engines. And, perhaps most hair-raisingly of all, the pilot of a passenger flight from Manchester to London apparently shut down his engines, allowing his aircraft to glide in eerie silence for two minutes, while his four tight-lipped passengers stood awkwardly to attention in the cramped cabin.[16]

On the other hand, there seems to have been quite the kerfuffle at the offices of the *Workers' Dreadnought*, the weekly publication of the Communist Party edited by the socialist suffragette, Sylvia Pankhurst.[17] As the crowd on Fleet Street stood motionless, they were appalled to hear a frightful commotion from the windows above. An eyewitness claimed that two or three girls in the office had created a 'disgraceful' scene. 'They were singing, shouting, dancing and banging tin cans.' According to the newspapers, those below remained perfectly still and quiet until the Great Silence was over. Then there was a rush for the premises. One of the girls involved in the fracas was interviewed and declared: 'We were dusting the office. We certainly made some noise and we did not dream of people outside hearing, so we went on dusting the place. We were not interested [in the ceremony] as we don't believe in it. But a workman must have told the people we were here, and a lot of people rushed upstairs. And then some girls knocked us about. They kept on hitting us until the police came.'[18]

Elsewhere in London, the labourers on one building site appear to have more respectfully typified the heartfelt public response. 'At 11 o'clock the whistle blew on a busy excavation where steam diggers were tearing up the earth and hundreds of men were busy with pick and shovel,' observed a passer-by. 'The diggers ceased, the huge crane stopped in the middle of its swing, with a huge steel girder silhouetted against the pale amber sky. Shovels and picks were dropped, and every man took off his cap and stood quietly beside his job.' It was a deeply personal moment for many. 'The whistle blew once more, and the steam digger rattled and coughed at its job,' continued the eyewitness. 'An old navvy had stood bare-headed beside me. One of London's own, with corduroy breeches, knee straps, and moleskin waistcoat. He wiped his eye with the back of his hand as he picked up his shovel. "He may be my boy, sir. They never found him."'[19]

In Whitehall, which for these 120 seconds had become the epicentre of the universe, the grief was palpable. A writer for the *Yorkshire Post* perhaps best captured the mood:

For two awful minutes we had the soul of the race laid bare. More than any eloquence of tongue was this eloquence of silence. Greater than any funeral music was the message of the still sad voice of memory that whispered to aching hearts. I have stood by the tombs of Kings and Queens. I have seen statesmen and poets laid to rest. I have thrilled to the glad murmur of happy multitudes in times of national rejoicing. But never have I known any feeling comparable to that of today as I gazed on the flag-covered coffin that enshrined the sublime anonymity of a fallen soldier, from that to the simple but all-moving symbolism of

the Cenotaph, and from both to the living, palpitating, pathetic
multitude of mothers and wives stricken by the fell blow of war
in these recent years. They held sombre possessions. They were
packed together on the pavements, fatigued but bravely enduring. Wreaths, large and small, were clutched in trembling hands.
Surely such an amazing store of flowers was never seen before,
from the cheapest and lowliest chrysanthemums to floral designs,
ingenious and fantastic.[20]

For Philip Gibbs, who had been so struck by the sight of the steel
helmet on the Unknown Warrior's coffin, the silence offered a
chance for the renowned war correspondent to reflect on the harsh
realities of a conflict which he had once done his best to disguise.[21]

Following the disastrous first day of the Somme on 1 July 1916 –
the deadliest in British military history with over 57,000 British
casualties including 19,240 dead[22] – Gibbs had described an encounter with a lorry-load of wounded soldiers: 'They were all grinning
as though they had come from a "jolly" in which they had been
bumped a little. There was a look of pride in their eyes as they came
driving down like wounded knights from a tourney. The men who
were going up to the battle grinned back at those who were coming
out.' And to sum up that bloodiest of days, with its tens of thousands
of casualties, Gibbs had written: 'And so, after the first day of battle,
we may say with thankfulness: All goes well. It is a good day for
England and France. It is a day of promise in this war.'[23]

Gibbs appears to have been haunted by the gulf between the
things he had seen in the war and the way he had felt obliged to
censor his own reports. But his remarkable evocation of the Great
Silence on 11 November 1920, in which he found his own way to
bring the ghost of the Unknown Warrior back to life, was perhaps
an attempt to redress the balance:

There was a dead stillness in Whitehall, only broken here and
there by the coughing of a man or a woman, quickly hushed.
The Unknown Warrior! Was it young Jack, perhaps, who had

never been found? Was it one of those fellows in the battalion that moved up through Ypres before the height of the battle in the bogs? One could see the glow of their cigarette ends. It rained after that, beating sharply on the tin hats, pouring in spouts down waterproof capes. The shelling began, gas shelling, every old thing. Fellows dropped into shell holes, full of water. Some of them lay there in the pits, where the water was reddish.

There were a lot of unknown warriors in the bogs. They lay by upturned tanks and sank in the slime. Queer how the fellows used to drop and never give a sound, so that their pals passed on without knowing. In all sorts of places the unknown warrior lay down and was not quickly found. On the fields of the Somme they lay in the churned-up earth, in High Wood and Delville Wood. There was a boy lying in a tangle of barbed wire. He looked as though he were asleep, but he was dead, all right.

What is this long silence, all this crowd in London streets, two years after the armistice and peace? Yes, those were the old dreams that have passed, old ghosts passing down Whitehall among the living.[24]

At last, carving a path through the stillness, eight bugles sounded the mournful elegy of the Last Post. The King lifted his head and carefully replaced his cap. Behind him, the royal princes followed suit. Movement returned to a crowd stiffened by grief. There was a small commotion to one side and two stretcher-bearers hurried forward. A woman clutching a small bunch of lilies had fainted. Someone picked up her lilies and placed them on the stretcher beside her. She looked little more than a child.[25]

Now the King carried a wreath of white flowers to the foot of the Cenotaph. In his neat, inky handwriting, a stiff white card was inscribed: 'Buckingham Palace. In memory of the glorious dead. From George R. I. and Mary R. November the 11th, 1920.'

Among the onlookers stood a tiny woman in a black coat, her greying hair pinned beneath a black bonnet. The years had not been kind to 43-year-old Rose, Alec Reader's mother, who had made the short journey from the other side of the Thames carrying a wreath of laurel and summer roses from her own garden.[26] Four years after her 18-year-old son's death at High Wood, he and his copy of *Treasure Island* still missing, she was even now struggling to accept that she would never see him again. Her wreath looked pathetically small compared with the King's grand offering. So did her little card. There was so much to say. How could she encapsulate the life of her son – the child, the boy, the man? The soldier fighting and dying for his country, his body lost forever? It was hard to know where to start. In the end, she had simply written: 'My Alec, Rest in Peace.'[27]

A barked order. Hooves scraping on sand-sprinkled stone. And with a creak of leather, the gun carriage finally left the Cenotaph and began to rumble towards Westminster Abbey. A lady standing nearby was heard to cry softly: 'Goodbye, goodbye!'[28]

Much of the crowd was now weeping quite openly. In the midst of it all was the humble Unknown Warrior on his gun carriage, wrapped in Padre Railton's flag.

He had had quite a journey from the battlefields of France.

And it wasn't over yet.

CHAPTER THIRTEEN

'THE MAN IN THE COFFIN MIGHT BE MY DADDY'

WHITEHALL, LONDON
11 NOVEMBER 1920

As the great procession moved away from the Cenotaph, the ranks of the military were graced by the King taking up his role as chief mourner, walking stiffly behind the Unknown Warrior's carriage. In his wake came the princes, the bearer party, hundreds of servicemen, six abreast, with the veterans following behind.

This second leg of the procession, to Westminster Abbey and the grand state funeral and burial, had only been bolted onto the previously planned Armistice Day programme a few weeks earlier.

Like millions of others, I watched the state funeral of Her Late Majesty Queen Elizabeth II in 2022, glued to the television at home. A lump in my throat at times, but also fiercely proud to witness the unfolding spectacle. I can still see the Queen's coffin on *its* gun carriage, dragged by a team of sailors towards the abbey, with the new King, Charles III, marching slowly behind it, his loss palpable. There was a sombre magnificence to the procession, with the scarlet dress uniforms of the Guardsmen mirrored in the dazzling royal standard covering the coffin, with the orb and sceptre, and the Imperial State Crown resting on a lustrous purple cushion. The sumptuous wreath and its handwritten card trembling with the motion of the gun carriage – a reminder that this was not just a queen, but someone's mother too.

The similarities between her final journey and the Unknown Warrior's are writ large, and so are the differences. As he floated on a sea of khaki to Westminster Abbey, along the very same roads, between the very same buildings, beneath the same London sky, Padre Railton's battle-faded Union Jack had taken the place of the royal standard. Instead of the crown, orb and sceptre lay the workaday steel helmet, webbing and bayonet of a soldier. Even the modest wreath placed on the Warrior's coffin by King George V had a spartan quality to it, compared with the gorgeous rainbow of flowers that lay upon the Queen's a century later.

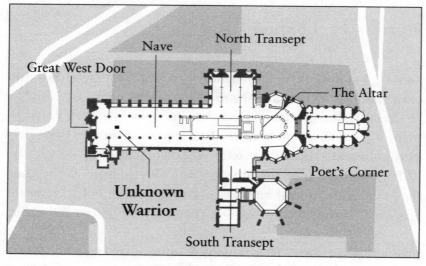

WESTMINSTER ABBEY

Waiting inside Westminster Abbey, those who had been granted tickets in the ballot had been arriving since the early hours, and, by 10AM, everyone was seated.

And what a congregation it was.

Lord Curzon had been careful to ensure that the Unknown Warrior's funeral did not become a society event. Getting the balance of the congregation in the abbey right was one of the most sensitive and controversial aspects of the entire undertaking. It had been re-evaluated many times during the run-up and, following a fierce press campaign, the committee had established three priority groups of possible attendees:

Women who had lost a husband and a son in action.

Women who had lost all their sons.

War widows who had 'only' lost a husband.

As in 2022 at Her Late Majesty's funeral, here were those recognised for their contribution to British life. But in 1920, their collective sacrifice had been their unplanned gift to the nation. And of these women, there was one group which trumped all others in a game that nobody wanted to win. A pitiful band of ninety-nine mothers distinguished by an almost unfathomable depth of loss. They had been selected for seats of honour because each one had lost her husband and *all* her sons.[1]

Of course, there were no special places reserved for bereaved fathers. And there was certainly no space for the 'young ladies' of the missing, such as Bert Bradley's bereft sweetheart, perhaps still biting back the tears as she pictured her first love falling in battle, never to be seen again. She had sent him the new pipe that he had been smoking shortly before he died, along with the half-pound of milk chocolate and tin of preserved cherries. Precious things, in those days. At least Bert had perished knowing that someone cared.[2]

Over 20,000 applications had been received for the roughly 1,600 places that had been made available at the abbey, with further spaces reserved at the Cenotaph and along Whitehall. Some 7,500 requests came from mothers who had lost either their only son, or all their sons; 4,042 came from widows.[3] Perhaps we should not be surprised by what may seem a low application rate from the hundreds of thousands of bereaved. In 1920, the widow of a private soldier would have received an army pension of just £1 per week, so a trip to London would have been well beyond the means of most who lived outside the city.[4]

Places had also been found for a hundred nurses who had been blinded or otherwise wounded while doing their duty, and for a little girl who had applied for tickets on the basis that she had lost nine brothers, either killed or missing. Perhaps most poignantly of all, the newspapers had come across a 12-year-old boy who had written his own plea to the authorities, ending his letter with the enduringly resonant thought shared by so many: *The man in the coffin might be my daddy.*[5]

Among all those with special claims for tickets, no one could have begrudged the benighted ranks of women who had shuffled grimly into the abbey that morning. 'Every kind of mother – brave and proud, pathetic and frail – made her way alone, humbly, and on foot, to the Abbey,' noted the *Daily Mirror*. 'They carried sad little handfuls of flowers that wilted through the long wait, and in the dim light of the Abbey, little was distinguishable save the blackness of their clothes and the whiteness of their faces. And how white they were! A little grey woman next to me showed me the medals she was wearing. "Five – one for each of my boys," she said with a smile.'[6]

Alongside the ninety-nine who had lost their husband and every single one of their sons, there was another remarkable group in the abbey: the honour guard known as the '100 VCs' – those awarded the Victoria Cross, or one of the other highest-ranking medals for bravery in the face of the enemy.[7] Though, on the day, illness had prevented four invitees from attending. 'The occasion forbade a cheer, and they passed in silently,' noted one observer as the ninety-six arrived. 'But what a cheer there might have been.'[8] The public in 1920 will have been acutely aware that to have assembled so many VCs was to bestow a very different kind of honour upon the Unknown Warrior. He already had the King as his chief mourner. He had the highest-ranking officers in the land as his honorary pallbearers. But the respect of the VCs was something else. These men were, after all, his peers, his comrades-in-arms. Not literally 'the bravest of the brave', for it is a sad truth of war that such a thing tends to be incompatible with longevity.

Having met some of the living recipients of the VC, I have no doubt they have something that sets them apart from the rest of us. To a man, they are humble, talk reluctantly, and only in general terms, of the day they won the nation's highest award 'For Valour'. But those of us who have faced the enemy in less noteworthy ways recognise a real hero in our midst, and these men are quietly revered in military circles. It was, therefore, a perfect inspiration on the part of Lord Curzon to assemble so many of them, for the Great British public, on the day it really mattered. 'Each of something striking in face and figure; each with the plain deep ribbon and the cross of supreme valour on his breast, this gallant band of brothers struck the keynote of comradeship,' declared one eyewitness.[9]

* * *

Representative of all those heroes waiting in the dim lights of Westminster Abbey for a fallen comrade was the diminutive figure of William Coltman, Victoria Cross (VC), Distinguished Conduct Medal (DCM) and bar, Military Medal (MM) and bar (denoting a medal awarded twice). A humble stretcher-bearer, who, by the end of the conflict in 1918 – and despite never having fired a single shot because of his strict Christian and pacifist beliefs, though not a conscientious objector – had become the most highly decorated 'other rank' in the British Army.[10]

Born on the outskirts of Burton-upon-Trent in 1891, Bill was the youngest of nine children. A market gardener and Sunday school teacher, he volunteered for the British Army in January 1915, arriving in France a few months later. His first Military Medal was awarded in February 1917 for rescuing a wounded officer stuck on barbed wire fencing in no-man's-land, jamming his own body between him and the enemy gunfire. He won his second that summer, for several separate instances of gallantry, including rescuing casualties at an ammunition dump hit by mortar fire and from a collapsed trench tunnel.

The London Gazette citation for his first award of the Distinguished Conduct Medal highlighted his 'conspicuous gallantry and devotion to duty in evacuating wounded from the front line at great personal risk under shell fire. His absolute indifference to danger had a most inspiring effect upon the rest of his men.' Although only five-foot-four, Bill was clearly a man of immense personal strength and courage, as the citation for his second DCM in September 1918 confirmed: 'He dressed and carried many wounded men under heavy artillery fire. He remained at his work without rest or sleep, attending the wounded, taking no heed of either shell or machine-gun fire, and never resting until he was positive that our sector was clear of wounded. He set the highest example of fearlessness and devotion to duty to those with him.' Only a week later, he won his VC, 'for most conspicuous bravery, initiative and devotion to duty. Lance Corporal Coltman, on hearing that wounded had been left behind during a retirement, on his own initiative went forward alone in the face of fierce enfilade fire, found the wounded, dressed them, and on three successive occasions carried comrades on his back to safety, thus saving their lives.'[11]

'Yours is one of the very few, if not the only case in the whole British Army, where a man has gained so many distinctions,' King George V had told Coltman, when he presented his Victoria Cross at Buckingham Palace in May 1919. 'I heartily congratulate you.'[12]

* * *

William Coltman and the honour guard of heroes had lined up on either side of the nave in Westminster Abbey while the ceremony at the Cenotaph had been taking place, and the extraordinary congregation waiting inside the ancient church took part in their own service. Some of those already immersed in the singing and the organ-playing had waited several years for this moment: a verifiable and public acknowledgement of their personal loss. The focal point of the Unknown Warrior's committal was not to be at the front of the abbey, close to the high altar. Instead, it would be almost at the back of the nave, where the light streamed through the stained-glass windows high above. So the seating had been reversed, the congregation facing the grave, backs to the altar. Between the first and second arches at the west end stood a broad, low platform, covered in purple silk with a white border. At its centre, the open grave.

And so they waited, the band of the Grenadier Guards playing softly for the congregation, a 'singularly appropriate'[13] programme of French and English music, including Sullivan's 'In Memoriam', Guilmant's *marche funèbre*, César Franck's *Rédemption*, and the slow movement 'Killed in Action' from Arthur Somervell's symphony *Thalassa*. A few minutes before 11AM, as the massed bands at the Cenotaph 400 yards away prepared to launch into 'O God, Our Help in Ages Past', the abbey organist pulled out his stops, ready to match them note for note. He, too, began by playing the first line as an introduction, 'and when he repeated it, everyone joined in singing this most helpful and encouraging of our familiar hymns'.[14]

The same thing was happening across Britain.

'It required very little imagination on the part of the thousands who crowded Holy Trinity Church this morning,' the *Hull Evening News* told its readers, 'to think that they were actually witnessing the burial of the Unknown Warrior in Westminster Abbey. The same hymn, full of consolation and hope, "O God, Our Help in Ages Past", was sung, and as the boom of the final stroke of 11 died, there was absolute silence, which allowed the vast congregation to visualise the scene at the Cenotaph and the Abbey.'[15]

As the final notes had faded away, the great bell of the abbey sounded the first stroke of the 11th hour of the 11th day of the 11th month, two years to the minute since the guns had fallen silent. As outside on Whitehall, in the shadows of the great abbey, the crowd fell silent and, 'for a little while,' reported *The Times*, 'the bereaved of a nation walked in spirit through the cemeteries of France and Flanders, Gallipoli and Mesopotamia, and stood before far-away wooden crosses.' At last a woman audibly sobbed, 'and the breakdown helped to release the tears which others had, with difficulty, held trembling on their eyelids'.[16]

A little more than six minutes after it had left the Cenotaph, the funeral procession made a slow and graceful turn in front of the iron gates outside the North Door of the abbey. The massed bands wheeled away into a side street and fell silent as the bearer party halted. There was a momentary hiatus, then the leather straps on the gun carriage were released and the heavy, zinc-lined oak coffin was lifted onto their shoulders.

It was time.

They carried their dead comrade slowly, feet-first, through two ranks of helmeted and overcoated policemen, past the split ranks of the firing party, marching with measured steps from the November sunlight into the gloom of the abbey's interior.

HORSE GUARDS PARADE, LONDON
SEPTEMBER 2023

The soldier responsible for the planning and smooth running of the Unknown Warrior's procession thus far must surely have allowed himself a moment of calm congratulation. The pressure to get everything right must have been intense, and it was nearly over.

Performing a similar role 102 years later for the Queen's funeral, Garrison Sergeant Major 'Vern' Stokes understands all too well the complexity of the role. 'You are fully aware that you're carrying out your work under the direct scrutiny of some of the most high-profile people in our country,' he tells me. 'And, more importantly, that many, many millions might be watching on TV here in the UK, and then countless more overseas. But I don't regard that as a burden of responsibility. I regard it as the *privilege* of responsibility.'[17]

Watching the old footage of the bearer party carrying the Unknown Warrior's coffin into the abbey, Vern reflects on the same task the Guardsmen accomplished in 2022, gaining worldwide acknowledgement. 'It's really important to understand that an event like the Queen's funeral, or the King's later coronation, might last a few hours when you watch it on TV. But the planning and rehearsals could have taken many weeks. Perhaps months, sometimes. The bearer party for Her Majesty were rehearsing relentlessly in the days before the funeral, practising day and night to ensure everything was perfect. Especially the final stages carrying the coffin into the chapel at Windsor. There was simply no room for error.' Having carried a coffin a couple of times, I vividly remember watching in awe – and with no little trepidation – the eight Grenadier Guardsmen inching their way meticulously up the steep steps of St George's Chapel at Windsor, carrying the monarch on their shoulders. Some reports estimated that her oak casket might weigh around 250kg, or a quarter of a tonne.[18]

Vern shakes his head, reliving the moment. 'We go through every aspect of a parade or procession, examining every single item that *could* go wrong, or how external factors might affect it. Everything from troops fainting, protestors getting in the way of the parade, horses going out of control, medical emergencies. For instance, if one of the cars conveying VIP attendees took a wrong turn and ended up blocking a route, we'd all be in serious trouble because everything is planned down to the second. That minutiae of detail has to be examined, explored and tested well before the day. We practise for everything, so that if something untoward does happen, we *already* know what we have to do to solve the problem.'

Of course, the organisers of the Unknown Warrior's funeral in 1920 did not have months in which to prepare. They barely had weeks. But as Vern reminds me, the troops of the era had had a different kind of training to today's soldiers learning the ropes for a ceremonial procession. 'I think that the military of 1920 was probably very comfortable with being completely flexible in what it did, and how it did it. They had been fighting a brutal war for many years and were quite used to being moved around the battlespace, marching from area to area to take up different positions. I think they probably had the ability to react very quickly when ordered to do something. The very different environment back then certainly lent itself to the military delivering such a memorable ceremony and parade at incredibly short notice.' And how does Vern think those in charge of the parade might have felt about the demand to deliver

such excellence? He spoke candidly to a newspaper in the hours
before the late Queen's funeral:

'I have occasionally had to pinch myself over the last few days as
the preparations unfold and I deal with the magnitude of what we
are embarking on. I was brought up in poverty on a council estate in
Shropshire. I left school at sixteen and just needed to get away from
home. My parents had split up and I sensed that if I didn't do something meaningful with my life, there wouldn't be much of a future
ahead of me. Joining the army provided the direction I needed; the
escape from my past. There were fifteen Prime Ministers during the
Queen's seventy-year reign, but only six Garrison Sergeant Majors,
with me as the sixth. The role has a much wider responsibility than
one may expect a Warrant Officer to have, and I certainly feel very
privileged to have it.' But as Vern acknowledged in the aftermath,
his role certainly came with an unprecedented level of expectation
and pressure. 'I was utterly exhausted; Her Majesty's funeral was a
global recognition of service, and it's something that will live with
me for a long time.'[19]

WESTMINSTER ABBEY, LONDON
NOVEMBER 1920

The bearer party halted by the platform above the grave, then
carefully laid the coffin on the stout wooden timbers placed across
the opening, which, as the *New York Times* pointed out, stood 'in
the pathway of kings, for not a monarch can ever again go up to
the altar to be crowned, but he must step over the grave of the man
who died that his kingdom might endure'.[20] A precedent was being
set, a challenge to the future for the kings, queens, presidents and
commoners who would follow the Unknown Warrior's journey
down that aisle.

After the bearer party had stepped away, the King, Dean Ryle and
the honorary pallbearers moved into position, almost shoulder to
shoulder, around the grave. Behind the funeral party, other dignitaries, including Prime Minister Lloyd George and his predecessor

Herbert Asquith, took up their places in the front row, while the ninety-nine widows were arranged in two bleak groups of tearful longing on either side. The King stood to attention at the Unknown Warrior's feet, facing the Great West Door. Dean Ryle and the Archbishop of Canterbury waited, backs to the door, facing the high altar.

One crucial figure, not standing at the graveside, was the man who started it all, Padre David Railton. It is a measure of the man that he recorded little of his experiences that day, but we do know he was in a prime location at the abbey from a note he wrote later in his anonymous memoir using the voice of his flag: 'The Dean had the courtesy to give him a special place on Armistice Day, close to the grave.'[21] And years later, further evidence of his ringside seat came from a lady who said her husband was related to Railton, and claimed that 'Railton sat beside King George V and Queen Mary in the Abbey'.[22]

The brief service that followed was, according to *The Times,* 'the most beautiful, the most touching and the most impressive that, in all its long eventful story, this island has ever seen'.[23] A fitting conclusion then to the more than half a million stories which had lain unfinished since the end of the war.

Beethoven's mournful 'Three Equali for Four Trombones', played by the brass of the Grenadier Guards, set the tone. Choosing a German composer to initiate the ceremony was perhaps an act of calculated forgiveness and redemption. And, at the same moment, flowers were placed on the grave of a German prisoner at Whittington near Oswestry.[24] Less controversial, perhaps, was the singing of Psalm 23, whose soul-soothing language would have been comfortingly familiar to the congregation:

> The Lord is my shepherd; I shall not want ...
> Yea, though I walk through the valley of the shadow of
> death, I will fear no evil: for thou art with me.

How often, in the mud-spattered, blood-caked abyss of the trenches, must desperate soldiers have muttered these lines to themselves?

They had certainly been in the hearts of Anthony French and Bert
Bradley when the two friends had first arrived in the blasted, corpse-
strewn landscape near High Wood in September 1916. 'We skirted
the carcasses and the craters. Here on the threshold of stark tragedy
all light-heartedness fled,' recalled French. 'A shell screamed above
us and burst over the hill. Still in step we plodded on. The macabre
surroundings strangely affected me. I thought of the pale horse in
Revelation, and of him that sat up on it. Clinging to calmness but
desperate for sympathy, I broke the silence and asked Bert what he
thought of it all.'

Bert had given his friend a wry smile, before answering with that
familiar biblical quotation. 'Though I walk through the valley of
the shadow of death . . .' he began.

'That's it!' replied French. Then to himself: 'I will fear no evil . . .
No evil . . . I will fear no evil.' He was, he recorded, 'soon comforted'.[25]

After the Psalm, Dean Ryle read a lesson from the Book of
Revelation, about the beautiful life of those in heaven. 'These are
they which came out of great tribulation. They shall hunger no
more, neither thirst anymore.'[26]

As the next hymn was sung, the bearer party removed the helmet,
webbing, bayonet and Padre Railton's flag from the coffin, leaving
the iron shield and Charles ffoulkes's crusader's sword attached.
The Unknown Warrior would not be weaponless in the afterlife.

The Guardsmen held the coffin steady on ropes as the transverse
timbers were pulled away, then the heavy medieval casket was lowered gently into its final resting place.[27] 'There it lies on sand which
has apparently been untouched since the Abbey was built,' noted
The Times. 'The diggers of the grave found there no remnants of
other humanity.'[28]

Dean Ryle began to intone: 'For as much as it hath pleased
Almighty God of his great mercy to take unto himself the soul of
our dear brother here departed: we therefore commit his body to
the ground.'

A gleaming silver shell filled with the soil taken from the battlefields was handed to the King, who sprinkled a small amount over

the coffin with his fingers, before reverently tipping the rest into the grave as the Dean continued: 'Earth to earth, ashes to ashes, dust to dust, in sure and certain hope of resurrection to eternal life, through our Lord Jesus Christ, Amen.'

An odyssey which had begun in one of the flayed battlefields of France – and then proceeded via a night in the tinpot chapel at Saint-Pol, a bumpy ride north in a motor ambulance, a peaceful night under French guard in the great château of Boulogne, a mile-long parade through the thronged streets of the French port, an epic salute on the quayside from Maréchal Foch, a foggy Channel crossing aboard a torpedo destroyer under escort, an emotional welcome at Dover, a floral-scented train ride through the darkened English countryside with supporters at the wayside, a final night under guard on a deserted platform at Victoria Station and a martial parade up The Mall to the Cenotaph – had finally reached its conclusion.

Bring him home, they said.

And they had brought him home.

* * *

Once again, it was the organist who had the task of stirring the congregation, and the rousing notes of 'Abide with Me' rang out. Incredibly, it is still possible to hear the congregation mournfully singing the words over a century later.

Special permission had been given to two ex-RAF officers to record the service using their experimental audio system. Four carbon microphones had been placed inside the abbey, with cables running to a technical van parked in the street outside, where the two intrepid sound engineers sat amid their Heath Robinson-style array of heating ovens and cutting lathes. The system was, for its time, a colossal innovation. Simple acoustic recordings, made on the spot, had existed since Edison. But this new remote technique was the harbinger of the 'outside broadcasts' which became the focal point of TV coverage of later state occasions.[29]

The results were sadly underwhelming. Thirty-six single-sided discs were cut during the service, but the Columbia record company rejected all but two: 'Abide with Me' and Kipling's 'Recessional', which ended the service. These distorted, lurching affairs were released as two sides of a 12-inch record, of which 500 copies were pressed, and sold by the abbey for seven shillings and sixpence in aid of its restoration appeal.[30] Crackly and indistinct as they sound, it is eerie to think that these are the voices of bereaved widows and battle-scarred VCs, their grief and yearning echoing into the vaulting of the abbey, to be captured, preserved and cherished in the next millennium. Kipling had written 'Recessional' for Queen Victoria's Diamond Jubilee in 1897, and the haunting refrain of 'Lest we forget, lest we forget' had quickly been taken up by those who mourned. Though it is difficult to tell with any clarity, it appears to have caused quite a stir in the abbey. 'The great wave of feeling which that hymn always arouses could be felt surging through the whole congregation,' observed The Times. 'It could be seen in many a woman, and even some men, finding expression in tears.'[31] As one mother in the congregation recalled, 'If tears came to me during the service as they came to many, they were mingled with gladness, for in that beautiful building and that music that thrilled my soul I felt very near to my lost boys.'[32]

The Times reporter was transfixed by the rush of sound that followed. 'From somewhere far away in the great church, a scarcely audible whisper began to steal upon us. It swelled, with absolute smoothness, until we knew it for the roll of drums. Then the whole Abbey was full of the reverberating roar; and then it began to die away, and died into a whisper so soft that no one could say for certain when it stopped.'[33] Finally, there came the clear, rousing bugle call of 'Reveille'. 'A cheerful challenge carrying us on to the life that must be lived in action,' as the Guardian described it, before the Great West Door was flung open, 'to let the chilly mist of the London day and the noises of the street in upon that warm-coloured splendour; that calm of recollection'.[34]

* * *

The King strode out of the abbey, with a procession of soldiers, sailors, airmen, dignitaries and statesmen in his wake. Each cast a glance into the open grave as he passed. Next, the VCs broke ranks and became 'just comrades looking their last upon a comrade'.[35]

Then the women left their seats, and began that long, slow file-past of the bereaved. 'West End and East End; the rich woman and the poor; all was one in this democracy of memory,' observed one eyewitness.[36] One lady plucked a white chrysanthemum from a bunch she carried and threw it into the grave. Others followed and soon the purple and white carpet around the tomb was thickly scattered with flowers of white and red.[37] After the last of the congregation departed, the doors of the abbey were closed. The grave was covered with the white and gold embroidered silk of the Actors' Pall, presented by the Actors' Church Union in memory of their fallen comrades. Padre Railton's flag was then spread on top.

Outside, the Great Pilgrimage was already underway.

As soon as the ceremony on Whitehall had ended, even before the Unknown Warrior was entombed, the public were filing past the Cenotaph.

The first pilgrims had been two legless men in hospital blue, who rattled and whirred along on their hand-powered tricycles. Then came six green motor coaches, filled with injured veterans also in hospital blue. One carried men who had lost limbs. Blinded soldiers filled another. Many were so severely injured they could not rise in salute as they passed by. They had come from Scotland, Ireland and Wales, from the Outer Hebrides and from the Shetland Isles. Two wounded soldiers had walked 60 miles to lay wreaths at the Cenotaph; both had lost a brother in the war.[38] Many remote towns sent a special representative carrying tributes from multiple families.

Most of those queueing seemed to have brought wreaths or bunches of flowers to place at the base of the memorial. But, sadly, there is no Pathé newsreel of this extraordinary sight, no visual record of a pilgrimage that appears to have put even the outpouring of public grief following the death of the Queen in the shade. 'Why did the movie cameras stop?' asked the *Daily Graphic*, with a mixture of sadness and outrage. 'They could have photographed the *via dolorosa* of all the little people who really won the war – the men, the women, the children, the ones who suffered most. You cannot invent drama like that. It happens. Nor can you invent a world's misery.'[39]

Further epic queues carried the hardiest pilgrims onward to Westminster Abbey where the doors were reopened at 12:40PM. Slowly and softly, the grateful public filed past the Unknown Warrior's grave, around 40,000 of them before the doors were finally closed, an hour later than normal, at 11PM.[40] Over the week that the grave remained open, people stood for hours, day and night, in queues stretching for 7 miles, just for the chance of a few seconds at the graveside. One wreath bore the inscription: 'From the Commander-in-chief, Atlantic Fleet, Flag Captain, Officers and Ship's Company. H.M.S. Queen Elizabeth.' Next to it lay a tiny bunch of lilies with a card attached: 'In loving memory of Tom, from Dad and Mum.'[41]

Classless it may have been, but the Great Pilgrimage to both the Cenotaph and Unknown Warrior was a severe test of endurance. 'I looked to my right and, there again, I saw the hungry eyes of people who live on memory; faces that betoken ever-threatening collapse,' said one bystander on Whitehall. 'Within three-quarters of an hour, nine women and girls fainted in my neighbourhood.'[42]

This wasn't like the Queen's lying-in-state, a century later, when the Great Queue became almost an art installation in its own right. It helped that years of planning meant that the logistical system was a well-oiled machine by then, with snaked railings at pinch points, and state-of-the-art communications predicting the current waiting time, calculated to the minute and broadcast across the media. Back in 1920, packed together in a dense throng extending halfway up Whitehall, the massed mourners of Britain's war dead were left at a standstill for hours on end.

In the queue to honour the Queen, an atmosphere of warm

kindred-spiritedness prevailed. In the queues for the Cenotaph and abbey in 1920, something bleaker could be felt. The long rows of women, dressed almost entirely in black, presented a sombre sight. 'One old lady came from the far north of Scotland,' noted a policeman who was struck by the number of women who had come from very remote villages to pay their respects to the dead. 'She carried a bunch of withered flowers, and told me with tears in her eyes that the flowers came from a little garden which her boy had planted when he was only six.'[43] Another in widow's weeds, who had come up to London by train with her 10-year-old boy, had burst into tears when she heard she could not be admitted to the earlier ceremony. 'I wrote for a place and had no answer. But I *did* think they would help me, and thought it would be all right if I came up,' she sobbed. 'My husband came over from India to enlist, and brought me and the boy with him. He was wounded three times, badly enough to be excused from service, but each time he volunteered again. The last time, he never came back.'[44]

One widow of twenty-one – though she looked more like sixteen – was philosophical about the length of the queue. 'I'm going to put my wreath on the Unknown Soldier's grave,' she declared. 'And if I've got to wait here all day, I'll do it in the end.'[45] The long queues, still waiting at the Cenotaph past midnight, made an extraordinary sight. 'The vast sweep of the road was almost silent, save for the ceaseless murmur of footsteps,' recalled one witness. 'Under the brilliant glare of the lamps that were softened by the foggy air, the long, dark lines of people stretched from Trafalgar Square to the Cenotaph, from whose base they could be seen vanishing into the distance: two narrow lines of slowly moving people, separated by a wide pathway on which stood, here and there, vague figures of policemen on horseback.'[46]

Next day, 200,000 people passed through the abbey. On the Saturday, many of the far-flung football fans travelling by train down to London to support their local teams took the opportunity to pay their respects at the Cenotaph, with cohorts from Blackburn, Blackpool and Sheffield standing out among them.[47]

For some, however, the emotions aroused by the ceremony and subsequent pilgrimage were simply too much. After returning from the Cenotaph that evening, one mourner went to visit a friend. 'Goodbye,' he had said as he was leaving. 'This is the last time you will see me.' His body was found later that night on a railway line in Middlesex. Returning a verdict of 'Suicide while of unsound mind', the coroner said that the scenes at the Cenotaph had no doubt preyed on the old man's soul, 'particularly in view of the fact that he had lost a son in the war'.[48]

* * *

In London and beyond, the events of 11 November 1920 were both haunting and redemptive. The cautiously pessimistic King George V pronounced himself pleased with the way things had turned out. Back at Buckingham Palace, the King wrote in his personal diary: 'Got home at 12 o'clock, everything was most beautifully arranged and carried out.'[49] Later adding: 'The whole ceremony at the Cenotaph was most moving and impressive. I then followed the gun carriage on foot to Westminster Abbey where the burial took place; the grave was filled in with soil brought from France. The Service was beautiful and conducted by the Dean.'[50] His private secretary sent a note of thanks to Dean Ryle that evening: 'The King was deeply impressed with today's unique ceremony the inception of which was your own ... His Majesty sincerely thanks you and all concerned for the perfect manner in which everything was carried out.'[51] Prime Minister Lloyd George also expressed his gratitude, writing:

> *I wish to express on my own behalf and on behalf of His Majesty's government, our grateful appreciation of your courtesy in allowing last Friday's [sic] service to be held in your old and historic building, whose record is so intimately associated with many great events in our country's history. The service at the Abbey was by general acceptance in its*

dignity and solemnity fully adequate to the occasion. It
was a striking tribute to the memory of those gallant men
who were so foully murdered in the performance of their
duties and a true expression of grief felt by all classes in the
country.[52]

Perhaps one of the most remarkable personal narratives of the
Unknown Warrior's funeral was published shortly after the event,
apparently written as 'a claiming of individual grief among the
collective'.[53]

'The most terrible words in all writing used to be *There they
crucified Him*. But there is a sadder sentence now – *I know not
where they have laid Him*. Surely "missing" is the cruellest word in
the language.' While filled with the most intimate, specific details
about the family of the dead soldier – whom the writer refers to
simply as 'John' – it must have struck a powerful chord with all
those families desperate to feel their own private connection with
the man who had just been buried in Westminster Abbey. The
sentiments expressed will certainly be representative of all who
were there that day:

The Evening of November 11 1920

Boy dear, I am so happy I have found you at last. I am sure the
authorities did all they could, but oh, I am so thankful that the
long and bitter disappointment of opening official envelopes is
ended. I am so thankful that I shall never again have to read those
cruel words, 'Regret – No Trace . . .'

I have found you at last. Today I stood by your grave. It
seemed such a little grave for your great heart. The King and all
the mighty of the land were about us, but it was my arms you
felt around you as you sank to sleep. When the bugles blew the
Reveille, I almost cried 'Hush!' for I had just heard your drowsy
sigh of content. Sleep well; it has been such a long and tiring day.
You will be rested when morning breaks.

Your father was the proudest man in all Britain today. His eyes were sparkling gems, almost too vividly bright in his statuesque face as he stood like a Guardsman on parade. And your mother, as ever, understanding everything. 'We must take care not to be late, my dear. This is a great day, we must be off in good time.'

I never understood what 'Death swallowed up in victory' meant until I watched your father by your grave. For even he had never pictured you lying among the greatest of his people's heroes, beside Royal bones, taking your own proud place in his country's history, yourself history too. 'Buried in Westminster Abbey – my son John.'

Your mother? How can I hope to tell you of her thoughts in the Abbey? Does anyone really know what any mother thinks on such a day as this? 'It is strange,' she said in that matter-of-fact way of hers, 'how sometimes, without warning, something quite unexpected gets past one's guard and cuts through all one's defences.'

Of myself I do not write, boy dear. You know without my telling you I was always proud of you and I am prouder than ever today. But as always, still a little jealous for you too. I hate to share you with anyone, even the greatest in the land. I cannot yield my place as mourner even to the King. I loved the crowds for the homage they paid you, but you are mine and mine alone.

Tonight when it is very dark, when all the statues are asleep and the Abbey silent as the grave, I shall steal through the portal of the mansion of the Dead, past the rows of famous warriors, and I will whisper to you words that no one else shall ever hear.

And kiss you goodnight.[54]

It had been a day of healing, a day of hurt, a day of forlorn memories and of flowers wet with untold tears. A day that marked, at last, the end of an exceptional journey for an unknown man; a man nobody could now ever forget.

CHAPTER FOURTEEN

THE SEARCH CONTINUES

1920–1925

For many thousands of families, the funeral of the Unknown Warrior had, at last, brought some of the equilibrium they had so desperately sought. As one writer neatly put it: 'The Cenotaph is the token of our mourning as a nation; the Grave of the Unknown Warrior is the token of our mourning as individuals.'[1]

Following the ceremony, the authorities had planned for a pilgrimage lasting three days, after which the tomb would be closed. But, as the *Yorkshire Post* reported, 'No one could have foretold how surely the emblem to the glorious dead and the symbolic grave would capture the imagination of the people.'[2] So the candles around it remained lit and the 7-mile queue of mourners, standing four-deep, waited to pay their respects.[3] One-legged veterans on crutches, faces disfigured by shrapnel, stood alongside children, parents and uncles. 'There were little ones in their mother's arms who had never known their daddy,' wrote one commentator. 'Boys and girls who had only experienced during a fleeting ten days' leave all that daddy meant to them. But each mother told her child that daddy had now returned, and hundreds of these children placed a simple bouquet at the foot of the national monument.'[4] By Sunday, the base of the Cenotaph was buried beneath 100,000 floral tributes, which rose 10 feet up its flanks.[5] There were grand wreaths from regiments and home-made affairs from the slums of Rochester and Reading. And a myriad of single red roses, the most vivid shade of crimson, each symbolising a lost love and combining into a carpet of arterial blood. The bittersweet aroma of loss wafted the length of Whitehall. By Monday, it was estimated that a million and a half people had paid their respects at the Cenotaph, and at least half a million at the abbey.[6]

One little boy who stooped to place a posy at the foot of the Cenotaph made even the policemen standing guard blink back tears. 'Oh look, Mummy,' he cried with delight. 'What a lovely garden my daddy's got!'[7] Curiously, the fact that some well-meaning parents had succeeded in persuading their children that the body inside the coffin in Westminster Abbey really *was* their father caused its own complications.

After all, they couldn't *all* be right, could they?

One soldier's 7-year-old son was so impressed by what his mother had said that he told all his schoolfriends about the high honour which had been bestowed upon his father. To his amazement and indignation, another small boy claimed that it was *his* daddy who had been followed to Westminster Abbey by the King and buried with regal splendour. 'A spirited altercation ended in a personal encounter,' reported the local newspaper, 'in which the children displayed all the courage of their fathers. Both are now in hospital undergoing repairs.'[8]

Other children, meanwhile, had to watch their remaining parent's life slowly fall apart. After attending the official ceremony at the Cenotaph, young Donald Overall and his family had headed to St Bride's Church near Fleet Street, where his father's regiment had gathered a congregation of veterans, widows, orphans and parents. 'The organ was playing with the regimental band in accompaniment, and the one hymn they played was "Oh Valiant Hearts". My mother was in tears once more. I can't forget that day. I was feeling for my mum, and I'd never had to confront those feelings before.'[9]

* * *

In the midst of this tumult of emotion was the body of the Unknown Warrior, his open grave still covered by the Actors' Pall and Padre Railton's battle-worn flag. Dean Ryle had announced that it would finally be sealed on the night of Wednesday, 17 November, but as the deadline approached, the numbers of people attempting to visit the abbey grew and grew. Bowing to the will of the public, Ryle agreed to postpone its closure for one more day. Finally, at 4PM on Thursday, 18 November, in the gathering dusk of a wintry afternoon, the great doors were finally locked against the procession of frozen mourners still hoping to be allowed inside.

One hundred sandbags of soil from the battlefields of France and Flanders, which had accompanied the casket aboard HMS *Verdun*, were now emptied over it, rendering war poet Rupert Brooke's 'corner of a foreign field' both literally and symbolically 'forever England'.[10]

Then a slab of white marble temporarily sealed the tomb. On it was chiselled the gilded inscription:

A BRITISH WARRIOR WHO FELL

IN THE GREAT WAR 1914–1918
FOR KING AND COUNTRY.

GREATER LOVE HATH NO MAN THAN THIS.

The Bible-literate public of the day would have had no difficulty completing the last line: 'that a man lay down his life for his friends'.[11]

For almost a year, between three and four hundred tributes were still being laid at the Cenotaph every week.[12] And the space around the Unknown Warrior's grave remained festooned with flowers and lovingly scrawled cards, alongside David Railton's flag.

Railton himself was now too busy helping the homeless and unemployed he encountered on a daily basis in Margate to give much thought to symbolism, however potent. He was punishingly aware of the worsening plight of ex-servicemen countrywide. He even

undertook a lengthy pilgrimage around Cumberland disguised as
a tramp to experience his ex-comrades' struggle to find a way back
through the wreckage of their past lives, having given up everything
to defend their homeland.[13] In May 1920, unemployment stood at
less than 3 per cent. A year later, it was running at almost 24 per
cent. Times were not just hard. For many, they were near impossible.

Railton had set out with a shilling in the pocket of his shabby
overcoat, stopping at houses and farms along the way, asking for
work. Some nights he slept rough and, at least once, in a doss-
house. The poor, more often than not, were the first to offer
small gifts of food and money. Worse, perhaps, than the physical
hardship for the transparently honest Railton, would have been
the need to pretend to be something he was not. Above all, he was
shocked to discover, because of the large numbers of returning
veterans, how hard it was for ex-servicemen to find a job and adjust
to so-called 'normal' life. For those with disabilities, it could be a
non-starter. With characteristic vision, he had managed to shine a
light on a series of uncomfortable truths. His 'Vicar Turns Tramp'
story attracted attention around the world, prompting at least one
newspaper to acknowledge that 'his experiences induce the belief
that the position of the ex-serviceman seeking work is well-nigh
hopeless'.[14]

* * *

The flowers and wreaths were eventually cleared from the Unknown
Warrior's grave in October 1921. America had conferred upon
him the Congressional Medal of Honor, the greatest award it
could bestow, for actions performed 'at the risk of life, above
and beyond the call of duty'.[15] Their ambassador informed the
Foreign Office in August that the Supreme Commander of the
American Expeditionary Forces, General Pershing, would come to
Britain in person to present it, throwing the British establishment
into something of a quandary. How to respond? The American
Unknown Warrior was due to be buried in Arlington Cemetery,

near Washington DC, in a few weeks' time, and it would be churlish for George V not to decorate *him* in similar fashion.

Lloyd George advised the King that 'no decoration but the Victoria Cross will suffice'. Horrified, he refused. The VC had only ever been awarded for conspicuous gallantry under enemy fire. Even the British Unknown Warrior had not been thus honoured. 'His Majesty considers that to compare the Victoria Cross, the highest military decoration in the world, as an equivalent to the Congress Medal, which has only now been struck and with no history behind it, is to lose sight of all proportion.'[16] This was probably a bit harsh, since the VC, introduced by the eponymous Queen in 1856, only pre-dated the Congressional Medal by a matter of five years. In any event, Lloyd George eventually persuaded his monarch to send a telegram to President Harding declaring, 'I greatly wish to confer upon your Unknown Warrior our highest decoration for valour, the Victoria Cross.'[17]

General Pershing duly arrived on 'a thick foggy morning'[18] with his 470-strong guard of honour, along with a detachment of seventy-five sailors from the USS *Olympia*, which would later collect the body of their own unknown soldier from Le Havre. The American naval contingent were carrying their rifles, much to Dean Ryle's disapproval, who forbade them from being brought inside.[19] Pershing described the 'overpowering emotion' he felt upon entering Westminster Abbey for the medal ceremony on 17 October, surrounded by the graves of so many distinguished men and women. 'As they pass in memory before us,' he said, 'there is none whose deeds are more worthy, and none whose devotion inspires our admiration more than the Unknown Warrior. In this holy sanctuary, in the name of the President and the people of the United States, I place upon his tomb the Medal of Honor, in commemoration of the sacrifices of our British comrade and his fellow countrymen.'[20]

After carefully arranging 'with reverent hands' the medal's wide blue ribbon of watered silk on the tomb, he stepped two paces back and saluted.[21]

* * *

Around the same time, Dean Ryle was formally inviting David Railton to the upcoming Armistice Day service in Westminster Abbey on 11 November 1921, during which another ceremony would be held to dedicate and hang his treasured flag. With Railton in attendance in the abbey three weeks later, the white and gold Actors' Pall which had covered the Warrior's grave a year earlier was drawn back to reveal the sombre yet striking new gravestone, 7 feet long and 4 feet wide, hewn from a solid lump of black Tournai marble, quarried in Belgium. The inscription was carefully inlaid using brass melted down from shell and bullet cases retrieved from the battlefields of France and Flanders. Dean Ryle had apparently written the words 'with painstaking care, embodying in it, the texts which had accompanied wreaths sent on the first Armistice Day':[22]

BENEATH THIS STONE RESTS THE BODY

OF A BRITISH WARRIOR

UNKNOWN BY NAME OR RANK

BROUGHT FROM FRANCE TO LIE AMONG

THE MOST ILLUSTRIOUS OF THE LAND

AND BURIED HERE ON ARMISTICE DAY

11 NOV: 1920, IN THE PRESENCE OF

HIS MAJESTY KING GEORGE V

HIS MINISTERS OF STATE

THE CHIEFS OF HIS FORCES

AND A VAST CONCOURSE OF THE NATION

THUS ARE COMMEMORATED THE MANY

MULTITUDES WHO DURING THE GREAT

WAR OF 1914–1918 GAVE THE MOST THAT

MAN CAN GIVE LIFE ITSELF

FOR GOD

FOR KING AND COUNTRY

FOR LOVED ONES HOME AND EMPIRE

FOR THE SACRED CAUSE OF JUSTICE AND

THE FREEDOM OF THE WORLD

THEY BURIED HIM AMONG THE KINGS BECAUSE HE

HAD DONE GOOD TOWARD GOD AND TOWARD

HIS HOUSE

David Railton stepped forward to the altar and handed his flag to Lord Haig, who presented it in turn to Dean Ryle. 'This flag,' declared the Dean, 'which was carried in France during the Great War and has rested for 12 months at the grave of the Unknown Warrior, we herewith dedicate to the glory of God, and in perpetual memory of all who gave their lives fighting on land and sea and air for their King, for Great Britain and Ireland, and for the Dominions beyond the seas.'[23]

Outside, people were gathered at the Cenotaph, once again in their thousands, waiting for Big Ben to trigger the start of another Great Silence. And once again, 'the hush that ensued was profound, and for the first minute the world seemed soundless. Strong men standing bareheaded allowed tears to course unchecked down their cheeks. Their womenfolk, bending before the rush of affectionate memories, could not withhold the sobs that racked them. Mercifully, when the tension became more than could humanly be borne, the crackling of a maroon [an exploding flare] signalled the end of the period of silent prayer.'[24]

Inside the abbey, too, the silence was highly charged. Especially for Railton, seeing his flag on the high altar, bringing together the martial and spiritual aspects of his life, which had so often been in bitter conflict. After the silence, the procession, including Dean Ryle, Lord Haig and Railton himself, moved back down the nave to stand by the grave of the Unknown Warrior. Gathered there, too, were soldiers from the 47th (London) Division, with whom Railton had served at High Wood. The old unit of Anthony French and his dead friend, Bert Bradley, and of young Alec Reader, the promising young cross-country runner who never did take his copy of *Treasure Island* back to the school library.

'All eyes now turned to the grave,' wrote one witness. 'The flag already dedicated was handed to a soldier, who mounted a ladder and placed it in position on a pillar, from which it will hang over the tomb of the Unknown.'[25]

* * *

While the burial of the Unknown Warrior had brought public relief and even a hint of closure to many families, it was not a miracle cure. The missing were still missing. The bereaved were still wondering. And, even three years after the war, there were still bodies lying on the former battlefields, sometimes in plain sight, waiting to be collected. And yet the authorities were preparing to call off the search. In the summer of 1921, an official report certified that, almost without exception, 'the whole of the battlefield areas of France and Belgium have been finally searched for isolated graves, both British and German. It cannot be guaranteed that no graves remain in the area. Some 204,654 remains had been [located].'[26] Yet by autumn 1921, 300,000 men were still unaccounted for.[27] Questions were asked in Parliament: was enough being done to find the bodies of the missing? The exhumation parties could have given their own answer, but it would undoubtedly have been unprintable. The lives of those continuing with that epic task were not to be envied. Even the resourceful and highly decorated Lieutenant Colonel Edward Gell, General Wyatt's companion in the chapel at Saint-Pol on the night the Unknown Warrior was chosen, was beginning to feel the strain. In August 1921, his senior officer had written to say that he had sent him away on leave as he was showing initial signs of a mental breakdown.[28]

The headquarters of the Directorate of Graves Registration and Enquiries at Saint-Pol were to be closed down at the end of September 1921, with responsibility for the exhumation work passed on to the Imperial War Graves Commission, which would provide a more limited service. The stalwart individuals who had worked together to attempt to bring order to the chaos of the body-strewn battlefields began to say their goodbyes.

For Vere Brodie – who, a year earlier, had witnessed the bodies arriving for selection – it was a sad time. 'Leaving St Pol meant leaving what had become a very happy home to everyone,' she said later. 'By September 1921, our uniforms, which had never been renewed, were very much the worse for wear, and only just held together. But I look back on those days very often. They were full of interest and good friends.'[29] On Monday, 26 September, Brodie and her female colleagues marched out of camp with the rest of 'the boys'. Local French people came to their doors to watch the little parade go past and call 'Au revoir' and 'Bon voyage'. Arriving in London the next day, they were finally demobilised at the War Office. 'This was the official end,' wrote Brodie. 'But the members unanimously felt that they would, as their last act, like to take some flowers to the Cenotaph.' They laid their wreaths at its foot, 'to the boys who, unlike ourselves, would not come back'.

Then they made one last pilgrimage. To the grave of one boy who had come back against all the odds. 'We, from St Pol, have a special feeling towards the Unknown Warrior, as it was in our camp that he was chosen from other unknown soldiers. And it was in our camp chapel that he lay before being carried to England and Westminster Abbey.'

Vere does not mention in her diaries that she also had a very personal reason for paying her respects at the tomb. She had lost a brother and a cousin during the war, along with several loyal estate workers employed at the family's Scottish home. Her cousin's grave, destroyed in subsequent fighting, was lost. Like so many others, her family were still wondering where their very own Unknown Warriors lay.

* * *

With the search parties in the process of being disbanded, the Secretary of State for War was finally forced to make a statement in *The Times* attempting to ease public anxiety. 'Since the Armistice, the whole battlefield area in France and Flanders has been systematically searched at least six times. Some areas in which the fighting had been particularly heavy, were searched as many as 20 times.' He explained that the early ventures had been fairly straightforward, owing to the number of 'surface indications' – often visible bones and body parts, or a patch of vegetation, thriving because of a decomposing body a few inches below. Since then, however, 90 per cent of the bodies found had been in 'invisible graves', only discovered thanks to the skill and experience of the exhumation parties. 'It is probable that a number of these invisible graves have not yet been found,' he continued, 'and are likely to be brought to light during the work of reconstruction and in the opening up of areas at present inaccessible owing to the thickness of undergrowth, the marshiness of the land, etc. The searching, however, was most thorough.'[30]

It is hard to imagine that any bereaved family still hoping for news of a loved one was reassured by this. And they were unlikely to know that bodies *were* still being found – and in large numbers, too. When the officials of the IWGC convened for their thirty-seventh meeting on 18 October 1921, one commissioner had quietly observed: 'If it was known to the public that bodies were being found at the rate of 200 a week at the time the search parties were disbanded, the public would want an explanation.'[31]

It wasn't as if that public could be kept at arm's length, either. The very first civilians had travelled to the battlefields in France in December 1918, and the number of visitors was growing all the time. Many travelled with charitable organisations such as the Church Army, who had taken 5,000 family members by the summer of 1920, the Salvation Army, who made it possible for 18,500 people to travel between 1920 and 1923, and the YMCA, who helped 60,000 bereaved to travel to France and Flanders between 1918 and 1923. Others made the journey by themselves, and by 1921 the French tyre company, Michelin – famous for its iconic guidebooks – had published fifteen English-language visitor guides to the battlefields. Clever marketing, considering how many tyres would need to be replaced after battling with the rutted, shrapnel-studded and shell-strewn roads and tracks of northern France.[32]

Worst of all, for the families of the missing, was the thought of the numbers still lying in those foreign fields until their corpses were unearthed by weather conditions or scavenging animals. Once the search parties had left an area, who was going to mark a British grave, let alone endeavour to identify a body? On 26 May 1922, one of them wrote to the press expressing his horror at the 'hundreds, if not thousands' of British bodies still lying exposed in France. 'The whole circumstances are a disgrace to our nationhood,' he thundered.[33]

He had a point. Between 1921 and 1928, another 28,000 bodies were found, of which only a quarter were able to be identified. And 10,000 more were discovered in the years up to 1937, at least half of them by labourers hunting for scrap metal. Almost a third were dug or ploughed up by farmers working their fields.[34]

* * *

Some of those making their way across the Channel to visit the grave of their loved one had been planning the trip from the moment they had received the worst of all possible news. Others, relatives of the missing, had no clear destination. The personal quest, the unquenchable desire for answers, remained, for many, an open wound. Perhaps he was lying forgotten in a hospital or asylum? Perhaps, shell-shocked, he had forgotten his own name?

Henry Hamilton confessed that he was 'haunted by the idea that there is a bare possibility that my son is alive and might be found somewhere, possibly the victim of an aphasia'.[35] Had the Canadian been a poor man, circumstances might have forced him to accept his loss. But, as Richard van Emden says in *Missing: The Need for Closure after the Great War*, 'wealth could be its own curse, condemning families to open-ended investigations with almost no chance of success, while paralysing lives that would otherwise continue, albeit under a veil'.[36] Hamilton was no stranger to that curse. Before the war, he had been an energetic barrister and the former mayor of a large town near the Great Lakes. Logical and highly intelligent, he simply didn't understand how a body could just vanish into thin air. Particularly when that body belonged to his youngest son. On one level, Hamilton was no different from the thousands of other bereaved parents unable to accept their son's death. On another, he would demonstrate just how far a determined father could go, with sheer dogged tenacity. And hard cash.

The last anyone had heard of 20-year-old Robert Hamilton was that he was being treated for injuries at a dressing station on 8 August 1918, the first day of the Battle of Amiens. He and another young Canadian, a carpenter before the war, had suffered severe head wounds when a German shell exploded and killed five of their comrades. The carpenter died at the dressing station soon afterwards. But Robert Hamilton's fate remained a mystery. He seems to have simply disappeared.

It is one thing to vanish in the endless, clinging mud of no-man's-land during an offensive. But to do so while being treated in hospital is a very different matter.[37] Undaunted by the thousands of miles of ocean that separated Canada from France, Hamilton Sr set about finding his son. He conducted his own investigation of unit records and battle reports, sharing his wishful conclusion with the Imperial War Graves Commission: 'The weight of evidence appears to be that Gunner Hamilton is still living.' This was only the beginning. Hamilton then contacted those who had staffed various field hospitals and smaller medical units in the vicinity. He produced an incredibly detailed map of the key stages in his son's journey, convinced that Robert and his fellow casualty had actually been moved to a different dressing station, known as White Chateau. He presented his evidence to the Red Cross and the Canadian military. As his investigations continued, Hamilton appears to have grudgingly accepted the possibility that his son might, after all, be dead. But if that were the case, where was the body? Hamilton's hunch was that, despite having succumbed to his injuries in a hospital bed, Robert must have been buried mistakenly as one of the thousands known only 'unto God'.

In July 1919, Hamilton pursued a lead that surfaced in Rouen. An unidentified soldier had died on 15 August 1918, exactly a week after his son had been wounded, and was buried in the town's St Sever Cemetery. Despite his failing health, Hamilton agreed to attend the proposed exhumation. Alas, the exhausting journey and the gory dig were in vain. The body wasn't Robert's.

In early 1920, he learned that an unknown Canadian had been buried close to a medical facility near his son's possible last port of call. Another grave was dug up, but, once again, fruitlessly disturbed, although the marker was changed to an 'Unknown British Soldier', presumably because some personal equipment had helped identify the body's nationality, if not his name. Next, Hamilton uncovered something even more remarkable. A Canadian soldier named Gillis, whose details were clearly marked on an Amiens headstone, was actually alive. After further bureaucratic tussles, the opening of very-much-alive Gillis's grave was undertaken. But, yet again, its decaying contents did not belong to Robert Hamilton.

In November 1920, just as the selection process for the Unknown Warrior was gathering momentum and the four bodies were being brought to Saint-Pol, Hamilton prompted yet another exhumation, this time having come across an unidentified Canadian who had died in hospital on 9 August 1918, the day after his son was wounded. Again, the black earth did not give up the body of his son.

On and on it went.

I can only imagine what this quest was like for Henry Hamilton, as he repeatedly attended the exhumations of rotting corpses in the hope that one of them might be his son. A writer who had fought in the war recalled one such experience where he heard a comrade gasp: '*What is that face? His face? It isn't his face.* In place of his face we found the hair. The corpse was broken, and folded the wrong way,' later writing of another, 'the legs came unstuck at the knees, and his [breeches] tore away. There was me with a full boot in each fist. The legs and feet had to be emptied out.'[38] Henry Hamilton must have immersed himself in these gut-wrenching ordeals on many occasions. If the burial of the Unknown Warrior in Westminster Abbey had offered some closure to many, it was never going to be enough for him. In July 1921 – nearly three years after his son's death – he persuaded the IWGC to sanction another exhumation, and this time sent his nephew from Canada to attend the dig; still no joy. These endless journeys would not have been lightly undertaken. A transatlantic steamship crossing took between five and nine days, depending on fog and ice, and a second-class return cost some £200 (about £11,000 today).[39]

Now Hamilton began to focus on the grave of the young carpenter who had died of his wounds following the shell blast that had also injured his son. Permission to dig up the carpenter was refused by the IWGC, but an illegal exhumation appears to have been carried out at Longueau Cemetery, near Amiens, in 1921. Robert wasn't there either.

Unflagging, Hamilton now began to consider the graves of German unknowns at Longueau. What if his son were buried in one of those? He had evidence that an enemy soldier with a head wound had sought help from one of the Canadian dressing stations in 1918. Once again, he sent his long-suffering nephew to Europe on a voyage of fruitless exhumation. The officers of the IWGC were becoming exasperated. There would and could be no more exhumations. But another long letter from Hamilton in August 1922 swayed them into agreeing to an exhumation of *nine* unknown German graves in what Hamilton argued was the final resting place for those who didn't survive White Chateau dressing station.

The powers that be in the IWGC assured Hamilton, in their tight-lipped response, that his presence would not be necessary. He made the journey anyway and must have derived a certain grim satisfaction from the discovery that two of the unknown 'German' graves actually contained British soldiers. As a barrister, this was gold dust. If the witness could be proved unreliable on one point, how could any of his testimony be trusted? Now he went for the jugular, demanding that *all* German graves at Longueau be dug up. This was scheduled for January 1924, more than five years after Robert's death. No trace of Gunner Hamilton could be found.

By July, Henry Hamilton still hadn't lost his zeal for more exhumations. He wrote a fifteen-page letter, laying out his claims, counter-claims, accusations, observations and demands. A month later, a further eleven bodies were uncovered. More applications to the IWGC followed, but on 7 November 1925, four days before the anniversary of the Armistice that had come three months too late to save his son, Henry Hamilton died. His long battle for answers had come to an end, leaving behind a foreign field littered with the disinterred remains of no fewer than fifty-five graves. His widow and their two surviving sons did not continue his hopeless quest.

But many of the rest of the bereaved were still desperate to connect with their loved ones.

* * *

Elizabeth French – an impoverished widow living in Scotland – was one of the 'lucky ones' who did have a grave to visit. But, unlike Henry Hamilton, she did not have the resources to do so. Her 22-year-old son Joseph had been killed on the first day of the Third Battle of Ypres in July 1917. A battlefield padre had broken the news to her in a letter from the front, which Elizabeth kept for the rest of her life:

> *Dear Mrs French,*
> *I have a very sad and painful piece of news to break to you, which I am afraid you will indeed find hard to bear.*
> *You will have read in the papers that a great battle was fought in Belgium on Tuesday 31st July, and that that battle resulted in a great victory to our army.*

*But such a victory has its cost, and it grieves me to have
to tell you that your son No. 265123 Pte J. French was buried
by a shell during that action.*

*The loss of a son must always be a very hard one for a
mother to bear.*[40]

The loss of her son was indeed very hard for her to bear. From the
moment Joseph was killed, she had been determined to visit his
grave, and when she read that the YMCA Red Triangle League was
offering a scheme to help bereaved parents do just that, she quickly
wrote to them. A grant to cover the journey was duly approved,
with the cost estimated at £13 5s 10d (roughly £830 today), along
with a passport for Elizabeth which had to be signed by the local
policeman once she had glued her photograph, taken at a professional studio, inside.

Elizabeth's husband had died in 1920, so she would be travelling
alone on what would be her first trip abroad. Just three weeks after
Railton's flag was dedicated and hung in Westminster Abbey on
11 November 1921, Elizabeth spent a night at the Euston Hotel in
London, in readiness for an early ferry to Belgium the following day.

A month before he died, her son Joseph had come home on leave.
He, too, had stopped in the capital on his way back to the front line:

Dear Mother,

*I arrived here in London today about 10AM after a fairly
decent journey and not much the worse – only a wee bittie
homesick, that will soon pass away once I am back with
the boys. I felt the coming away getting hard this time,
and although I was maybe looking pretty bright, I was not
altogether all right. Well, I hope the war will soon be finished
and us all back again very soon to bonny Scotland and home.*

Elizabeth was keenly aware, all these years later, that she was about
to retrace Joseph's final footsteps, and she kept a comprehensive
diary of her journey:

'This is the Ypres party here,' our host said, and led me to a table where three ladies and a young man sat. We quickly ascertained where we had all come from, and which cemeteries were to be visited. Our party consisted of an old lady and her son, on their way to visit the eldest son's grave; two sisters on the way to visit the grave of their only brother who fell in action after being only nine weeks at the front, and myself.

Next morning, a smiling guide approached the travellers' table and led them out to catch the underground line to Victoria Station. 'This was another new experience for me, although to my companions it was nothing new, and they smiled indulgently when I told them so.'

From Victoria, Elizabeth and her party caught the South Eastern and Chatham Railway train to Dover, making the Unknown Warrior's homecoming journey in reverse. From Dover their ferry took them east towards Belgium. It was a rough crossing, and everyone was seasick. Disembarking at Ostend, they scanned the crowd anxiously for their Red Triangle guide. 'Just at the end of the gangway we picked him out,' she said, 'noting with pitying eyes that the khaki sleeve at his right side hung empty, poor fellow. A splendid specimen of English manhood he must have been, until war had maimed him for ever. Oh, how glad we were to reach *terra firma* again, and to hear our guide's cheery greeting: "Come along, Red Triangles, follow me."'

They caught a train to Ypres, a weary slog after their long day, the air so icy that their carriage windows were frozen over. But perhaps the hardship helped, as Elizabeth's thoughts began to turn to Joseph's last few weeks in this harsh landscape. 'Until now, I, and I think the others also, had kept thoughts of our destination at bay. Now it gripped us relentlessly, and our little jokes and pleasantries fell from us. We sat in silence, seeing visions and dreaming dreams of our young heroes who had led the way before us, whom we had nursed in their infancy, and watched with fear in our hearts as they marched lightly away on that never-to-be-forgotten day, to meet death on these battlefields through which we were now speeding.'

Elizabeth found herself struggling to make sense of the bitter mystery of it all. 'Many, many times have I vainly tried to reason out the eternal why and wherefore of such awful happenings, and with ruthless force it gripped my heart again. Why had this dear lad, whose grave I had journeyed so far to see, who had just opened his eyes 26 years ago, and who had lived a quiet and blameless life, been fated to come to this far away land of Belgium to die?'

It helped, perhaps, that others in the group were struggling, too. A shared solidarity in grief. 'Just as I had reached the blank wall of unanswering silence again, our dear old lady whispered with white lips: "My poor Peter had to come a long way to die." We drew together and, until Ypres was reached, spoke in hushed tones of our boys, telling their all-too-short life stories and their little youthful pranks. It comforted us all and helped to draw our thoughts from these awful fields we knew lay out there about us.'

Finally, the brakes began to groan as the train clattered towards Ypres, and Elizabeth and her frozen companions saw the scattered lights of the ruined town. A plank bridge across a trench led them to their lodgings, where their guide pushed open a door, letting in a blast of icy wind which nearly extinguished the swinging lamps in the large dining room. 'Oh, how cold you must be.' Their new host held out a welcoming hand. 'Come to the stove at once.' Elizabeth noted her prematurely grey hair and sad eyes. But there was cheer too. 'There seemed to be a crowd about the tables and a babble of talk was going on as we thawed our numbed hands and feet before the fine stove. As soon as dinner was over, we formed a wide circle about the huge fire and quickly found ourselves at home.' But now Elizabeth began to pick up details about how the DGR&E contingent from Saint-Pol were spending their time. 'It came to me with a shock that my immediate neighbours on the couch were calmly talking of the exhuming of bodies.' Just that day, she heard, sixteen had been dug up and buried in a nearby cemetery. One lady in the hostel had fainted on seeing one of the corpses being carried past. Elizabeth had been focused on Joseph, but now she began to feel that 'war with its attendant horrors' was all around her.

But there was worse to come, in their cramped quarters. 'Oh, that terrible night of cold! I do not think any of us will ever forget it. The sheets were like ice. And ice, solid to the very bottom, was in our jugs. In fact, jugs generally split in two there, we were informed. Our little old lady suffered terribly in the other bed as she was still weak from a recent severe operation.' Elizabeth was haunted by the thought of what it must have been like for their sons. 'In the trenches and on the bare hillsides they had endured this bitter weather in all its variations, and my wonder now is that so many of our surviving boys returned with sane minds and in many cases cheery souls.'

Elizabeth's destination the next day was the cemetery at Boezinge, about 5 miles north of Ypres. The trench system there still attracts battlefield tourists today. When it was excavated between 1998 and 2000, some 155 corpses, undisturbed since the First World War, were unearthed. Only one could be identified: Frenchman François Metzinger, who had died on 21 May 1915. The others were Unknown Warriors.

That afternoon, her new YMCA guide, Tommy, arrived to drive her the final stretch of her pilgrimage. She hurried to get everything ready. 'I brought from our room a wreath of holly and other greenery which I had carried from home for my grave, made for me by a father who had given two sons to his country's cause. On my family's behalf, I purchased from Mr Marston a lovely cross of white artificial flowers which they wished me to lay on their brother's grave.' They set off. 'And only when I was stepping into the car did I remember that I had never been in one before.' Elizabeth had laughingly said as much to her son on his last leave, and he had promised to take her for a ride himself. After the war was over. Now, she reflected, 'my joy ride was to visit his grave'. Even an experienced passenger would have found it a terrifying journey. 'Now be sure to grip the seat well as it's an awful road,' Tommy told her as they headed off. 'Dodging a shell hole here and a huge pile of debris there, sometimes with one wheel up and the other deep in a frozen rut, we tore through the town. It seemed to me as we sped on that human ingenuity would never cope with the havoc, and that Ypres must forever lie as one of the ruined cities of the world.'

At last Tommy stopped the car and they stumbled across several ploughed fields before finally reaching 'the lonely little spot' she had travelled so far to see. They passed through a small white gate with a painted sign: 'No Man's Cottage Cemetery, British'. First used at the end of July 1917, Joseph French, killed on 31 July, must have been one of its first occupants. Today, it contains seventy-nine graves, of which just two are unidentified. Tommy handed Elizabeth her wreaths, then whispered, 'Give me your passport and I will find your grave.'

Elizabeth would later write that she could not really describe the 'all too few minutes, precious to mothers beyond all others' she spent at Joseph's graveside. But she certainly evoked the desolate scene as best she could, perhaps conscious that her description of her own pilgrimage might be the closest that some bereaved mothers might ever come to visiting their own son's grave:

It lies on the ridge of a long, bare slope below which the war had raged bitterly. In every direction, as far as the eye can reach, rise the white columns of stone erected at the cessation of hostilities. All round lie trenches, which in course of time will no doubt be filled in, and on the left, lies ruined Ypres. 'No Man's Cot' contains only three rows of crosses. I do not think there are more than a hundred men buried there altogether. There is no road to it yet. Even the permanent fence has not been erected; simply a strand or two of barbed wire encloses this quiet and lonely little God's area where surely our boys sleep as quietly as they would at home in Morayshire. At the rear of the cemetery, in a little square of fence, stands the memorial recording the sacrifice of the men who lie there. With numbing fingers, I tied my white cross to that other cross below the seven names. Tying my holly wreath also, for a rising wind warned me that they would not lie long on the grave, I took my last lingering farewell and turned away.

This last paragraph comes as a shock to me. We do not know if Elizabeth was expecting to find a single, neatly tended grave, with a trim white headstone engraved with her son's name. But from her description of seven names on a memorial 'in a little square of fence', it sounds as if Joseph must have been entombed in a mass grave with the soldiers he died alongside. Perhaps the crater left by the shell that had taken their lives now provided their final resting place.

Elizabeth French died six years after visiting her son's grave, aged just fifty-three. I truly hope she had found some comfort in her personal voyage of discovery.

BERKSHIRE
SUMMER 2023

All too quickly, before the wounds of the previous conflict had really healed, Britain found itself tumbling into the next one.

Exhausted by the demands of his parish work and perhaps still carrying the corrosive fatigue of his wartime service, David Railton had resigned from his position in Margate in 1925. He took on a number of roles before arriving as Rector of Liverpool in 1935, as new, sinister forces were beginning to shake the foundations of European nations. When war broke out in 1939, Railton, true to character, immediately offered himself for active service. He was fifty-five, but still dismayed by the polite response from the War Office. 'Sir, I am directed to reply to your letter and thank you for your offer of service. I am, however, to inform you that a candidate for a commission as a temporary chaplain for service in the event of war must be under the age of 40. In the circumstances, it is regretted that you cannot be considered for appointment.'[41]

Determined to serve his country once more, he explored various other avenues and eventually, in 1943, the Royal Air Force appointed him as one of seven prominent clergymen or 'super chaplains'. He would spend two weeks a month visiting squadrons and facilities, doing what he could to boost the men's spiritual health and morale, as well as holding services. Much the same work he had done twenty-five years earlier as a battlefield padre in the trenches.

His only son, Andrew, had been preparing to go up to Balliol, his father's old college at Oxford, when the Second World War broke out. Instead, he enlisted and was posted to the Western Desert of North Africa in 1940. Aged just twenty, Andrew Railton appears to have had a truly hair-raising time of it. No doubt having inherited his father's sense of humour and powers of persuasion, he was given command of a company of 120 Ethiopian Patriots whose task was to carry out raids and rally their tribal chiefs. Making do with First World War equipment, young Railton had no radio and his nearest British military support was 30 miles away. Communication was by runner; a request for air cover necessitated a 40-mile trip by mule. Described as an 'unorthodox soldier', he was later posted to India and northern Burma, and captured briefly by the Japanese.[42]

* * *

Eighty years later, surrounded by photographs and memorabilia, I listen in amazement to Margaret, Padre David Railton's daughter-in-law, as she describes her late husband Andrew's military career. He was clearly hewn from the same stone as his father. Sitting in her living room, I see this rather frail 94-year-old light up when she recalls those years. 'Of course, I didn't know Andrew *during* the war, but it must have been very, very difficult for his parents to have their only son away for so long. During the six years he served overseas, they had no personal contact with him at all, from what I understand.'[43]

I am stunned. I have interviewed many hundreds of Second World War veterans, including a great number of prisoners of war, and have never heard of even sporadic contact being impossible. *None at all?* I ask. *For six years?* 'They did get an official letter every now and then to say he was still alive and on operations,' she replies. 'But, no, because of the nature of his work, and his movements around the world, they didn't hear anything from him personally until he came home after the war.' We both consider this for a while. Or, at least, I am considering it. Margaret is looking into the distance, enjoying the view of her garden flowers in the dazzling sunlight. I am thinking about the incredible efforts that David Railton went to in the trenches, the hundreds of letters he wrote, to his family and to those in his care he had buried. And then being stuck at home in Liverpool, on the other end of it all, enduring a silence that lasted for six years. The past is another country, I remind myself; they do things differently there.

Margaret, breaks the silence. 'It's almost impossible to understand what it must have been like not to hear from their only son for so long. Their terrific faith must really have helped them during that difficult time.' So she has been considering it, too. She asks me to hand her one of the yellowing envelopes piled on the sofa and withdraws an old black-and-white photograph of a weary-looking David Railton doing his best to smile in the ruins of a bombed-out church. 'This picture of my father-in-law standing in the remains of Saint Nicholas Church in Liverpool is quite telling; representative of his experience of yet another war.' Railton's church had been hit during a German bombing raid over Christmas 1940. A local newspaper reported: 'Mr Railton distinguished himself when his church was hit, by dashing into the blazing building and rescuing some of the altar vessels.'[44] The bravery he had shown during the First World War still evident in the Second.

With the end of the war came the return of the prodigal son. Far from being apologetic about any shortcomings as a correspondent, Andrew Railton had other things on his mind, as Margaret recalls with a chuckle. 'He was quite annoyed at his parents after his return, because they had allowed moths to get into his wardrobe and make holes in his kilt. And they had also sold his motorbike.' Suddenly she is serious again. 'But at least he came home.'

Like his father, Andrew had won the Military Cross for unstinting courage in the face of the enemy. Letter writing might not have run in the family, but bravery certainly did. I can see that Margaret is thinking again. Still weak from a recent illness, her mind has lost none of the brilliance that earned her a double first in archaeology and anthropology at Cambridge University in 1951. She has that Railton-esque interest in people; a vivid warmth and wisdom that shine through everything she says and does. She quizzes me about my own military service, especially my time as a prisoner of war in Iraq. Most people are too embarrassed to ask about the brutality I suffered, but Margaret has no such qualms and we happily chat about the harsh realities of military life. And death. 'I was lucky that Andrew came home from the Second World War safely,' she tells me. 'Even though he was in a bad way, and weighed only 6 or 7 stone, he still came home. So I do reflect on all those widows and parents from the previous war, who were not fortunate like me. And when you think about how many people flocked to the Unknown Warrior's tomb in 1920, you truly understand just how important the project was; how much it meant to so many people. It brought a finality to their personal experience of war.'[45]

David Railton was honoured with a seat in Westminster Abbey for the Queen's coronation, while Margaret and Andrew stood on Park Lane to watch the procession. 'It's curious to think that the parade we watched in 1953, and then King Charles's coronation procession seventy years later, had some similarities with the procession when the Unknown Warrior returned in 1920. It's really quite strange how these things are echoed through time.'

David Railton himself conducted their 1952 marriage service in London's Eaton Square, and he christened their daughter, Diana, three years later. A few days later, on 28 June 1955, he came to stay with them before heading north to Scotland. 'It was a lovely evening,' Margaret recalls wistfully. 'We had dinner together and chatted. A neighbour with a very beautiful garden had sent the most wonderful box of fresh strawberries, which we all enjoyed after dinner.' The next day, Railton went up to London to catch the sleeper to Fort William, where he now lived with his wife Ruby. 'He had done it so many times before,' Margaret says. 'It was just a normal day.'

As the train sped through the countryside on its journey north through York, Durham and Newcastle, Railton ate dinner and read the evening papers before moving down to his compartment. As he neared his destination the following morning, he donned his coat and hat, collected his suitcase and overnight bag from the luggage rack, then stepped out into the corridor.[46] As the train began to slow, a few hundred yards from the platform, he was standing in the corridor, chatting to a friend, and moved aside to let another passenger pass.[47] The carriage bumped and swayed as its wheels jolted over a set of points. Railton lost his balance and fell heavily against the door, which burst open and sent him tumbling backwards into thin air.[48]

Someone pulled the emergency cord. But it was too late. By the time they reached him, the Reverend David Railton MC was dead. There was nothing anybody could do to save the man who had lived through two world wars, surviving gas attacks and artillery bombardments, machine-gun and sniper fire.

There was no telegram. No dreaded letter from the postman. For Andrew and Margaret Railton, who had been having breakfast with him just twenty-four hours earlier, it all happened much faster. 'We received a telephone call later that day to tell us the awful news. It was quite unbelievable. Such an incredible shock.'

DEATH RIDDLE OF 'UNKNOWN SOLDIER' PADRE screamed the *Daily Mirror* headline, before quoting a police officer who added little in the way of detail: 'Mr Railton was standing in the corridor as the train was slowing down. The door opened – how, we don't know – and he was killed instantly. We do not know the full circumstances and we are still investigating the accident.'[49]

Andrew Railton immediately caught the first train north to identify his father's body and to be with his mother. 'It was all so very sad,' Margaret sighs. 'I was on my own with the baby, so couldn't travel. Our golden retriever, Duff, simply would not settle. Andrew phoned me that night to explain what had happened.' Identifying the broken body must have been an excruciating experience. He was even able to see traces of their beloved dog's fur on his father's trousers. 'My darling Duff simply howled and howled that night.'

Margaret flinches at the memory. 'It was as if he *knew*. Eventually I brought him upstairs and allowed him on the bed. He lay there where my husband normally did and just went to sleep beside me. He must have known that I needed the company and comfort. Dogs can sense grief.'

The little church close to Railton's house in Scotland was packed to overflowing for the funeral. I know from the many I have spent time with during my search for answers surrounding the missing just how precious and valuable it is to hold a funeral after a loved one is killed; how much it helps those left behind to properly grieve and find closure. I know, too, how bruising it is when the circumstances of a death render such a thing impossible. Wasn't this what David Railton's idea for the Unknown Warrior was all about?

So it is with the profoundest sense of irony – and very real sadness – that I discover his beloved wife Ruby, to whom he had confided his innermost thoughts in hundreds of fond letters from the trenches, and with whom he had shared forty-five years of happy and harmonious marriage, had not attended his funeral.

'It was all too much for her.' Margaret looks down at her hands. 'She was so devastated. She just couldn't bring herself to go.'

CHAPTER FIFTEEN

WE WILL REMEMBER YOU

WHITEHALL, LONDON
11 NOVEMBER 2023

Pigeons scavenging for scraps scatter as I hurry through Trafalgar Square on a bright November morning. I follow a small group down Whitehall, huddled in overcoats, medals and poppies pinned to their chests. We pass through the crowds lining the pavements, and yellow-jacketed police officers stopping the traffic. It is 103 years since the Cenotaph was unveiled, and just a matter of months since I stood on the Somme battlefields, trying to imagine what it must have been like to fight and die there. Today, I am truly honoured to have been invited by the Western Front Association to be their guest of honour at their annual service of commemoration at the Cenotaph, marking the precise moment the guns fell silent in 1918. As one veteran tells a TV news crew, 'Armistice Day has been a beacon for remembrance in all eras.' Age-wearied veterans stand alongside teenage military cadets in army khaki and air force blue. A large crowd is gathered behind the barriers waiting in the sunshine. Representatives from schools as far afield as Glasgow and Grantham have made the journey to be part of the service. For me, this is what 'remembrance' is all about. Acknowledging the service of those who went before us, never allowing their sacrifice to be forgotten.

My quest for the genesis of the Unknown Warrior, and his subsequent journey home, has become a deeply resonant, multi-layered voyage of discovery, during the course of which the past has spread its subterranean roots into the present. It was Padre David Railton's deep understanding of the need for a symbol, for answers, that national yearning for closure, that impelled him to act. To give one of the dead – and thus every one of the dead – a proper resting place.

And his timely interventions have equal relevance today, as bodies of the missing are still recovered, as they did more than a century ago.

* * *

Lance Corporal John Morrison was born in 1885, four years after Vere Brodie, who served at Saint-Pol during the selection process for the Unknown Warrior. He had grown up on Vere's family's grand estate in Scotland, where his father was headkeeper. By the age of fifteen, and a gamekeeper himself, he pursued a life close to nature until the war intervened in November 1914, when he joined the Black Watch, one of a host of Vere's family, friends and estate workers who followed her in the service of their country.[1]

Just two months later, on 25 January 1915, a heavy enemy attack threatened the line north of Arras, and Morrison's battalion was sent forward in a desperate attempt to stabilise the position. John suffered a serious leg wound during the ferocious fighting, but still went to the aid of a wounded officer. 'Some gallant fellow crawled up to me shortly after I was hit,' recalled the Lieutenant in a letter to John's brother a few weeks after the event:

> He attempted to assist me off with my pack. But, owing to the nature of my wound, I was unable to turn my neck to see who it was. I heard he was hit and asked him if it was so. He replied, "Yes, sir." When I enquired again later, I received no reply. I could just touch his hand by reaching back, and

found he was dead. From the sound of his voice, I thought it was your brother. I hoped it wasn't so, and that I had made a mistake, for he was one of my most valued men. His end was a gallant one.

The battalion lost fifty men that day, with a further 161 wounded. John's body was lost in the battle and he was later commemorated on the Le Touret Memorial, alongside his other comrades with no known graves. One of his sergeants wrote to Morrison's parents, telling them their son had died 'a hero's death'.

I wonder if Vere Brodie, who was so intimately linked to the story of the Unknown Warrior, and presumably knew of her estate worker's fate, connected these personal losses to the ceremony she had witnessed in 1920?

John Morrison was missing for 100 years until a French farmer was working the land in 2014. 'While ploughing our field, we saw a bone,' he said. 'Out of curiosity, we scratched and found ammunition. And then a spoon. We called the Commonwealth.'

In the first instance when remains are discovered, the Commonwealth War Graves Commission (CWGC) secures the site, checking for unexploded ordnance which, even today, can still pose a deadly danger. They then work meticulously to ensure any remains are recovered with due respect, carefully recording where any body parts or artefacts lie before they are collected and labelled. Back at base, human remains are cleaned and, if possible, reassembled into anatomical order, then assessed to establish the age range and likely height. Any artefacts are stabilised, logged and examined for markings.

The CWGC then utilise information from their own archive to build up a picture of what action occurred at the recovery location throughout the duration of the war, then curate a list of names of the missing who might have died there. Depending on the extent of their findings, the report is then passed to the appropriate government authority.[2]

With more human remains and military items uncovered from the site where John Morrison fell, the Ministry of Defence's so-called 'War Detectives' then set to work.

The 'Joint Casualty and Compassionate Centre' (JCCC) – the same department that springs into action when someone dies on active service today – includes an extraordinary team that deals with the dead of previous wars, investigating human remains found on old battlefields and in aircraft wrecks. They started with the spoon, which was faintly engraved with a service number: 5181. Excavation of the site had revealed enough indications of a particular regiment to give the War Detectives a sporting chance of making a positive identification. The Black Watch Museum in Perth was able to confirm that a soldier with that army number had indeed died in the area at the time the artefacts suggested. Now they had a name, the War Detectives were able to trace some of John's surviving relatives: a 90-year-old nephew, Ian, and 92-year-old cousin, Sheila. DNA samples showed a match.

Lance Corporal John Morrison was finally laid to rest with full military honours in July 2016, 101 years after his death. The service was led by a padre from the Black Watch, with soldiers of the Royal Regiment of Scotland serving as pallbearers, firing the salute and playing the pipes. Two of John's great-nieces and a great-nephew were also there to pay their personal tribute. One of the missing had at last been honoured and buried as he deserved, with a gravestone to mark the spot. A Warrior, no longer Unknown.

* * *

Alongside the Commonwealth War Graves Commission, the War Detectives' success stories continue to this day, with the remains of thousands of the missing – from both wars – being recovered, re-searched, painstakingly identified if possible, and given the dignity of a military funeral. Even 'unknown' bodies in existing graves can be formally named, and the headstone changed, if enough evidence is presented by researchers to establish who the remains must belong to. Though some might question the time, expense and effort involved, the comfort these cases bring for even distant relatives cannot be underestimated, and such ceremony will never become more than those who gave their lives for our country deserve.

Twenty-three-year-old stretcher-bearer Robert Malcolm was serving with the 140th Field Ambulance during the Third Battle of Ypres in 1917, collecting the wounded around Fusilier Wood south of Ypres and carrying them back to dressing stations down the line. It was a 'wood' in name only by then, as three years of fighting had left little more than a wasteland of churned earth and blasted stumps. Robert's task was both dangerous and arduous, coping with badly injured casualties as the battle raged on in the filthy weather and clogging mud around him.[3] On 5 August, the Royal Fusiliers had already repulsed a number of enemy raids, but continued shellfire and soaring casualties meant that Robert's unit was called further forward to give emergency support. It was the last anyone heard of him. He was reported missing the following day. Believed killed during the intensive bombardment, the Flanders mud had claimed him, leaving nothing but a name on the Menin Gate Memorial to the Missing.

In 2019, fragments of the uniform found with an unidentified body at Fusilier Wood included a brass cap badge – a snake wrapped around a staff – of the Royal Army Medical Corps (RAMC). A decayed medical orderly cloth patch, with its distinctive red cross, offered a further clue. We know how hard it was to identify bodies recovered after the war, already in an advanced state of decomposition, but a century later? Today, finely honed investigative techniques and the advent of modern DNA testing have opened new doors. So, too, have the loving care and forensic expertise now applied to each individual discovery, unlike the hurried battlefield clearances and clumsy exhumations of a century ago. But it can be a lengthy and complex process. In 2023, *four years* after the remains were first discovered, they were finally identified as Robert Malcolm, and he could be laid to rest.

'The identification of Private Malcolm was indeed a long and at times complicated task,' declared War Detective Rosie Barron. 'So it is very satisfying to have organised his burial service. Stretcher-bearers were vital to the war effort. Without their dedication and bravery, many more men would have died on the battlefields.' Her team had discovered that Robert belonged to a family of twelve children from Stockton-on-Tees and had followed his father into the shipbuilding industry as a rivet heater before enlisting in 1914. His parents and his siblings all died without ever knowing what had happened to him. Sadly, the War Detectives also learned that his service medals, posted to his mother after his death, had never been delivered, and were returned to the authorities to be destroyed. Perhaps those three gleaming decorations – his Mons Star, British War Medal and Victory Medal – might have brought her a little comfort when she most needed it?

In a final act of his nation's recognition and gratitude, the missing medals were restruck and reissued, taking pride of place on his coffin alongside an RAMC service cap and poppy wreath. Private Malcolm was carried to his grave by a bearer party of serving soldiers from his old regiment, watched by two of his relatives. 'It has been a privilege to have his great-great-nieces here today to see him laid to rest,' said Rosie Barron. 'And to know that he will be remembered by future generations of his family, who will now be able to visit his grave.' After the ceremony, the new medals were presented to his descendants, along with the Union Jack which had covered his casket.

For family members, being given the opportunity to honour one of their own after so many years can feel like a rare privilege. 'It is overwhelming for us,' said one of Robert's great-great-nieces, who had provided her own DNA during the process. 'As Private Malcolm had been missing for so long, it was amazing and quite emotional to see the care that all those in the wider army family have taken to identify and honour him.' She went on to echo Padre David Railton's inspiration for the Unknown Warrior; the belief that one funeral might stand for many, that one man brought in from the cold could, in some strange way, bring them all. 'We feel this [funeral] is for everybody who has lost somebody, and hasn't got a final resting place for them. It is our way of acknowledging the sacrifice that he and so many others made in the service of our country.'

As well as reconnecting the dead with their own families, there is a wider significance, too, in identifying Unknown Warriors after all these years, as the army padre who conducted Private Malcolm's funeral explained. 'The continuing work of identifying the remains of those killed in the First World War, and bestowing upon them the full honours of a proper burial, are key to reminding ourselves that, despite the unimaginable numbers lost in the conflict, each soul whose life was cut short was a precious human being, and loved by someone. This can so easily be forgotten when death, back then, was meted out on such an industrial scale.'

* * *

The nineteenth-century Prime Minister William Gladstone is said to have declared: 'Show me the manner in which a nation cares for its dead, and I will measure with mathematical exactitude the tender mercies of its people, their respect for the laws of the land, and their loyalty to high ideals.'[4] From my personal experiences in the military, and the journey I have now taken, I am all too aware that how the nation honours and respects its war dead is still deeply significant for serving members of our Armed Forces.

'Swede' Williams has served a number of operational tours in Afghanistan with the Royal Artillery, and his experiences of death, and its aftermath, have left him with a searing insight into sacrifice and its memorialisation. 'Some of my colleagues died in truly awful circumstances,' he says. 'The brutality of what they endured still sits heavily with me. My father and grandfather both taught me about remembrance, and I think it's incredibly important. It is the promise from the nation to those who serve that what they do is respected and appreciated.'[5]

Swede has created his own rituals of remembrance to honour the comrades he has lost. 'For my best friend, I slip away alone to a bar on the day he died and order us both a pint. I raise my glass to his in salute, and then drink mine. When I'm finished, I'll leave a note saying "RIP, Brother" next to his full pint.' On Remembrance Sunday itself, 'I pop down to the Mess and leave a bottle of port on the table for anyone who wants to toast their memory, or the memory of their own friends. These sacrifices were made out of love, and respect for our culture and our values. You cannot put a price on that sense of duty and dedication. And it should never be forgotten.' As we speak, I need no reminding that the terrible things Swede witnessed, the losses he suffered, have deeply affected him. And I fully understand the rituals he describes, which are widespread across the military family. My fellow Gulf War POWs and I gather every year on the anniversary of our release to celebrate our freedom and survival. Amid the revelry, an important tradition is always observed before dinner, when we stand, observe a moment's silence, and drink a toast to our 'absent friends' who, unlike us, were not lucky enough to come home.

'There are two leaps of faith we take when we serve our country,' Swede continues. 'The first is that our families, our nearest and dearest, will be properly looked after if we perish. The second is that our sacrifice, our death, will be remembered.' In recent years, Swede has focused that recognition of service, of remembrance, on those from the Great War, in whose footsteps he follows. 'I have never had much of an interest in history, but in 2014 my wife and I realised that it was the centenary of the start of the war and we did not want to miss the opportunity to mark the sacrifice. I decided to learn more about the soldiers who served one hundred years earlier.'

During their research, Swede and his wife, Hannah, a reservist in the Royal Artillery, read about the Christmas Truce of December 1914, when the guns fell silent and troops from both sides met in no-man's-land to smoke, have a kickabout and exchange gifts. 'We thought it was a beautiful moment in the chaos of war and decided we would spend our Christmas at Ypres, to remember the fallen and commemorate that iconic event.' During their trip, they attended the Last Post ceremony at the Menin Gate and toured the battlefields. 'We stopped at lots of memorials, relating the stories we read to the ground around us, trying to imagine how it was for those young men. We reflected on how different our life in today's military is, compared to what they went through.' Then on the day itself, they set out on their pilgrimage. 'It was a curious and sombre way of celebrating Christmas,' he recalls with a wry smile. 'I was anxious, nervous, perhaps worried about not doing the moment justice.'

In the first light of dawn, he and Hannah laid their crosses in the trenches close to the memorial. Then, in silence, they sat and watched the sun rise over no-man's-land, picturing the scene a century earlier, remembering the men who had shivered there before them. 'We were thinking about what it looked, felt, and smelled like. What were *their* hardships and luxuries? I thought about my own time in Afghanistan and the death of friends. But we enjoyed good times too: playing cards, crowding round a small laptop to watch a dodgy copy of the latest movie that we had managed to buy in a local market. Singing songs, building furniture from scrap and moaning about crap kit. Telling stories and piss-taking. Laughing with mates. I realised they had done the exact same stuff, but in a different time and different environment. We were no different.'

As the light grew, Swede and Hannah waited. Expecting others to arrive to mark the anniversary, they had brought some chocolate and tobacco to share. Swede had also brought a football, ready for a kick-about in no-man's-land – a centenary replay of the legendary game.

They waited. And waited.

No one came.

'It broke our hearts.' Swede shakes his head at the memory. 'It was that moment which drove us to do more to remember the past. I was simply not prepared for people not caring enough to be there. It pained us that no one else had come. I genuinely felt that we had let down the men who *were* there a hundred years earlier.' He thinks about this for a moment, and his voice softens. 'I don't think it's because people don't care. It's because the stories don't get told enough, are almost forgotten. People simply do not know the reality of what happened.' Over the following years, he and Hannah did all they could to commemorate the various centenaries that marked the turning points of the Great War. On the anniversary of the first day of the Battle of the Somme they attended the remembrance service at the Memorial to the Missing at Thiepval. And there, Hannah took Swede by surprise. 'She had secretly unearthed the story of a great-uncle of mine who had been killed in the second week of the Somme. Hannah described his story to me, in the very fields where he had fought and died.'

Standing just five-foot-five in his socks, with a passion for keeping pigeons, Private William Brown had lied about his age to enlist when he was seventeen. He had been at Beaumont-Hamel, one of the haunted sites I visited myself, with his Worcestershire Regiment and been involved in that worst job of all, clearing the dead who were clogging the battlefield. On 10 July 1916, William himself was killed during the fighting north-east of Albert. The postman delivered a letter to his parents, Harry and Ada, laying out the bald facts about his death. There had been a German artillery bombardment. He was missing, presumed dead. That was all that was known. William was just eighteen.

Discovering that his great-uncle was an Unknown Warrior lit a lamp in Swede's mind. 'He really made us think about all those who never came home, and what the grave in Westminster Abbey really means.'

Like me, the more Swede discovered about the Unknown Warrior, the more he was captivated, and the centenary of the burial in 2020 presented the perfect opportunity for a significant act of recognition. He and a group of friends decided they would carry a weighted stretcher, wrapped in a Union Jack, along the exact route the Unknown Warrior had been taken from Saint-Pol to Westminster. 'We would remember him at all the significant spots – Boulogne, Dover, Victoria Station, the Cenotaph, retracing his precise journey one hundred years later, *to the second*, just as we had done with the Christmas Truce.'

Crowds had been organised to gather at each key stage. The vast steam locomotive *Tornado* would haul nine Pullman carriages of veterans from Dover to Victoria. The original Cavell Van, now fully restored and recertified for track service, would be attached to the epic train. The most senior Warrant Officers from the four armed services had been enlisted to provide an honour guard. At Victoria Station, members of the Household Cavalry would stand guard. It was hoped a member of the royal family would attend the final stage, placing a wreath on the stretcher at the Cenotaph, then escorting the team to Westminster Abbey. 'Organising it all was the single greatest achievement of my life.'

Sadly, the global pandemic intervened. 'The Covid restrictions were just too great. It was going to be impossible and the grand event had to be cancelled. I really felt as though I'd failed.'

In an effort to rescue something from the wreckage, he and Hannah carried out the journey alone. 'We were there at every significant point from Saint-Pol to the Cenotaph.' On 11 November itself, there was a small service at Westminster Abbey. Swede and Hannah had been allowed to enter, alongside a handful of VIPs, including selected members of the royal family. 'Separately, of course,' he says with a chuckle. 'London was a ghost town that day, hardly any noise, like something out of a disaster movie. We felt so insanely honoured to be allowed into the abbey. The only people who were allowed to pay their respects that morning were us and the future King.' They had brought a wreath, of bay leaves and roses, an exact replica of the one King George placed on the Unknown Warrior's coffin a hundred years earlier. 'I remember we trod so lightly, as if we were sneaking in. It was so silent, every tiny noise could be heard, and we felt as if we shouldn't be there.' When they arrived at the tomb, a single wreath had already been placed, signed by Charles, Prince of Wales.

'We felt so privileged. I got goosebumps as I watched Hannah lay our wreath at the other end of the tomb.' Together, wearing their face masks, they spent a few minutes of silent remembrance in the company of the Unknown Warrior, then slipped quietly back into the deserted streets. 'We felt so sad that this was the end of the journey,' Swede tells me, ruefully. 'I still feel as if I didn't do enough to make it all work. But we will try to set an example around remembrance for the rest of our lives. We will continue to tell the stories of the dead and the missing and explain their importance to anyone who will listen.'

WHITEHALL, LONDON
11 NOVEMBER 2023

A military band of drummers and pipers, kilts swaying, marches towards the Cenotaph. An honour guard from the King's Colour Squadron of the Royal Air Force stamps into place. More uniformed men and women appear, from all branches of the services. Behind the crash barriers, the crowds look on in respectful silence. It is a distillation of the great procession that carried the Unknown Warrior's gun carriage to his funeral 103 years ago. The massed bands, the dense crowds, the honour guard representing every regiment, ship and squadron in the land, the senior officers and the veterans. I take a deep breath and consider how my own journey from ignorance about how and why the Unknown Warrior arrived here in 1920 has brought me to being the Western Front Association's guest of honour in the very same spot, on 11 November 2023, waiting, alongside the country's Secretary of State for Defence, to lay my poppy wreath in memory of the fallen of the Great War.

I stare up at the smooth white flanks of the Cenotaph. I have stood here many times on Remembrance Sunday, contemplating my lost comrades. Men and women I *knew*. If I am honest, the dead of a different war, a century earlier, always felt strangely remote. The gap between now and then too great for my imagination to bridge.

I couldn't claim any genuine sense of loss, because I didn't think I knew the people who had died.

Now I do.

Big Ben begins to chime eleven o'clock, just as it rang out over the crowds gathered here a century ago. So begins today's Great Silence, and I think about young Donald Overall, just one of perhaps 360,000 children who lost their father during the Great War.[6] Back in November 1920, Donald and his mother must have been standing very close to where I am now. He could still remember the smell of his father's pipe tobacco on his khaki tunic as he carried him upstairs.

As an adult, Donald fought in the Second World War as a flight engineer on Halifax bombers. Sometimes, as they flew over northern France, he would look down through the darkness, imagining his father 'down there', and promising himself that – one day – he would visit his grave. Ninety years after his father's death in 1917, he finally made the trip. 'I'm an old man, I am supposed to be tough,' he said. 'I thought I was hard, but I'm not. He's my dad. I miss him. I missed him as a boy, and I miss him as an old man. I was really proud of my dad and I always wished I could be like him. I didn't know his faults; he must have had them. He must have had weaknesses, but I didn't know them either. It is very important that I have come back. I feel closer now than I have ever been. That time he carried me to bed was the last time, and this is the next time, 90 years on. I don't know how much longer I will live, but I will never forget him. To me he was everything, he was a man that I wanted to be like. I've never forgotten, I never will, never will.'[7]

I think about the fatherless children of the other – more recent – Unknown Warriors whose stories I discovered which have touched me so deeply. Of Mary Fowler, whose father was killed when HMS *Coventry* was sunk in the Falklands in 1982. 'I remember him taking apart and fixing my hairdryer,' Mary told me. 'He showed me how the different parts functioned, even explaining what the bi-metallic strip was. I still remember that to this day. Dad is still a

missing presence for me. His picture is in the hall and if my grandson asks, "Where's Great-grandad Mike?" I tell him he's looking
down, keeping watch over us from the stars.'[8]

And I think of those 'lucky enough' to have a resting place to
visit and how their lives have been touched by war, of Nikki Scott's
children, after their amazing dad was killed in Afghanistan in
2009. 'I tell them that the grave is their daddy's place,' she said.
'Where they can talk to him, laugh or cry with him, tell him their
hopes and their dreams and their fears. He will always be waiting
for them at his grave.'[9]

In the chill air of Whitehall, the bright notes of 'Reveille' shake
us from our reveries and remembrances.

The procession of wreath-carriers advances to lay their scarlet poppies on the smooth, pale-cream stone at the base of the Cenotaph.
Then, a few paces to my right, the Parade Marshal begins to recite
the familiar words of Laurence Binyon's famous poem, 'For the
Fallen'. I feel as if I am hearing it for the first time.

They shall grow not old, as we that are left grow old.

No longer are the 'they' to whom the poem refers abstract and
blurred. I now know *they* are Anthony French and Bert Bradley,
exchanging fearful glances as they took their last tot of rum before
going over the top.

They are Tom Kettle, his hand shaking, writing one last, loving
sonnet for his baby daughter before striding out to die.

And they are Padre Rupert Inglis, the brilliant rugby player,
widowing his wife in the bid to bring one last wounded man in from
the darkness.

As I listen to Binyon's attempt to find comfort and consolation in
the idea of men dying before their time, I can almost hear the low,
mellifluous voice of David Railton doing his utmost to console and
comfort a terrified Denis Blakemore, found guilty of cowardice, in
the last minutes before the poor boy was shot at dawn.

Having spent the past year deeply immersed in the story of the
Unknown Warrior, and in following his progress up to this very

hour of this very day, I feel as if – for the first time – I can finally stand at the Cenotaph and connect with the never-ending sacrifice of Our Glorious Dead.

And when the Parade Marshal reaches the famous line of the poem, I am finally saying it from the heart: *We will remember them.*

We bow our heads for a few seconds, turn and retreat.

It is time to move on.

Westminster Abbey, London
December 2023

Like the numberless pilgrims who came here in 1920, it feels only right to end my journey where it began.

While the tourists take selfies at the main entrance to the abbey, I picture the honour guard of ninety-six VCs lining up behind them a century ago. Nearby, the choir had sung 'I Am the Resurrection and the Life' as the bearer party from the Coldstream Guards slowly carried the 'Treasure Chest' past the policemen in their overcoats, through the great oak door and into the velvet shadows. I take a moment to absorb my surroundings, savouring the familiar aroma of hymn books, molten wax and oaken solemnity. A hushed Communion service is taking place, even as we visitors shuffle down the aisles. If Padre Railton was able to hold services in the trenches during an artillery bombardment, then why not in peacetime at Westminster Abbey, with a few hundred tourists on the loose?

I walk slowly towards the nave, noting old details with new eyes.

Encased in a stout display cabinet of glass and oak fixed to a pillar near the tomb, I admire the complex and ornate five-pointed star of the Unknown Warrior's American Congressional Medal of Honor. Embossed with the single word 'VALOR' in block capitals, it is suspended on a star-spangled ribbon of grey-blue watered silk.

Hanging nearby is HMS *Verdun*'s ship's bell, the last remaining relic of the destroyer that carried the Unknown Warrior's body back from France. When she was broken up in 1946, it was acquired by an enterprising young officer and on Remembrance Sunday 1990 he presented it to the abbey to commemorate her part in the historic crossing from Boulogne to Dover.[10]

I turn to face the neat rectangle of poppies that delineates the Warrior's grave and ask one of the attendants in a scarlet cassock what the most special part of the abbey is for her. She looks at me for a moment, and smiles. 'The heart of the abbey is the shrine of Edward the Confessor,' she says. 'But you know, after working here for ten years, I find this tomb for the Unknown Warrior is the most poignant.' We pause to gaze at the black marble slab. She tells me she comes from Brazil, where they have their own grave to an Unknown Warrior. 'And this one connects me with the one at home, with the sacrifices of my own people. It is hard to describe, but it is very moving. People come here from all over the world, and it means something different to each of us.'[11] More than sixty other countries now have their own tomb, each echoing the sentiments of the one here at Westminster and its blood-brother in Paris. The attendant tells me that young recruits from the British military are often brought here to show them the grave as part of their training. I find this reassuring. I can think of no better teacher for the soldiers of this generation than a man who gave his life for King and country a century ago, and whose sacrifice we still honour today.

I am privileged to have been invited to meet the thirty-ninth Dean of Westminster, The Very Reverend Dr David Hoyle, so am ushered past the tourists and up ancient stone steps into the heart of the abbey. Sitting in the Dean's office, surrounded by hundreds of religious and historical books, we discuss the importance, and ongoing legacy, of the Unknown Warrior.

'There are just over 3,300 graves in Westminster Abbey; a huge assembly of the dead,' he tells me over coffee. 'Of course, we do have some extraordinary burials here; Edward the Confessor, Henry III, Henry V; it goes on and on. But the Unknown Warrior is probably the principal memorial in the abbey. It is the one that stops all our visitors in their tracks. I sometimes watch as people walk down the nave after evensong. They invariably pause at the tomb to read the words, and reflect on what they mean. It is a deeply, deeply significant part of the fabric of the abbey. I have stood at the door for some truly extraordinary events in the life of our country, Her Late Majesty's state funeral and the King's coronation to name just two. I have watched some of the most important people in the land enter and it is still incredibly significant for me to see them walk around that single grave. No foot ever falls on what is incredibly sacred ground. I have to keep reminding visitors that it is a real grave; a person lies beneath that slab, which makes it very different from other war memorials that commemorate death and sacrifice.'

Dean Hoyle pauses for a moment to retrieve a curiously shaped picture frame from a windowsill crammed with family photos and images from his long career in the Anglican Church. He hands me the envelope-sized smooth wooden artefact which contains a black-and-white photograph of someone climbing into a First World War Sopwith Camel biplane. He tells me it is part of a propeller from his grandfather's aircraft and points out a bullet hole on the edge. 'History is important to all of us. My father's father flew in the Royal Flying Corps; I believe he was shot down and injured. My mother's father served in one of the Lancashire infantry regiments and was shot at Passchendaele before being captured. Only recently a cousin told me about a letter he had written from a prisoner of war camp in Germany, saying that one bullet had hit his cigarette case, another hit the Bible in his breast pocket which had saved his life.'

We take a moment to contemplate how close both his grandfathers came to death, how very differently life might have turned out. 'I know almost nothing about them; they were a generation that simply did not talk about their experiences. War is about bravery, sacrifice, loyalty, comradeship and much else, and we rightly commemorate that. We can read historical accounts of those who were there, but I think that it is truly difficult to fully comprehend what they went through, what they saw, the incredible levels of death and destruction they endured. So there is an element to the story of the Unknown Warrior, and the staggering toll of loss it signifies, which in some ways takes us to the limits of our understanding of death – it speaks to all of those thousands upon thousands of names on memorials like the Menin Gate and Thiepval, all those graves in countless cemeteries in France and Belgium where the occupant is unknown.'

With an imposing portrait of the man at the centre of the project gazing down on us from above a fireplace, we discuss the background of the man Dean Herbert Ryle had buried just yards away, and over 100 years earlier. 'There have been various proposals to DNA-test the remains, with an idea of trying to find out more about who lies there. With modern research and records, there could even be a slight possibility of establishing exactly who he was.'

And what of the theories, based on the limited accounts of the 1920 selection process, about who the Unknown Warrior *could* – or *could not* – have been? 'As a historian, I love uncovering the experiences of our past; research can bring us to the limits of what we know, but I feel it is important to pause and allow the mystery of some subjects to remain. Yes, we could establish more, but why would we? The mystery of what the Unknown Warrior represents is sacrosanct – a platform on which to reflect on those vast wartime losses over a hundred years ago. A unique story of the scale of death during that conflict, a scale, even knowing the numbers involved, that frankly beggars our imagination. The whole point about the concept was that it could, just could, be anybody. So when a grieving widow visited the tomb back in 1920 she might say, *This could be my husband*. She could tell her children, *This could be your father*. That's what it was all about.

Trying to find out more information about who might lie there diminishes that concept, that story, the very reason for having a tomb of an Unknown Warrior. A man who was everyone and no one, and lived a life as important as your life and mine.'

Back down in the nave, I glance up to the Union Jack, now hanging in the tiny St George's Chapel a few yards away, above the great Coronation Chair which has been in use since 1306. Today, it looks more like a veil of red, white and blue gossamer than the stout cotton flag that David Railton's mother-in-law gave him to take to France. But it has not lost its majestic power to transport one back to the blood-soaked, shell-shocked, mud-flooded hell of the trenches.

Padre Railton's grandson, also David, tells me that he, too, always looks up at it whenever he visits Westminster Abbey. 'It has real significance for me, and is such a tangible link to my grandfather,' the distinguished barrister says. 'Don't forget, John, this was *his* flag, used in battle. As you know, it was an item of immense importance that travelled with him throughout the war. He and that flag saw and experienced so much: the harsh reality of war, the suffering and loss of comrades. It obviously meant a great deal to him, and to see it hanging there over a hundred years later now means a huge amount to me and his family too.' He pauses. 'Sadly, the flag is now fading, which, of course, the black marble slab will never do.

'I think my grandfather would be surprised, probably amazed, that over a hundred years after the event we are still talking about his role. I am sure he would not want our discussion to be about *him*, but I think he'd be pleased that we are still acknowledging the underlying issues – the death, the grief, the sacrifice – of which he experienced so much.'[12]

While it must have been a proud moment for David Railton Sr to see his flag hanging in the nation's parish church, his humility is still evident on the bronze plaque which avoids any mention of his name in explaining its remarkable provenance:

This Union Jack, sometimes called the Padre's Flag, was used day-by-day on a flag post or improvised altar or as a covering for the fallen on the Western Front during the Great War 1914–1918. It covered the coffin of the Unknown Warrior at his funeral on November 11th 1920. After resting for a year on the grave, it was presented to the Abbey on Armistice Day 1921 by the Chaplain who used it during the war.[13]

Reading between the lines, I wonder if Railton insisted that his name be kept off the plaque, just as he was always reticent to claim credit for the idea for which he is now remembered. His flag memorialised his dead and missing comrades, not the man who ministered to them. 'I think my grandfather was uniquely placed, in the eye of the storm of the First World War, to truly understand what was needed,' says his grandson, as we reflect on how a humble army padre set in motion an idea which offered solace to the yearning, and the possibility of healing, for an entire nation. 'He had seen every aspect of warfare and battle. Great loss and great suffering, he and his flag burying so many comrades. Then he had written so many letters to countless parents and wives, explaining how their loved ones died, hoping to offer just a glimmer of comfort. So my personal feeling is that he had a truly unique insight into what was needed, and why.'

I am intensely grateful to have had the opportunity to speak to the grandson of a man I had never even heard of before I began this journey, yet have now come to admire so greatly. I wonder if perhaps Padre Railton himself was something of an unknown warrior?

I think of his remarkable daughter-in-law and David's mother, Margaret Railton. Sadly, only two weeks after our conversation in the summer, she died peacefully at home. I treasure the time I spent with her. She knew she was ill and, although fragile, was sparklingly alive and delighted – determined – to talk about her father-in-law. 'He really was a *most* remarkable man; a very gentle person,' she said. 'Ideally suited to life as a military padre. He was always concerned about *other* people. Caring for them. Helping them. He had a natural empathy, easily connecting with others, and they with him.'

She had raised her eyes and smiled, almost as if picturing her father-in-law standing with us. 'When he was alive, he certainly never mentioned anything about his involvement to me or, as far as I can remember, to anybody in his family. But now, we are *incredibly* proud of what he achieved, both during the war and in the aftermath. We always just think of his role with the Unknown Warrior as a family story, but when I talk about it to you, John, I begin to understand that it is really a story of our country, how important it was a hundred years ago, and how important it still is today.'

I contemplate Margaret's words as I read and reread part of the gilded inscription on the Warrior's grave:

... A BRITISH WARRIOR

UNKNOWN BY NAME OR RANK

BROUGHT FROM FRANCE TO LIE AMONG

THE MOST ILLUSTRIOUS OF THE LAND ...

THUS ARE COMMEMORATED THE MANY

MULTITUDES WHO GAVE THE MOST THAT

MAN CAN GIVE LIFE ITSELF[14]

In the midst of this place where names are so important, I like the fact that this most important grave of all – the one upon which even kings and queens never walk – belongs to the one man resting here whose name nobody knows. Representing all the unknowns.

People are standing around the tomb now, listening to their audio guides with pursed lips and downcast eyes. I want to talk to them about what I have learned. That this polished slab of black marble is not just a symbolic memorial. It is the gravestone of a flesh-and-blood human being who fought and died for his country. I want to tell them that his bones are just beneath our feet. About his astonishing journey from the battlefield to lie here among kings. I want to tell them how important this grave, this man became in offering a scrap of comfort to the bereaved.

He could have been anyone. He could have been everyone.

'Buried in Westminster Abbey – my son, John,' as one proud father put it in 1920.[15] Or, in the words of that small boy whose unarguable logic had touched so many when he wrote to apply for a ticket to the ceremony in 1920: 'The man in the coffin might be my daddy.'[16]

In a different time, he could have been me.

I shut my eyes. I can almost hear the soft Scots accent of Professor Dame Sue Black, the forensic anthropologist, who helped me understand the harsh reality, and very real necessity, of recovering the long-dead. 'I absolutely understand that visceral need to have your relative's body; to know where they lie, and to have a grave to visit and to contemplate.'

I think about all the Unknown Warriors, from the First World War and beyond, whose stories I have discovered. About the families whose fathomless grief is focused on this tomb. In the silence of Westminster Abbey, I whisper to this single warrior, the one with no name:

Thank you. We will remember you.

ENDNOTES

NB: **JN** = John Nichol; **WFA** = Western Front Association;
IWM = Imperial War Museum

Prologue

1 https://www.tudorsociety.com/28-april-1603-elizabeth-funeral/
2 In 2011, Captain Bowes-Lyon's grandson produced information that his
    grandfather had actually been buried in Quarry Cemetery, Vermelles. The
    evidence was accepted and a special memorial headstone to Captain
    Bowes-Lyon was erected, inscribed 'Buried near this spot' as there is no
    certainty about the precise location of his remains within the cemetery:
    https://www.westernfrontassociation.com/on-this-day/27-september-1915-
    captain-fergus-bowes-lyon-8th-black-watch
3 First part of the inscription.
4 https://www.census.gov/history/pdf/reperes112018.pdf
5 These figures vary depending on sources and can change as bodies are
    identified: https://www.britannica.com/event/World-War-I/Killed-wounded-
    and-missing
6 https://blog.forceswarrecords.com/
    the-unknown-warrior-gone-but-never-forgotten/
7 Michael Fowler letter to Mary Fowler, written 17 April 1982. Edited.

Chapter 1: Death at High Wood

1 Anthony French, *Gone for a Soldier* (The Roundwood Press, 1972). Some
    quotes and scenes edited for brevity.
2 National Records of Scotland: https://www.nrscotland.gov.uk/research/
    learning/first-world-war/the-battle-of-the-somme
3 https://www.history.com/news/10-things-you-may-not-know-about-the-
    battle-of-the-somme

4 Alan Maude, *The History of the 47th (London) Division 1914–1919* (Naval & Military, 2009).

5 Second Lieutenant F. W. Beadle, Royal Artillery, in Lyn Macdonald, *Somme* (Penguin, 2013).

6 Adapted from Terry Norman, *The Hell They Called High Wood* (Pen & Sword, 2014).

7 Guy Chapman, *A Passionate Prodigality* (Buchan & Enright, 1985).

8 https://ww1richmond.wordpress.com/2016/05/20/boy-soldier-private-alec-reader/

9 Private papers of T. H. Farlam, IWM documents.4863, consulted at: https://www.iwm.org.uk/collections/item/object/1030004870

10 www.scarboroughsmaritimeheritage.org.uk/article.php?article=552

11 John Buchan, *Memory Hold-the-Door* (White Press, 2015).

12 Kettle's account and letters are constructed from: https://thehistoryofparliament.wordpress.com/2016/09/09/died-not-for-flag-nor-king-nor-emperor-thomas-michael-kettle-1880-1916/; https://www.rte.ie/centuryireland/index.php/articles/tom-kettles-words-of-war; UCDA LA34/402 Papers of Tom Kettle; T. Burke, 'In Memory of Tom Kettle', *Journal of the Royal Dublin Fusiliers Association*, Vol. 9, 9/2002.

13 *Guardian* article on letters of fallen soldiers, 30 June 2016.

14 David Railton letter to Ruby Railton, 1 August 1916.

15 http://inglis.uk.com/diaryofrupertinglis.htm

16 W. J. Bradley letter to Andrew Scott Railton, quoted in Andrew Richards, *The Flag* (Casemate, 2019).

17 David Railton letter to Ruby Railton, 31 July 1916.

18 Tom Kettle, 'Rhapsody on Rats' from *The Ways of War* (Project Gutenberg eBook, 2021).

19 Document in Cambridge University Library, reproduced at: https://musicb3.wordpress.com/2016/08/05/arthur-bliss-125-wwi-and-the-somme/

20 IWM docs: L. W. Pratt, typescript manuscript, quoted in Peter Hart and Nigel Steel, *The Somme* (Weidenfeld & Nicolson, 2008).

21 Adapted from Chapman, *A Passionate Prodigality*, op. cit.

22 E. Dalton, quoted in T. Burke, 'In Memory of Tom Kettle', op. cit.

23 Corporal H. F. Hooton, quoted in Norman, *The Hell They Called High Wood*.

24 IWM docs: J. H. Reynolds, typescript memoir, quoted in Hart and Steel, *The Somme*, op. cit.

25 IWM docs: L. Gameson, typescript, 15/8/1916–9/9/1916, quoted ibid.

26 Chapman, *A Passionate Prodigality*, op. cit. 'Very lights' are often called 'Verey lights'.

27 Adapted from Richards, *The Flag*, op. cit.

28 David Railton letter to Ruby Railton (edited), 12 September 1916.

29 UCD archive; quoted at: https://www.irishtimes.com/culture/heritage/thomas-michael-kettle-an-enduring-legacy-1.2640866

30 Conversation extrapolated from Bingham's letter to Kettle's family.

31 Edited extracts from Kettle's letters.

32 Hart and Steel, *The Somme*, op. cit.

33 Adapted from French, *Gone for a Soldier*, op. cit. Some quotes edited for clarity.

34 P. Davenport et al., *The History of the Prince of Wales' Own Civil Service Rifles* (Project Gutenberg eBook, 2016).

35 Sidney F. Major, *The First World War History of the 1/18th Battalion.* Found at: https://www.londonirishrifles.com/index.php/first-world-war/ 1-18th-battalion-in-the-first-world-war/

36 Rifleman Donald Cree, 1/8th Battalion (Post Office Rifles), London Regiment, 140th Brigade, 47th Division. IWM docs – DDS Cree, typescript memoir, quoted in Hart and Steel, *The Somme*, op. cit.

37 M. J. 'Paddy' Guiton, quoted in Davenport et al., *The History of the Prince of Wales' Own Civil Service Rifles*, op. cit.

38 This is only a very condensed account of the battle of High Wood that day.

39 Letter edited for brevity.

40 Maude, *The History of the 47th (London) Division 1914–1919*, op. cit. It is recorded that *after* casualties from High Wood had been replaced, the strength of the division was 8,500.

41 Letter from the field of Waterloo (June 1815), as quoted in Edward Shepherd Creasy, *Decisive Battles of the World* (Dover, 2008).

42 This figure is quoted in a number of different sources, including: https://www. ww1battlefields.co.uk/somme/high-wood

43 Quoted in Norman, *The Hell They Called High Wood*, op. cit.

Chapter 2: The Glorious Dead

1 Maude, *The History of the 47th (London) Division 1914–1919*, op. cit.

2 French, *Gone for a Soldier*, op. cit. Some quotes edited for clarity.

3 Lieutenant Etienne de Caux, 1/8th Battalion (Post Office Rifles), London Regiment, quoted in Hart and Steel, *The Somme*, op. cit. De Caux was the French interpreter attached to the 1/8th Londons.

4 As reported by de Caux, ibid.

5 Author's interpretation of events.

6 Rupert Inglis letter to his wife, 16 September 1916, from collected letters at: http://www.inglis.uk.com/diaryofrupertinglis.htm

7 Captain Roger Bulstrode, 20th Division, quoted in Hart and Steel, *The Somme*, op. cit.

8 Chapman, *A Passionate Prodigality*, op. cit.

9 Andy Smith, JN interview, 2023.

10 David Railton, *The Story of a Padre's Flag, Told by the Flag*, unpublished memoir.

11 Letter to Ruby Railton, 26 April 1916. Some of Railton's words have been edited for brevity and clarity. Railton uses the term 'Verey'.

12 George Kendall, *Daring All Things* (Helion & Company Ltd, 2016). Edited for clarity.

13 David O'Mara, 'Identifying the Dead: A Short Study of the Identification Tags of 1914–1918': https://www.westernfrontassociation.com/world-war-i-articles/identifying-the-dead-a-short-study-of-the-identification-tags-of-1914-1918/

14 David Railton letter to Ruby Railton, 24 September 1916.

15 CWGC: 'London Cemetery and Extension, Longueval', quoted in Richards, *The Flag*, op. cit.

16 Adapted from Richards, *The Flag*, op. cit.

17 https://www.heritage.nf.ca/first-world-war/articles/beaumont-hamel-en.php

18 Information from: https://www.ww1battlefields.co.uk/somme/beaumont-hamel/

19 Revd E. C. Crosse, quoted in Peter Hodgkinson, 'Battlefield Clearance and Burial' (article for the University of Birmingham's *Journal of First World War Studies*), at: https://www.longlongtrail.co.uk/burial-clearance-and-burial/

20 J. N. Grissinger, US Medical Corps, in document at: http://www.worldwar1.com/dbc/burial.htm

21 Captain Dunn, Medical Officer with the 2nd RWF, quoted in Norman, *The Hell They Called High Wood*, op. cit.

22 Fabian Ware, 29 June 1917, quoted in Hodgkinson, 'Battlefield Clearance and Burial', op. cit.

23 Michael Moynihan (ed.), *God on our Side* (Leo Cooper/Secker & Warburg, 1983). Edited for clarity.

24 This and the following testimony from Alf Hayes are drawn from both the padre's personal diary and from JN interview.

25 https://blogs.icrc.org/intercross/2022/09/27/identifying-argentina-s-unknown-soldiers-almost-40-years-later/

26 Convention for the Amelioration of the Condition of the Wounded and Sick in Armies in the Field, Geneva, 6 July 1906, at: https://ihl-databases.icrc.org/en/ihl-treaties/gc-1906?activeTab=historical

27 Major W. E. Frye, quoted at: https://arstechnica.com/science/2022/08/were-bones-of-waterloo-soldiers-sold-as-fertilizer-its-not-yet-case-closed/

28 Quoted at: https://www.historynet.com/civil-war-soldiers-looted-their-dead-enemies-of-swords-boots-undies-and-more/

29 For further analysis, please see: https://www.tandfonline.com/doi/full/10.1080/15740773.2021.2051895

30 Quoted in Joe Turner, 'The Bones of Waterloo', 4 March 2015, at: https://medium.com/study-of-history/the-bones-of-waterloo-a3beb35254a3

31 Ibid.

32 R. W. Holloway, letter to the editor of *Cairn's Post* (Australia) in 1917, quoted by Joe Turner at: https://medium.com/study-of-history/the-bones-of-waterloo-a3beb35254a3

33 Private McCauley, IWM docs 97/10/1, quoted in Hodgkinson, 'Battlefield Clearance and Burial', op. cit.
34 https://www.nam.ac.uk/explore/1916-year-attrition

Chapter 3: The Yearning

1 French, *Gone for a Soldier*, op. cit. Text edited for brevity.
2 Kendall, *Daring All Things*, op. cit. Author's italics.
3 Richards, *The Flag*, op. cit.
4 Lieutenant Patrick Campbell MC, quoted in Richard Garrett, *The Final Betrayal* (Buchan & Enright, 1989).
5 Vera Brittain, *Testament of Youth* (Phoenix, 2014). Some text edited for brevity.
6 Quoted in Justin Saddington, 'Peace and Commemoration: Britain after the First World War', in WFA magazine *Stand To!*, No. 120 – Unknown Warrior Special, November 2020.
7 IWM, papers of J. Bennett 83/14/1, quoted in Jay Winter, *Sites of Memory, Sites of Mourning* (Cambridge University Press, 2010).
8 Lucy Easthope, *When the Dust Settles* (Hodder & Stoughton, 2022).
9 Sue Black, *All That Remains* (Doubleday, 2018). And JN interview.
10 Richard van Emden, *Missing: The Need for Closure after the Great War* (Pen & Sword, 2019).
11 Philip Longworth, The Unending Vigil (Pen & Sword, 2010).
12 Ibid.
13 Van Emden, *Missing*, op. cit.
14 Longworth, *The Unending Vigil*, op. cit.
15 Jill Stewart, 'Sir John Edward Fowler – The Last Repatriation from the Western Front in 1915?': https://www.westernfrontassociation.com/world-war-i-articles/sir-john-edward-fowler-the-last-repatriation-from-the-western-front-in-1915/
16 Ibid.
17 Lieutenant Engelberg, Pionier-Btl 13, Staden, 27 September 1917 (letter, private collection, R. Schäfer), quoted at: https://www.the-low-countries.com/article/how-missing-soldiers-regain-their-identity

Chapter 4: Closure?

1 Jean-Yves Le Naour, *The Living Unknown Soldier* (Metropolitan Books, 2004).
2 Central Statistical Office (1920s), quoted at: www.longlongtrail.co.uk. Figures can change as new remains are discovered or old bodies identified.
3 Longworth, *The Unending Vigil*, op. cit.
4 Sue Black, JN interview.
5 Juliet Nicolson, *The Great Silence* (John Murray, 2009).

6 Haig, March 1916, quoted in van Emden, *Missing*, op. cit.

7 Report by Arthur Hill, assistant director of the Royal Botanic Gardens at Kew, quoted in Longworth, *The Unending Vigil*, op. cit.

8 *The Times*, 14, 15, 27, 29 November 1918.

9 Rudyard Kipling, *The Times*, 17 February 1919.

10 Gail Braybon (ed.), *Evidence, History and the Great War* (Berghahn Books, 2008).

11 Fabian Ware, quoted in Longworth, *The Unending Vigil*, op. cit.

12 Winter, *Sites of Memory, Sites of Mourning*, op. cit.

13 *Hansard*, 4 May 1920.

14 Maud Selborne, 'National Socialism in War Cemeteries', *National Review*, July 1920, quoted in Mark Connelly, 'Sarah Smith, the British War Graves Association and the Issue of Repatriation', WFA magazine *Stand To!*, No. 128, November 2022. Lord Robert Cecil, also known as Lord Salisbury, served as Prime Minister three times over a total of thirteen years.

15 Lady Selborne, letter to *The Times*, 23 December 1919.

16 Sarah Smith, letter to *Yorkshire Evening Post*, 12 April 1919.

17 Sarah Smith and the British War Graves Association, petition for the repatriation of British bodies, May 1919 (CWGC/1/1/5/21).

18 CWGC, April 1919, undated petition to the Prince of Wales, quoted in Connelly, 'Sarah Smith, the British War Graves Association and the Issue of Repatriation', op. cit.

19 Sue Black, JN interview.

20 Private W. F. Macbeath, quoted in Hodgkinson, 'Battlefield Clearance and Burial', op. cit.

21 Van Emden, *Missing*, op. cit.

22 Lieutenant Colonel Gell, senior IWGC representative in France, quoted in Hodgkinson, 'Battlefield Clearance and Burial', op. cit.

23 Hodgkinson, 'Battlefield Clearance and Burial', op. cit.

24 Van Emden, *Missing*, op. cit.

25 Black, *All That Remains*, op. cit.

26 Hodgkinson, 'Battlefield Clearance and Burial', op. cit.

27 Jill Stewart, 'Clandestine Exhumations, Bringing the Dead Home', WFA magazine *Stand To!*, No. 128, November 2022: https://www.westernfrontassociation.com/latest-news/2022/november-2022/just-out-stand-to-no-128

28 Colin Fenn, 'The Inconvenient Dead', at: https://inconvenientdead.wordpress.com/2018/12/21/twentieth-century-body-snatching-who-owns-the-body/; and Stewart, 'Clandestine Exhumations, Bringing the Dead Home', op. cit.

29 Veronica Maddocks, 'Peel, Anna Bella (Durie)', in *Dictionary of Canadian Biography*, Vol. 16, University of Toronto/Université Laval, quoted by Colin Fenn, op. cit.

30 Black, *All That Remains*, op. cit.

Chapter 5: The Need for a Symbol

1 Based on photograph of scene at: http://wwıcentenary.oucs.ox.ac.uk/body-and-mind/lloyd-georges-ministry-men/

2 Ibid.

3 https://hansard.parliament.uk/Commons/1927-07-28/debates/5baa696f-65ca-4ddo-9ec2-ec9621321ae7/PopulationStatisticsEnglandAndWales

4 Ibid.

5 https://www.historic-uk.com/HistoryUK/HistoryofBritain/Thankful-Villages/

6 Arthur Mee, *The King's England*, quoted at: https://heritagecalling.com/2018/11/11/an-introduction-to-thankful-villages

7 Casualty figures vary greatly depending on source. This figure is from: https://www.census.gov/history/pdf/reperes112018.pdf

8 The story of the Souls family is taken from: https://www.bbc.co.uk/gloucestershire/focus/2002/10/soulsbrothers.shtml; https://www.bbc.co.uk/gloucestershire/focus/2002/10/soulsbrothers2.shtml

9 Letter edited for brevity.

10 *Gloucestershire Echo*, 9 January 1935.

11 Maude, *The History of the 47th (London) Division 1914–1919*, op. cit.

12 David Railton to Ruby Railton, 4 October 1916.

13 Supplement to the *London Gazette*, 11543, 25 November 1916.

14 Margaret Railton, JN interview.

15 *Our Empire* magazine, November 1931, Vol. VII. Account edited for brevity.

16 Ibid.

17 Railton, *The Story of a Padre's Flag*, op. cit.

18 https://adb.anu.edu.au/biography/melba-dame-nellie-7551

19 Nicolson, *The Great Silence*, op. cit.

20 Virginia Woolf, *The Diary of Virginia Woolf, Vol 1: 1915–1919* (Mariner Books, 1979).

21 War Cabinet Peace Celebrations Committee, Minutes of Meeting, 1 July 1919, quoted in Hanson, *The Unknown Soldier*, op. cit.

22 'The Story of the Cenotaph' by Eric Homberger, quoted in Hanson, ibid.

23 Sir Alfred Mond, First Commissioner of Works, 1916–1921.

24 Nicolson, *The Great Silence*, op. cit.

25 Ibid.

26 https://encyclopedia.1914-1918-online.net/article/war_widows

27 The National Archives WORK 21/74: Letter of 25 June 1919, quoted in Andrea Hetherington, 'Up in Smoke: Britain's War Widows and the Conflict of Commemoration', WFA magazine *Stand To!*, No. 120 – Unknown Warrior Special, November 2020.

28 The National Archives WORK 21/74: Letter of 8 July 1919 to Sir Lionel Earle.

29 Mike Hally: https://www.westernfrontassociation.com/world-war-i-articles/19th-july-1919-peace-day-in-britain/ – letter edited for clarity.

30 Ibid.

31 Harold Nicholson, *King George V* (Constable, 1984). Haig was promoted to Field Marshal in January 1917.

32 https://www.westernfrontassociation.com/world-war-i-articles/19th-july-1919-peace-day-in-britain/

33 Nicolson, *The Great Silence*, op. cit.

34 https://www.english-heritage.org.uk/visit/places/the-cenotaph/history

35 *Daily Mail*, 12 November 1919.

36 *Manchester Guardian*, 21 July 1919.

37 *Morning Post*, 20 November 1919.

38 *The Times*, 21 July 1919.

39 *Daily Mail*, 23 July 1919.

40 *The Times*, 7 November 1919.

41 Nicolson, *The Great Silence*, op. cit.

42 Evelyn Waugh, *The Diaries of Evelyn Waugh* – 11 November 1919 (Weidenfeld & Nicolson, 1976).

43 Richards, *The Flag*, op. cit.

44 *Our Empire* magazine, November 1931, Vol. VII. Account edited.

45 Ibid.

46 Railton, *The Story of a Padre's Flag*, op. cit.

47 Maurice H. Fitzgerald, *A Memoir of Herbert Edward Ryle* (Macmillan, 1928). Edited quote. Those writing at the time tended to capitalise 'Abbey'.

48 Dean Herbert Ryle letter to David Railton, 16 August 1920, quoted in Richards, *The Flag*, op. cit.

49 *Our Empire* magazine, November 1931, Vol. VII.

50 Dean Ryle letter to Lord Stamfordham, October 1920, Westminster Abbey Archive.

51 Lord Stamfordham, the King's private secretary, letter to Dean Ryle, 7 October 1920, Westminster Abbey Archive. Edited quote.

52 M. P. A. Hankey, Secretary to the Cabinet, letter to Dean Ryle, 15 October 1920, Westminster Abbey Archive.

53 Dean Ryle to David Railton, 19 October 1920, Railton family archive.

54 Railton, *The Story of a Padre's Flag*, op. cit.

55 *Our Empire* magazine, November 1931, Vol. VII.

56 *The Times*, 22 October 1920.

57 Dr Tony Trowles, JN interview.

58 *Yorkshire Evening Post*, 25 October 1920, and several other newspapers.

59 Dean Ryle to David Railton, 25 October 1920.

60 Fitzgerald, *A Memoir of Herbert Edward Ryle*, op. cit. Edited quote.

61 *Daily Express*, 16 September 1919.

62 *The Comrades' Journal II*, November 1919.

63 Various newspapers, 26 October 1919. Quoted in Robert Sackville-West, *The Searchers* (Bloomsbury, 2021).

64 Saddington, 'Peace and Commemoration', op. cit. Edited quote.

Chapter 6: Missing – Fate Unknown

1 https://www.in2013dollars.com/uk/inflation/1919

2 Mary Fowler, JN interview, 2023.

3 David Hart Dyke quoted at: www.ssafa.org.uk/support-us/
our-national-campaigns/falklands-40/falklands-40-david-hart-dyke

4 Russell 'Eli' Ellis, Chief Petty Officer, HMS *Coventry*, JN interview.

5 Documentary: *HMS Coventry – Sea of Fire*, Windfall Films. Some
quotes edited for brevity and clarity. https://www.youtube.com/
watch?v=bnJ_S3AIylQ

6 Ibid.

7 From 'The Long Endurance' chapter in Kettle's *The Ways of War*, op. cit.
Edited for brevity.

8 Documentary: *HMS Coventry – Sea of Fire*, op. cit.

9 https://www.ssafa.org.uk/support-us/our-national-campaigns/falklands-40/
falklands-40-david-hart-dyke

10 https://weatherspark.com/h/d/45062/1982/5/25/Historical-Weather-on-
Tuesday-May-25-1982-in-London-United-Kingdom#Figures-Temperature

11 Understandably, there are conflicting reports of the final few seconds of the
attack. Resolved here where possible.

12 This is Captain Hart Dyke's testimony; some accounts say that the bomb did
not explode.

13 Post-war crew correspondence with the Argentinian pilots.

14 https://www.express.co.uk/news/uk/1773939/hms-coventry-sinking-
falklands-war-royal-marines-chris-howe-spt and conversation with JN.

15 Documentary: *HMS Coventry – Sea of Fire*, op. cit. Some testimony edited for
clarity.

16 Ibid.

17 Ibid.

18 https://www.hmscoventry.co.uk

19 Michael Fowler letter to Mary Fowler, written 17 April 1982. Edited for
brevity.

20 Jenny Green, JN interview.

21 Linda Schaffner, quoted in JN, *Eject! Eject!* (Simon & Schuster, 2023).

22 *Sydney Morning Herald*, 9 November 1920.

Chapter 7: The Chosen One

1 A conservative estimate, based on more than 500,000 missing soldiers/sailors/
airmen, and taking into account the fact that some families lost more than one
man. https://www.gov.uk/government/news/interesting-facts-about-our-
work

2 https://www.saintpolsurternoise.fr/articles/histoire-de-la-ville

3   Cedric Hardwicke, *Let's Pretend: Recollections and Reflections of a Lucky Actor* (Grayson & Grayson, 1932).

4   Vere Brodie, *Tea & Talk*, typescript memoir, National Army Museum Collection 1998-01-26-2. Supplied by Mark Scott. Account edited for brevity. The Women's Army Auxiliary Corps was later renamed Queen Mary's Army Auxiliary Corps.

5   The words are repeated in French. The date of the selection on the headstone is incorrect. The inscription uses the term 'interned' instead of 'interred'.

6   *Nottingham Evening Post*, 21 October 1920.

7   *Daily Mirror*, 23 October 1920.

8   *Daily Mirror*, 22 October 1920.

9   *Nottingham Evening Post*, 29 October 1920.

10   In military parlance, titles such as Brigadier General are regularly shortened to simply 'General'.

11   CWGC Archive file no. ADD6/1/16, 1/11/1920-22/10/2009.

12   Interview with Laetitia Hardie (née Wyatt) in the *Guardian*, 13 October 2018.

13   General Wyatt, notes from his personal papers, 28 November 1935.

14   Chesterfield WFA newsletter, Issue 24.

15   https://archive.cwgc.org/Record.aspx?src=CalmView. Persons&id=DS%2FUK%2F74

16   Chesterfield WFA newsletter, Issue 24.

17   General Wyatt letter to the *Daily Telegraph*, 11 November 1939.

18   Dean Herbert Ryle to David Railton, 25 October 1920.

19   Account by John Sowerbutts in *The Undertakers' Journal*, November 1920, reprinted in *Funeral Director Monthly*, June 2021. https://www.nafd.org. uk/wp-content/uploads/2021/06/Unknown-Warrior-Centenary.pdf – some sections edited for brevity.

20   Ibid. Edited for clarity.

21   *Daily Telegraph*, quoted in the *Staffordshire Sentinel*, 27 October 1920.

22   *Daily Mirror*, 29 October 1920.

23   Ibid.

24   *The Times*, 29 October 1920.

25   *Birmingham Gazette*, 30 October 1920.

26   *Daily Mirror*, 30 October 1920.

27   http://www.brunswickironworks.co.uk/centenary-1906-1931.html

28   https://historypoints.org/index.php?page=site-of-brunswick-ironworks

29   http://news.bbc.co.uk/local/northwestwales/hi/people_and_places/history/ newsid_9181000/9181534.stm

30   CWGC Archive file no. ADD6/1/16, 1/11/1920-22/10/2009. The body was eventually transported to Boulogne, not Calais.

31   David Railton, *Our Empire*, November 1931, Vol. VII.

32   Postcard by Revd Railton in Railton family archive, quoted in Richardson, *The Flag*, op. cit.

33 Various, including *Western Daily Press*, 3 November 1920.

34 Ibid.

35 Railton, *The Story of a Padre's Flag*, op. cit.

36 *The Times*, 10 November 1920. Edited for brevity.

37 David Railton, Army Book 152 – Correspondence Book (Field Service), Railton family archive, quoted in Richards, *The Flag*, op. cit.

38 An excellent account of Blakemore's trial and its aftermath appears in Richards, *The Flag*, op. cit.

39 The National Archives, Field General Court Martial – Blakemore, D. J., WO71/569, quoted in Richards, *The Flag*, op. cit.

40 Railton, *The Story of a Padre's Flag*, op. cit. Edited for brevity.

41 The National Archive, Field General Court Martial – Blakemore, D. J., WO71/569, quoted in Richards, *The Flag*, op. cit.

42 https://www.iwm.org.uk/blog/research/2017/04/second-lieutenant-george-arthur-nicholls-he-always-played-the-game

43 There is some dispute about the actual provenance of this sword – the matter will be addressed later.

44 https://www.iwm.org.uk/memorials/item/memorial/47966

45 Adjutant General's instructions document headed 'G1-2-3/133, DGR&E France, Unknown Warrior'.

46 Adjutant General's instructions document headed 'G1-2-3/133, DGR&E France, Unknown Warrior' by AAG Lieutenant Colonel H. Miller, War Office, 33–38 Baker Street, 22 October 1920 and handwritten notes by unknown author headed 'Unknown Warrior', stipulating '20/10 AG instructed that "body to be only bones"', UW WA 1920-1939 file, CWGC.

47 Kendall, *Daring All Things*, op. cit. Edited for clarity.

48 Brodie, *Tea & Talk*, op. cit.

49 Kendall, *Daring All Things*, op. cit.

50 Mark Scott, *Among the Kings* (Colourpoint Books, 2020).

51 https://www.theguardian.com/world/2018/oct/13/story-of-choosing-unknown-warrior

52 L. J. Wyatt letter to the *Daily Telegraph*, 11 November 1939. Curiously, Wyatt seems to have muddled the date of the selection, placing it on 7 November 1920 (which simply doesn't fit with the known chronology). Yet he had correctly dated it to 8 November in a handwritten, signed and dated account of the event written in 1935. It is perhaps for this reason that the commemorative headstone in Saint-Pol and many accounts use the wrong date.

53 John Sowerbutts article in *The Undertakers' Journal*, November 1920, reprinted in *Funeral Director Monthly*, June 2021.

54 Ibid. Edited.

55 Author's assessment of the process.

56 Personal recollection by Wyatt's daughter, Laetitia Hardie, who visited Saint-Pol with her father just before the Second World War, *Guardian*, 13 October 2018.

57 L. J. Wyatt letter to the *Daily Telegraph*, 11 November 1939. Edited for clarity.

58 L. J. Wyatt notes from personal papers, 28 November 1935.

59 *Time* magazine, June 1930.

60 'Bringing the Unknown Warrior Home', *The Undertakers' Journal*, November 1920.

Chapter 8: The Burning Chapel

1 *Guardian*, 9 November 1920.

2 L. J. Wyatt letter to the *Daily Telegraph*, 11 November 1939.

3 John Preston, 'The Unknown Warrior: A Hero's Return', *Daily Telegraph*, 9 November 2008.

4 Scott, *Among the Kings*, op. cit.

5 National Archives, Acc 2013/002, quoted in Scott, *Among the Kings*, op. cit. Letter edited for clarity.

6 Scott, *Among the Kings*, op. cit.

7 Ibid.

8 Ibid.

9 Major General Sir Cecil Smith letter to Revd Collings, 15 November 1980, Westminster Abbey Muniment 63774B; second letter from Cecil Smith to Revd Collings, November 1980, Westminster Abbey Muniment 63774B, quoted in Scott, *Among the Kings*, op. cit. The contents of the two separate letters are combined and edited.

10 Brodie, *Tea & Talk*, op. cit.

11 https://www.extremeweatherwatch.com/cities/paris/year-1920#november

12 *Penrith Observer*, 9 November 1920.

13 Curriculum Vitae of Ernest Fitzsimon, 1 June 1942, Fitzsimon family archive, quoted in Scott, *Among the Kings*, op. cit.

14 *Belfast Telegraph*, quoted in Scott, *Among the Kings*, op. cit.

15 Fitz is pictured in a photograph circa 1921 having found his brother's grave, in Scott, *Among the Kings*, op. cit.

16 Brodie, *Tea & Talk*, op. cit.

17 WAAC Unit Administrator Vere Brodie, IWM Q 109517.

18 *The Undertakers' Journal*, November 1920.

19 Brodie, *Tea & Talk*, op. cit. The phrase 'simple little wooden coffin' is Brodie's, too.

20 Michael Gavaghan, *The Story of the British Unknown Warrior* (M&L Publications, 2006).

21 *The Undertakers' Journal*, November 1920. Account edited.

22 Gavaghan, *The Story of the British Unknown Warrior*, op. cit.

23 *The Undertakers' Journal*, November 1920. The inscription actually reads 'who fell' rather than 'who died'.

24 20 September 1920.
25 *Leeds Mercury*, 10 November 1920.
26 *Hartlepool Northern Daily Mail*, 10 November 1920.
27 *Westminster Gazette*, 10 November 1920.
28 *Evening Standard*, 10 November 1920.
29 Lady Lucy French, 'Never Such Innocence: Remembrance for a New Generation', WFA magazine *Stand To!*, No. 120 – Unknown Warrior Special, November 2020.
30 *Evening Standard*, 10 November 1920.
31 WFA magazine *Stand To!*, No. 120 – Unknown Warrior Special, November 2020.
32 Christina Holstein, 'The Repatriation and Burial of French Soldiers After the First World War', WFA magazine *Stand To!*, No. 128, November 2022 Special Edition.
33 Scott, *Among the Kings*, op. cit.
34 *Pall Mall Gazette*, 10 November 1920.
35 *Westminster Gazette*, 10 November 1920.
36 Public Records Office WO 32/3000.
37 *Westminster Gazette*, 10 November 1920.
38 Richards, *The Flag*, op. cit.
39 *Westminster Gazette*, 10 November 1920.
40 *The Undertakers' Journal*, November 1920. Text edited for clarity.

Chapter 9: The Warship of the Dead

1 *Staffordshire Sentinel*, 11 November 1920.
2 http://www.doverwarmemorialproject.org.uk/Information/Educational/Unknown%20Warrior.pdf
3 https://www.raf100schools.org.uk/resource/41/the-origins-of-the-raf
4 *Dover Express* and *East Kent News*, November 1920.
5 *Daily Telegraph*, 11 November 1920. Some newspaper quotes in this chapter edited for brevity.
6 *The Times*, 11 November 1920.
7 *The Rime of the Ancient Mariner* by Samuel Taylor Coleridge, quoted in the *Daily Telegraph*, 11 November 1920.
8 *The Undertaker's Journal*, November 1920.
9 Professor Alison S. Fell, 'The French Unknown Soldier: Contexts and Controversies', WFA magazine *Stand To!*, No. 120 – Unknown Warrior Special, November 2020.
10 Memo from General Erich von Falkenhayn to Kaiser Wilhelm II in late 1915.
11 https://www.history.com/news/10-things-you-may-not-know-about-the-battle-of-verdun#
12 Ibid.

13 Filmed interview with Auguste Thin, 1965, l'Institut national de l'audiovisuel: https://www.facebook.com/watch/?v=1457225964669019. Some articles spell his name as 'Thien'.

14 *Daily Telegraph*, 11 November 1920.

15 *Daily Herald*, 10 November 1920.

16 *Daily Mirror*, 11 November 1920.

17 *The Undertakers' Journal*, November 1920.

18 *Daily Mirror*, 11 November 1920.

19 Ibid.

20 *Dover Express*, 11 November 1920.

21 *Daily Mirror*, 11 November 1920.

22 *Daily Telegraph*, 11 November 1920.

23 *Westminster Gazette*, 10 November 1920.

24 Ibid.

25 Chandler's story is constructed from a number of sources: https://livesofthefirstworldwar.iwm.org.uk/story/79840;
    Chandler was Harold's great-uncle, according to: https://www.iwm.org.uk/collections/item/object/30082803;
    https://www.mirror.co.uk/news/uk-news/unknown-warrior-every-husband-son-3945259;
    https://www.theguardian.com/world/2018/jul/22/rose-from-unknown-warriors-coffin-to-be-part-of-exhibition-about-national-mourning

26 Helen Judson, 'Edith Cavell', *The American Journal of Nursing*, July 1941.

27 https://www.iwm.org.uk/history/who-was-edith-cavell

28 Moya Peterson, 'Edith Cavell – Nurse and Martyr', University of Kansas School of Nursing, 2018.

29 https://www.historytoday.com/archive/edith-cavell-reburied-norwich

30 https://www.wrexham-history.com/s-s-wrexham-captain/

31 *De Telegraaf*, 16 July 1916.

32 Quoted at: https://en.wikipedia.org/wiki/Charles_Fryatt

33 Gavaghan, *The Story of the British Unknown Warrior*, op. cit.

34 *Daily Telegraph*, 11 November 1920.

35 Ibid.

36 https://www.steamlocomotive.com/locobase.php?country=Great_Britain&wheel=4-4-0&railroad=sec#9445

37 *Daily Mirror*, 11 November 1920.

38 *Evening Post*, 11 November 1920.

39 *Daily Telegraph*, 11 November 1920.

40 Richards, *The Flag*, op. cit.

41 *Daily Mail*, 11 November 1920.

42 *Daily Mirror*, 11 November 1920.

43 *The Undertakers' Journal*, November 1920.

44 *Sheerness Guardian*, 13 November 1920.

45 *Daily Mirror*, 11 November 1920.
46 Ibid.
47 *Daily Mail*, 11 November 1920.
48 Ibid.
49 *Guardian*, 11 November 1920.
50 Ibid.
51 *Daily Mirror*, 11 November 1920.
52 *Gloucester Echo*, 11 November 1920.
53 *The Times* and *Guardian*, 11 November 1920.
54 *Daily Mirror*, 11 November 1920.
55 *Guardian*, 11 November 1920.
56 *The Times*, 11 November 1920.
57 *Daily Mirror*, 11 November 1920.
58 Ibid.
59 *The Times*, 11 November 1920.
60 *The Undertakers' Journal*, November 1920.
61 *Guardian*, 11 November 1920.

Chapter 10: Welcome Home, Boys

1 Nikki Scott, JN interview, and *A War Widow's Story* video for the charity Scotty's Little Soldiers: https://youtu.be/NkMuR4v_7AE
2 Major Charlie Burbridge, EGYPT Squadron Leader, quoted at: www.gove. uk/government/fatalities/corporal-lee-scott-of-2-rtr-killed-in-afghanistan
3 Jarra Brown MBE, *46 Miles: A Journey of Repatriation and Humbling Respect* (Menin House, 2015). And conversation with JN.
4 The exact sequence of the development of events at Wootton Bassett varies depending on the source consulted.
5 Lieutenant Colonel David O'Kelly of the Yorkshire Regiment, describing Sergeant Lee Johnson, killed by a mine in Afghanistan, 8 December 2007. Quoted in Brown, *46 Miles*, op. cit.
6 Debbie Mackin to Jarra Brown, quoted in *46 Miles*, op. cit.
7 *Guardian*, 14 July 2009.
8 https://www.networkrail.co.uk/who-we-are/our-history/iconic-infrastructure/ the-history-of-london-victoria-station/
9 Easthope, *When the Dust Settles*, op. cit.
10 https://www.wherearethepoppiesnow.org.uk/poppy/david/ – there are a number of different and conflicting accounts of Sumpter's involvement.
11 *Southall Gazette*, 10 November 1989.
12 https://www.warhistoryonline.com/world-war-i/encounters-enemies-7-peaceful-meetings-opposing-sides-world-war-mm.html
13 https://the-rearview-mirror.com/2014/12/25/the-christmas-truce-of-1914/
14 *Guardian*, 4 August 1994.

15 *Southall Gazette*, 10 November 1989.
16 *Pinner Observer*, 9 November 1989.
17 *Daily Telegraph*, 5 August 1994.
18 Ibid.

Chapter 11: Dawn at Last

1   Richard van Emden, *The Quick and the Dead* (Bloomsbury, 2011). Account edited for brevity.
2   *Guardian*, 12 November 1920.
3   Ibid.
4   Ibid.
5   *The Times*, 12 November 1920.
6   The majority of this group held the Victoria Cross; some had also been awarded the Distinguished Service Order, Distinguished Service Medals and more. A few of the group had been awarded the Conspicuous Gallantry Medal or the Distinguished Conduct Medal.
7   *Daily Telegraph*, 11 November 1920.
8   Details provided by Colin Dean, archivist to the Royal Military School of Music.
9   Exact details of who formed up where vary depending on the source. The official orders appear to suggest some were outside the station. But the next day's press reports have almost all of the action occurring inside.
10 Curzon MSS, F112/318, Unveiling Cenotaph/Unknown Warrior Committee, 19 October 1920, quoted in David Cannadine, *Aspects of Aristocracy* (Yale University Press, 1994).
11 *Guardian*, 12 November 1920.
12 Cannadine, *Aspects of Aristocracy*, op. cit.
13 Hallie Eustace Miles, quoted in Jonathan Grun, 'A Walk with the Unknown Warrior', WFA magazine *Stand To!*, No. 120 – Unknown Warrior Special, November 2020.
14 Information from Colin Dean, archivist to the Royal Military School of Music, and from his paper: 'The Unveiling of the Cenotaph and the Interment of the Unknown Warrior'.
15 https://blog.nationalarchives.gov.uk/planning-the-burial-of-the-unknown-warrior/
16 https://www.bmmhs.org/the-unknown-warrior/
17 Official medal citation, quoted at: https://www.bmmhs.org/the-unknown-warrior/
18 https://en.wikipedia.org/wiki/1908_Pattern_Webbing – some reports also describe a 'soldier's sidearm' being used.
19 It is unclear at what point Railton's Union Jack was positioned on the coffin.
20 The official orders state: 'The Gun Carriage will be drawn up on the west side

of the Carriage Road opposite the Railway Station' but all the press reports has it inside the station.

21 *Westminster Gazette*, 10 November 1920.
22 The (archaic) lower-case spelling of 'ffoulkes' is correct.
23 Author's italics.
24 Letter from ffoulkes to Sir Lionel Earle, 29 October 1920, quoted in Sarah Barter Bailey, 'Charles John ffoulkes: Master of the Armouries 1913–38', *Royal Armouries Yearbook*, Vol. 5, 2000.
25 I am indebted to Dr Iason Tzouriadis, Assistant Curator of European Edged Weapons at the Royal Armouries in Leeds, both for this description, based on the IWM's photograph of the two swords, and for the information about ffoulkes's role in providing the swords.
26 Quoted in Barter Bailey, 'Charles John ffoulkes: Master of the Armouries 1913–38', op. cit.
27 Q31485, IWM Photo Archive collection.
28 James Bone, 'When the Cenotaph was Unveiled', in John Hammerton (ed.), *The Great War – I Was There*, Part 48 (Amalgamated Press, 1939).
29 *Otago Daily Times*, 19 March 1928.
30 *Daily Mirror*, 31 July 2014.
31 The Royal Flying Corps became the Royal Air Force in 1918.
32 Gavaghan, *The Story of the British Unknown Warrior*, op. cit.
33 *Guardian*, 11 November 1920.
34 *Daily Telegraph*, 12 November 1920.
35 Ibid.
36 David Lloyd, *Battlefield Tourism* (Berg, 1998).
37 Bone, 'When the Cenotaph was Unveiled', op. cit.
38 *Daily Mirror*, 11 November 1920.
39 Garrison Sergeant Major Andrew 'Vern' Stokes OBE MVO, JN interview.
40 *The Times*, 12 November 1920.
41 *Guardian*, 11 November 1920.
42 *Sunday People*, 14 November 1920.
43 *Daily Herald*, 12 November 1920.
44 *Globe*, 10 November 1920.
45 https://anthonycarew.org/lowerdeck.html
46 Van Emden, *The Quick and the Dead*, op. cit. Edited for brevity.
47 *Guardian*, 12 November 1920.
48 *The Times*, 12 November 1920.
49 *Birmingham Evening Despatch*, 11 November 1920.
50 *Sunday People*, 14 November 1920.
51 *The Times*, 12 November 1920.
52 Jimmy's exact position and role in the parade is unclear. https://blog.nationalarchives.gov.uk/planning-the-burial-of-the-unknown-warrior/

53 Comment from J. Eric Nolan, grandson of James Dunn, 6 November 2020, at: https://blog.nationalarchives.gov.uk/planning-the-burial-of-the-unknown-warrior/

54 *Yorkshire Post*, 12 November 1920.

55 *The Times*, 12 November 1920.

56 Bone, 'When the Cenotaph was Unveiled', op. cit.

57 *Daily Mirror*, 12 November 1920.

58 http://www.burnleyinthegreatwar.info/youngkitchene12.htm

59 https://towneley.org.uk/online_exhibition/foreword/jennie-jackson-1909-1997/

60 Van Emden, *The Quick and the Dead*, op. cit. Some quotes edited and amalgamated from Richard van Emden's extensive interviews.

61 Bone, 'When the Cenotaph was Unveiled', op. cit.

62 *The Times*, 12 November 1920.

63 *Yorkshire Post*, 12 November 1920.

64 Philip Gibbs, *The Soul of a Nation*, reprinted by the *Toronto Globe*, 1920.

65 Ibid.

66 https://royalcentral.co.uk/features/how-the-influence-of-her-beloved-grandfather-king-george-v-is-seen-in-queen-elizabeth-iis-final-journey-180985/

67 *The Times*, 12 November 1920.

Chapter 12: The Great Silence

1 *Daily Mirror*, 12 November 1920.

2 https://edencamp.co.uk/blog/forgottenfriday-royals-at-war/

3 Heather Jones, *For King and Country* (Cambridge University Press, 2021).

4 Ibid.

5 https://www.rct.uk/collection/68932/king-george-vs-field-marshals-uniform – edited quote.

6 *Yorkshire Post*, 12 November 1920.

7 *Evening Post*, 12 November 1920.

8 Van Emden, *The Quick and the Dead*, op. cit.

9 Gibbs, 'The Soul of a Nation', op. cit.

10 *The Times*, 11 November 1920.

11 Gertrude's story is constructed from: Van Emden, *The Quick and the Dead*, op. cit.; 'The Life and Death of Harry Farr', *Journal of the Royal Society of Medicine*, September 2006; *Guardian*, 14 November 1991 and *Independent*, 10 November 2017. The Regimental Sergeant Major's words are reported in a number of sources, including https://staffblogs.le.ac.uk/crimcorpse/2016/10/03/shot-at-dawn

12 Van Emden, *The Quick and the Dead*, op. cit.

13 *Nottingham Evening Post*, 11 November 1920.

14 Hanson, *The Unknown Soldier*, op. cit.

15 WFA magazine *Stand To!*, No. 120 – Unknown Warrior Special, November 2020.
16 Homberger, 'The Story of the Cenotaph', op. cit.
17 https://en.wikipedia.org/wiki/Workers%27_Dreadnought
18 *Hull Evening News* and *Birmingham Evening Despatch*, 11 November 1920.
19 *Guardian*, 12 November 1920.
20 *Yorkshire Post* and *Leeds Intelligencer*, 12 November 1920. Edited for brevity.
21 Gavin Fuller, *The Telegraph Book of the First World War* – Introduction (Aurum Press, 2014).
22 https://www.iwm.org.uk/history/what-happened-on-the-first-day-of-the-battle-of-the-somme
23 *Daily Telegraph*, 3 July 1916.
24 Gibbs, *The Soul of a Nation*, op. cit. Edited for brevity.
25 Bone, 'When the Cenotaph was Unveiled', op. cit.
26 Hanson, *The Unknown Soldier*, op. cit.
27 Ibid.
28 *Daily Mirror*, 12 November 1920.

Chapter 13: 'The Man in the Coffin Might Be My Daddy'

1 Andrea Hetherington, 'Up in Smoke: Britain's War Widows and the Conflict of Commemoration', op. cit.
2 French, *Gone for a Soldier*, op. cit.
3 Hetherington, 'Up in Smoke', op. cit. And National Archives, WORK 20/1/3, quoted at: https://blog.nationalarchives.gov.uk/planning-the-burial-of-the-unknown-warrior/
4 Hetherington, 'Up in Smoke', op. cit.
5 *Fulton County Tribune*, 31 December 1920: https://chroniclingamerica.loc.gov/lccn/sn87076552/1920-12-31/ed-1/seq-2/; and *Sherbrooke Daily Record*, 11 November 1920: https://numerique.banq.qc.ca/patrimoine/details/52327/3100229
6 *Daily Mirror*, 12 November 1920.
7 Other awards that day included the Conspicuous Gallantry Medal, the Distinguished Service Cross and the Distinguished Service Medal.
8 *The Times*, 12 November 1920.
9 *Evening Post*, 12 November 1920.
10 *Derby Telegraph*, 5 November 2018.
11 https://victoriacrosstrust.org/grave/william-harold-coltman/
12 *Derby Telegraph*, 5 November 2018, and Lt Col. Ken Roberts RAMC (retd): https://www.westernfrontassociation.com/world-war-i-articles/britains-most-decorated-soldier-in-the-first-world-war/ – citations edited for brevity.
13 *Evening Post*, 12 November 1920.
14 *The Times*, 12 November 1920.

15   *Hull Evening News*, 11 November 1920.

16   *The Times*, 12 November 1920.

17   Vern Stokes, JN interview.

18   https://www.forces.net/royals/queen/
why-queens-lead-lined-coffin-weighs-same-about-dozen-55lb-bergens

19   Vern Stokes interview in the *Daily Express*, 18 September 2022 (quote edited and includes parts of JN interview).

20   *New York Times*, 12 November 1920.

21   Railton, *The Story of a Padre's Flag*, op. cit.

22   *British Legion Journal*, October 1961.

23   *The Times*, 12 November 1920.

24   *Birmingham Gazette*, 12 November 1920.

25   French, *Gone for a Soldier*, op. cit. Edited for clarity.

26   Revelation 7:9–16, King James Version (excerpt).

27   A sketch showing this sequence later appeared in *The Illustrated London News*.

28   *The Times*, 12 November 1920.

29   https://www.worldradiohistory.com/Archive-All-Audio/Archive-Studio-Sound/70s/Studio-Sound-1977-06.pdf

30   https://www.recordedchurchmusic.org/historic-recordings/experiments-in-electrical-recordings

31   *The Times*, 12 November 1920.

32   *Daily Mail*, 12 November 1920.

33   *The Times*, 12 November 1920.

34   *Guardian*, 12 November 1920.

35   Ibid.

36   Ibid.

37   Ibid.

38   *Daily Express*, 12 November 1920.

39   *Daily Graphic* – Unknown Warrior Special, 12 November 1920.

40   Lloyd, *Battlefield Tourism*, op. cit.

41   Van Emden, *The Quick and the Dead*, op. cit.

42   *Daily Graphic*, 12 November 1920.

43   *Daily Telegraph*, 12 November 1920.

44   *Daily Graphic*, 12 November 1920.

45   Ibid.

46   *Daily Mail*, 12 November 1920.

47   Lloyd, *Battlefield Tourism*, op. cit.

48   *Birmingham Gazette*, 16 November 1920.

49   Extract from King George V's diary, quoted in Gavaghan, *The Story of the British Unknown Warrior*, op. cit.

50   Personal notebook of George V, quoted at: https://www.royal.uk/
centenary-grave-unknown-warrior-and-cenotaph

51 Letter to Dean Ryle, 11 November 1920, Westminster Abbey Archive. Edited.
52 Lloyd George to Dean Ryle, 29 November 1920. Westminster Abbey Archive. Edited letter. The ceremony occurred on Thursday, 11 November 1920, not a Friday, as Lloyd George wrote.
53 Anonymous, *To My 'Unknown Warrior'* (Hodder & Stoughton, 1920).
54 Ibid. Text edited for brevity.

Chapter 14: The Search Continues

1 Herbert Jeans, 'In Death's Cathedral Palace', *British Legion Journal*, Vol. 9, No. 5, November 1929.
2 *Yorkshire Post*, 13 November 1920.
3 *Daily Mirror*, 15 November 1920.
4 *Evening Despatch*, 13 November 1920. Edited.
5 Hanson, *The Unknown Soldier*, op. cit.
6 *Yorkshire Post*, 15 November 1920.
7 *Daily Herald*, 13 November 1920.
8 *Leicester Evening Mail*, 18 November 1920. Edited.
9 Van Emden, *The Quick and the Dead*, op. cit.
10 From the sonnet 'The Soldier' by Rupert Brooke (1887–1915).
11 John 15:13, King James Version.
12 *The Times*, 24 August 1921.
13 Richards, *The Flag*, op. cit.
14 *Evening Standard*, 19 November 1921.
15 *The Times*, 18 October 1921.
16 Both quotes from Lord Stamfordham letter to Lord Curzon, quoted in John Gore, *King George V* (John Murray, 1949).
17 *The Times*, 18 November 1921.
18 Fitzgerald, *A Memoir of Herbert Edward Ryle*, op. cit.
19 Ibid.
20 *The Times*, 18 October 1921. Edited.
21 *Daily Mirror*, 18 October 1921.
22 Fitzgerald, *A Memoir of Herbert Edward Ryle*, op. cit. Edited quote.
23 *Evening Standard*, 11 November 1921.
24 *Yorkshire Post*, 12 November 1921.
25 Ibid.
26 Colonel Commandant for the DGR&E, 6 August 1921, quoted in Hodgkinson, 'Battlefield Clearance and Burial', op. cit. Some quotes edited.
27 Ibid.
28 Colonel Goodland letter to Major Chettle, August 1921, quoted in van Emden, *Missing*, op. cit.
29 Brodie, *Tea & Talk*, op. cit. Quotes edited.
30 *The Times*, 10 November 1921.

31 Sir Robert Hudson, quoted in Hodgkinson, 'Battlefield Clearance and Burial', op. cit.

32 Van Emden, *Missing*, op. cit.

33 Mr Chapman of Mailly-Mallet, quoted in Hodgkinson, 'Battlefield Clearance and Burial', op. cit.

34 Ibid.

35 CWGC//8/1/4/1/2/25-1 File CCM 8933 Pt 2 page 4, quoted in Jill Stewart, 'The Disappearing Gunner', at: https://www.westernfrontassociation.com/world-war-i-articles/the-disappearing-gunner/

36 Van Emden, *Missing*, op. cit.

37 The narrative that follows is distilled from the excellent article 'The Disappearing Gunner', op. cit., by Jill Stewart, honorary secretary of the WFA. Some letters and quotes edited.

38 Henri Barbusse, *Under Fire: The Story of a Squad* (J. M. Dent & Sons, 1917). Edited for brevity.

39 https://www.ggarchives.com/Immigration/ImmigrantTickets/PassageContractsByYear-1920s.html

40 Elizabeth French's account is taken from Jill Stewart's article, 'A Mother's Pilgrimage to Ypres, 1921': https://www.westernfrontassociation.com/world-war-i-articles/a-mother-s-pilgrimage-to-ypres-1921. Some letters and quotes edited.

41 War Office letter to David Railton, 12 September 1939, quoted in Richards, *The Flag*, op. cit.

42 *Daily Telegraph* obituary, 11 November 1920.

43 Margaret Railton, JN interview.

44 Unknown newspaper clipping, 23 July 1942, Railton family archive, quoted in Richards, *The Flag*, op. cit.

45 Margaret Railton, JN interview, August 2023.

46 Richards, *The Flag*, op. cit.

47 *Daily Mail*, 1 July 1955.

48 Richards, *The Flag*, op. cit.

49 *Daily Mirror*, 1 July 1955.

Chapter 15: We Will Remember You

1 John Morrison story from: https://www.pressandjournal.co.uk/fp/past-times/2645743/john-morrison-the-moray-hero-whose-body-was-lost-for-100-years/; www.nts.org.uk/stories/brodie-castle-the-community-during-wartime

2 Information taken from: https://www.cwgc.org/find-records/commemorations/finding-and-rebuying-our-war-dead/

3 Robert Malcolm story from:

https://www.cwgc.org/our-work/news/
world-war-one-stretcher-bearer-buried-in-belgium/;
Independent, 11 May 2023;
https://www.standard.co.uk/news/uk/dna-ypres-jordan-british-
belgium-b1080218.html;
https://www.military.com/daily-news/2023/05/10/wwi-soldier-finally-finds-
resting-place-flanders-fields.html;
https://eu.usatoday.com/story/news/world/2023/05/12/
wwi-soldier-buried-flanders-fields-belgium/70210982007/;
BBC regional news (Tees), 10 May 1923, consulted at: https://www.bbc.co.uk/
news/uk-england-tees-65553011

4 Amnesty International newsletter, 27 September 2011, quoting State Human
Rights Commission (SHRC) report on unmarked graves.

5 Swede Williams's personal account and JN interview. Some quotes edited for
brevity. Swede is now training to be an RAF pilot.

6 Van Emden, *The Quick and The Dead*, op. cit.

7 Ibid. Edited quotes.

8 Mary Fowler, JN interview, 2023.

9 Nikki Scott, JN interview.

10 www.westminster-abbey.org/media/6173/passing-ww1-generation-service.pdf

11 Personal conversation with Westminster Abbey attendant, 2023.

12 David Railton KC, JN interview.

13 Edited text on plaque in St George's Chapel, Westminster Abbey.

14 Edited inscription on tomb of Unknown Warrior in Westminster Abbey.

15 Anonymous, *To My 'Unknown Warrior'*, op. cit.

16 Quoted in various newspapers.

BIBLIOGRAPHY

Black, Sue, *All That Remains: A Life in Death* (Doubleday, 2018)

Blunden, Edmund, *Undertones of War* (Penguin Modern Classics, 2010)

Braybon, Gail (ed.), *Evidence, History and the Great War: Historians and the Impact of 1914–18* (Berghahn Books, 2008)

Brittain, Vera, *Testament of Youth* (Phoenix, 2014)

Brown, Jarra, *46 Miles: A Journey of Repatriation and Humbling Respect* (Menin House, 2015)

Buchan, John, *Memory Hold-the-Door* (White Press, 2015)

Cannadine, David, *Aspects of Aristocracy: Grandeur and Decline in Modern Britain* (Yale University Press, 1994)

Chapman, Guy, *A Passionate Prodigality* (Buchan & Enright, 1985)

Coleridge, Samuel Taylor, *The Rime of the Ancient Mariner* (Vintage Classics, 2014)

Creasy, Edward Shepherd, *Decisive Battles of the World* (Dover, 2008)

Davenport, P. et al., *The History of the Prince of Wales' Own Civil Service Rifles* (Project Gutenberg eBook, 2016)

Easthope, Lucy, *When the Dust Settles: Searching for Hope after Disaster* (Hodder & Stoughton, 2022)

Feilding, Rowland, *War Letters to a Wife* (Spellmount Classics, 2001)

Ferguson, Niall, *The Pity of War* (Allen Lane/The Penguin Press, 1998)

Fitzgerald, Maurice Henry, *A Memoir of Herbert Edward Ryle* (Macmillan, 1928)

French, Anthony, *Gone for a Soldier* (The Roundwood Press, 1972)

Fuller, Gavin, *The Telegraph Book of the First World War* (Aurum Press, 2014)

Garrett, Richard, *The Final Betrayal: The Armistice, 1918 ... and Afterwards* (Buchan & Enright, 1989)

Gavaghan, Michael, *The Story of the British Unknown Warrior* (M&L Publications, 2006)

Geurst, Jeroen, *Cemeteries of the Great War by Sir Edwin Lutyens* (010 Uitgeverij, 2009)

Gilmour, David, *Curzon: Imperial Statesman* (Penguin, 2019)

Graves, Robert, *Goodbye to All That* (Penguin Classics, 2000)

Gregory, Adrian, *The Silence of Memory: Armistice Day 1919– 1946* (Bloomsbury Academic, 1994)

Hanson, Neil, *The Unknown Soldier: The Story of the Missing of the Great War* (Corgi, 2007)

Hardwicke, Cedric, *Let's Pretend: Recollections and Reflections of a Lucky Actor* (Grayson & Grayson, 1932)

Hart, Peter and Steel, Nigel, *The Somme* (Weidenfeld & Nicolson, 2008)

Hart Dyke, David, *Four Weeks in May: A Captain's Story of War at Sea* (Atlantic Books, 2007)

Hope, Anna, *Wake* (Transworld, 2014)

Inglis, Rupert Edward, *War Diaries* (Privately published, date unknown)

Jones, Heather, *For King and Country: The British Monarchy and the First World War* (Cambridge University Press, 2021)

Kendall, George, *Daring All Things* (Helion & Company Ltd, 2016)

Kettle, Tom, *The Ways of War* (Project Gutenberg eBook, 2021)

Knight, Jill, *The Civil Service Rifles in the Great War* (Pen & Sword, 2004)

Le Naour, Jean-Yves, *The Living Unknown Soldier: A Story of Grief and the Great War* (Metropolitan Books, 2004)

Levine, Joshua, *Forgotten Voices of the Somme* (Ebury Press, 2009)

Lloyd, David, *Battlefield Tourism: Pilgrimage and the Commemoration of the Great War in Britain, Australia and Canada, 1919–1939* (Berg, 1998)

Longworth, Philip, *The Unending Vigil: The History of the Commonwealth War Graves Commission* (Pen & Sword, 2010)

Macdonald, Lyn, *Somme* (Penguin, 2013)

Maude, Alan, *The History of the 47th (London) Division 1914–1919* (Naval & Military, 2009)

Moynihan, Michael (ed.), *God on our Side: The British Padre in World War 1* (Leo Cooper/Secker & Warburg, 1983)

Nichol, John, *Tornado* (Simon & Schuster, 2021)

Nicholson, Harold, *King George V* (Constable, 1984)

Nicolson, Juliet, *The Great Silence: 1918–1920 – Living in the Shadow of the Great War* (John Murray, 2009)

Norman, Terry, *The Hell They Called High Wood* (Pen & Sword, 2014)

Orpen, William, *An Onlooker in France 1917–1919* (Project Gutenberg eBook, 2006)

Peterson, Moya, *Edith Cavell: Nurse and Martyr* (University of Kansas School of Nursing, 2018)

Railton, David, *The Story of a Padre's Flag, Told by the Flag*, unpublished memoir

Richards, Andrew, *The Flag: The Story of Revd David Railton MC and the Tomb of the Unknown Warrior* (Casemate, 2019)

Rogerson, Sidney, *Twelve Days on the Somme* (Greenhill Books, 2006)

Rose, Kenneth, *Curzon: A Most Superior Person* (Papermac, 1985)

Sackville-West, Robert, *The Searchers: The Quest for the Lost of the First World War* (Bloomsbury, 2021)

Scott, Mark, *Among the Kings: The Unknown Warrior – An Untold Story* (Colourpoint Books, 2020)

Souhami, Diana, *Edith Cavell* (Quercus, 2015)

Van Emden, Richard, *Missing: The Need for Closure after the Great War* (Pen & Sword, 2019)

Van Emden, Richard, *The Quick and the Dead: Fallen Soldiers and their Families in the Great War* (Bloomsbury, 2011)

Waugh, Evelyn, *The Diaries of Evelyn Waugh* (Weidenfeld & Nicolson, 1976)

Western Front Association, *Stand To!*, No. 120 – Unknown Warrior Special (Western Front Association, November 2020)

Winter, Jay, *Sites of Memory, Sites of Mourning: The Great War in European Cultural History* (Cambridge University Press, 2010)

Woolf, Virginia, *The Diary of Virginia Woolf, Vol 1: 1915–1919* (Mariner Books, 1979)

PICTURE CREDITS

9. Coffin at Boulogne Castle: Imperial War Museum; procession and cart at HMS *Verdun*: Hulton Deutsch/Contributor
10. Coffin at Victoria Station: Topical Press Agency/Stringer; grave in Westminster Abbey: Dean and Chapter of Westminster
11. Both images: Scotty's Little Soldiers
12. Unveiling of the Cenotaph: Imperial War Museum; both Donald Overall photos: Richard van Emden
13. Author at Beaumont-Hamel: John Nichol; Swede and Hannah Williams: Swede Williams
14. Procession at Westminster Abbey: Topical Press Agency/Stringer; author with GSM Stokes: John Nichol; Stokes leading the royal family: PA Images/Alamy Stock Photo
15. King placing wreath: PA Images/Alamy Stock Photo; crowds in Westminster Abbey: Dean and Chapter of Westminster
16. Padre's Flag: Picture by Picture Partnership/Andrew Dunsmore

INDEX

Page references in *italics* indicate images.

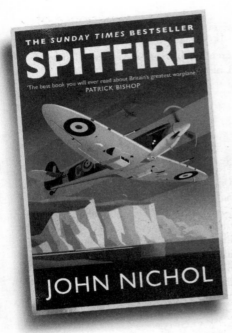

'A thrilling and moving tribute to some of its greatest heroes'
Daily Mail

'The best book you will ever read about Britain's greatest warplane'
Patrick Bishop,
author of *Fighter Boys*

'Leaves us marvelling yet again at the bravery, stoicism and sheer level-headedness of our forebears'
Daily Telegraph

'Don't miss this very special book; it's so good'
Rowland White,
author of *Vulcan 607*

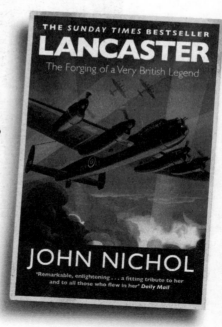

Available now

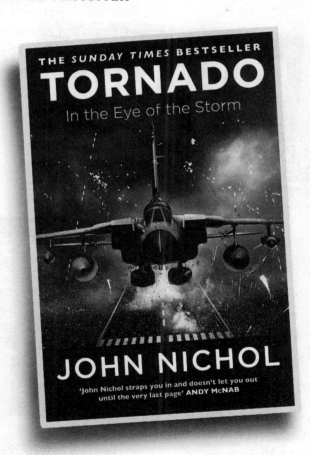

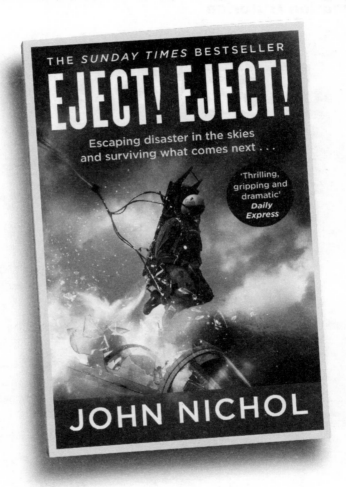